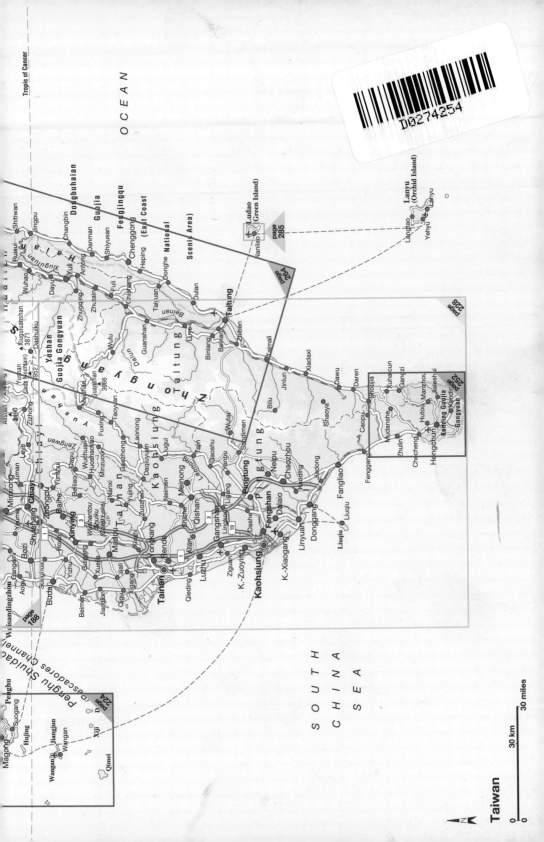

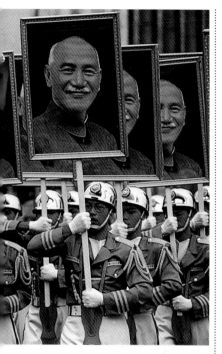

Shopping, the feature on Taiwan's Top Hikes and the Insight On... picture story on Night Markets.

The remaining features – Geography, People, Tribal Minorities, Contemporary Culture, and Arts and Crafts – were either updated or written afresh by **Chris Taylor**, a Taipei-based journalist and guidebook writer who has spent the past decade in Taiwan – including a stint with the English-language daily *Taipei Times*. Taylor also wrote the Insight On... picture story on the Mazu Festival.

The latest version of this guide was thoroughly updated by **Rick Charette**. As editorial director of *Travel in Taiwan*, a bimonthly guide for visitors, and a writer published widely in local and international travel publications, Canadian-born Charette also took on the demanding job of overhauling and updating the Travel Tips section.

Finally, lending her expertise was **Julie Gaw**, managing editor with a Hong Kong-based travel magazine, who wrote the two picture stories on Betel Nuts and Meinong's Umbrellas.

The current edition builds on the excellent foundations created by the editors and writers of previous editions, most notably **Daniel Reid**, **Bernd Hans-Gerd Helms**, **Linda Chih-Ling Hsu**, **John Gottberg Anderson**, **Paul Zach**, **Keith Stevens**, **Andy Unger** and **Jon-Claire Lee**.

Much of the new photography was contributed by **Chris Stowers**, and supplemented by pictures from **Brent Hannon**, **Chris Taylor**, **Glyn Genin**, **H. Rogers**, **R. Retter** and **Bill Wassman**. **Paula Soper** edited the text in the Insight London office and **Susan Howarth** proofread the book.

The contributors

This edition of *Insight Guide: Taiwan* was edited by **Vivien Kim**, a Singapore-based editor, and supervised by managing editor **Francis Dorai** from Insight Guides' Singapore office. The book was completely restructured, and builds upon the earlier edition put together by **Scott Rutherford**.

The services of a number of Taiwan-based journalists were enlisted for this new edition. The Modern Taiwan history chapter and feature on Cross-Strait Relations, which help explain the conflict between China and Taiwan, were written by **Brent Hannon**, a Taipei-based American freelance writer who has spent seven of his 12 years in Asia in Taiwan. Hannon also contributed the chapters on Food and Drinks, and

Map Legend

▬ ▪ ▪	International Boundary
▬ ▬ ▬	Provincial Boundary
▬ ▪ ▬ ▪	National Park/Reserve
▬ ▬ ▬	Ferry Route
◉	MRT
✈ ✈	Airport: International/Domestic
🚌	Bus Station
❶	Tourist Information
✉	Post Office
🏛 ✝ ⌐	Church/Ruins
✝	Monastery
☾	Mosque
✡	Synagogue
🏰 🏚	Castle/Ruins
⌂	Mansion/Stately Home
∴	Archeological Site
⌒	Cave
𝗜	Statue/Monument
★	Place of Interest

The main places of interest in the Places section are coordinated by number with a full-color map (e.g. ❶), and a symbol at the top of every right-hand page tells you where to find the map.

INSIGHT GUIDE
TAIWAN

CONTENTS

Maps

Distinctive Dao
fishing boat on
Lanyu (Orchid Island)

Insight on ...

Information panels

Places

Travel Tips

THE BEST OF TAIWAN

*From family outings and unique attractions, to the best street markets
and temples. We tell you what this fascinating island has to offer.
Plus some money-saving tips to fit your budget.*

HIGHLIGHTS OF TAIWAN

Visit some of Taiwan's dazzling must-see sights.

- The **National Taiwan Democracy Memorial** *(see page 138)* Long called the Chiang Kai-shek Memorial, A work of art complex built on an imperial scale that rivals Beijing's Forbidden Palace for magnificence.
- **Taipei 101** *(see page 135)* Taipei Financial Center, 101 stories tall, is the world's highest building and a wonder of engineering.
- **National Palace Museum** *(see page 147)* Home to the world's greatest repository of Chinese art, collected over a thousand years ago by China's emperors.
- **Taroko Gorge** *(see page 271)* A 19-km-long canyon with rugged rocks, cascading water and lofty marble-laced cliffs. It's a breathtaking sight with an abundance of wildlife.
- **Kenting National Park** *(see page 250)* This top tourist destination is a natural playground of exotic flora and fauna with sandy beaches. There is a strong emphasis on conservation.

ONLY IN TAIWAN

- **Beef Noodles** Sold everywhere, marinated chunks of meat in steaming broth with noodles. North China dish brought by Chiang Kai-shek's peasant soldiers.
- **KTV** Karaoke Taiwan style. Private rooms mean inhibitions are left at the door.
- **Kaoliang** Fiery Kaoliang (sorghum) liquor is the local version of Maotai. You'll meet it when locals fete you and wish to test your mettle. Beware, prepare. *Ganbei!*
- **Betel nut Beauties** On the outskirts of Taipei you'll see these sexy femmes fatales in neon-lit glass kiosks selling cigarettes and mildly toxic Chinese chewing gum.
- **Beerhouses** Raucous, often cavernous theme spots, where the night-market snacks are washed down by kegs of draft.

ABOVE: a betel nut beauty.
LEFT: the National Taiwan Democracy Memorial.
RIGHT: Taipei 101 towers above the city.

BEST HIKES AND TRAILS

● **Qingtiangang** *(see page 160)* Found high on Yangmingshan, this wide plateau with ocean views passes fumaroles and idyllic pastures of water buffalo.
● **Yushan** *(see page 219)* With over 30 peaks to climb, you will be amply rewarded by the wonderful views.

● **Butterfly Corridor** *(see page 160)* The most popular trail on Yangmingshan, with the chance of spotting some of the area's 151 species of butterfly.
Qilai Ridge *(see page 221)* Qilai Ridge is one of the most popular and challenging of the hiking locations in the Central Mountain Range.

BEST MARKETS

Taiwan's markets – unique and colorful – give you a taste of authentic street life.

● **Dihua Street** *(see page 136)* Taiwan's oldest wholesale market, over 100 years, lined with heritage-site shophouses.
● **Guanghua Market** *(see page 110)* Jam-packed with stalls stocking every kind of electronic gadget your heart can desire, at Asian prices.
● **Shilin Nightmarket** *(see page 142)* The Taiwanese love their night-time snacking. Here you will find the quintessential Taiwan

experience in three floors of eating. In a month of visits you need not eat the same snack twice.
● **Taipei Holiday Flower Market** *(see page 139)* All kinds of exotic plants, flowers and bonsai are sold here.
● **Taipei Holiday Jade Market** *(see page 108)* The flower venue's twin sister, a mecca for jade-lovers with about 850 vendors. Be prepared to brave the crowds.

BEST ARCHITECTURE

● **The Grand Hotel** *(see page 130)* This classical Chinese palace, sitting on a plateau overlooking Taipei, was long the city's defining icon.
● **85 Sky Tower** *(see page 239)* Looking like a giant rocket about to launch, the tower houses a hotel in the upper half. Many love it, many hate it.
● **Lin An Tai Homested** *(see page 133)*

See how the rich lived hundreds of years ago in an expansive preserved residential complex.
● **Baoan Temple** *(see page 132)* This architectural masterpiece is amongst Taiwan's most elaborate.
● **Longshan Temple** *(see page 140)* Built in the 1730s, this is among the world's premier examples of exquisite Chinese temple art.

ABOVE LEFT: Yangmingshan hiking trail.
ABOVE : the stunning Longshan Temple.
BELOW: snacks galore at Shilin Nightmarket.

TAIWAN FOR FAMILIES

These attractions are popular with children and adults alike.

- **Taipei Astronomical Museum** *(see page 150)* You can easily spend the day here. The star attractions are the iWERKS Theater (polarized 3D glasses used), the IMAX Dome Theater and the Observatory Dome.
- **Guandu Nature Park** *(see page 161)* A protected wetlands near Taipei has a wide marsh area with guided birding tours and boardwalks. Look out for the miniscule version of the fiddler crab native to Taiwan's mudflats.
- **Hualien Ocean Park** *(see page 266)* Dolphin and seal shows, water rides and street parades. With eight themed zones, what more could a child ask for?

- **Leofoo Village Theme Park** *(see page 179)* Travel to the Wild West, Arabia, Southeast Asia, and through a safari park, plus carnival rides, entertainers and much more.
- **National Museum of Marine Biology and Aquarium** *(see page 256)* Huge aquariums big enough for beluga whales, amazing eco-environment recreations, live underwater feedings, and animal displays.
- **Window on China** *(see page 179)* Walk like a giant among countless recreations of the world's great architectural wonders, including the Forbidden Palace, the Sphinx and the Leaning Tower of Pisa.

ABOVE: the Taipei Astronomical Museum, four floors packed with constellations, space science and technology, and ancient astronomy.
BELOW LEFT: view from a teahouse at Muzha.

BEST VIEWS

- **Alishan** *(see page 217)* At 2,400 meters up, witness sparkling sunrises over majestic Yushan and other great peaks to the east. The renowned "sea of clouds" at your feet.
- **Jiufen** *(see page 171)* A former mining town now filled with artists and old teahouses. Buildings cling to the steep hillside, and below are views of the magnificent Pacific.
- **Muzha Tourist Tea Plantations** *(see page 153)* See the city sparkle and twinkle at night from the scores of teahouses perched on the highest slopes.
- **Suao-Hualien Highway** *(see page 263)* One of the world's

most exhilarating drives. Cliffs rising thousands of feet straight above, ocean breakers hundreds below, and you are on a two-laner etched from the rock.
- **Taipei 101 Observatory** *(see page 135)* On the 89th floor, Taipei becomes a giant scale model, and planes are flying by below your feet. You get a fantastic 360-degree panoramic view of the city. The outdoor deck, on the 91st, is even higher.
- **Four Animals Mountain** *(see page 152)* From the westernmost peak of this mountain on Taipei's outskirts, the view of the city below is not to be missed.

BEST FESTIVALS AND EVENTS

- **Birthday of the City of God** *(see page 136)* Enjoy raucous processions, opera, puppet shows, and other fun at Xiahai City God Temple.
- **Birthday of Mazu** A celebration of Taiwan's most popular deity, the Goddess of the Sea who protects sailors and fishermen. Colorful pageantry and fireworks.
- **Spring Scream Festival** *(see page 253)* This is no traditional party. It's a multi-day alfresco rockfest in set in Kending National Park.
- **Taipei Lantern Festival** Celebrate the end of the Chinese New Year holidays with the locals. Traditional foods, arts, crafts, and music.
- **Baosheng** *(see page 132)* This lively tribute to the God of Medicine is a week-long celebration, including lion and fire-walking stunts.

ABOVE RIGHT: burning incense at Xingtian temple.
BELOW: dressing up for the Baosheng Festival.

FREE TAIWAN

- **Hiking** The national parks and scenic areas are laced with well-maintained hiking paths, many blazed hundreds of years ago.
- **Magazines** Pick up free tourist-oriented *Travel in Taiwan* copies from all Tourism Bureau service centers, *Discover Taipei* at City Hall and MRT stations, *This Month in Taiwan* from hotels and other public places.
- **Temples** There is always an open invite to the nation's countless Daoist, Buddhist, and Confucian worship sites, large and small.
- **Parks and Gardens** Taipei's many public parks, such as Sishoushan Community Forest, 228 Memorial Peace Park, Daan Forest Park and the Botanical Garden, all do not charge admission fees.

MONEY-SAVING TIPS

Night Markets Though a bit greasy for sensitive stomachs, Taiwan's night-markets are clean but dirt cheap. Visitors can feast on all sorts of traditional Taiwanese snack foods and drinks, and still come away with change from an NT$500 bill. *See page 144.*

More Cheap Eats and Drink *Biandang* are Taiwan's answer to lunchboxes. *Biandang* outlets are ubiquitous; for NT$50–80 you can feast on a bed of rice in a disposable, sealable box, with a choice of three/four toppings from a buffet selection of 15–20, a chicken drumstick or pork chop. Cheap and tasty.

Museums If not free, many island public museums have only nominal entrance fees.

Subways Taipei and Kaohsiung have systems. There's no better or more economical way to move around these cities. Day passes and free transfers to buses make it even better.

Shopping Refunds Foreign travelers spending at least NT$3,000 on the same day, and from the same Tax Refund Shopping (TRS) store, can have the 5 percent VAT refunded.

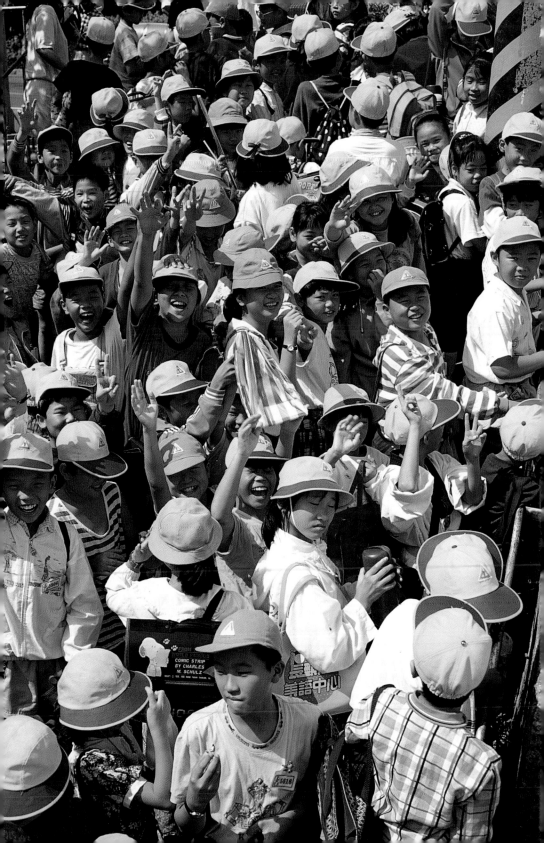

THE BEAUTIFUL ISLAND

This fertile island is no longer a mere bolthole for refugees

but a surprising, independent land with its own identity

Few people think of Taiwan as a travel destination. Its place in the popular imagination of the West is more as a producer of computer chips and peripherals, as a political thorn in the side of China, and, for those who keep abreast of current events, as the small island that sprinted from the starting line of martial law to attain fully-fledged democracy in little more than a decade.

But for those who take the time to make the journey and do some exploring, Taiwan is far more than the headlines would suggest. The ruggedly mountainous island that the Portuguese named *Ilha Formosa* – the "beautiful island" – more than four centuries ago may have had its beauty tarnished by rapid industrialization and booming population growth, but it remains a place of pleasant surprises. To be sure, the densely populated western plains are largely one long urban corridor punctuated by factories, but just a short distance inland such scenes give way to pristine mountain views. Meanwhile, the craggy east coast of the island remains for the most part unspoilt, as are Taiwan's less-visited offshore islands.

Lying less than 200 km (120 miles) east of China, the island that for thousands of years was inhabited only by tribes of head-hunting aborigines became a refuge for Chinese migrants escaping legal and political persecution around four centuries ago. Pirates and political exiles, traders and adventurers, farmers and fishermen left behind the crowded coastal areas of China – most often the southern region of Fujian province – to start new lives in Taiwan. They found that food grew abundantly in Taiwan's soil, a significant concern for a people accustomed to frequent famines and chronic food shortages. Furthermore, the island was fat with mineral resources – coal, sulfur and iron – not to mention jade, opal and coral.

Small surprise, then, that they were joined by enterprising émigrés blown to the island by the political storms of the mainland. Disgruntled mandarins and merchants, fed up with the factional vagaries and chronic interference of court politics, made their way to the island. The minority Hakka came from the northern Guangdong coast to escape persecution; Ming loyalists came to defy Qing rule. And in the mid-20th century Taiwan became a refuge for those who lost the mainland to the Chinese Communist Party. In the end, it is probably that image – Taiwan as emblem of a divided China – that figures largest in the Western mind.

Note: Chinese usage in this book follows the Hanyu Pinyin transliteration standard, widely used in Taiwan; non-Hanyu forms are used when official or more familiar.   ❏

PRECEDING PAGES: nun strikes a pose at Foguangshan, northeast of Kaohsiung, a center of Buddhism in Taiwan; the lion dance is performed to usher in good fortune.
LEFT: a school outing for kids in Taipei.

Decisive Dates

ISLAND SETTLEMENT

Circa 10,000 BC Primitive utensils found in caves prove there was prehistoric life on the island.

206 BC The most ancient Chinese historical record referring to Taiwan indicates that the island was called the "Land of Yangzhou."

AD 239 The earliest attempt to establish a Chinese claim to Taiwan is made when the Kingdom of Wu sends a 10,000-man expeditionary force.

AD 1000 Ethnic Chinese settlement appears to have commenced, mainly by the Hakka people.

ILHA FORMOSA

15th and 16th centuries Taiwan becomes a haven for marauding pirates and traders. The island is known as *Ilha Formosa* or "beautiful island," a name bequeathed by admiring Portuguese sailors.

1593 The first Japanese attempt to annex Taiwan.

COLONIAL INTERESTS

1622 Dutch forces capture the Pescadores archipelago (Penghu Islands) and attempt to control traffic through the Taiwan Strait.

1624 The Dutch agree with the Chinese government to evacuate the Pescadores archipelago in return for the right to settle on Taiwan, marking the start of Dutch colonial rule on the island.

1626 Spanish forces seize Keelung and from there expand control in northern Taiwan.

1642 The Dutch capture major Spanish settlements in northern Taiwan, thereby consolidating control over the island.

1652 Chinese revolt against Dutch-imposed poll tax; nearly 3,000 Chinese are slaughtered.

THE ZHENG DYNASTY

1661 Zheng Cheng-gong (Koxinga; Guoxingye) attacks the Dutch forces, bringing an abrupt end to Dutch rule and the beginning of the Zheng dynasty in Taiwan.

1662 Koxinga dies. His son and grandson maintain rule over Taiwan until 1683, which marks the beginning of China's governance of Taiwan under the Manchu or Qing dynasty.

COLONIAL INTRUSIONS

1786 Major rebellion against Chinese rule occurs.

1839 China takes up arms to suppress the foreign opium trade in Canton (Guangzhou).

1858 Treaty ending the Second Opium War opens four Taiwanese ports to foreign trade.

1867 25 foreign traders settle in northern Taiwan at Danshui and Keelung. Trade booms, doubling in volume by 1869, and doubling again by 1870.

JAPANESE OCCUPATION

1874 The Japanese attack Taiwan, mounting a punitive campaign against local aborigines for killing Japanese sailors.

1894 A full-scale war between Japan and China breaks out when the Japanese invade Korea, long a Chinese vassal state. The Treaty of Shimonoseki in 1895 concludes the Sino–Japanese War; Taiwan is ceded to Japan.

1945 On October 25, Taiwan becomes part of the Republic of China as a result of Japan's defeat in World War II.

1947 February 28 Incident sparks suppression and killing of thousands of Taiwanese by Kuomintang (Guomindang); beginning of White Terror period.

THE REPUBLIC OF CHINA

1949 The government of the Republic of China flees to Taiwan after being defeated on the mainland. Taipei becomes the provisional capital of the Republic of China.

AMERICAN INVOLVEMENT

1950 Taipei breaks diplomatic relations with the UK after the latter establishes formal ties with Peking (Beijing). The Korean War breaks out and

Taiwan is placed under American protection against possible Communist attacks, and also receives substantial economic aid.

1955 The US and Taiwan ratify the Sino–American Mutual Defense Treaty, and President Eisenhower is authorised to use US forces to defend Taiwan.

1958 On August 23, the second Offshore Island Crisis begins with forces of the People's Republic of China on the mainland bombarding Kinmen.

1959 On August 7, Taiwan experiences its worst floods for more than half a century. Later in August, Taiwan receives Nike-Hercules missiles from the US.

1965 The Republic of China and the US sign an agreement on the status of the US military in Taiwan. There is a critical test of strength for Taiwan and its leadership as its preferential trade status with the US is terminated. Nevertheless, industrialization, modernization and economic progress accelerate.

CHIANG'S LAST YEARS

1966 The National Assembly elects Chiang Kai-shek (Jiang Jie-shi) to a fourth term as president.

1971 The Republic of China loses its membership in the United Nations as the China seat is given to the People's Republic of China.

1974 The island's population reaches 16 million, twice what it was in the early 1950s.

1975 Chiang Kai-shek dies.

THE GROWTH OF DEMOCRACY

1978 Chiang Ching-kuo (Jiang Jing-guo), Chiang Kai-shek's son, is elected president.

1978 The US announces its recognition of the People's Republic of China, and ends official diplomatic relations with Taiwan.

1979 The Kaohsiung Incident galvanizes the Taiwanese against martial law and is a turning point in the democratization of Taiwan.

1980 The US–Republic of China Defense Treaty is terminated.

1986 The Democratic Progressive Party (DPP) establishes itself as an opposition force.

1987 Martial law is lifted.

1988 President Chiang Ching-kuo dies and the National Assembly officially elects Lee Teng-hui (Li Deng-hui) as the island's first Taiwan-born president.

1991 Taiwan replaces Japan and the US as the number one investor in the People's Republic.

PRECEDING PAGES: a depiction on silk of a procession of the Ming emperor Wuzong. **LEFT:** Chiang Kai-shek (standing) with his mentor, Dr Sun Yat-sen, 1924. **RIGHT:** statue of Chiang Kai-shek at Sun Moon Lake.

TENSION RISES

1993 The first official governmental contacts between Taipei and Beijing take place in Singapore.

1996 Taiwan holds its first fully democratic elections for presidency and the Taiwanese vote in their first elected president, 73-year-old Lee Teng-hui.

2000 On March 18, 54 years of Nationalist (Kuomintang) rule comes to an end with the election of DPP candidate Chen Shui-bian as president.

2001 KMT loses position as majority party in legislative elections, and thus control, with DPP emerging as largest party.

2002 After a 10-year effort, Taiwan gains entry into WTO on January 1; China is also accepted in

December 2001 after insisting on being first.

2002 US president George W. Bush ratifies largest arms package for Taiwan in decades. Pundits once again assess what this means for cross-strait military balance and future security of Taiwan.

2004 Chen Shui-bian pulls out a surprise victory against a united KMT-led opposition, emerging as a majority president with a paper-thin 0.228 percent victory margin. The opposition rejects the outcome and takes to the streets in violent protest. It very gradually acquiesces.

2008 Taiwan's status remains an explosive issue. Officially, Beijing considers the island a renegade province, while Taiwan has never officially declared independence from the mainland. ❑

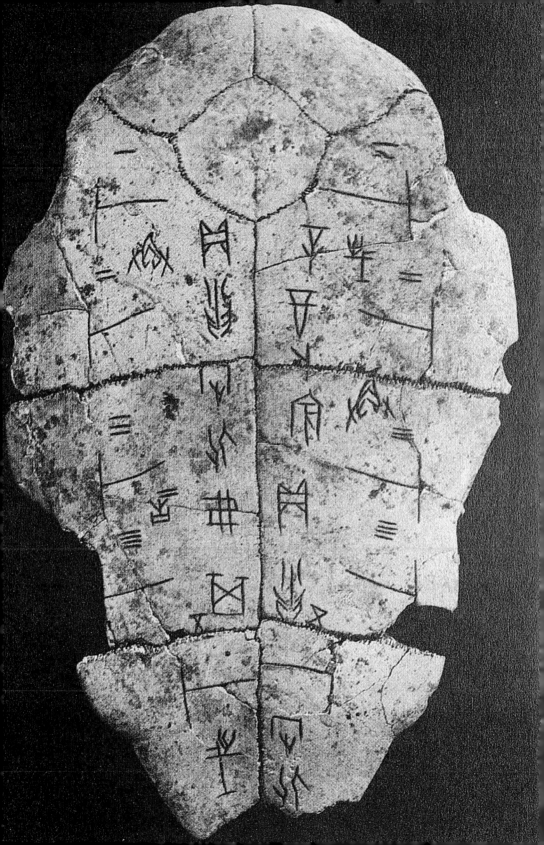

ISLAND SETTLEMENT

The Portuguese may have openly declared its beauty, but they were by no means the first or the last people to stake a claim on this bountiful island

lha formosa! Ilha formosa! Portuguese sailors shouted with admiration from their ships as they sailed past Taiwan, en route to Japan during the 16th century. The island thus became known to the West by the Portuguese word *formosa*, or beautiful.

This island off China's southeast coast has lured successive waves of people from Austronesia, Chinese immigrants from the mainland, explorers and exploiters from the West, and aggressive imperialists from Japan. All desired to possess the island of Taiwan.

But of all Taiwan's suitors, China proved to be the best match for the feisty and fertile island. The marriage of China's sophisticated and aesthetic culture with Taiwan's bountiful beauty and rich natural endowments has produced one of the most dynamic lands in Asia. Like *yin* and *yang*, ancient Chinese heritage and the island's indigenous charms are the inseparable elements that define Taiwan.

Prehistoric development

Little is known about Taiwan's earliest history. Radioactive carbon dating of primitive utensils found in caves and other sites has indicated that prehistoric people appeared on the island at least 10,000 years ago. Archeologists believe Taiwan's links with mainland China may be just as old. They have identified four stages of prehistoric tool development that match those of the mainland. They have also identified two later stages suggesting that other prehistoric Southeast Asian cultures arrived on the southern and eastern coasts of Taiwan. Early peoples, whose descendants now form an important part of Taiwan's culture, are believed to have Malaysian and southern Chinese Miao ancestry.

The most ancient Chinese reference to Taiwan indicates that the island was called the Land of Yangzhou, during the rise of the Han dynasty, in 206 BC. There may even have been an attempt at

LEFT: Chinese characters from the Shang dynasty written on an oracle shell from a tortoise.
RIGHT: scene from Taiwan's prehistoric past.

that time to explore the island, according to the *Shiji* (historical records), which referred to Taiwan as Yizhou. The earliest attempt to establish a Chinese claim apparently occurred in AD 239, when the Kingdom of Wu sent a 10,000-man expeditionary force, according to the ancient *Sanguoji*, or the *History of the Three Kingdoms*.

In the early 1400s, a eunuch magistrate and navigator from the Ming court, Zheng He (Cheng Ho), reported his "discovery" of the island to the emperor of China. The name used went down in the record books as "Taiwan," which some think means terraced bay. But despite the obvious fertility of the land, an imperial rule prevented the Ming empire's populace from emigrating to Taiwan – or elsewhere.

Two distinct groups of peoples were living on Taiwan at the time of the Chinese arrival. One group lived a sedentary existence on the rich alluvial plains, practicing hunting, fishing, and swidden cultivation, the majority in the central west and southwest. The others were semi-nomadic mountain tribes fighting incessantly among themselves, and practicing ritual tattooing and head-hunting.

Enter the Hakka

Although it is not known exactly when the Chinese first began to settle on Taiwan, the first mainland immigrants came from an ethnic group called the Hakka – literally "guests" or "strangers." The Hakka, a minority group relentlessly persecuted in China since ancient times, were driven from their native home in Hunan province about 1,500 years ago and forced to flee south to the Fujian and Guangdong coasts of the

mainland. There, they successfully engaged in fishing and trading, activities that eventually brought them to the Pescadores archipelago, now known as Penghu, and then later to Taiwan. By AD 1000, the Hakka had probably established themselves in the southern part of Taiwan, driving the indigenous tribes from the fertile plains and up into the mountains. The Hakka grew sugarcane, rice and tea, and engaged in active trade with the mainland. Today, the Hakka rank among Taiwan's most enterprising people.

Other Chinese also set their sights on Taiwan. During the Ming dynasty (1368–1644), immigrants from Fujian province began to cross the

A PIRATES' PARADISE

During the 15th and 16th centuries, Taiwan was a haven for marauding pirates and freewheeling traders plying the eastern Chinese coast, from both China and the Japanese archipelago. The distinction between pirates and traders was gratuitous, as ships plied both trades and operated freely in Taiwan's waters. In fact, because it was close to the trading centers and shipping lanes of China and Japan, yet free of outside political control – the populace governed itself on clan and village lines, without interference from Peking (Beijing) or elsewhere – Taiwan turned into a pirates' paradise. When times were good, they traded. When times were bad, they raided.

Taiwan Strait in ever-increasing numbers. They pushed the Hakka further inland and usurped the rich western plains. Chinese settlers adopted the term *benshengren*, which means "this-province people," or natives, to differentiate themselves from both the Hakka and the original indigenous peoples, whom they called "strangers." Even today, the descendants of these early immigrants from Fujian refer to themselves as *benshengren*, thereby distinguishing themselves from the late 1940s influx of mainland refugees, who are called *waishengren*, or "outside-province people," by the old-timers.

Still, the only true natives of Taiwan are the aborigines. Like the Indians of America and the

Aborigines of Australia, they have been shunted off to special reservations, though many have chosen to live among the Han in search of work or education. The majority of Taiwan's populace, in contrast, is descended from various groups of mainland Chinese immigrants. Even the Taiwanese dialect of Chinese is an offshoot of southern Fujianese.

Colonial interests

In 1590, the Portuguese arrived on the north coast of Taiwan and established a trading settlement and port facilities. The Japanese first attempted to annex Taiwan in 1593, after the

The Dutch imposed heavy taxes and labor requirements on the island's inhabitants in areas they controlled, and imported missionaries to preach Christianity. The Dutch East India Company gained exclusive commercial rights to the island, importing opium from Java (Batavia), which was part of the Dutch East Indies. The Dutch taught islanders to mix tobacco with opium and smoke it. The habit rapidly took root in Taiwan, later spreading to the mainland. (Two centuries later, opium would play a notorious role in the fall of the Qing dynasty, and would become the catalyst for war between China and Britain.)

warlord Hideyoshi Toyotomi unsuccessfully tried to conquer China by way of Korea. Hideyoshi's designs on Taiwan fared no better, as it proved too unruly to control.

This did not seem to put off the Europeans, however. The Dutch turned to Taiwan after they failed to wrest Macau from the Portuguese. At first, in the early 1600s, the Dutch were primarily interested in the Pescadores, but in 1624 they established a fort and settlement on the southwestern coast of Taiwan.

LEFT: bronze pitcher from China's Spring and Autumn period (722–481 BC). **ABOVE:** the Dutch Fort Zeelandia (Anping Gubao), near Tainan, Taiwan, in the mid 1600s.

Meanwhile, in 1626, the Spanish took control of the natural harbor and surrounding area at Keelung, later building a fort in Danshui. The jealous Dutch, wishing to achieve complete control over the island's foreign trade, drove the Spanish out of Taiwan in 1642. Two years later, the Manchu conquest of the mainland began, an event that exerted lasting impact on Taiwan.

For a while, the Dutch lived in relative harmony with both local residents of Taiwan and mainland immigrants. But the Dutch then sought to collect a poll tax, leading the Chinese to revolt in 1652. The revolt was easily suppressed, but nearly 3,000 Chinese were killed.

China's Ming dynasty reigned for 276 years, under 16 emperors. The creative arts and sciences flourished. But its glory faded under an administration that became increasingly corrupt. At the same time, Manchu leaders built a strong base of support and a huge army in what are today's northeastern provinces. They swept south, advancing against the crumbling Ming armies.

Before the Manchu reached Peking (Beijing), a Han Chinese rebel army took the capital. The emperor hanged himself, a humiliating final act in the saga of a glorious era. Loyalist Ming forces allowed the Manchu past the Great Wall to push the rebels from Peking, but soon found

the Manchu had greater designs. As they were pushed south the Ming loyalists brought a southeastern pirate named Zheng into their cause.

Son of Zheng

Zheng's forces, especially his navy, proved effective. He also took a Japanese wife, who bore him a son. The son inherited the Ming banner and with it a new name: Koxinga (Guoxingye) – Lord of the Imperial Surname.

With an army of 100,000 men and an armada of 3,000 ships, Koxinga carried on the mainland fight against the Manchu from 1646 until 1658. At one point, he almost recaptured the ancient capital of Nanjing. But the Manchu finally

forced Koxinga to retreat to the island bastion of Taiwan, an event that eerily foreshadowed Chiang Kai-shek's (Jiang Jie-shi) retreat across the Taiwan Strait three centuries later.

In Taiwan, Koxinga encountered the Dutch, who discounted him as a mere pirate, incapable of mounting a serious threat. But Koxinga's spies, aided by Dutch deserters, provided valuable intelligence. In 1661, Koxinga sailed from Penghu with 30,000 armed men, engaging 600 Dutch settlers and 2,200 Dutch soldiers at the two southwestern coastal forts. Koxinga captured Fort Zeelandia (Anping Gubao), near present-day Tainan, and graciously permitted the Dutch governor and his surviving men to leave the island. Thus, Dutch rule in Taiwan ended four decades after it began.

Taiwan became the personal domain of Koxinga. He gave the island its first formal Chinese government, turning it into a Ming enclave that continued to defy the Manchu, who by now had established firm control over the mainland. Koxinga's reign was brief but influential. He set up his court and government at Anping, and launched transport and education systems. Great strides were also made in agriculture. Tainan became the political and commercial center, and Anping grew into a prosperous harbor.

Perhaps Koxinga's greatest and most lasting contribution to Taiwan was his love for most things Chinese. His entourage included more than 1,000 scholars, artists, monks and masters of every branch of Chinese culture. He ushered in a renaissance of numerous ancient Chinese laws, institutions, customs and lifestyles.

Koxinga died suddenly in 1662, aged 38, less than a year after his conquest of Taiwan. Centuries later, he was named a national hero and is venerated in Taiwan as a *junzi*, perfect man. His son and grandson maintained rule over Taiwan until 1683, when the Manchu finally succeeded in taking control of the island, snuffing out the last pocket of Ming patriotism. Taiwan officially became an integral part of the Chinese empire when the Manchu, or Qing, court conferred the status of *fu*, or prefecture, on the island. But Qing rule remained nominal at best. Manchu officials sent to govern Taiwan usually succumbed to intrigue and self-indulgence. ❏

LEFT: porcelain jar from Qing dynasty, at Taipei's National Palace Museum. **RIGHT:** portrait of Taiwan's first Chinese ruler, Koxinga, painted by one of his descendants.

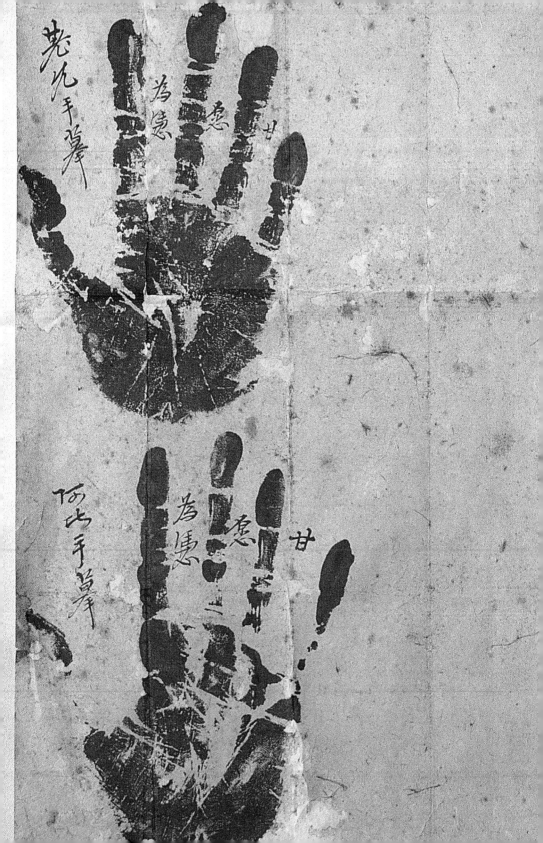

COLONIAL INTRUSIONS

As China's grip on Taiwan weakened, foreign powers
battled for control of this strategic and fertile island

Despite strict prohibitions from the imperial court against further emigration to Taiwan, colonists continued to pour across from the mainland. During the first 150 years of Qing rule, the island's population increased sevenfold. Karl Gutzlaff, a Prussian missionary visiting Taiwan in 1831, observed: "The island has flourished greatly since it has been in the possession of the Chinese. The rapidity with which this island has been colonized, and the advantages it affords for the colonists to throw off their allegiance, have induced the Chinese to adopt strict measures... The colonists are wealthy and unruly..."

One early point of contention between China and the West concerned the fate of shipwrecked European sailors who were frequently washed ashore on Taiwan. These involuntary visitors were routinely beaten, imprisoned and often beheaded, either by the Chinese authorities or by aborigines on the island. Whenever the Western powers sued the court of Peking (Beijing) to intervene in such incidents, they discovered that Peking had little real authority over island affairs, and even less interest. So Western nations resorted to gunboat diplomacy to punish locals for mistreatment of their crews, and dealt directly with the islanders rather than with Peking.

Economic potential

One of the first foreigners to recognize Taiwan's economic potential and to advocate its outright annexation was Dr William Jardine, scion of the powerful British trading firm Jardine Matheson and Company. Jardine was alarmed when China took up arms in 1839 to suppress the British opium trade in Canton (Guangzhou). He informed the British foreign secretary that "we must proceed to take possession of three or four islands, say Formosa, Quemoy (Kinmen) and Amoy (Xiamen), in order to secure new markets and new footholds in China."

LEFT: handprints of a tribal member used to transfer property to new Chinese settlers, Dongshi, 1866. **RIGHT:** Matteo Ricci, an Italian Jesuit, was influential in the Chinese court.

When the first conflict, or Opium War, broke out between China and Britain, it further strained the relations between China and the West. Crews of British vessels subsequently shipwrecked off Taiwan faced even harsher treatment. The ships were plundered, then burned. The crews were stripped naked and

forced to walk painful distances to captivity.

The British were not the only foreign power to show an interest in Taiwan during the 19th century. Several American traders and diplomats also advocated annexation of the island. They included Commodore Matthew Perry, who understood Taiwan's strategic importance in East Asia. Gideon Nye, a wealthy American merchant and a leading member of his country's expatriate community in Canton, proposed in 1857 that "Formosa's eastern shores and southern point... in the direct route of commerce between China and California and Japan, and between Shanghai and Canton, should be protected by the United States of America."

Nye also had personal reasons for his proposal: he suspected that his brother, who mysteriously disappeared on the opium clipper *Kelpie* in 1849, had been captured and killed in Taiwan.

The treaty ending the Second Opium War, in 1858, opened four Taiwanese ports to foreign trade: Danshui and Keelung in the north, and Taiwan Fu (Tainan) and Dagao (Kaohsiung) in the south. During the ensuing decade, foreign trade in Taiwan grew rapidly, involving British and American firms. Primary export products were camphor, tea, rice, sugar, lumber and coal. The primary import, sometimes exceeding exports in value, continued to be opium.

By 1867, 25 foreign traders lived in northern Taiwan at Danshui and Keelung, and another dozen lived in the south at Tainan. Trade boomed, doubling in volume by 1869 and doubling again by 1870. Expatriate communities flourished around Taiwan's ports and they maintained close ties with their counterparts in Hong Kong, Canton and Xiamen.

Increased violence

A negative aspect of the trade boom was the increased frequency of violent incidents, corresponding to the greater number of foreign trading vessels that called at the island's ports.

MISSIONARY MAYHEM

The law and order situation was further aggravated by the arrival of foreign missionaries in the early 1870s. Zealous preachers from various sects of Christianity fanned out over the island and staked out territorial domains, which created more confusion than their conflicting religious doctrines. The missionaries, backed by their home countries, competed for exclusive territories in much the way traders competed for monopolies of major exports. Attacks on missionaries and their converts led to the same futile wrangling between local magistrates and foreign officials as incidents in the commercial sector. Only displays of force produced settlements.

Brawls between drunken foreign sailors and the local Chinese usually ignited the violence, and vendettas followed. Local magistrates refused to act in such cases, insisting that the foreigners petition authorities in Peking. But, because of Peking's lack of influence and interest in the island's affairs, nothing was accomplished through such "legal channels."

Yet one thing was clear to all the squabbling parties: Taiwan was indeed an alluring beauty. It was rich in resources and strategically located, but it was also untamed. There was a need for law and order that Peking could not provide. Expatriates clamored for foreign governments to step in. The Japanese did just that.

The Japanese

In 1871, a Japanese ship foundered and sank off the coast of Taiwan. Three of its crew drowned, and only 12 of the remaining crew eventually survived. The rest were slaughtered by Botan aborigines. When the news of the killings reached Tokyo, Japan immediately prepared to launch a punitive expedition against the Botan tribe. Only Foreign Minister Soyeshima Taneomi held back the impending attack, deciding first to try to work out a diplomatic resolution with Peking.

Soyeshima was accompanied on his trip to Peking by Charles Le Gendre, an advisor to the

Soyeshima obtained a formal audience with the Chinese emperor, a significant accomplishment. The emperor tacitly admitted that the minorities inhabiting parts of eastern and southern Taiwan were beyond his political control. All of Japan hailed that disclosure as a diplomatic victory, but Soyeshima's return to Tokyo was marred by factional fighting over the military's long postponement of intervention in neighboring Korea, a Chinese vassal state. Soyeshima wiped his hands of the Taiwanese affair in disgust. In 1873 several sailors were killed by a Taiwanese tribe. A violent revolt of samurai protesting Meiji reforms in February 1874 finally impressed upon

planned military expedition to Taiwan who had earlier resigned as American consul to Amoy in order to enter the service of Japan's new Meiji emperor. Le Gendre had extensive experience in the island, negotiating settlements involving several American ships wrecked there, and in some cases also dealing directly with ethnic-minority tribes. But Washington had always ignored Le Gendre's calls for greater American vigilance in Taiwan. So Le Gendre advised Tokyo that it should prepare for war if its foreign minister's mission to Peking turned out to be unsuccessful.

Left: the Qing emperor receives a foreign envoy in Peking.
Above: the British negotiate to open China's ports to trade.

the Japanese Government the urgent need for a foreign adventure to vent frustrations of dissatisfied, and now masterless, samurai. So on April 27 that year, 2,500 troops, 1,000 laborers and several foreign advisors, led by Le Gendre, boarded warships bound for Taiwan.

The military expedition landed at two points in southern Taiwan, one clearly within Chinese jurisdiction. Japanese troops made a few forays into the mountains to punish the offending tribal groups, but their continued presence in the south prompted strong Chinese protests and a willingness to negotiate. After protracted talks in Peking, the Chinese Government agreed to pay Japan to compensate the families of the dead crewmen, and four times as much additionally for the expenses incurred by the military expedition. In return, Japanese forces withdrew from Taiwan and returned to Tokyo in triumph.

China continued to run Taiwan as a prefecture of Fujian province for more than a decade after the departure of the Japanese. But the repercussions of the Japanese occupation continued to resound through the island. For one thing, Japan's bold military move, for the first time in the island's history, had created a semblance of law and order on parts of the island. In fact, some foreign traders even seemed to wel-

ing desire for an overseas empire. In the 1894–5 war, China suffered total and ignoble defeat at the hands of a nation it had considered inferior and barbaric. China's navy had been made a complete mockery of in the war.

Not long before the war, vast sums of money that had been earmarked for modernizing China's navy had, in fact, been diverted by the greedy Qing dynasty's Empress Dowager Cixi to restore the Summer Palace, northwest of Peking. Therefore, it came as no surprise to outsiders when the out-gunned and humiliated Chinese Navy was annihilated in the Sino-Japanese war.

come the Japanese occupation of 1874, as it forced Chinese authorities to take more interest in the island's affairs and virtually eliminated attacks on its foreign settlements. Meanwhile, militarists in Tokyo soon began rattling their swords and demanding annexation of Taiwan, Korea and the Ryukyu Islands (Okinawa).

Fighting between Japan and China again broke out in 1894, when the Japanese invaded Korea, which had long been a loyal Chinese tributary state. China sent battleships to Korea's aid, but the Japanese sank them in a humiliating rout. Earlier, China had managed to buy off Japan to avert war, but this time nothing short of territorial gains would satisfy Japan's burn-

Cession to Japan

The Treaty of Shimonoseki, written by Japan, ceded possession of the Ryukyu Islands, Taiwan, and the Pescadores to Japan. It marked the start of half a century of Japanese rule over Taiwan and much of Northeast Asia, giving Japan a decisive role in Korea that would culminate in its annexation 15 years later.

Japan's takeover of Taiwan did not go down well with some locals, who resisted for several months; over 7,000 Chinese soldiers and several thousand civilians were killed during early resistance. (Later, in 1915, some 10,000 Chinese lost their lives during the Tapani revolt against the Japanese, again without success.)

The Japanese undertook an intensive modernization of Taiwan's infrastructure. A domestic network of railways and roads was constructed, linking major points of the island for the first time. The Japanese also built schools, hospitals and industries, and updated agricultural methods. Most importantly, strict Japanese rule ended the factional bickering and futile debates that had always marked island politics and commerce. Still, Japanese occupation proved oppressive and ultimately unpopular.

THE 22ND PROVINCE

After Japanese withdrawal in 1874, Taiwan was declared the 22nd province of China in 1885 and the population surpassed 2.5 million.

own image and to sever the island's ancient Chinese cultural roots. But, as in Korea, such cultural brutality would fail.

Retrocession Day

Taiwan toiled under Japanese occupation until the end of World War II. After Japan surrendered, Taiwan was restored to Chinese sovereignty on October 25, 1945, a date still recognized annually as Retrocession Day.

Following this return to Chinese sovereignty, hordes of adventurers from mainland China

Between 1918 and 1937, Japan consolidated its regime in Taiwan, exploiting its rich natural resources exclusively for the benefit of Japan. Resident Japanese officers and officials enjoyed elite privileges which were denied to local citizens. In the last stage of occupation, the naturalization of all Taiwanese as Japanese nationals was enforced. As in occupied Korea, the Japanese required everyone in Taiwan to adopt Japanese names and speak the Japanese language in an effort to remold Taiwan in its

FAR LEFT: Qing dynasty's Empress Dowager Cixi.
LEFT: France and China went to war in 1884.
ABOVE: civil war on the mainland drew a motley group.

stormed across the Taiwan Strait, dismantling the industrial infrastructure left by Japan and shipping items of value back to Shanghai.

Meanwhile, civil war had broken out on the mainland. The struggle for control matched the Communist Party of Mao Zedong and Zhou Enlai against the Nationalist Party, or Kuomintang (KMT; Guomindang). The KMT head was a fiery leader named Chiang Kai-shek (Jiang Jie-shi). The struggle for control of the mainland preceded World War II by decades, but both sides had reluctantly joined efforts to defeat the Japanese. With both the Japanese and the earlier colonial powers gone, China now had the opportunity to set its own course. ❏

THE RISE OF THE REPUBLIC

The successful post-war emergence of Taiwan as an economic power
while remaining a preserve of Chinese tradition is the legacy of one man

Chiang Kai-shek's (Jiang Jie-shi) association with Taiwan bears striking similarities to the saga of Koxinga (Guoxingye) centuries earlier. Both men fought to preserve the traditional order in China, and both established a bastion of that order in Taiwan, in defiance of their adversaries on the mainland. Most

significantly, both men successfully launched a renaissance of classical Chinese culture, which has made Taiwan a living repository of China's most ancient and cherished traditions.

Birth of a nationalist

Chiang Kai-shek was born on October 31, 1887, in Zhejiang province, China. His mother was a devout Buddhist; his father, a salt merchant, died when Chiang was only eight. Then, when he was at the tender age of 14, Chiang's mother arranged for him to marry Mao Fu-mei. In 1908, she gave birth to Chiang's first son, Chiang Ching-kuo (Jiang Jing-guo).

At the time, the Chinese imperial system was

disintegrating. Nationalism became the dominant force, and revolution was in the air. Caught up in the rapidly changing swirl of events, young Chiang took up military studies – in Japan, ironically. It was there that he first met a revolutionary called Sun Yat-sen (Sun Yi-xian).

Chiang participated in Sun Yat-sen's revolutionary forays into China, completing his military studies in Japan in 1912. That same year, Dr Sun Yat-sen became the first provisional president of the Republic of China (ROC), when Puyi abdicated as emperor, ending the Qing dynasty and closing the history books on China's 50 centuries of imperial rule. Chiang returned to China shortly after his second son, Chiang Wei-kuo (Jiang Wei-guo), was born, out of wedlock.

Two episodes left permanent imprints on the character of young Chiang after his return. For 10 years he resided in Shanghai, where he socialized with the wealthy merchants and bankers of that commercial city, as well as, reputedly, its underworld elements. Those contacts helped Chiang to forge a political power base that would carry him through two decades of warfare, and also provided him with the backbone for the Nationalist, or Kuomintang (KMT; Guomindang), successes in Taiwan. He loved Shanghai, and Taipei was largely built in its image. The second influential episode occurred in 1923, when Sun Yat-sen sent Chiang to Moscow as his emissary. Chiang returned from this mission with a deep distrust of the Russians and Communist doctrine.

Chiang Kai-shek has been labeled a conservative revolutionary. His concept of changing China was to foster nationalism and end China's humiliation at the hands of foreign powers. Nevertheless his vision of a modern China remained grounded in traditional Confucian social values. A born-and-bred Confucian, he cherished values like loyalty and obedience. He believed that the rebirth rather

LEFT: Chiang Kai-shek in 1930.
RIGHT: Lugang in 1934. The Japanese tried hard to eliminate Taiwan's Chinese identity.

than the destruction of traditional culture was the answer to China's woes.

After the successful Northern Expedition against the warlords who had partitioned China into personal fiefdoms, Chiang rode into Shanghai to consolidate his power. In 1927, Soong (Song) Mei-ling became his second wife. She was from a Shanghai merchant and banking family, one of China's most powerful, and younger sister of Sun Yat-sen's widow. (Dr Sun had died in Peking in March 1925, at the age of 59.) Madame Chiang, as she became known in the West, was an American-educated Christian. Before they married, Chiang Kai-

conducted from Japanese airfields in Taiwan. In 1943, the Generalissimo, as Chiang came to be called, met with American president Franklin D. Roosevelt and Britain's prime minister, Winston Churchill, in Cairo. The three men secretly pledged that Manchuria and Taiwan would be returned to China after the war.

Japan surrendered in 1945, but Chiang's problems continued. The Communists seized the opportunity of post-war chaos – and quantities of abandoned Japanese arms – to directly engage Chiang's Nationalist (Kuomintang or KMT) army in an all-out conflict. Civil war raged across the vast Chinese landscape for four long years. To

shek fulfilled a vow to her parents and converted to Christianity. His new wife and his conversion were important influences during the remainder of his life.

Constant conflict

The story of Chiang Kai-shek's campaigns against the Chinese Communists, and his war against the invading Japanese, has been well documented in many history books. The Japanese succeeded in occupying Manchuria in 1931. In 1937, they took Tianjin and Peking, captured Chiang's beloved Shanghai, and then overran Nanjing, which then was the capital of China. Their advance was bolstered by bombing raids

make things worse, Chiang's administration was plagued by corruption and incompetence.

Chiang Kai-shek was elected president of the Republic of China (ROC) in 1948. However, by then, the war was swinging in favor of the Communists; they eventually took Tianjin and Peking and established the rival People's Republic of China (PRC) in October 1949. Thus began the saga of the "two Chinas" – the PRC and the ROC.

Retreat to Taiwan

On January 21, 1949, Chiang Kai-shek resigned from the ROC presidency. After nearly a year of self-imposed solitude, in December 1949

Chiang returned to lead an exodus of Kuomintang soldiers and a rambling entourage of merchants, monks and masters of classical arts across the Taiwan Strait to Taiwan. Still calling his retreating government the Republic of China (ROC), Chiang's army defeated pursuing Communists in a last-stand battle on Quemoy (Kinmen), holding that island ever since.

Chastened by his defeat on the mainland, and knowing there was growing discontent in the military and civilian ranks – as well as being pushed by a disapproving US administration – Chiang was determined to reform Kuomintang policies in Taiwan. One of his first acts was to execute the rapacious governor-general Chen Yi, who was held responsible for the looting of Taiwan's wealth and the terrorizing of its people since 1945. In fact Chen Yi was the Kuomintang governor of Taiwan when the tragic February 28 Incident *(see box below)* occurred. Many Taiwanese were under the impression that Chen Yi was killed for his misdeeds in Taiwan, but in fact Chiang had Chen Yi promoted and sent to the mainland. It was only when Chiang later suspected Chen Yi of colluding with the Communists to overthrow him that he had him killed.

Next, Chiang initiated a land-reform policy that was as sweeping as the one instituted by

THE FEBRUARY 28 INCIDENT

Nationalist misrule on Taiwan led to a deep undercurrent of anger among the Taiwanese. On February 27, 1947, a minor incident led to a rupture of the dam holding back their discontent. On this fateful day, officials injured a poor widow on a Taipei street while attempting to confiscate her black-market cigarettes. A crowd rushed to her defense. In their panicked retreat, one of the monopoly bureau officers shot into the crowd – a man fell and died.

Word spread like wildfire. On the next day, the Taiwanese gathered in the streets, and there were more shootings. Around the island people rose in protest, and mainlanders caught alone and unprotected fell to the mobs.

An ugly and clearly KMT-orchestrated crackdown came, with summary executions and arbitrary massacres, and the educated, in the thousands, "disappeared." Between 18,000 and 28,000 Taiwanese are said to have been murdered. On March 10, 1947 martial law was declared, and remained in existence for the next 40 years.

The February 28 Incident, commonly known as "Er Er Ba" or "2-2-8," long defined the Taiwan independence movement and still lies at the core of embittered feelings toward mainlanders by the Taiwanese, the wounds only now slowly healing. Exactly 50 years after the February 28 Incident, in 1997, the day was proclaimed a national holiday.

the Communists on the mainland, but with one vital difference. Instead of vilifying and killing landlords, the Kuomintang government paid them for their land, then offered them funds and tax breaks to engage in non-agricultural business ventures. That move helped launch the industrial revolution that would become the catalyst for the island's phenomenal economic growth. Overnight, Taiwan found itself with an entrepreneurial elite of former landlords, who now had the money and the motivation to invest in Taiwan's future. Other reforms followed: the educational system was overhauled and students were sent abroad to absorb new technology and training.

Although national affairs remained firmly in the hands of the Kuomintang, democratic institutions were established at local levels.

Chiang nominally governed the island according to Sun Yat-sen's *Sanminzhuyi* (Three Principles of the People). Still honored today in both Communist China and Taiwan as the father of each respective country, Dr Sun built his framework for sensible government on three points: *minzu*, nationalism, or the liberation of China from foreigners; *minquan*, democracy; and *minsheng*, livelihood, or economic security for the people.

Of the three principles, Dr Sun considered nationalism the primary goal, and that the fastest way of obtaining that goal was through a democratic system that provided for the livelihood of the people. Chiang amplified on Dr Sun's interpretations of the Three Principles in his book, *China's Destiny*, published in 1943.

With the outbreak of the Korean War in 1950, Taiwan was placed under the American protective umbrella from possible Communist attacks, and received substantial economic aid, too. In 1955, the United States and Taiwan ratified the Sino-American Mutual Defense Treaty.

Chiang's last years

Chiang Kai-shek continued to maintain strict political discipline and social order, crushing

---

LEFT: Chiang Kai-shek and his wife at the Cairo Conference, 1943, with Franklin D. Roosevelt and Winston Churchill.
RIGHT: Chiang broadcasts the news of his Nationalist (Kuomintang) government's retreat to Taiwan, 1949.

DISUNITED NATIONS

In 1971, the Republic of China (ROC), a founding member of the United Nations, lost its membership and was replaced by the mainland's People's Republic of China (PRC).

all dissent, potential and real, in the White Terror period and shutting out almost all non-KMT political participation at the central and provincial levels.

Although Chiang gave entrepreneurs free rein in the economic sphere, the domestic market for large-scale concerns was largely restricted and directed to those loyal to the regime in the early years.

Enthusiasm for capitalism propelled the private sector to grow from less than 50 percent of Taiwan's economy in 1953 to 75 percent

in 1974, at the expense of state monopolies. During this time, the island's population doubled to 16 million.

The year 1965 proved a critical test of strength for Taiwan and its leadership. Financial aid from the United States, which had provided a springboard for economic development, was terminated. Nevertheless, industrialization, modernization, and economic progress continued to accelerate.

Chiang died shortly after midnight, on April 5, 1975. He was succeeded by the vice-president, Yan Jia-kan. In the next presidential election in 1978, Chiang Kai-shek's son, Chiang Ching-kuo, was elected president. ❑

MODERN TAIWAN

The transition to democracy has provided the framework for economic prosperity,
with far-sighted governments stealing a march on Taiwan's near neighbors

At the time of Chiang Kai-shek's (Jiang Jie-shi) death in 1975, Taiwan was a rising economic power, and had evolved from a pineapple- and sugarcane-growing country into a leading exporter of textiles, toys and shoes. But material success came at a price. The ruthless Chiang had allowed no freedoms and tolerated no dissent. His dictatorship was typified by executions without trial, midnight knocks on the door, long prison terms for political dissidents, and strict suppression of everything Taiwanese, including the Taiwanese and other native languages.

As the country prospered, and the people became richer and more educated, they grew restive. To the native Taiwanese, most of whose ancestors came from Fujian province in the 1600s and 1700s, Chiang and the China-born Nationalist (Kuomintang; Guomindang) Party "mainlanders" were outsiders. During the 1970s, despite the persecutions of the martial-law era, dissent percolated throughout Taiwan. Much of the resistance came from the southern part of the island, a native stronghold where Taiwanese was the common language, and where few mainlanders had settled. Resentment against martial law and the Nationalists boiled over in 1979, with the Kaohsiung Incident *(see box, page 38).*

Friendlier times

After the Kaohsiung Incident, the situation began to change. Chiang Kai-shek's son Chiang Ching-kuo (Jiang Jing-guo), who had become president in 1978, steered the country toward greater freedom. Unlike his autocratic father, the younger Chiang was friendly and personable, and made an effort to mix with the people. He also brought a number of native Taiwanese into the high echelons of the central government, including Lee Teng-hui (Li Deng-hui).

Chiang Ching-kuo was re-appointed president in 1984, and Lee became vice-president.

LEFT: changing of the guard at the Martyrs' Shrine (Zhonglie Zi), Taipei. **RIGHT:** girls on parade with Sun Yat-sen posters during National Day festivities.

Within the next few years, Chiang clearly saw the need for reform. Across Asia, the tide was turning in favor of democracy. The Philippines had overthrown dictator Ferdinand Marcos, and violent pro-democracy protests were underway in Korea and elsewhere. International pressure to end martial law was increasing as well.

As the island continued to prosper, Taiwan's people demanded a greater voice. In 1986, the Democratic Progressive Party (DPP) established itself as an opposition force. Although the new group was illegal, Chiang defied Nationalist hardliners and refrained from a crackdown.

In 1987 Chiang Ching-kuo announced the lifting of martial law, and allowed the people of Taiwan to travel to China for the first time since the end of the civil war in 1949. By the time Chiang died in 1988, Taiwan's transition from martial law to democracy was well underway. The ban on political parties ended the following year.

Lee Teng-hui took over as the island's president in 1988, and became party chairman the same year, outmaneuvering mainlander Nationalist hardliners. He continued the political reforms begun by Chiang Ching-kuo, but soon had to turn his attention to another issue: persistent bullying by mainland China, which considered Taiwan a breakaway province.

Years of resistance to the Nationalists had hardened the Taiwanese people, making them difficult to push around. The harsh rhetoric from China solidified their sense of a separate identity, and at the same time, the DPP was loudly demanding a formal declaration of independence from China. By this time too, millions of Taiwanese had visited China, and what they saw on the mainland shocked them: grinding poverty, harsh repression, and corruption.

Provocative politician

Throughout the 1990s, the Taiwan–China dialogue was shaped by master politician Lee Teng-hui, who was president and Nationalist Party chairman from 1988 to 2000. The Taiwan-born Lee did much to provoke China during his presidency, furthering his own pro-independence sentiments along with those of a solid segment of the populace.

Lee's high-profile US visit in 1995 helped galvanize support for independence in Taiwan,

THE KAOHSIUNG INCIDENT

The Kaohsiung Incident was *the* landmark event in the development of Taiwan's democracy. It took place in December 1979, when a pro-democracy journal called *Formosa Magazine* organized a rally in Kaohsiung, to commemorate Human Rights Day.

The rally was repeatedly interrupted by riot police using tear gas, and it soon became a violent confrontation between the martial-law government and the democracy activists, who numbered nearly 150,000. Between skirmishes, the protestors gave impassioned speeches, but the rally eventually turned into an all-out riot, and many activists and policemen were severely beaten.

Eight of the Kaohsiung rally organizers, including famous dissident Shih Ming-teh (Shi Ming-de) and later vice-president Annette Lu, were charged with sedition. They were defended by a team of lawyers including Chen Shui-bian, future president of Taiwan, and Frank Hsieh (Xie), later mayor of Kaohsiung and chairman of the Democratic Progressive Party (DPP). In the end the eight organizers were found guilty, and many received long jail terms. But the Kaohsiung Incident and subsequent trial received widespread publicity, and it galvanized the people of Taiwan against martial law. It was the crucible in which the DPP party was forged, and a turning point in modern Taiwanese history.

while his "Go Slow Be Patient" policy of 1996, which limited Taiwanese investment in China, stopped the two sides from building closer economic ties.

The Chinese had little success dealing with Lee, and even went to the extent of calling him names like "schemer." In 1996, as Taiwan prepared to hold its first direct presidential election, China tried to derail Lee's campaign by launching missiles near the island. But the move backfired, and Lee won by a huge majority, becoming the first presi-

> **DEMOCRATIC LANDMARK**
>
> Chen Shui-bian's victory in the March 2000 presidential election was the first democratic change of power in 3,400 years of recorded Chinese history.

2000 was a contest between old and new, as the Nationalist candidate Lien Chan (Lian Zhan) squared off against Independent James Soong (Song) and DPP candidate Chen Shui-bian. Chen won with just over 39 percent of the vote, to 36 percent for Soong and just 22 percent for Lien. This election ended 54 years of Nationalist rule, and marked the completion of Taiwan's journey from dictatorship to democracy. The Nationalists were further humiliated in the legislative elections of late 2001 when the DPP became

dent ever elected by the people of Taiwan.

In 1999, President Lee took the offensive again, saying Taiwan and China were two separate states. This was a sharp break from his previous position, which held that there was one state but with two governments. That speech shaped the subsequent campaign debate on China, by making the presidential candidates appear much more moderate than Lee.

Taiwan's presidential election on March 18,

LEFT: the Nationalist Party's Lee Teng-hui was president from 1988–2000. **ABOVE LEFT:** Chen Shui-bian of the DPP Party. **ABOVE RIGHT:** Ma Ying-jeou, of the opposition Kuomintang Party, was elected president in 2008.

the largest party and the KMT lost its majority.

In the 2004 presidential election the humiliation continued, the united Lien/Soong forces beaten by just under 30,000 votes by Chen's DPP. The losers called the election a fraud, claiming Chen had set up an assassination attempt on the eve of election that left him and his VP lightly wounded. The resulting violent street protests led to a further rift between the pro-China faction and the growing "Taiwan first" population.

In 2008, the KMT took back power, in large part because of DPP scandals. The public is waiting to see if the KMT's pro-China moves will bring economic and political benefits.

The economy

Taiwan's powerhouse economy is one of the envies of Asia. In the 1990s, the country's Gross Domestic Product (GDP) grew 6.2 percent per year, among the best in the world, compared with the US at 3.2 percent and Japan at just 1.2 percent. Even the Asian economic crisis of 1997–8, which plunged neighboring countries into recession, was barely a bump in the road for Taiwan.

Taiwan is a world-class producer of bicycles, plastics, chemicals and other products. Its exports earn foreign exchange reserves of about US$287 billion, the fifth-largest in the world after China, Japan, Russia and India. It is the

world's leading producer of laptop computers, while the value of its IT hardware industry tops US$80 billion a year. Taiwan also excels in the manufacture of computer chips: Taiwan Semiconductor Manufacturing Corporation and United Microelectronics are the world's top producers of made-to-order integrated circuit chips that drive the world's computers, cell phones and video games.

Much of the credit for Taiwan's economic success goes to the government, which avoided the prestige projects that typify other Asian countries. Instead, it built useful infrastructure that contributed to economic growth. In the 1950s, the government promoted agriculture through land reforms, and in the 1960s it emphasized the manufacture of labor-intensive exports such as textiles, paper and electrical goods. With its low labor costs and high quality control, Taiwan soon became a successful exporter. By the 1970s, the focus was on infrastructure projects like the first North-South Freeway, Chiang Kai-shek International Airport, railways, harbors, and a nuclear power plant. In 1980, in a stroke of far-sighted genius, and long before other countries in Asia realized the importance of electronics, government planners launched the Hsinchu Science-based Industrial Park (now Hsinchu Science Park), which became the epicenter of Taiwan's electronics industry.

In the 1980s, rising labor and land prices eroded Taiwan's advantage in cheap manufacturing, and much of such business fled to cheaper sites in China and Southeast Asia.

Decreased regulation

In the 1990s, the government's ambitious Asia-Pacific Regional Operations Center plan eased regulations and introduced competition to a variety of industries. The plan helped liberalize the economy, lower trade barriers and clear away useless red tape. Hundreds of areas were targeted, ranging from banks to foreign exchange and telecommunications.

By the end of the decade, much had been accomplished, from lower long-distance and cellular phone rates to lower charges for cargo shippers and easier access to the capital markets. Although many of the changes were incremental, together they added up to a significant package of reforms. Now, with Taiwan in the World Trade Organization, it is becoming even more competitive as it lowers trade barriers and ends subsidies to protected industries.

The economy is an important topic in Taiwan because it fuels a high-flying lifestyle of lavish Chinese restaurants, mobile phones, cars and designer-brand clothes. Per capita GNP averages about US$16,000 a year, less than half that of the United States and Western Europe, but far higher than countries such as Malaysia, Thailand, the Philippines and China.

Politics and Taiwan's bilateral ties with China therefore form a dicey game that could easily interfere with the island's enviable rate of economic growth. ❑

LEFT: Taipei 101 Financial Building.

Cross-Strait Relations

Taiwan's most enduring and intractable problem is its troubled relationship with China. The island's existence as a de-facto separate country is a humiliation to the mainland, which considers Taiwan a breakaway province. By insisting that Taiwan return to the motherland on its terms, and by threatening military force in order to achieve this, China has left itself little room for diplomatic maneuver.

Taiwan, on the other hand, wants independence. Polls show that the vast majority of people in Taiwan wish to remain separate from China. That stance has strengthened since the lifting of martial law, as the China-born "mainlander" generation has lost influence, and a pro-Taiwan identity has emerged.

The Taiwanese see no reason to return to China, which they view as a badly-governed country where business is dominated by corrupt officials, personal freedom is limited, and the quality of life is poor.

However, despite having opposite goals, the two sides have talked. In 1992 and 1993, discussions were held under a One China platform, which held that Taiwan and China were part of one country, but with two governments. But, in the mid-1990s, under Taiwanese President Lee Teng-hui, the relationship worsened. Lee introduced rules restricting Taiwanese investment in China and refused to re-open direct air and shipping links to China, which have been banned since 1949. In 1999, Lee broke from the One China policy, saying the two sides were separate states, and should negotiate as such.

The third major player in the relationship, the US, endorses the One China policy and does not support Taiwanese independence. But the Taiwan Relations Act, enacted by the US Congress in 1979, implies that America will provide Taiwan with defensive weapons and defend it against attack.

Meanwhile, Taiwan continues to behave like an independent country, conducting its own foreign policy. It is not a member of the UN, but it has 23 diplomatic allies, and almost every year requests admission to the world body.

Nor has Taiwan neglected its military forces. Its air force has approximately 150 Lockheed F-16 fighter jets and 58 French-built Mirage 2000 fighters, along with 130 home-made IDF jets. Conscription is mandatory, and over 300,000 soldiers

serve full time in the military. The US is pushing for greater professionalization, and under President George W. Bush agreed to sell Taiwan weaponry that was previously off-limits, including diesel submarines.

The war of words has done little to slow trade between the two countries. Indirect cross-strait business has grown steadily, and China is now Taiwan's top trading partner, followed by the US and Japan. Taiwanese investment in China has surged sharply since the mid-1990s.

But business is one thing, and politics is another. In March 2000, Taiwan turned in a dangerous result at the ballot box, electing an

independence-minded president, Chen Shui-bian. Just as they did in 1996, voters ignored threats from China, and elected the candidate most disliked by Beijing. China reacted cautiously to Chen's election, but repeated its main theme: There is One China, Taiwan is part of that China, and it can never be independent. President Chen said he was willing to discuss any topic, including One China, but the future of Taiwan should be decided by the people of Taiwan. The pro-KMT retook the presidency in 2008.

Chen pursued a policy of what Beijing calls "creeping independence." In March 2006 he closed down the National Unification Council, set up by the KMT, as an "undemocratic" body. ❏

RIGHT: sending a strong message to China.

GEOGRAPHY AND CLIMATE

A mountainous backbone, fertile plains, persistent volcanic activity

and a complex weather system provide the geographical backdrop to the island

The island of Taiwan straddles the Tropic of Cancer, separated from China by the Taiwan Strait, 160 km (99 miles) wide at its narrowest point. Taiwan lies 355 km (221 miles) north of the Philippines and 595 km (370 miles) southwest of Japan's Okinawa.

Taiwan is shaped like a tobacco leaf, with its tip pointing toward Japan. It stretches 390 km (242 miles) in length and is about 140 km (87 miles) wide at its broadest point. Its total area of nearly 36,000 sq km (13,900 sq miles) makes Taiwan about the size of the Netherlands.

Divisive mountains

Taiwan's most prominent topographical feature is the Zhongyang Shanmo (Central Mountain Range), a ridge of towering mountains that runs for about 270 km (167 miles) of the island's length and which was formed by ancient tectonic, and, to a lesser extent, volcanic activity.

The mountain range bisects the island from north to south, covers two-thirds of the country, and is almost impenetrable because of its extreme ruggedness. More than 200 of the island's peaks rise 3,000 meters (9,843 ft) or more in altitude. Taiwan's tallest peak is Yushan (Mount Jade) at 3,952 meters (12,959 ft). Heavy rainfall has deeply scarred its face with rugged gorges and valleys.

A narrow valley of rich alluvial soil, 160 km (99 miles) long, separates the middle bulge of mountains from a smaller line of crests that fronts the east coast. In many areas of the east coast cliffs drop sharply to the sea, forming the island's most spectacular scenery. The Central Cross-Island Highway dramatically slices its way through the central range to these east-coast escarpments.

Primeval plate activity pushed the island up from under the sea, as evidenced by coral from prehistoric seabeds lodged in igneous rock up to 610 meters (2,000 ft) high in the hills. While

the related fiery volcanic activity ended eons ago, bubbling pools of hot sulfurous water and hissing steam vents still punctuate the terrain.

The most densely populated areas of Taiwan are the plains, tablelands and basins. The broad, sea-level plains that spread across the west of Taiwan are fed by short, winding rivers that

bring rainwater and alluvial soil from the mountains, making them extremely fertile. The largest plain is the Chianan (Jianan) Plain, which extends from Changhua to Kaohsiung, a distance of 180 km (112 miles), and measuring 48 km (30 miles) at its widest point. The other two major plains are the Pingtung Plain and the Lanyang Plain of Ilan County.

Taipei, Taichung and Puli are situated in basins. The area stretching between Taoyuan and Hsinchu, on the other hand, is tableland.

The rivers flowing down from the mountains into the western plains of Taiwan not only deposit fertile alluvial soil but also turn much of the western coast into tidal mud flats, a feature that

PRECEDING PAGES: scenic Sun Moon Lake area. **LEFT:** Qilai Ridge, west-central Taiwan, offers a challenging hike. **RIGHT:** flooded rice field, central foothills of Taiwan.

military strategists claim would make the island very difficult to invade. Easier targets might be the two island groups administered by Taiwan in the Taiwan Strait, which are much closer to China than they are to Taipei. The small, hilly island of Kinmen (Quemoy) is close enough to China's Fujian province (only 2,310 meters/1½ miles) to afford views of the Chinese city of Xiamen, while Mazu lies close to the mouth of Fujian's Min River.

Also prominent are the Penghu Islands, or Pescadores, an archipelago of some 64 small

THE BIG SHAKE-UP

The 9-21 earthquake gave Taiwan such a shaking that it is thought that Yushan, the island's highest peak, may have gained a few meters in altitude.

islands located midway between China and Taiwan and formed by volcanic action forcing up basalt from the sea floor.

Taiwan is still characterized by seismological instability. The island sits where two plates grind together (the Eurasian Plate is folding under the Philippine Sea Plate at a rate of about 7 cm/3 inches a year), building up enormous pressure that occasionally results in earthquakes.

Hualien is closest to what geologists refer to as the subduction zone between the two plates, and indeed it is the east of Taiwan, in the vicinity of Hualien, that is most often rattled by tremors. Nevertheless, the entire island is riddled with fault lines, and major earthquakes

(Taiwan has recorded 19 quakes measuring over 7 on the Richter scale since 1906) can strike anywhere on the island, the biggest in recent history being the 9-21 (September 21) earthquake of 1999, which measured 7.3 on the scale.

Climate

Due to Taiwan's mountainous topography, its weather is as diverse as its landscape. In the low areas the climate is subtropical and in the far south tropical, while in the heights of the Central Range the thermometer can dip to temperatures that allow snow.

There are two distinct seasons: hot (May–October) and cool (November–March). Unfortunately, the island's excessive humidity exaggerates these seasonal changes.

During the summer months, with average daytime temperatures in the north rising to 35°C (95°F) and humidity seldom dropping below 75 percent, the island's low-lying coastal areas seem like a giant sauna, making it a good time to escape to the relative cool of the mountains. Likewise, winter temperatures usually do not fall below 10°C (45°F), but the dampness can chill the bones. It is a good idea to bring warm clothes during the winter months, even if you are going to be spending the majority of your time in southern Taiwan.

The most pleasant times of the year are the brief spells of spring and fall, during April and May, and October and November. Skies are generally clear, nights are cool and days moderate. But, at any time of year, Taiwan's weather may change dramatically. High and low temperatures can vary as much as 10°C (15°F) from one day to the next.

Nature wrings an average annual rainfall level of more than 1,000 mm (40 inches) from the cloak of humidity that hangs over Taiwan. In higher elevations, the average rainfall can be five times as great.

The northeast winter monsoon and the southwest summer monsoon provide the moisture. The northeast monsoon moves in from late October to late March, causing rain in the windward reaches of northeast Taiwan. The southwest monsoon takes its turn from early May until late September, causing wet weather in the south while the north enjoys drier spells. Nevertheless, it is not entirely wise to rely on such general formulations in predicting Taiwan's weather. Rain – often British-style incessant drizzle – is something to be prepared for at any time of the year.

The typhoon season

The most feared aberrations in Taiwan's moody weather are typhoons. *Taifeng* (the English word derives from the Chinese), meaning "great winds," tend to swell up in the Indonesian archipelago to the south, then sweep through the Philippines and storm northwards toward Japan, usually via Taiwan, before making landfall on the southern Chinese mainland.

at the southern city of Kaohsiung fell below 71 cm (28 inches), reportedly the lowest reading ever recorded in Taiwan. Winds of 250 km (155 miles) an hour battered the island. And in 1968, a typhoon drowned downtown Taipei in nearly 4 meters (13 ft) of water and made rowboats the only form of practicable transport.

Visitors caught in Taiwan during a typhoon need not panic, however. Taiwan's new steel-and-concrete structures and modern hotels are generally immune to any serious damage. But bear in mind that, while it's safe to watch the typhoon from the windows, it is still risky to walk the streets. ❑

The typhoon season lasts from mid-August until early October. During this time, no fewer than a half-dozen typhoons may cross or skirt Taiwan. At roughly three- to four-year intervals, a typhoon of major proportions crashes into Taiwan, with wind speeds of up to 160 km (99 miles) per hour or more. Such fierce storms can capsize ships, flood low-lying cities, trigger huge landslides, uproot trees and blow down dwellings.

One of the worst typhoons to hit Taiwan occurred in August 1911. Barometric pressure

LEFT: at the scene of the 9-21 earthquake.
ABOVE: a typhoon-induced landslide wreaks havoc along a narrow mountain road.

TYPHOON WARNING

Even without watching the television weather reports, most Taiwanese know instinctively when a typhoon is on the way. Formed by low-pressure regions out to sea, typhoons suck Taiwan's clouds and dirty air away long before they make landfall, usually blessing the island with a day or so of brilliant sunshine. A beautiful sunny day in the months of September through October will usually have people remarking to each other about "typhoon weather" – and invariably they're right. Two or three days later the island is battening down, and scouring winds will send torrential downpours lashing down on anyone foolhardy enough to venture outdoors.

THE TAIWANESE

The people of Taiwan may come from a variety of ethnic backgrounds, but they are united in their generous hospitality and their openness to visitors

Statistics released recently show the population of Taiwan stands at just under 23 million. With much of the island taken up by uninhabitable mountainous regions, those people are squeezed into a relatively small amount of space, making Taiwan 14th in the world in terms of population density, among countries with a population of at least 10 million.

Unsurprisingly, it is Taipei where this population density is at its highest, with 10,000 people per sq. km (nearly half a square mile). Having rapidly evolved from a largely agrarian society in the space of a few decades, close to 70 percent of Taiwan's population today can be found in urban metropolitan areas with populations of 1 million or over. The largest by far is the Taipei Greater Metropolitan Area, which has a population of just over 6.5 million, followed by the Kaohsiung Greater Metropolitan Area with 2.6 million and the Taichung-Changhua Greater Metropolitan Area with around 2 million.

The upshot of this is that Taiwan may be crowded, but, if you get out of the urban corridors into the mountains or the rural east coast, it suddenly becomes a lot more peaceful.

Ethnicity and politics

Taiwan's population is not as homogeneous as it might seem to the casual visitor, and the ethnic breakdown is an issue that is subject to sensitive political factors. Until very recently, asking someone whether they were Taiwanese was likely to result in a vehement denial, followed by the words "I'm Chinese." This is far less the case these days, and the opposite often applies, making it safer to ask people whether they are Taiwanese than Chinese.

The problem derives from the fact that, in modern times, the term Chinese refers to those mainland Chinese who fled with Chiang Kai-shek (Jiang Jie-shi) to Taiwan in 1949 as well as their descendants. Called *waishengren*, liter-

ally "outside-province people," or *daluren* ("mainlanders"), they comprise about 15 percent of Taiwan's population. The remainder of the population are called *benshengren*, or "this-province people" – whether Hakka, whose descendants arrived from China as early as AD 1000 (comprising around 14 percent of the population), aborigine (less than half a million), or descendants of the Minnan people of southern Fujian province. This latter group began settling in Taiwan around four centuries ago, have deeper connections with the island than do mainlanders, and are likely to perceive themselves as Taiwanese (as do the Hakka for the most part).

The decisive moment in this change of consciousness came with the lifting of martial law in 1987. Suddenly, after 40 years of suppression of Taiwanese language and culture, the question of Taiwanese identity was something that could be discussed openly. Today, the Taiwanese dialect can be heard in popular music, television, movies and news broadcasts. Former

---

PRECEDING PAGES: traditional Confucian rites at a temple.
LEFT: the friendly face of new Taiwan.
RIGHT: a trishaw can take you places in Kaohsiung.

president and Kuomintang (KMT; Guomindang) chairman Lee Teng-hui (Li Deng-hui), a Hakka who is more comfortable speaking Taiwanese than Mandarin, announced himself late in his tenure as a "New Taiwanese," a rallying cry that has become somewhat definitive of the new native sentiment prevalent on the island.

Taiwanese

Some 98 percent of Taiwan's population is ethnically Han Chinese, meaning at some point they or their ancestors crossed the Taiwan Strait from China and made Taiwan their home. The Han Chinese may share a general common culture, but linguistically they are a very diverse people. The Cantonese dialect spoken in Hong Kong and southern China, for example, is as different from Mandarin, the standard "national tongue" spoken in both China and Taiwan, as Dutch is from English. The same applies to Taiwanese, a polytonal dialect said to be older than Mandarin, which has evolved from the Fujian dialect known as Minnanyu.

Minnanyu-speaking immigrants from Fujian province started to arrive in Taiwan in large numbers early in the 17th century, a period that coincides with the earliest Dutch settlements on the island. When Koxinga (Guoxingye) fled

IT'S IN THE NAME

With increasingly large numbers of citizens preferring to call themselves Taiwanese *(taiwanren)*, the issue emerges of how to acknowledge the shared Chinese cultural legacy of the Taiwan people.

The Chinese term for the "Chinese" is *zhongguoren*, but many say that this refers to the people of China, which they argue is a separate political entity from Taiwan. Thus more and more people are using the term used by Malaysian and Singaporean Chinese to refer to themselves: *huaren*, a name that recalls the people who founded the legendary Hua dynasty near China's sacred Huashan (Mount Hua).

to the island in the 1660s, there were about 50,000 Fujian immigrants living on Taiwan. By the time his descendants were ousted by the Manchu some 20 years later, the number had jumped to 100,000. They continued to come, so that by the 1895 Japanese annexation of the island there were more than 3 million.

In the early days, they were very clannish, and communal conflicts tended to break out on a regular basis between immigrants from different parts of Fujian, or these two main groups against Hakka from northern Guangdong. By the 1860s, however, such conflicts had almost disappeared, as the population assimilated through intermarriage.

Unless you can hear the difference between Mandarin and Taiwanese, it is near impossible to distinguish between more recently arrived "mainlanders" and those who can trace their Taiwanese ancestry back through many generations. In general, however, away from the cosmopolitan sophistication of Taipei, Taiwanese tend to be earthier.

The men often chew *binlang* (betel nut), and communal meals are frequently accompanied by drinking sessions. Being deeply superstitious, they pay regular visits to temples to pray for good luck. In the aftermath of the 9-21 earthquake in 1999, Western-trained psychiatrists

Taiwan. The Hakka people have a well-known reputation for being thrifty and hardworking, and even more than most Chinese have a great love of education. Meinong claims to have produced more university graduates than any other village in Taiwan.

Traditionally, Hakka people live in villages made up of three-sided homes *(sanheyuan)* fronted by a wall to create a compound garden, reflecting what is perceived by other Chinese as their clannish nature. Most Hakka nowadays live in the same apartment blocks as other Taiwanese, but it's still possible to see such homes in the vicinity of Hsinchu and in Meinong.

from Taipei who went to the mostly Taiwanese-populated quake areas to offer counseling to victims largely found their services disregarded in favor of treatments by local shamans.

Today, Taiwan's Hakka population numbers around 4.5 million, though for the most part they are not a very visible minority. The exception is in traditional Hakka communities that have retained their language and customs, such as in the small village of Meinong *(see picture story on pages 246–7)* found in the south of

LEFT: a farmer in Mazu Islands with freshly harvested vegetables. **ABOVE:** Hakka children with traditional oil-paper umbrellas, Meinong village, south Taiwan.

Customs and etiquette

The Taiwanese like to think of themselves as *reqing*, a word that translates best as "warmhearted," and possessing a spirit of *renqingwei*, which means, loosely, "hospitality." Few visitors would be able to dispute these qualities. Unlike nearby Japan, where foreigners too often feel clumsy in the face of mysterious social rules, in Taiwan the visitor is invariably greeted warmly and made to feel at ease. Foreigners, after all, are considered guests, and the Taiwanese pride themselves on being *haoke*, or "good hosts." Don't be surprised when Taiwanese make you the object of uninvited hospitality or small favors. But, even if at times it seems a little overwhelming, try to enjoy it.

Taiwanese, like other Chinese, are at their most hospitable when you visit their homes or when they are hosting a meal in a restaurant. Visitors will probably be asked concerned questions about whether they can use chopsticks, or are used to eating Chinese food – even if they have been living amongst Chinese for years and speak Chinese fluently

Once such formalities are dispensed with, most likely the drinking will begin. For Taiwanese, drinking is a far more self-conscious social activity than it tends to be in the West, and is more rule-bound (see Food and Drink, page 98).

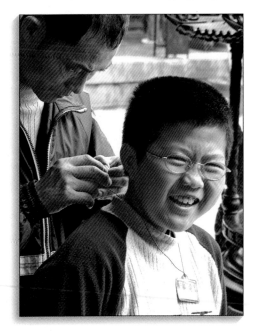

Another aspect of dining out with Taiwanese that sometimes confuses foreigners is when it comes to paying the bill. Taiwanese – unless they are young students – never "go Dutch." Dividing up a bill is considered unseemly, and it will always be the role of someone – the oldest person, perhaps, or most likely the person who suggested the venue – to qingke, or "get the bill." As a visiting foreigner, it's unlikely you will ever have this privilege. By all means make a show of fighting for the bill, but don't press the point too hard.

Much is made about the Chinese concept of "face" or mianzi as it's called in Chinese, but it's not a particularly complex concept. If, for

example, somebody were to toast you at a banquet and you didn't toast in return, it would be a loss of "face" for the toaster. If, on the other hand, you were to politely explain (with a smile) that you don't drink but would reciprocate the toast with some tea (which is invariably on hand), you would save the "face" of the person toasting you. In other words, face boils down to showing respect and not embarrassing people.

Politeness and smiles

Politeness and smiles go a long way in Taiwan, as they do throughout the East. In a sense, they are simply another way of "giving face," showing respect for the person you are addressing. If you need help, try not to look too flustered, and when dealing with officials a smiling air of humility invariably yields better results than petulance. Directness is not the virtue in Taiwan that it is sometimes in the West.

If you are invited to a Taiwanese home, it's polite to bring a gift. It need not be anything ostentatious – something small from your home country or a bottle of duty-free foreign liquor perhaps. Gift-giving is far less institutionalized in Taiwan than in Japan, but it's nevertheless an important part of the cementing of relationships. When offered a gift, always accept – you can always pass it on to someone else later.

One thing that can take some getting used to is the Taiwanese penchant for flattery. Learn a few words of Chinese and you will be undoubtedly besieged with compliments about your language skills. Flattery, like gift-giving, aims to ingratiate, but it also has the effect of creating a harmonious social atmosphere in which those who should receive respect receive it. Harmony, after all, is the supreme Confucian virtue, and Confucian virtues are to a certain extent still the bedrock of Taiwanese society.

Lastly, no social rules are carved in stone. Taiwan is a small island with 23 million people, and they are each different. Maintain an open mind and a smile, and you will find them exceedingly welcoming and generous, even if you make the occasional social gaffe or two. For the Taiwanese, such gaffes reinforce their sense of having a unique and special culture. ❑

LEFT: traditions are kept alive among the young.
RIGHT: standing proudly erect at the Martyrs' Shrine (Zhonglie Zi), Taipei.

TRIBAL MINORITIES

Taiwan's earliest settlers are now beginning to find their voice, shaking off
old, unfavorable reputations and fighting back from years of oppression

Amid all the debate of recent years as to who are the "real" Taiwanese, the voice of Taiwan's original inhabitants has been gathering strength. Once regarded by Taiwan's Chinese settlers as "savages," Taiwan's aboriginal tribes are finally beginning to be recognized as the victims of long oppression, and their arts and culture taken with new seriousness. With the formal recognition of four small tribes in the past few years, there are now officially 13 tribal groups.

Today, aborigines amount to about 2 percent of Taiwan's total population, numbering around 470,000. Until the 1990s they were called *shandiren*, or "mountain people," a name derived from the fact that Chinese occupation of the fertile plains initially left the mountain and other remote tribes untouched. Today, however, the preferred appellation is *yuanzhumin*, or "original inhabitants."

Most of Taiwan's aboriginal people have been assimilated into modern life to the extent that they have become almost indistinguishable from their Chinese counterparts. But it is still possible in remote, mountainous regions to find villages little changed from centuries ago. These villagers grow traditional crops like millet for brewing alcohol, sweet potatoes and taro, a kind of root vegetable. In recent times, cash crops like wild mushrooms, pears, peaches and plums have become a popular and lucrative form of income, though Taiwan's entry into the WTO has resulted in severe price competition. The tribes are also benefiting somewhat from enhanced tourism-income opportunities.

The tribes

The origin of Taiwan's minorities is disputed in anthropological circles. The consensus, however, is that the northern tribes are probably of southern China origin and the southern tribes of Austronesian origin. One thing is certain: archeological digs have shown that aborigines

have inhabited Taiwan for at least 15,000 years, much longer than their Chinese counterparts.

The largest ethnic-minority group is the Ami, which has just under 150,000 members. They populate the scenic valleys and flatlands near Hualien, on the east coast. The Ami are mainly farmers: their annual harvest festival, held dur-

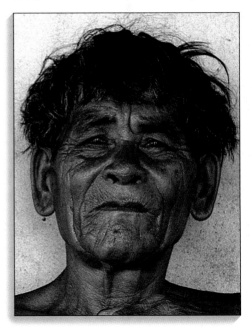

ing the last weeks of July and early August, brings out the best of their traditional dance forms, music, costumes and customs. Travelers can observe Ami traditions at a cultural center in Hualien *(see page 266).*

The minority group most accessible to visitors to Taipei are the Atayal, who live in the lush valleys of Wulai, just an hour's drive south of the capital, but who can also be found in Taoyuan, Nantou and other northern counties.

The Paiwan inhabit the mountains of eastern Pingtung and Taitung, in the south. The snake-worshiping cult of the *baibushe* (hundred-pacer) – victims, it is said, will only live 100 paces after being bitten – still remains strong

---

LEFT: harvest dance of the Rukai people, near Taitung.
RIGHT: Dao elder, Orchid Island (Lanyu).

in Paiwan tradition. The snake's visage appears in abstract form on almost all arts and crafts.

The Paiwan, in particular, are master wood-carvers, making totems, doors, eaves, beams, smoking pipes and other masterpieces from the trees of Taiwan's alpine forests. Another interesting tribe is the Rukai, whose largest cluster of hamlets is in Wutai, Pingtung county, where its 200 or so households engage primarily in agriculture. The social organization and customs of the Rukai resemble those of the Paiwan.

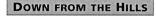

DOWN FROM THE HILLS

Although long called *shandiren*, or "mountain people," official statistics show that nearly half of Taiwan's aborigines have left the mountains to seek opportunities on the plains nowadays.

the arms of their most ardent admirers.

The Puyuma tribe has traditions similar to the Ami. They live mainly in the foothills of the Central Mountain Range, near Taitung, and occasionally congregate on the city's outskirts for major festivals that include swing contests.

Another island tribe of note are the Bunun, who live in the southern Central Mountain Range. The Bunun still practice a ritual form of night worship that remains essentially unchanged from ancient times.

An interesting feature of Wutai town is the buildings constructed from stone slabs quarried in the surrounding mountains. The architecture resembles the piled slate homes that dot the Himalayan highlands of western China, northern India and Nepal.

One fascinating display of Rukai prowess is seen in their traditional "swing contest," one of the most entertaining tribal rituals in Taiwan. Prospective brides mount an enormous swing, with their legs bound to prevent them from flailing. Burly tribesmen, dressed in full ceremonial attire, then swing the ladies until they sail like kites to dizzying heights. Afterwards, the girls are carried from their swings and dropped into

There are, however, two exceptions: severed pig heads have replaced disembodied human heads as sacrificial offerings, and electricity has replaced traditional torches for lighting.

The ethnic group that has been least affected by Taiwan's headlong plunge into the 21st century are the Dao, who live on Lanyu (Orchid Island), off the southeast coast, and who are the only seafaring minority found in Taiwan. For half a century during their occupation of Taiwan, the Japanese deliberately isolated Orchid Island as a living anthropological museum. Dao fishing boats, each hewn from a single giant tree, are beautiful vessels that glide over the waters of the Pacific.

Trial husbands

Of particular interest are the marriage customs of the Dao. Women significantly outnumber the men on the island and have parlayed their numbers into a potent social force.

Upon engagement, the male moves into the family home of the female for a one-month trial marriage. During that time, the prospective groom must prove his prowess in hunting and fishing, exhibit his ability to build boats, and demonstrate other skills. If he fails the tests, he is sent packing in disgrace and another suitor is brought in. Even when the man successfully wins the bride, he is expected to continually

Popular Puyuma singer A-Mei has achieved much success with her R&B-influenced hits in Taiwan and throughout the Chinese world and was chosen to sing the national anthem at Chen Shui-bian's presidential inauguration in 2000.

Museums and often tacky theme parks have also drawn attention to aboriginal arts and crafts, in particular weaving, a tradition carried on by the women of all 13 Taiwan tribes. Bold patterns are used for capes, shawls, shirts, vests, shoes and sandals. The weaving of red on black is a dominant style, and motifs incorporate elements of the two regions from where anthropologists believe the tribes' ancestors may have come. ❑

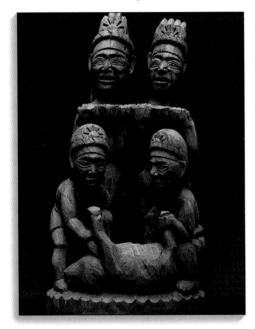 

prove his worth to his wife and her family. Otherwise, the Dao woman may exercise her unilateral right to divorce her husband – at any time and on any grounds – and seek a new mate.

Creativity

Taiwan's aborigines have been taking an increasingly active role in politics in recent years, but it is their creativity as singers and dancers, and their arts and crafts, that have chiefly caught the public eye in Taiwan.

LEFT: portrait of Rukai marital bliss. **ABOVE:** wooden carving of hunters, by Paiwan artist of southern Taiwan. **RIGHT:** Rukai bride-to-be harnessed to a ceremonial swing.

SO CLOSE, YET SO FAR

Orchid Island's Dao (also called 'Yami') people speak a language that is mutually intelligible with the language spoken by minority tribes on the Philippines Batanes Islands. Some anthropologists think the word "Yami" is an ancient Austronesian word meaning "north." Orchid Island lies north of the Batanes, though the Dao themselves refer to their island as Botel Tobago. Whatever the case, the Dao people are separated from their Philippine neighbors by politics today. A journey that could once be made on festive occasions by boat in a day, today requires flying from either Taipei or Kaohsiung to Manila and then a long journey to the north of the Philippines.

RELIGION AND RITUALS

Ancestor worship, Daoism, Buddhism and popular folk religion have bequeathed
a mix of mysticism and ritual that underscores the lives of the Taiwanese

Traditional religion has flourished in Taiwan, despite the rapid development from a rural society into an industrialized complex of urban enclaves. Indeed, the temples of Taiwan are as much a feature of the skylines as are factories and office buildings.

Ancestor worship

The ancestor worship of the Chinese is based upon the assumption that a person has two souls. One of them is created at the time of conception, and, when the person has died the soul stays in the grave and lives on sacrificial offerings. As the corpse decomposes, the strength of the soul dwindles, until it eventually leads a shadow existence in the underworld. However, it will return to earth as an ill-willed spirit and cause damage if no more sacrifices are offered.

The second soul only emerges at birth. During its heavenly voyage post-death, it is threatened by evil forces, and is also dependent upon the sacrifices and prayers of living descendants. If the sacrifices cease, then this soul, too, turns into an evil spirit. But if the descendants continue to make sacrificial offerings and graves, the soul of the deceased may offer them protection.

Originally, ancestor worship in Chinese history had been exclusive to the king. Only later did peasants also begin to honor their ancestors. At first, people believed that, during the sacrificial ritual, the soul of the ancestor would search for a human substitute – usually the grandson – as an abode. Until 2,000 years ago, when genealogical tablets were introduced as homes for the soul during sacrificial acts, the king and noblemen used human sacrifices.

Even today, the Chinese worship their ancestors and offer the deities sacrifices of food. However, the original religion of the people focused on the worship of natural forces. Later, people began to worship the Jade Emperor, a figure from Daoism who became the highest

LEFT: temple altar at Tucheng Shengmu Miao, Tainan.
RIGHT: ancestor worship is commonly practised; seen here are photographs of the dead with urns containing ashes.

god in the popular religion after the 14th century. Among the many other gods in popular Chinese religion, there were also earth deities, and every town worshipped its own unique city god. There were demons of illness, spirits of the house and deities of streams and rivers. Apart from Confucianism (which scholars consider a code of ethics rather than a formal religion), Daoism and Buddhism, there was also a working-class religion known as Daoist-Buddhism.

Daoism

Only when the Qin dynasty won over its rivals in 221 BC did the first emperor over a united China come to power. At the time, there were various schools of philosophical thought, but only Confucianism and Daoism gained wide acceptance in China.

Central concepts of Daoism are the *dao*, which basically means way or path, but also has a second meaning of method and principle, and *wuwei*, which is sometimes simply defined as "swimming with the stream." The concept of *de* (virtue) is closely linked to this, as a virtue that manifests itself in daily life when *dao* is put into practice. The course of events in the world is determined by the forces *yang* and *yin*. The masculine, brightness, activity and heaven are considered to be *yang* forces; the feminine, weakness, darkness and passivity are *yin* forces.

Laozi was the founder of Daoism. He is said to have been born in a village in the province of Henan in 604 BC, the son of a distinguished

FUSION OF RELIGIONS

As Buddhism became more and more popular, it borrowed ideas from Daoism, and vice versa, to the point where one might speak of a fusion between the two.

The ordinary people were not particularly attracted by the abstract concepts and metaphysical reflections of Daoism. Even at the beginning of the Han period (206 BC–AD 220), there were signs of both a popular and religious Daoism.

Religious Daoism developed in various directions and into different schools. The ascetics retreated to the mountains and devoted their time to meditation, or lived in monasteries. In the Daoist world, priests were important medicine men and interpreters of oracles. They carried out

family. For a time, he held the office of archivist in the capital of Luoyang. But Laozi later retreated into solitude and died in his village in 517. Since the 2nd century AD, many legends have been told about Laozi and experts argue about his historical existence.

The classic work of Daoism is called the *Daodejing*. It seems certain that this was not written by a single author. The earliest, and most significant, followers of Laozi were Liezi and Zhuangzi. Liezi (5th century BC) was particularly concerned with the relativity of experiences and strived to comprehend the concept of *dao* through meditation. Zhuangzi (4th century BC) is famous for his poetic allegories.

exorcism and funeral rites, and read mass for the dead or for sacrificial offerings.

Historical and legendary figures were added to the Daoist pantheon. At the head were the Three Commendables. The highest of the three deities, the heavenly god, is identical to the Jade Emperor, worshipped by the common people.

Buddhism

The Chinese initially encountered Buddhism at the start of the first century, when merchants and monks came to China over the Silk Road.

The type of Buddhism prevalent in China today is the *Mahayana* (Great Wheel), which – as opposed to *Hinayana* (Small Wheel) promises all creatures redemption through the so-called *bodhisattva* (redemption deities). There were two aspects that were particularly attractive to the Chinese: the teachings of karma provided a better explanation for individual misfortune, and there was a hopeful promise for existence after death. Nevertheless, there was considerable opposition to Buddhism, which contrasted sharply with Confucian ethics and ancestor worship.

At the time of the Three Kingdoms (AD 220–280), the religion spread across each of the three states. After tribes of foreign origin had founded states in the north, and the gentry from the north had sought refuge in the eastern Qin dynasty (317–420), Buddhism developed along very different lines in the north and south of China for about two centuries. During the rule of Emperor Wudi (502–549), rejection and hostility towards Buddhism spread among Confucians. And during the relatively short-lived northern Zhou dynasty (557–581), Buddhism was officially banned for three years.

Buddhism was most influential in Chinese history during the Tang dynasty (618–907), when several emperors officially supported the religion. During the years 842 to 845, however, Chinese Buddhists also experienced the most severe persecutions in their entire history: 40,000 temples and monasteries were destroyed, and Buddhism was blamed for economic and moral decline. In the course of time, ten Chinese schools of Buddhism emerged, but only two remain influential today.

Key figures

In Chinese Buddhism, the center of religious attention is the Sakyamuni Buddha, the founder of Buddhism who was forced into the background in the 6th century by the Maitreya Buddha (who is called Milefo in China, or redeemer of the world). Since the 7th century, a *bodhisattva* deity has been a popular female figure of devotion in China. She is known as Guanyin, a motherly Goddess of Mercy to the ordinary people. Guanyin means "the one who listens to complaints."

From the 14th century onwards, the Pure Land (Amitabha Buddhism) school has domin-

FAR LEFT: image of the Jade Emperor (Yuhuang Dadi).
LEFT: Buddhist monks at Jinguashi.
RIGHT: Buddhist image on tapestry, Qing dynasty.

ated the life and culture of the Chinese people, but the most influential Buddhist school has been the so-called School of Meditation (called Chan in China, Zen in Japan), which developed during the Tang dynasty. It preaches redemption through Buddhahood, which anyone is able to reach. It despises knowledge gained from books or dogmas, as well as rites. Guided meditation is used in order to lead disciples toward enlightenment, but the most important method is dialogue with the master, who asks subtle and paradoxical questions, to which he expects equally subtle and paradoxical answers.

In 1949, the year the People's Republic of China was founded, there were approximately 500,000 Buddhist monks and nuns, and 50,000 temples and monasteries, in China. A number of well-known Buddhist temples were classified as historical monuments. But, during the Cultural Revolution started in 1966, it seemed as if the Red Guards were intent on completely eradicating Buddhism. Nominally autonomous Tibet – which practiced Tantric Buddhism or Lamaism, introduced from India in the 7th century AD – was hard-hit by these excesses. (Lamaism features Brahman and Hindu gods in its pantheon, as well as Buddhist deities; magic, repetitive prayers and rituals help achieve redemption.)

Popular religion

Chinese folk religion is a blend of practices and beliefs that have developed out of animism, ancestor worship, Confucianism, Daoism, Buddhism and various folk beliefs. In Taiwan, these forms of worship are generally similar to those still practiced by Chinese elsewhere in Asia. But despite the common thread that runs through traditional beliefs and rituals, and the fact that the island is comparatively small with good communications, local practices in Taiwan differ considerably from region to region.

Although Taiwan has separate Buddhist, Daoist and Confucian temples, the common person blends the practices of all three with a measure of superstition and ancestor worship. To further confuse matters, peasant devotees refer to this religious blending by the umbrella term Buddhism, even as they regularly visit local folk-religion temples to worship heroes and deities unknown to Buddhism. There is little concern for strict dogmatism in folk religion.

Most of the time incense is burned in temples, and devotees light paper offerings to the deities or seek advice through the use of divining blocks or sticks. Religious solemnity is not a quality of temples, which are often retreats from the heat and where women and the elderly

CATALOGUE OF DEITIES

A huge pantheon of gods and goddesses are found in traditional Chinese religion, and the origins and legends that surround these deities go deep into Chinese history. Most are the heroes and notables of Chinese myth, legend and history, deified either by imperial order or popular choice (not unlike Christian saints). Some of these deities are so well-known that their images are found in many or most temples; others are unique to a single temple. Some communities even have cult followings, which have developed around a particular historical figure who is believed to have protected or guided the town, or to have worked a miracle in the locality.

meet and chat with acquaintances, relax or play cards. Some village temples even double as schools, stores and recreation centers.

Because the supernatural and human worlds coexist in the folk religion of Taiwan, temples represent the place where the two worlds can meet and communicate. The living devotees provide the resident deities with incense, oils and food offerings; in exchange, they receive advice and protection against demonic influences responsible for such earthly sorrows as plagues, disasters and illnesses. ❑

ABOVE: a medium enters into a trance during a temple puppet show, Taipei.

Taiwanese Temples

Many of Taiwan's temples were built in the 18th and 19th centuries by craftsmen. They range in size from small shrines containing one or two images or tablets to large establishments with several main halls flanked by minor ones, each holding separate altars. As a rule, a temple is named after the chief deity on the main altar.

Insight into Chinese folk religion can be gleaned from the architecture and decor of the buildings themselves. One important element is the ornate roof, alive with images of deities, immortals, heroes and mythological animals, all of which attract good fortune and repel evil.

The center of a temple roof is usually crowned with one of five symbols: a pagoda, representing a staircase to heaven; a flaming pearl, symbolizing the beneficial *yang* spirit; the sun, usually flanked by two dragons; a magic gourd, which is said to capture and trap evil spirits; or the Fu, Lu, and Shou, gods of Prosperity, Posterity and Longevity. These roof symbols reflect the role of the temple's main deity. Beside them are the fantastic assortment of figures associated with Chinese temples, including the phoenix, said to appear only in times of extreme peace and prosperity, and the dragon, symbol of strength, wisdom and good luck.

These exterior features are, at first glimpse, very much the same in Buddhist and folk-religion temples. Inside, however, the differences are obvious. Buddhist temples contain few images, with one to three significant gilded Buddhas on a main altar. Confucian temples, severe by comparison, do not contain any images. Once drab with age, many old temples now have been renovated. In some cases, their new ornamentation has transformed them into exotic curiosities. Modern folk-religion temples have also been built, especially in central and southern Taiwan. These are invariably large and costly buildings, with only one or two images.

The interior decoration of folk-religion temples varies considerably. Many of them contain fascinating murals of scenes from Chinese mythology and history. Pillars and balustrades may be intricately carved. Most temples have guardians painted on the outside of the main doors. The main altar bears the image of the temple's major deity, attended by aides or servants. Fronting the principal deity is a smaller image of the same god; this miniature is taken from the temple occasionally to bless devotees in their home doorways, or is carried aloft during festivals to other temples.

Beneath the main altar, at ground level, are two forms of small altar. One contains a tablet dedicated to the protective spirit of the temple itself; the other contains stone or wooden "white tigers" – the bringers or destroyers of luck. There are always five items on the table before a temple's main altar, the most sacred being a large incense pot. Filled with ash accumulated by years of worship, it is the repository for the spirit of the venerated Jade Emperor.

In addition to the gods, ancestors are also commonly at the receiving end of offerings. Traditionally, ancestral tablets were kept in family homes, (sometimes in ancestral halls) and respects were paid at a living-room altar. These tablets bear the ancestors' names and sometimes photographs, and are given regular offerings, lest they become troublesome hungry ghosts. Increasingly, however, families pay temples to house the ancestral tablets.

Like those of the human world, the inhabitants of the underworld require food, money, clothes and a house. Food offerings give symbolic sustenance, and spirit money – bundles of "Bank of the Underworld" notes – and paper artifacts representing material items are burned to release their essence. ❑

RIGHT: (from right to left) Fu, Lu, Shou – gods of Prosperity, Posterity and Longevity.

DAJIA MAZU: PAGEANTRY ON PARADE

Gongfu (Kungfu) exhibitions, dancing dragons, exploding firecrackers, crowds and lots of noise are all hallmarks of the annual Mazu pilgrimage

Every year, around midnight on a pre-determined day before the 23rd day of the third month of the lunar calendar, Taiwan's Dajia Mazu pilgrimage gets underway. Over the following week, tens of thousands of pilgrims will walk, cycle and drive with Mazu – the most popular goddess in Taiwan – as bearers carry her statue over a loop more than 280 km (174 miles) around central Taiwan. By the time the pilgrimage is over, more than a million people will have watched the procession pass by.

The pilgrimage is easily Taiwan's grandest, noisiest and most grueling – a mass exercise in medieval pageantry and a celebration of all that is uniquely Taiwanese. Chinese opera singers do wailing battle with the tinny trumpeting of marching bands. Knots of "devil boys," their faces painted and tiger-like fangs protruding over their upper lips, jostle the crowds with spears and clubs, beating themselves on their heads so that blood streams down their faces and stripped upper bodies, while spirit mediums go into convulsions by the roadside. Entire villages will make offerings of food and burning incense to Mazu, and jostle for position to prostrate themselves in seemingly endless lines for the good fortune of having Mazu's statue pass over them.

THE CULT OF MAZU

It is thought that the worship of Mazu originated in coastal China and then spread throughout Southeast Asia. Some scholars think Mazu was a woman named Lin Mo-niang, who was born during the Song dynasty (960–1127) on the island of Meizhou, in China's Fujian province, and died at the age of 28. In Taiwan, she is known as the Goddess of the Seas, or the Heavenly Mother, and has become the island's patron saint and most widely worshiped folk deity.

△ **SONG AND DANCE**
One of the many performing troupes that precede Mazu's arrival at a stop on the 280-plus km (174-mile) pilgrimage route around central Taiwan.

▷ **WIELDING THE WHIP**
Although frowned upon by pilgrimage organizers, *jitong* (spirit mediums) can still be seen during the festival flagellating themselves until they bleed.

PRAYERS AND PILGRIMS

△ GODDESS ON THE GO
Mazu makes her triumphant return home to Dajia's Zhenlan Gong after eight days of traveling and being watched by up to a million people.

▽ FLYING THE FLAG
The Embroidered Flag Troupe leads the way for Mazu's entry into the town of Xingang, the half-way point of the spectacular pilgrimage.

At the front of the Mazu pilgrimage procession is the *Bobe-a*, who bangs a gong to notify the temples, villages and towns along the procession route that it's time to light incense in anticipation of Mazu's arrival. *Bobe-a* (in Taiwanese) is an outlandish figure dressed in a conical, helmet-shaped hat, sheepskin vest and a black pajama-like costume. With a pig's trotter and a bunch of spring onions tied to his waist, his attire is completed by wearing a sandal on one foot and nothing on the other. Behind the *Bobe-a* are flag-bearing troupes of pilgrims from all over Taiwan, including the 36 Expectants and the Embroidered Flag Troupe. The performing troupes that follow the *Bobe-a* lend the pilgrimage much of its color and excitement. They include a troupe called the Holy Infants, comprising huge dancing babies, and the Drunken Buddha Troupe, who cavort drunkenly along the street taking imaginary swigs from hip flasks.

△ LUCKY STEPS
Villagers prostrate themselves in the streets to receive the good luck of having Mazu's statue pass over them.

◁ BEAT THE DRUM
The Mazu pilgrimage is an aural assault, with firecrackers exploding every step of the way and truckloads of loud drummers crowding the streets.

▷ MONEY TO BURN
In Xingang, bundles of paper offerings ("spirit money") pile so high they have to be shoveled into trucks and burnt outside town for fear of sparking a major conflagration.

THE ROLE OF CONFUCIANISM

One man born over 2,500 years ago continues to shape Chinese society

with his philosophy of benevolence and social propriety

"When friends visit from afar,
Is this not indeed a pleasure?"

For more than 2,000 years, Chinese scholars aspiring to government office were required to memorize *The Analects*, or *Lunyu*, the most hallowed of all Confucian classics. Today, copywriters with Taiwan's Tourism Bureau often borrow the above opening lines of the *Lunyu* for obvious reasons. The fact that Confucius began his great work with such a disarmingly simple and welcoming maxim emphasized the importance the philosopher placed on friendship and social etiquette.

Confucius believed that true pleasure cannot be found in selfish, sensual abandon or in personal gain, but in generosity to friends, in social intercourse and in social hierarchy. Thus, hospitality has long been one of China's finest arts.

Master Kong

Confucius, known to the Chinese as Kong Fuzi, or Master Kong, was born in the kingdom of Lu, near modern Shandong, in 551 BC. As a child, he demonstrated profound interest in ancient rituals. People admired his erudition and sincerity but, because he lived in a time of internal chaos, few men of influence were willing to adopt his pacifist ideas.

Without a platform from which to address the masses, Confucius set out to peddle his ideas on his own. While still a young man, he traveled throughout the Chinese empire, taking his message of peace, friendship and reform to the various petty princes. Most received him with interest and hospitality, but few showed intentions of changing their warring ways. While traveling, Confucius also gathered and studied materials that revealed the secrets of the earlier golden ages of Chinese culture – the Xia, Shang and Zhou dynasties. One of the men who assisted him was Li Dan, known to pos-

LEFT: portrait of Confucius.
RIGHT: Laozi, founder of Daoism, is often depicted riding on his water buffalo.

terity and philosophy as Laozi, the Old One.

Laozi was the founder of Daoism. He was also in charge of the imperial archives of the Zhou dynasty, which housed all the surviving documents detailing events from the 23rd century BC up to his time. The records were preserved in archaic script on tiles, bamboo and

tortoise shells. Laozi permitted Confucius to use the archives and copy as many records as he wished. The ancient documents formed the basis for his so-called Confucian classics.

"I never created or wrote anything original," Confucius claimed. Instead, he considered himself an interpreter and transmitter of the profound ideas and deeds of the ancient kings of China's golden age. He is generally credited with putting the documents of the imperial archives into a common, contemporary language, and with publishing them.

The five classics of Confucianism, known as the *Wujing*, consist of the *Yijing* (Book of Changes), *Shijing* (Book of Poetry), *Shujing*

(Book of History), *Liji* (Book of Rites) and *Chunqiu* (Spring and Autumn Annals). Later works published by Confucius or his disciples and believed to contain original philosophies of the master were the *Great Learning*, *Doctrine of the Mean* and *Classic of Filial Piety*.

The *Lunyu* consists of a collection of the notes and journals of the master's conversations, teachings and journeys. Believed to have been compiled by the disciples of his school, it is often regarded as the basic "scripture" of Confucianism. Publication in itself was

> ### WORSHIPED THINKER
>
> Although Confucianism is not generally considered a religion, temples to the great sage abound in Taiwan, always called "Kong Miao."

a bold move for Confucius. Never before in Chinese history had anyone but kings and ministers published books. But Confucius was a commoner, or at most, a member of an impoverished noble family. His years of writing and interpretation of hallowed doctrines were followed by 44 years of teaching – yet another revolutionary course. Before he arrived on the scene, only aristocrats and royalty received formal education. Confucius, however, welcomed to his school of thought anyone who demonstrated a keen intellect and a sincere desire to learn.

By the time of his death at the age of 72, some 3,000 students had been attracted to the teachings of Confucius. Around 70 disciples are believed to have carried on his work, building on his ideas during the period of intellectual fervor known as the One Hundred Schools Period. Thousands of books were published, and tens of thousands of students educated as a result of the example set by Confucius.

Among them was Mencius. Considered second only to Confucius among the great sages of ancient China, Mencius further advanced the concepts of his predecessor and reaffirmed basic Confucian principles, particularly the notion that government should be conducted for the benefit of the people and not the ruler, and that human nature was basically good.

Dark ages

In 221 BC, the enlightened age of Confucius and Mencius was buried under the militant Qin dynasty, which swept down from the northwest. Led by founding emperor Qin Shi Huangdi, China was united for the first time under a bureaucratic government. But Qin Shi Huangdi was contemptuous of learning and viewed the contending schools of philosophy as potential sources of sedition and a threat to his empire. He executed hundreds of scholars and ordered most books to be burned. Only tomes on agriculture, divination and medicine were spared.

It is a testimony to the strength and endurance of Confucius's doctrines that his works somehow survived. Private editions were secreted in walls and underground vaults. After the demise of the Qin dynasty, the subsequent Han dynasty collected the hidden works of Confucius during the 2nd century BC, and declared his writings to be the official canons of a new state philosophy. Until Confucian studies were formally abandoned in 1905, the Confucian classics remained the most sacrosanct source of knowledge and moral authority for every Chinese ruler and bureaucrat.

Etiquette and people

Confucianism is far too complex to cover in detail here. But a few highlights reveal its wisdom. Confucius's most celebrated concepts were those of *li* and *ren*. *Li* has been translated by various scholars as rites, ceremonies, etiquette and propriety. Its combined implications underline all social behavior in the Chinese system, providing the appropriate behavior for every situation a person may face in life. If *li* conflicts with the law, a superior man will not hesitate to follow the dictates of *li*. *Li* also incorporates the many formal rituals by which a person symbolically expresses propriety, like sacrificial rites that honor deceased ancestors.

Even more important is the Confucian concept of *ren*. Its written form or character consists of the symbols for person and the number two. *Ren* thus dictates social relations. It can be roughly interpreted in English as benevolence and kindness. For Confucius, if all humankind followed the virtues of *ren* and *li*, all social behavior would become appropriate

the absolute obedience of inferior to superior. Such common traits of Chinese society as authoritarian government, filial piety, patriarchal family structure, primogeniture and the importance of friendships – all save the first are still important within the social life of Taiwan today – can be traced to the Five Cardinal Relationships.

Confucius also formulated a version of the universal Golden Rule. But like many things Chinese, it takes an opposite tack from the Western concept. "Do not do unto others what you would not have them do unto you" is a reasonably accurate translation of the Confucian version. To "do unto others," as the West does,

and benevolent, and the sources of friction among people would be eliminated. In his utopian prescription for humanity, he promoted peace and social harmony.

Confucius established the Five Cardinal Relationships as a guide to the social behavior that would motivate followers to his utopia. These rules governed relations between subject and ruler, husband and wife, parent and child, elder sibling and younger sibling, and between friends. The last is the only social relationship of equality possible in a Confucian society. The rest demand

would be far too aggressive and presumptuous. The practice of actively performing good deeds is considered a form of social interference in traditional Chinese society. Instead, the Chinese prefer simply to refrain from doing bad deeds.

Any individual who successfully follows the precepts of Confucian teaching can attain the goal of the master's philosophy – ie, becoming a superior person. Confucius stressed that the superior individual was not necessarily an aristocrat or powerful politician, but simply a person of virtue. Learning is the key to that process. "The superior man makes demands on himself; the inferior man makes demands on others," the wise Confucius is said to have concluded.

LEFT: Qin Shi Huangdi, who suppressed Confucianism.
ABOVE: aristocratic life during the Ming dynasty.

In practice, this concept led to the system of appointing learned Confucian scholars to administrate China on behalf of the emperor, thus diminishing the role of hereditary princes and royal relatives. Rule by men of knowledge and virtue managed to hold the unwieldy empire together from the 2nd century BC until the birth of the republican form of government in 1912. The Confucian concept of the superior man also explains the respect that the Chinese have always maintained for the learned and scholars.

TEACHER'S DAY

September 28 has been designated Teacher's Day, honoring Confucius. Teacher's Day is celebrated with elaborate ceremonies at Taiwan's many Confucian temples.

concerns lay in this life were widely adopted, religious matters receded and social issues moved to the fore. Since Confucius's time, the Chinese have continued without feeling the need for a single omnipotent god or an exclusive, all-embracing religion. They have simply referred to the powers above as "heaven," an impersonal, inscrutable force that drives the universe. Meanwhile, for the most part they have welcomed all religious faiths to their land – as long as they do not interfere with social or governmental

Confucianism, as practiced by the Chinese, is not a religion in the strict sense of the word. Technically, it is not even a philosophy. It is a way of life with equal importance placed on theory and practice. Confucius himself rarely expounded on religious subjects. He did not deny the existence of gods and obviously felt there was some universal force on the side of right. But he felt that people should steer away from spiritual concerns and concentrate on creating a harmonious society in this world.

The people of his day were extremely superstitious, spending an inordinate amount of time on formal sacrifices that invoked spirits. When Confucius's ideas that humanity's most pressing

concerns. But, to be on the safe side, many still pay homage to a variety of gods.

Contemporary influences

The most lasting of the legacies of Confucius has been the perseverance of the primacy of family and friends. This legacy persists in Chinese communities throughout the world. Family and friends provide many of the social and economic services performed by courts, police, banks and lawyers in the West.

It is the family, not the individual, that has been the basic unit of social organization in China since the Zhou dynasty established the system of *baojia* during the 12th century BC.

Society was divided into units of 10, 100, 1,000 and 10,000 families, according to neighborhoods and districts. Each unit chose a leader from its ranks who was responsible for the behavior and welfare of all families under his jurisdiction. This leader reported directly to the leader of the next highest *baojia* unit.

If someone committed a crime, the head of his household would initially be held accountable, followed by the head of the ten-family unit, then the leader of the 100-family group, and so on. Thus, minor crimes rarely were reported beyond the *baojia* organization. In this way, too, the entire family assumed collective responsibility for the conduct and well-being of its members.

Guanxi

In Chinese society, family comes first, state and occupation second. Close connections are maintained with all family members, even those who have moved halfway around the world. Such extended networks provide sources of warmth and comfort, as well as a secure form of social welfare and future business links.

Friends form the other half of the Chinese social equation. People of Chinese descent have a network of carefully cultivated friendships, their *guanxi* or connections. Good *guanxi* in the right places often helps get things done on both sides of the Taiwan Strait. It can open doors and help cut through red tape.

Westerners often view the cultivation of such connections as a form of cronyism, but the Chinese believe it is perfectly natural to perform favors for friends. Years of experience have taught the Chinese to trust friends and relatives to get things done, but they feel uneasy asking favors of strangers. The betrayal of a personal friend is a heinous social offense, which can have serious repercussions throughout the offender's network of *guanxi*. That network is only as strong as its weakest link, so each new relationship is given careful consideration.

Confucian-style relationships proliferate in the Chinese business world – and virtually prevent it from unraveling. People of Chinese descent routinely select business associates from among established family members and friends,

unlike Westerners, who tend to choose their friends from business or professional groups.

A Chinese businessperson can invoke the social pressures of a *guanxi* network whenever an associate defaults on contracts, thereby eliminating the need for expensive court actions. Similarly, people have been encouraged to settle personal disputes within their own families, neighborhoods and occupational groups rather than impose their problems on the public. They understand a member's behavior and motivations better than a court, and share collective responsibility.

Banks are another Western innovation fre-

quently bypassed by the *guanxi* system. In Taiwan, most people participate in small private investment associations, called *biaohui*. Friends, relatives and colleagues pool their money to form a mutual fund, from which each member may take turns borrowing. As with commercial loans, the money must be repaid with interest. The personal closeness of the group minimizes fraud.

Taiwanese and Chinese communities overseas often appear to be paradigms of lawfulness. In truth, they suffer their share of criminal activities. The peaceful appearances are in part a result of the traditional preference to settle matters among themselves. ❑

LEFT: children at a ritual ceremony honoring the birthday of Confucius. **RIGHT:** *guanxi*, a network of cultivated friendships, goes a long way in business.

ARTS AND CRAFTS

Taiwan's artistic heritage may owe much to Chinese tradition, but its galleries

display a wealth of artworks in various materials, and of varied inspiration

Many visitors to Taiwan associate the island's art and crafts with the kind of traditional Chinese arts that can be found in the Gugong Bowuguan (National Palace Museum). Yes, Taiwan is perhaps the best place in the world to admire China's artistic tradition, but it is also worth remembering that Taiwan has its own artistic trends and traditions.

Calligraphy

Almost without exception, the artist of early China was a calligrapher, and from a privileged class. Otherwise, he would never have had the endless hours of time needed to acquire skill with the *maobi*, the brush used to write characters. Competence with the brush was an important reflection of an education in ancient China.

The Chinese have always regarded calligraphy as the highest of the arts. With its abstract aesthetic, it is certainly the purest. In times past, the strength of a man's calligraphy was one of the most important elements in passing examination. Writing was regarded as a window to the soul. Few examples of ancient calligraphy still exist. Most ancient inscriptions are rubbings taken from cast-metal vessels, and the earliest examples of Chinese writing in Taipei's National Palace Museum *(see page 147)* are Shang-period oracle inscriptions, incised on tortoise shells or the scapulae of oxen.

The earliest examples of work by famous calligraphers on display at the museum include the *Bing-fu tie (On Recovering from Illness)*, by Lu Ji (261–303). Samples of post-Eastern Qin calligraphy are more common. Wang Xi-zhi, who lived during that dynasty, is regarded as the patriarch of the art of calligraphy.

The Song dynasty saw the rise of calligraphers carving on wood or stone, then making rubbings on paper and compiling their works as copybooks, a practice that became a popular method of studying an artist's style.

LEFT: finishing touches on a Chinese character.
RIGHT: temple etching of an unusual form of ancient calligraphy on the human body.

Even the short-lived Yuan dynasty produced several noted calligraphers. But the 300 years of the Ming dynasty generated numerous masters and masterpieces. The Qing dynasty introduced two distinctive styles of calligraphy, one that marked the era from 1796 to 1820, the other from 1851 to 1874.

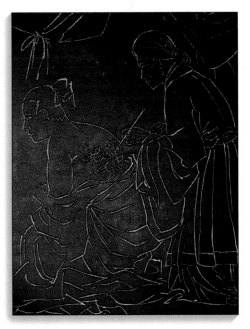

Porcelain

The Chinese invented porcelain sometime in the 7th century – 1,000 years before the Europeans obtained the secret. The most widespread form of ancient Chinese porcelain was celadon – a product made from a blending of iron oxide with a glaze that resulted, during the firing stage, in a characteristic greenish tone.

Sancai ceramics – ceramics with three-color glazes from the Tang dynasty – became world-famous. The colors were mostly strong green, yellow and brown. *Sancai* ceramics were also found among Tang-period tomb figurines in the shape of horses, camels, animal or human guardians, ladies of the court and officials.

The Song-period celadons – ranging in color from pale or moss green, pale blue or pale grey to brown tones – were also technically excellent. As early as the Yuan period, a technique from Persia was used for underglaze painting in cobalt blue (commonly known as Ming porcelain). Some common themes seen throughout the subsequent Ming period were figures, landscapes and theatrical scenes. At the beginning of the Qing dynasty, blue-and-white porcelain attained its highest level of quality.

Since the 14th century, Jingdezhen has been the center of porcelain manufacture, although today relatively inexpensive porcelain can be bought throughout China. However, antique pieces are still hard to come by because the sale of articles older than 100 years is prohibited by the Chinese government.

Jade

With its soft sheen and rich nuances of color, jade is China's most precious stone. The Chinese have known jade since antiquity, but it became widely popular only in the 18th century, when it began to be mined in China. Colors vary from white to green, but there are also red, yellow and lavender jades. In China, a clear emerald-green stone is valued most highly.

The oldest jades so far discovered come from the neolithic Hemadu culture (about 5,000 BC). The finds were presumably ritual objects. Among them were circular disks called *bi*, given to the dead to carry with them into the afterworld. Centuries later, the corpses of high-ranking officials were clothed in suits made of more than 2,000 thin slivers of jade sewn together with gold wire.

Since the 11th century, the Jade Emperor has been revered as the godhead in folk religion. Today, the ring disk – a symbol of heaven – is still worn as a talisman, and jade bracelets are worn for good luck throughout Taiwan.

> ### CALLIGRAPHIC SET
>
> Taipei's National Palace Museum has an extensive collection of calligraphy, with many rich examples from the Yuan, Ming and Qing dynasties.

Lacquerware

The oldest finds of lacquered objects date back to the 5th millennium BC. The glossy sheen of lacquerware is not only attractive to the eye but is also appealing to the touch.

The lacquer tree *(rhus verniciflua)* grows in central and southern China. When the bark of the tree is cut, it exudes a milky sap, which solidifies in moist air, dries and turns brown. This dry layer of lacquer is impervious to moisture, acid and scratches, and is ideal protection for materials such as wood or bamboo.

Bowls, tins, boxes, vases and furniture made of various materials (wood, bamboo, wicker, leather, metal, clay, textiles, paper) are coated with a skin of lacquer. A base coat is applied to the core material, followed by extremely thin layers of the finest lacquer which, after drying in dust-free moist air, are smoothed and polished to a glossy sheen.

In the dry lacquer method, the lacquer itself dictates the form: fabric or paper is saturated with lacquer and pressed into a wood or clay mold. After drying, the mold is removed and the piece coated with further layers of lacquer. Items were already being made in this way in the Han period.

During the Tang dynasty, large Buddhist sculptures were produced by the lacquerware process. If soot or vinegar-soaked iron filings are added to the lacquer, it will dry into a black color; cinnabar turns it red. The color combination of red and black, first thought to have been applied in the 2nd century BC, is still considered a classic by aficionados of Chinese art.

In the Song and Yuan periods, simply shaped monochromatic lacquerware was valued, and during the Ming period, the manufacture of lacquered objects was further refined.

The carved lacquer technique, which began at the time of the Tang dynasty, reached its highest peak during the Ming and Qing periods. The core, often of wood or tin, is coated with mostly red layers of lacquer. When the outermost coat has dried, decorative carving is applied, with the knife penetrating generally to the lowest layer so that the design stands out

and was then rediscovered in the 13th century. In the cloisonné technique, metal rods are soldered to the body of the metal object. These form the outlines of the ornamentation. The spaces between the rods are filled with enamel paste and fired in the kiln. Finally, metal surfaces not covered with enamel are gilded.

As a craft material, ivory is as old as jade, and early pieces can be traced to as far back as 5,000 BC. During the Bronze Age, wild elephants were not a rarity in northern China as they are today and the old artist-carvers regarded elephant tusks as a most desirable material. As a result, the once-large herds of

from the background in relief. The most well-known lacquerware is the Peking (Beijing) work, which goes back to the imperial courts of the Ming and Qing dynasties. Emperor Qianlong (1736–95) had a special liking for carved lacquerware; he was even buried in a coffin magnificently carved using this technique.

Cloisonné and ivory

The cloisonné technique – used to create metal objects with enamel decor – reached China from Persia in the 8th century AD, was lost,

LEFT: carved lacquer plate, circa 18th century.
ABOVE: an intricate carving in ivory.

elephants shrank to a small number, and eventually ivory had to be imported. Ming dynasty carvings exemplified excellent craft skills and superior taste; during Qing times, ivory carving was further improved. Most countries today, seeking to reduce animal poaching, ban the import of items carved from ivory.

Painting

Chinese painting first blossomed during the Tang dynasty, from 618 to 907. The figure and horse paintings of the Tang period were particularly exquisite. Few of them, however, have survived the centuries, but Taiwan's National Palace Museum in Taipei has 65 paintings in its collection that date from the Tang dynasty and earlier.

Flowers, birds and landscapes were the favorite subjects of artists who painted during the Five Dynasties and Song periods. Two of the greatest masters of the Southern Song imperial painting academy were Ma Yuan and Xia Gui. Their styles, which became popular in Japan, are typically asymmetrical. All the landscape elements and human figures are placed to one corner, the empty remaining surfaces suggesting an enveloping mist. Such masterpieces as Ma's *Springtime Promenade*, painted between 1190 and 1225, and Xia's *Chatting With a Guest by the Pine Cliff*, which dates between 1180 and 1230, are typical examples.

Because of the short duration of the Yuan dynasty, the number of paintings produced was relatively small. One Yuan-era painting in the National Palace collection is the masterpiece *Autumn Colors on the Qiao and Hua Mountains*, dated 1295.

The Ming dynasty saw the revitalization of traditional Chinese institutions, including painting. Among the myriad notables was Wu Wei, an ardent Daoist who so fully comprehended the mysteries of the *dao* that he came to be regarded as an immortal. Also prominent were Wen Zheng-ming, who excelled at images of

old trees, and Dong Qi-chang, one of the most important artists of the late Ming period.

The Qing period saw the flourishing of the so-called Individualists, including Zhu Dao, Dao Ji, Gong Xian, Kun Can and Hong Ren.

A Jesuit priest named Giuseppe Castiglione, who went to China as a missionary and was called to the imperial court, also became famous as a painter of figures, flowers, birds and horses. Lang Shi-ning, as the priest became known, blended European naturalism with Chinese composition and media. ❑

ABOVE: *Quails among the Chrysanthemums*, by Song-dynasty artist, 1131.

Contemporary Art

While the treasures of the National Palace Museum showcase artworks produced throughout China's long history, it is the Taipei Fine Arts Museum that most succinctly shows how Taiwanese artists have interpreted the immense changes that Taiwanese society has undergone over the past century.

Taiwanese artists first came into contact with the new trends in Western modern art when the Japanese annexed the island in 1895. This was an exciting time in Japan. After centuries of seclusion, the country was at the height of the Meiji Restoration, a period in which Western learning was embraced with a fervor that made Japan hungry for all things new. In terms of the arts, that fervor was soon to spread to Taiwan through the man who has come to be called the "father of modern Taiwanese art," Ishikawa Kinichiro.

Ishikawa took Taiwanese disciples with him on his travels around Taiwan in search of subjects to paint in what has been described as "lyrical" watercolors. Most famous of these were Ni Jiang-huai, Chen Cheng-bo, Li Mei-shu and Li Shi-jiao. Much influenced by French impressionism, these artists produced landscape drawings of Taiwan's subtropical rural scenes, and have had a lasting impact on successive generations of Taiwanese artists. Their work has, to a certain extent, become definitive of what is described as "national style."

The efforts of these early pioneers were continued through the Japanese era by artists like Liao Ji-chun (1902–76), whose impressionist painting *The Courtyard* is much beloved as an expression of Taiwanese home life and whose *Oluanpi Lighthouse* is regarded as a classic rendering of Taiwanese landscape. The impressionist oil paintings of Liao and other contemporaries were enormously influential, coming to be known as the *xiangtu*, or "native soil" school, a rallying point for artists (and writers) that has continued to exert influence in Taiwanese art ever since.

The work of these Taiwanese artists, however, fell into obscurity with the arrival of Chiang Kai-shek's Nationalists in 1949. The new Kuomintang government favored the restoration of traditional Chinese ink painting, sponsoring exhibitions of traditional Chinese artistic subjects such as bamboo and misty mountain peaks dotted with fir trees.

One of the few artists of this era to break new ground and produce genuine works of art was Zhang Da-qian, whose monumental "splash ink" landscapes are genuinely awe-inspiring productions.

By the late 1950s and early 1960s, classicist approaches to art were being spurned once again by a new generation who were inspired by developments in the West and influenced by everything from abstract to pop art. A period that most commentators refer to today as "blind enthusiasm" for Western modern art followed. However, this period did not last long. By the late 1960s, Taiwanese artists were once again turning their eyes on their "native soil" and emulating the movement that had

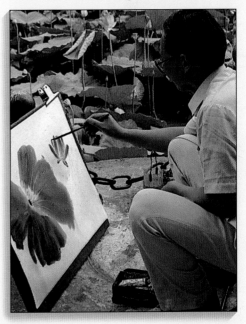

extolled it in the Japanese era. An influential figure during this period was Xi De-jin, who, upon returning from study abroad, abandoned abstract art and instead turned his attention to painting local Taiwanese scenes and folk traditions.

Recent years have seen a democratic intermingling of styles, with many different schools of art jostling for exhibition space in Taiwan. Highly influential in the early 1980s was the 101 School, which struggled to reflect what was then a nascent Taiwanese consciousness that has subsequently flowered into an island-wide movement.

Besides the Taipei Fine Arts Museum, there are several other galleries which feature the best in modern Taiwanese art (*see panel opposite*). ❑

RIGHT: modern artist paints in the old style.

CHINESE OPERA

Although initially strange to the Western ear and eye, Chinese opera has many conventions and traditions that ease the appreciation of its drama and spectacle

Westerners usually cringe when first encountering the somewhat shrill tones of traditional Chinese opera. To the ears of aficionados, however, the high-pitched notes lend emotional strength to song lyrics, and the prolonged wails accentuate the singers' moods. When added to the traditional accompaniment of drums, gongs, flutes and violins, the end result is an ancient sound so abstract it might have been concocted by an avant-garde composer of the 21st century.

The music provides the beat and the backing for a visual spectacle of electric shades of painted faces, glittering costumes, exquisite pantomime and impossible acrobatics – a unique blend of sight and sound called *jingxi*, capital opera, better known as Beijing opera.

Beijing opera was formally established in 1790. That was the year the most famous actors from all corners of the Chinese empire gathered in Peking (Beijing) to present a special variety show for the emperor. The performance proved so successful that the artists remained in the capital, combining their ancient individual disciplines of theater, music and acrobatics into the form of Beijing opera that continues today.

Teahouse spectaculars

The first venues for these spectaculars were the teahouses of the city. With greater popularity and increasingly complex performances, the teahouses evolved into theaters. Yet, the carnival atmosphere of the small teahouses persisted, and continues to do so even today.

Foreigners visiting an opera may be stunned to find that audiences eat, drink, and gossip their way through the show, only to fall silent during famous scenes and solo arias. But since audiences in Taiwan and in other Chinese communities know all the plots by heart – and all the performers by reputation – they know exactly when to pay undivided attention to the action.

LEFT: mask-like painted face of a heroine.
RIGHT: fastidious preparation begins before the show.

Chinese opera has no equivalent in the West, and bears only minor similarities to European classical opera. Thematically, the stories play like high melodrama, with good guys and bad guys who are clearly defined by costumes and face paint. The themes are drawn from popular folklore, ancient legends, and historical events.

It is in terms of technique, however, that Chinese opera emerges unique among the world's theatrical forms. The vehicles of expression blend singing, dancing, mime and acrobatics, and utilize sophisticated symbolism in costumes, make-up and stage props.

Each of the vehicles of Chinese opera is an art form in itself. The use of face paint, for instance, is divided into 16 major categories representing more than 500 distinctive styles. Proper application of the paint imparts a character with a clear identity.

History credits the invention of the make-up techniques to Prince Lanling, a ruler of the Northern Wei kingdom during the 6th century.

As his own features were so effeminate, the prince successfully designed a fierce face-mask to improve his appearance and his chances on the battlefield. His savage mask was later adapted for dramatic use. To facilitate the actors' movements and their ability to sing, the design was painted directly onto their faces.

Each color applied possesses its own basic properties: red is loyal, upright and straightforward; white denotes craft, cunning and resourcefulness – even a clown or a criminal; blue is vigorous,

OPERATIC SAINT

Tang dynasty emperor Xuanzong is the patron saint of Chinese opera. His fickle consort Yang Guifei is celebrated in the popular opera *The Drunken Concubine*.

tal conditions. These long, white armlets of silk are attached to the standard sleeves of the costume and trail down to the floor when loose.

Although it is merely an extra length of cloth, the expressive power of the water-sleeve can be remarkable when flicked by expert wrists. To express surprise or shock, a performer simply throws up his arms. The sleeves fly backwards in an alarming manner. An actor wishing to convey embarrassment daintily holds one sleeve across the face, as if hiding behind it.

wild, brave and enterprising; yellow dominates an intelligent but reserved character; brown suggests strong character with stubborn temperament; green is reserved for ghosts, demons and everything evil; and gold is the color of gods and benevolent spirits.

Water-sleeves and props

The extensive use of pantomime in Chinese opera virtually eliminates the need for elaborate stage sets. The few backdrops and props that are incorporated are put to ingenious uses.

One inventive prop that is actually part of a performer's costume is the water-sleeve, often used to mime emotion and imply environmen-

The range of symbolic gestures made possible by the water-sleeve is endless. These complement other expressive gestures in mime. Performers dust themselves off to indicate that they have just returned from a long journey. They form the sleeves into a muff around the clasped hands as protection against the cold weather of a winter scene. To cope with hot weather, the sleeves are flapped like a fan.

Simple devices like the water-sleeve, with its wide range of expression, make stage props generally unnecessary. The few that are used have obvious connotations. Spears and swords come into play during battle and action scenes. The long, quivering peacock plumes attached to the headgear of some actors identify them as warriors. Ornate riding crops with silk tassels tell any tuned-in audience that the actors are riding horses. Black pennants carried swiftly across the stage symbolize a thunderstorm, but four long pennants held aloft on poles represent a regiment of troops. A character riding a chariot holds up two yellow banners horizontally about waist high, each painted with a wheel. An actor bearing a banner with the character for *bao*, meaning report, is a courier delivering an important message.

Chinese opera also employs single props for a variety of uses. As simple an item as a chair is exactly what it appears to be when sat upon. But when placed upon a table, a chair is transformed into a mountain. Or it can be used as a throne. If an actor jumps off a chair, he has committed suicide by flinging himself into a well. After that, long strips of paper may be hung from just above his ears to indicate he has become a ghost.

With some basic grounding in the rich symbolism of the costumes, props, face paints and mime gestures, even a spectator who doesn't understand a word of Chinese may be able to follow the outline of the plot.

Rousing acrobatics

While neon-colored costumes and dazzling make-up can enthrall audiences for hours, the long intervals of song and dialogue can invariably induce bouts of boredom. But just as attention begins to drift, the performances are punctuated by rousing feats of athletics and prestidigitation. In fact, it is often difficult to distinguish the magic tricks from the acrobatics.

Chinese operas don't unfold on a stage. They leap, bound and bounce into action. Performers appear to have an uncanny knack for doing one midair somersault more than is humanly possible before they return to earth. Hands become feet and inverted stomachs become grotesque faces as two or more acrobats link arms and legs to become one fantastic creature.

The most thrilling portions of Chinese opera are the battle scenes. They employ every form of martial art and acrobatic maneuver conceivable. Sabers, axes and fists fly around in a way that would end in buckets of bloodletting

amidst novices. A sword flung high in the air, quite miraculously, can be caught in the razor-thin slit of its scabbard.

Traditionally, female roles in Chinese opera were performed by men, but modern performances today usually employ women to play women. Ironically, the old impersonators perfected such stylized feminine gestures that aspiring actresses have to learn to imitate a man imitating a woman.

The route to becoming an accomplished performer is a grueling one. Most children attend classes in opera schools as early as age seven, and instruction requires at least eight years. ❑

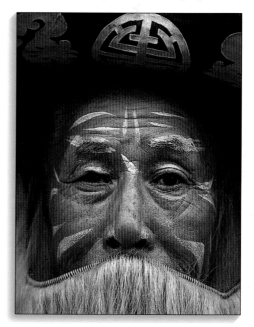

TAIWANESE OPERA

In addition to Beijing opera, an offshoot called Taiwan opera has become popular. It is usually performed outdoors on stages in the island's markets and temples and incorporates bright costumes and elaborate backdrops. Innovations in Taiwan opera range from the use of Taiwanese dialect, instead of the difficult Hubei dialect of Beijing opera, to disco-style robes and Western make-up techniques. These changes have broadened the popularity of opera among the general public. Traditional Chinese puppet shows are also staged frequently in Taiwan, and are based on the themes, roles, music and costumes of Beijing opera.

LEFT: a TaipeiEYE performance of Chinese opera.
RIGHT: heavily painted face, a distinguishing feature of all forms of Chinese opera.

MARTIAL ARTS

Chinese martial arts have a far softer, more deeply spiritual basis than the high-kicking, brick-smashing antics that the movie world tends to suggest

A scene long played out in the hills of Taipei behind the Grand Hotel: it's three o'clock in the morning. An old man strides vigorously up to Round Mountain Park. There he begins the dance that wakes the dawn. His arms arch upward slowly in a giant circle that symbolically splits the primordial unity of the cosmos into *yin* and *yang*. He moves his hips, spine and limbs in a harmony that animates the mystical ballet of *taiji*. With his circular movements synchronized to his abdominal breathing, he absorbs the potent *yang* energy that peaks between midnight and dawn.

The sun begins to rise. The old man, looking as spry as the new day, finishes with a regimen of *gongfu*. Back home, he sips the first of many cups of an herbal brew containing white ginseng and red jujube, sweetened with raw sugar, to help maintain the level of vital energy that pulses through his legs, spine and nervous system. By the time Hong Wu-fan – head of a family world-renowned for its contribution to martial arts – begins breakfast each morning, all Taipei has come alive with people jogging through the streets, stretching in the parks and egging their bodies into heightened consciousness with an array of exercise. Today in downtown Taipei, 2-28 Peace Park is a particularly popular spot for this impressive display of physical culture.

From the slow-motion flourishes of *taiji* and the graceful thrusts and parries of classical sword-fighting, to innovative fighting techniques and Chinese versions of aerobic dancing, spirited residents of Taipei display an impressive range of athletic abilities.

Many of the movements hark back to that most noble of Chinese institutions, the martial arts. Contrary to popular misconception, the Chinese martial arts are collectively called *guoshu*, or national arts, not *gongfu*, which literally translates as "time and energy spent on cultivating an art or skill." In fact, it can refer to

any skill. A great calligrapher has good *gongfu*. So does a master chef or master fighter.

The secrets of the martial arts have been handed down from master to disciple in an unbroken tradition reaching across tens of centuries. Many great masters joined the exodus to the island of Taiwan in 1949, bringing their

secrets and skills with them. Here, they trained a new generation of experts.

The dragon awakens

Two of the greats who came from the mainland were Zhang Jun-feng and Chen Pan-ling. Hong Wu-fan welcomed these homeless and destitute masters to his wealthy household. In gratitude, Zhang Jun-feng began to school Hong's five sons in the ways of the ancients. Subsequently, Chen let the Hong family in on the secrets of his mastery of *shaolin* and *taiji*.

Among Hong's five sons, the two masters discovered a sleeping dragon, someone with enormous talent not yet developed. Under the

---

LEFT: on-guard posture during filming of a martial-arts movie. **RIGHT:** a martial arts master practices his technique.

tutelage of Chen, Zhang and 15 other renowned masters, the dragon awoke. Hong Yi-xiang, before his death in the 1990s, was considered one of the greatest masters of the ancient arts. His legacy still defines the martial-arts world in Taiwan.

Hong Yi-xiang defied the typical image of a *gongfu* master. Packing more than 90 kg (198 lbs) of powerful bulk into a compact 1.7-meter (5 ft 6 inch) tall body, he looked more like a stevedore than a master of the martial, medical and fine

ANIMAL INSPIRATION

The Chinese developed fighting forms by imitating the movements of animals, and it is said that *taiji* was invented when a master fighter stumbled upon an eagle and a snake locked in mortal combat.

animal postures, and internal breathing methods is the model for all Chinese martial arts.

These arts are based on the cosmic principles of *yin* and *yang*, and on the five elements of the cosmos: earth, water, metal, wood and fire. The most fundamental concept is *qi*, which translates as vital energy or life force. But it also means air and breath. *Qi* is an invisible element contained in air, food, water and every living thing on Earth. Martial arts exercises like *taiji* cultivate *qi* through deep breathing and direct it around

arts. But to watch him perform his *taiji* forms, or demonstrate the circles of *bagua*, was like watching a gentle wind stir willow branches. Each move was smooth and fluid, yet swift and very sudden.

In the 5th century, the Indian pilgrim Bodhidharma, known to the Chinese as Damo, introduced Zen Buddhism to China and enhanced Chinese fighting forms by teaching the deep-breathing methods of yoga. Damo also taught the Chinese that martial arts should be cultivated for spiritual development, not for superficial shows of force, and should be used exclusively for defense, never for offense. His blend of external fighting forms, derived from

the body with rhythmic motions. *Qi* is the force that fuels the martial arts. Proper breathing must be correctly cultivated before a student moves on to complex external movements.

Soft and round

The essence of classical Chinese martial arts can be defined in two words: *rou* (softness) and *yüan* (roundness). By remaining soft and loose at all times, a person conserves vital energy while an opponent expends his by thrashing about. By using round, circular movements, the master combatant deflects his opponent's direct linear attacks, and all his parries naturally flow the full circle to become counterattacks.

Softness and roundness are maintained and enhanced through rhythmic breathing. Breathing also permeates the body with *qi* during combat. The hard linear movements glorified by the modern Chinese *gongfu* movies do not promote the circulation of *qi*. Hard styles like Japanese *karate*, Korean *taekwondo* and Chinese *shaolin* are better known in the West, but the soft rhythmic Chinese styles like *taiji*, *xingyi* and *bagua* are more traditional.

Legacy of Master Peng

Hong Yi-xiang's mastery over his own *qi* came to the forefront under his last and greatest teacher, Master Peng. Peng was a mainlander who had never accepted a single student after fleeing to Taiwan until, growing old, he realized he had to reveal his precious secrets before his death, or they would be lost to posterity. Scores of hopefuls rushed to his home in Taichung to be interviewed for the honor.

Master Peng conducted his audiences in a stark, dark room lit by a single candle. The candle stood on a low table between himself and his visitors. One by one, the eager hopefuls filed in, spoke briefly with the master, then left. Little did they know that they had been judged before uttering a word. Only one man passed the test. He managed to enter the room, approach the master and pay his respects without once causing the candle to flicker, so revealing full control of his *qi*. Master Peng had found his disciple: Hong Yi-xiang.

Master Hong not only took up the mantle of his great teachers, he also developed his own system of martial arts. Hong called his school *tangshoudao*, the Way of the Hands of Tang. It blends the finest elements of *xingyi*, *bagua*, *taiji* and the more difficult *shaolin*. It takes its name from the so-called golden age of Chinese culture, the Tang dynasty of the 7th to early 10th centuries, which was also the formative age of Chinese *gongfu*. *Tangshoudao*, which is Chinese *gongfu* at its classical best – internal, subtle and linked to Daoist philosophy – was Hong's personal attempt to restore Chinese martial arts to their authentic forms and traditions.

Master Hong, like Damo, believed that health and longevity are the true goals of martial arts. He said that self-defense techniques using martial arts can indeed increase longevity and promote health by protecting one from bullies, but he emphasized that if one's internal powers of *qi* are strong and steady, the bullies will instinctively steer clear. "The most accomplished martial artists are those who never have to fight. No one dares challenge them," Master Hong said. "Concentrate on the inner meaning, not the outer strength." He also elaborated on the apparent paradox that in softness there is strength. Hong noted that water eventually wears down the hardest rock, and that, when properly applied, "four ounces of strength can topple 1,000 pounds." ❑

LEFT: young martial arts trainees in combat.
RIGHT: a martial artist limbering up.

CONCRETE PROOF

Master Hong once demonstrated the truths of the *Dao* and the sudden explosions of power that his training enabled him to summon at will. Challenged to prove his might, he took on the task of smashing three solid cement blocks with a single blow. The blocks were stacked flush and placed on a solid flat surface, rather than up on blocks. Focusing his *qi* within, Hong mustered intense concentration then raised his fist high and brought it down with a single devastating blow. He didn't break the blocks. He shattered them. A film replay showed that, at the moment of impact, every hair on his right arm and shoulder was erect – the power of *qi*, he later explained.

TRADITIONAL MEDICINE

Time-honored herbal concoctions and physical techniques
both play their parts in keeping the Taiwanese healthy and vital

Consider the case of the curious goatherd, who one day noticed that several of his billy goats were behaving in an unusually randy manner, mounting the nearest females repeatedly in remarkably brief spans of time. Concerned by their amorous behavior, perhaps even a bit envious of their prowess, the goatherd, in time-honored scientific tradition, kept careful watch on his horny herd for a few weeks. He soon detected a pattern. Whenever a billy goat ate from a particular patch of weeds, the goat's promiscuous proclivities peaked.

Before long, Chinese herbalists had determined what goats had long known: that a plant of the *aceranthus sagittatum* family was one of the most potent male aphrodisiacs. Many of China's most efficacious herbal remedies were discovered in precisely the same manner, and Chinese medicine now has the world's most comprehensive pharmacopoeia of herbal cures.

Historical roots

Historians have traced the beginnings of herbal medicine to Shen Nong, the legendary emperor also known as the Divine Farmer, for his teaching of agricultural techniques, around 3,500 BC. References to various diseases and their herbal remedies first appeared on Shang dynasty oracle bones, circa 1,500 BC. They prove that medicine was a formal branch of study in China as long as 3,500 years ago. Later, books on medicine were among the few tomes spared during the infamous burning of books by Qin Shi Huangdi, in 220 BC.

The first volume that summarized and categorized the knowledge of herbal cures in China is first mentioned in the 2nd century BC. *The Yellow Emperor's Classic of Internal Medicine* contained the world's first scientific classification of medicinal plants, and is still used today.

The quintessential herbal doctor Sun Si-mo appeared 800 years later. He established a

LEFT: weighing out herbal medicine.
RIGHT: a physician administers Chinese traditional medical treatment with suction cups.

pattern of practice still followed by Chinese physicians. "Rich and poor, old and young, high and low are all alike in the clinic," Sun wrote. Three emperors invited Sun to be their personal physician. He declined, preferring to practice among the commoners. Previously only the high and mighty had access to profes-

sional medical care, but Sun applied the Confucian virtue of *ren*, or benevolence, to his trade. He established the great tradition of *ren-shu renxin* (benevolent art, benevolent heart) that has guided Chinese physicians ever since.

Sun Si-mo was also the first dietary therapist. "A truly good physician first finds out the cause of the illness, and … first tries to cure it by food," he wrote. "Only when food fails does he prescribe medication." Sun diagnosed the vitamin-deficiency disease beriberi 1,000 years before European doctors and prescribed a remarkably modern-sounding dietary remedy: calf and lamb's liver, wheatgerm, almonds, wild pepper and other vitamin-packed edibles.

Another milestone in the history of herbal medicine was the publication of *Ben Cao Gang Mu (Treasures of Chinese Medicine)* in the 16th century. This authoritative work was compiled by physician Li Shi-zhen, who classified and analyzed 1,892 entries, including drugs derived from plants, animals and minerals. The book was used by Charles Darwin while developing his system for classifying species in nature.

The theory and practice of traditional Chinese medicine takes an approach to disease and

A GOOD DIET

In Chinese medicine, part of the prevention of illness is correct diet, but not as one in the West might think. The concern is with how foods and drinks encourage or dissipate moods within the body.

ilies retained family doctors. The doctor was paid a set monthly fee and made regular rounds to dispense herbal remedies and medical advice tailored to the needs of each family member. When someone fell ill, the doctor was held responsible for failing to foresee and prevent the problem. Payments were stopped. Only when he cured the patient at his own expense did his normal fee resume. The system stressed the importance of preventive care. It also served as a deterrent to malpractice, as doctors profited

therapy that is diametrically different from Western ways. The Chinese prefer preventive techniques; the West concentrates on cures. The Chinese regard medicine as an integral part of a comprehensive system of health and longevity called *yangsheng*, which means "to nurture life." The system includes proper diet, regular exercise, regulated sex and deep breathing, as well as medicinal therapies and treatments. Unlike Western medicine, which has become increasingly fragmented into specialized branches, Chinese medicine remains syncretic. The various combinations of therapies must be mastered by every Chinese physician.

Prior to the 20th century, most Chinese fam-

by keeping their patients healthy and happy rather than sick and dependent.

Look for the cause

Modern families in Taiwan can no longer afford to keep a physician on the payroll, but the precept of prevention prevails. The Chinese trace and treat root causes of weakness and disease rather than their superficial symptoms. The physician draws a medical picture that encompasses everything from the weather and season to a patient's dietary and sexual habits. And true causes are often found far from the symptoms.

For instance, Chinese medicine traditionally traces eye problems to liver disorders. Such symptomatic connections are rarely established in the West, where the eyes and the liver are treated by two separate specialists.

The theoretical foundations of Chinese medical arts, like those of the martial arts, are rooted in the cosmic theories of *yin* and *yang*, the five elements (earth, water, metal, wood, fire), and the concept of *qi*, or vital energy. Essentially, Chinese doctors manipulate a patient's internal balance of vital energies by using herbs, acupuncture and other methods. By re-establishing the optimum balance and restoring harmony among the body's vital organs, a physician can keep his patient healthy.

Herbal therapy encompasses more than 2,000 organic medicines, but only about 100 are commonly used. The rest are reserved for the rarest conditions. Herbal prescriptions routinely contain at least a half-dozen ingredients (many common in Western kitchens, like cinnamon, ginger and licorice), some added simply to counteract the side-effects of more potent additives. The old adage "fight poison with poison" originated in this branch of Chinese medicine. Some of humanity's most virulent ailments are fought with such potent toxins as jimsonweed, centipedes, scorpion tails and mercury. Herbal prescriptions come in a variety of forms. There are pills, brews, powders, pastes, medicinal wines, serums and refined concentrates.

Acupuncture and massage

Acupuncture is probably the most widely used of Chinese therapies in the West. Acupuncturists stick fine steel needles into "vital points" along the body's "vital-energy" network. The insertion of a needle produces a specific therapeutic effect on a specific organ, gland, nerve or other body part. The points are connected to the internal organs and glands by energy channels called meridians. While many of the secrets of acupuncture mystify physicians in the West, they acknowledge that it can be effective in treating some ailments. It has also proven to be effective as an anesthetic.

Massage, called *tuina* (push and rub), is applied to joints, tendons, ligaments and nerve centers, as well as to vital points and meridians. *Tuina* can help relieve and gradually eliminate arthritis, rheumatism, slipped discs, nerve

LEFT: the fine points of modern massage.
RIGHT: a herbalist displays his cure-alls.

paralysis and energy stagnation and dissipation.

Guasha, or skin-scraping, involves the use of a blunt spoon or coin, dipped in wine or salt water, and rubbed repeatedly across vital points on a patient's skin until a red welt appears. In cases of heat stroke, colds, fever, colic and painful joints, the practice draws out "heat energy," hopefully eliminating the cause of the problem.

In *bagua*, suction cups made from bamboo or glass are briefly flamed with a burning wad of alcohol-soaked cotton to create a vacuum, then pressed over a vital-point. Skin and flesh balloon into the cup, drawing out evil energies by pressure. The method has been found effec-

tive in the treatment of rheumatism, arthritis, bruises, abscesses and such ailments.

As bizarre as these and other Chinese medical treatments may sound, all are utilized with apparent success in Taiwan. For many common ailments, the Chinese approach puts faith in natural and organic curatives. However, Chinese medicine does not dispute the superiority of Western medicine in the treatment of certain acute traumatic ailments, injuries and emergency cases. In fact, physicians in Taiwan today blend Chinese theories and practices with Western technology, and conversely, Chinese therapy and Western diagnosis in a system of medical care called the New Medicine. ❏

CONTEMPORARY CULTURE

New-found wealth, the opportunities of travel and the lifting of martial law have jointly provided the impetus for Taiwan's thriving arts scene

The past two decades have been a period of explosive creativity for Taiwan's contemporary artists. The end of martial law in 1987, the ever increasing affluence of the island and the large numbers of Taiwanese returning from overseas study and travel have all conspired to create a vibrant arts scene, much of it exploring the troubled nature of Taiwanese identity. Even areas such as cinema, which has seen a decline from its popular boom in the 1960s, have managed to steadily produce artists who garner awards at international competitions. Meanwhile, in areas such as popular music, the island has emerged as an Asian center, far belying its small size and relatively small population.

Cinema

Cinema is one of the few areas where contemporary Taiwanese culture has had some overseas impact, though this has been restricted to the art-house circuit, in which Taiwanese offerings frequently receive acclaim. This is a fairly recent development. In the 1960s and 1970s Taiwan had a very healthy movie industry, very much in the mold of centers like Bombay, Hong Kong and, of course, Hollywood. But with the opening up of Taiwan to foreign cinema, audiences grew tired of the often predictable romances and dramas produced locally, and in the last two-plus decades local cinema has become almost entirely the provenance of the art-house set.

Directors of the early 1980s were influenced by the *xiangtu* – "native soil" – literary movement, which had also in its turn influenced a great many local painters. One of the most representative movies is *A Time to Live and a Time to Die* (1985), directed by Hou Xiao-xian, who went on to win the Golden Lion award at the Venice Film Festival in 1989 for his depiction of the oppression of native Taiwanese by the Nationalists in *City of Sadness*. *A Time to Live and a Time to Die*, which is a coming-of-

LEFT: a Cloud Gate Dance Theater performance, undeniably New Age. **RIGHT:** Hollywood blockbusters at a high-tech movie theater in Ximending, Taipei.

age depiction of childhood in rural Taiwan during the 1950s and 1960s, movingly depicts the changes that swept across the island in its headlong rush from an agrarian to an urbanized and industrialized society.

Hou is internationally the most famous of Taiwan's so-called "new wave" directors, but

his nativist meditations on Taiwan's rural roots do not entirely match the scope of the new directions in which 1980s filmmakers were taking Taiwanese cinema. Edward Yang's *Taipei Story* (1985), for example, is a bleak look at youths whose lives seem bereft of meaning in the rainy urban landscape of modern Taipei.

Hou continues to make movies, remaining true to his artistic vision despite local public disinterest and a scarcity of funds. Meanwhile, a second generation of directors (inevitably called the "second new wave"), whose visions tend to be less brooding, reflect perhaps a new sense of buoyancy that has come with the lifting of martial law and increased affluence.

The work of Cai Ming-liang, whose *Vive L'Amour* took the 1994 Venice Golden Lion, bears some resemblance to that of Yang, usually examining urban loneliness, but directors such as Ang Lee (who has gone on to international Hollywood success, with Oscars for *Crouching Tiger, Hidden Dragon* and *Brokeback Mountain*) have taken on broader issues such as homosexuality in *The Wedding Banquet* (1993), and the Chinese obsession with food in *Eat Drink Man Woman* (1994). *The Wedding Banquet* broke all the rules of Taiwanese art-house cinema by entering the US mainstream movie circuit, grossing more than 30 times the amount it cost to make the film, and ironically, due to its US success, even reaching mainstream audiences in Taiwan itself.

PEOPLE, NOT POLITICS

Despite the fact that Hou Xiao-xian has never backed away from politically sensitive subjects – filming his early movies in Taiwanese despite a Nationalist injunction against doing so, and portraying political oppression by the Nationalist forces in *City of Sadness* – he denies that he is a political filmmaker. "What really interests me is people," he has been quoted as saying. "I am emotional about people. Only people move me." For anyone who has seen his films, with their moving depictions of ordinary people struggling against circumstance and history, such words ring true. His films leave an emotional residue that lingers long after the screening.

Dance

Cai Rui-yue is generally acknowledged as the mother of modern dance in Taiwan. In 1936, at the age of 16, she left Taiwan for Tokyo to study with Ishii Midori, one of Japan's most famous modern dance instructors. She returned in 1945 and established Taiwan's first school of ballet in Tainan. Evicted from the premises on the grounds that Western-style dance was "indecent," she soon shifted to Taipei. Shortly after marrying in Taipei, her husband was deported for his political views and she herself was imprisoned for two years. Upon her release, she opened the China Dance Academy on Taipei's Zhongshan North Road where it served as a center of dance until it burnt down in late 1999.

The most famous of Cai's students today is Lin Hwai-min, whose Cloud Gate Dance Theater has toured to international acclaim. Lin, who also studied in the US under Martha Graham, initially set out to combine modern Western dance, Chinese opera and an expression of Taiwanese identity in the early 1970s. His later work, however, has embraced influences from as far afield as India, Java and Tibet, taking on subjects – such as China's Tiananmen massacre in *Requiem* – that are not restricted to Taiwanese themes. A Cloud Gate performance is a breathtaking experience, providing a far more exhilarating insight into the vibrancy of contemporary Taiwanese arts than tourist-oriented performances such as Beijing opera.

Lin's Cloud Gate has been enormously influential in Taiwan, spawning many imitators and innovators. Most successful of these has been Liu Shao-lu's Taipei Dance Circle, whose oiled, near naked, squirming dancers caused controversy but won Liu the National Award for Culture and Arts nonetheless.

Lin Xiu-wei is another Lin protégé that has gone on to success with her Taigu Tales Dance Theater, whose brooding, studied performances have been compared to Japan's Butoh dance.

Puppetry

Taiwan's glove-puppet theater, or *budaixi*, seems an unlikely candidate for a modern revival, but a modern revival of what was once one of the island's most popular forms of entertainment is precisely what has happened. In part the excitement is due to a feature-length, glove-puppet movie, *Legend of the Sacred Stone* (1999), a hit amongst Taiwanese young and old, but the real reason lies with the group behind the movie, the High Energy Puppet Theater, which has its own cable TV channel devoted to nothing but glove-puppet dramas.

Reprising a 583-episode puppet TV series from the 1970s, High Energy has had enormous local success, spawning fan clubs and

piece of cinema that little anticipated the art form's revival in fortunes. Nevertheless, at the time the movie was made, some 200 puppet troupes were still active around Taiwan, usually reserving their performances for local festivals.

While it's possible to find performances of glove puppets today by channel surfing on Taiwanese television, nothing beats seeing an outdoor performance. The makeshift stage is usually a grandly colorful affair covered in swirling gold designs that

leading to the unexpected spectacle of glove puppets sharing shelf space with Hello Kitty dolls in Taiwan's toy shops and hand-crafted puppets fetching hefty sums in antiques boutiques.

Until this recent excitement, *budaixi* was just one of the many of Taiwan's folk arts that had fallen into decline. In 1993, director Hou Xiaoxian made a movie about one of the island's leading protagonists, Li Tian-lu (now deceased), called *The Puppetmaster*, an elegiac

make it look like the entrance to a temple. Meanwhile, the characters themselves strut about the stage in richly embroidered cloaks, carrying out pitched battles, intrigues and romantic affairs.

Manga

The Japanese word *manga*, meaning comics, is pronounced *manhua* in Chinese, and, like many things Japanese, took the island by storm in the 1990s. As in Japan, comics have been a staple in the Taiwanese "literary" diet for several decades, but recently this enthusiasm has reached fever pitch, leading to many local artists trying their hand at the art.

LEFT: Lin Hwai-min, award-winning choreographer and helmsman of the Cloud Gate troupe. **ABOVE:** a collection of traditional hand puppets.

Japanese *manga* remain the most popular variety in Taiwan in spite of (or perhaps because of) their sometimes quite racy content that frequently features soft porn and sometimes surprisingly explicit sex. But a new generation of Taiwanese *manga* artists (or *manga-ka* in the parlance of fans, borrowing from Japanese) emerged in the late 1990s, some of them breaking into the Japanese market. Notable among them is Chen Wen, whose adaptations of Chinese *gongfu* novels (*wuxia xiaoshuo*) have been a hit in Taiwan, Hong Kong and Japan. For a glimpse of *manga* culture at its most vibrant, a stroll through Taipei's youth district of Ximen-ding will turn up numerous *manga*-devoted shops as well as colorful youngsters sporting *manga*-inspired clothing designs.

Pop scene

Despite the perennial success of Hong Kong singers – most of whom release their albums in both Cantonese and Mandarin these days – Taiwan has emerged as the center of the Mandarin pop, or Mandopop, universe in recent years. It is a phenomenon that has led local cultural critics to point out that, while the two sides of the Taiwan Strait are divided politically, unification took place long ago on the cultural front.

ALTERNATIVE MUSIC

One side of Taiwan that few visiting foreigners see is its exciting alternative music scene. Whereas most Asian music cultures are almost entirely dominated by the corporate marketing of saccharine melodies, in Taipei indie fans have difficulty keeping track of the many bands jostling for attention in the vibrant local circuit.

Take Fish and the Bedroom Riot, which brings rock, theatre, and audiovisual experimentation to the stage. Band members include two artists from the now defunct Ladybug, Taiwan's near legendary all-girl quartet that one US reviewer described, when the band toured there in late 1998, as sounding "like Shonen Knife and The Jesus And Mary Chain covering The Go-Go's on 45 rpm." Or take the energetic band Sugar Plum Fairy, whose crunchy instrumental thrash sound seems to come directly from the US post-rock scene.

Throw into the mix bands like 88 Guava Seeds and Hohak Band, whose roots are clearly more Taiwanese, and you have an extremely eclectic line up.

The alternative band scene was kick-started in 1994 with the opening of Scum, a dingy, basement Taipei bar in which, musically, almost anything went. Today, performances take place in a number of more salubrious venues, which are listed in the Friday editions of Taiwan's English-language newspapers and on www.taiwannights.com.

The front-runner in the explosion of Taiwanese pop in the Chinese world was the late Teresa Deng, who, sharing the same surname as China's late party chairman, Deng Xiaoping, used to be jokingly referred to as Taiwan's "little Deng." Her popularity coincided with the reforms that began in 1978 in China, and her nostalgic, Mandarin love songs struck a popular chord on both sides of the strait.

The Taiwan music scene has, however, come a long way from the days when it was content to simply export sweet love songs. The local music scene began to diversify in the 1980s, when Taiwan's so-called "campus folk scene" started to permeate the corporate music world. The unofficial spokesman for this generation of singer-songwriters, who voiced social concerns through music, was Luo Da-you, who influenced Beijing rocker Cui Jian, among others.

Broadening horizons

It was only in the 1990s that the Taiwanese pop industry truly started to broaden its horizons and come into its own. Corporate-groomed stars continued to be a phenomenon throughout this period, but the industry was also marked by a large number of innovators who were able to turn their musical talents to considerable popular success. Musicians such as Wu Bai, who writes his own music and performs with a Western-style band featuring an American drummer, went from playing Taipei pubs to playing stadiums. His music is what he calls Taiwanese rock – melodic, foot-stomping crowd-pleasers sung in Taiwanese. His presence – if not his music – has inspired more musically adventurous songwriting bands like Luantan.

At the same time, the maverick Chen Mingzhang has devoted his musical career to exploring the notion of what it is to be Taiwanese through near-forgotten Taiwanese folk forms combined with modern electric influences. He engineered a surprise hit for the Kinmen Wang (the Kings of Kinmen), a blind duo whose Chen-penned *Drifting to Danshui* was hugely successful.

More surprises have occurred in the willingness of recent pop artists to break taboos and deal with subjects other than the Mandopop

staples of broken hearts and wistful love. Zhang Zhen-yue, an aboriginal singer-songwriter, broke onto the scene with *Boring Day* in 1997 and then took the island by storm in 1999 with *Mom, Pa, Give Me Money*, a song that reflected Taiwanese society's materialism but was considered so unfilial overseas that it was banned in Malaysia.

More mainstream, but nevertheless breaking new musical ground, is aboriginal pop diva A-Mei, who surprised audiences with her gutsy, R&B-influenced voice when she released *Bad Boy*. A-Mei has since become one of Taiwan's most successful musical exports in the Chinese world, although China banned her for a year

after she sang the national anthem at the presidential inauguration of Taiwanese independence supporter Chen Shui-bian in 2000. She has since made successful visits.

In terms of unabashed sugar-laced pop, the boy-band phenomenon has hit Taiwan's shores. JVKV, Taiwan's answer to Irish boy-band Westlife, has elevated "groupism" to an art form. The four gorgeous long-haired boys with their fairytale princely personas have spawned a multimillion-dollar industry – and brazen copycats (male and female) like 5566, Energy, K-One, and S.H.E. When it comes to solo acts, edgy Jay Chou and surgically created Jolin Tsai currently occupy the thrones of pop royalty. ❑

LEFT: home to a fevered pop music scene, Taiwan plays host to regular rock concerts. **RIGHT:** local son Wu Bai's repertoire ranges from blues to hard rock.

FOOD AND DRINK

Few places can match Taiwan for culinary expertise now that the secrets of ethnic cuisines from the mainland have been unlocked for Taiwanese chefs

Many Taiwanese claim that their country has the best Chinese food on earth, and there's little point in arguing. The island has a huge selection of simple, undecorated restaurants, many of them local secrets and most of them serving great food.

When immigrants flooded into Taiwan after

the civil war in China in 1949, they brought with them regional cuisines from all over the mainland. Many of the first restaurants in Taiwan were opened by retired soldiers, who plied their trade over hot woks in simple kitchens.

As Taiwan prospered, the people retained their taste for the regional dishes of China. Prosperity has brought a refined palate and an excellence seen only in the world's great dining cities. Taiwan is now a paradise for food lovers, and eating out is the top recreation.

Just about every type of Chinese food is available in Taiwan, including steamed Shanghai dumplings, salty beerhouse food, northern Chinese wheat-based snacks, Mongolian barbecues,

Sichuan hotpots, night-market noodles, barbecued squid, Cantonese dim sum, dried Hunan honeyed ham – the list is virtually endless. No matter how many times you eat out in Taipei, every meal will feature something original: a new dish, a new ingredient, a new preparation.

Most Chinese restaurants in Taiwan are very casual. The lighting and decor are unremarkable, and the staff tend to be informal and friendly. Each dish arrives steaming hot as soon as it's ready, with little regard for order or decorum. The meals themselves are a frenzy of chopsticks and rice bowls, and afterwards the tablecloths are often badly stained and piled high with remnant bones and spilled food.

Gourmets will argue endlessly about Chinese regional cuisine: what dish belongs to which place, how the regions should be divided up, where the best seafood comes from, and so on. But generally speaking, five major types are represented in Taiwan: Canton (Guangdong), Sichuan, Hakka, Shanghai and Beijing.

Cantonese

Food-wise, the Cantonese have long been ahead of their time. In the past couple of decades, the world has discovered the virtues of fresh food with simple ingredients, quickly cooked and lightly seasoned. The Cantonese have been doing this for centuries. The classic Cantonese dish is lightly steamed fish, doused in red-hot oil and topped with a mild sauce of fresh coriander (cilantro), ginger, pepper, sesame and soy sauce. Other famous Cantonese dishes are too numerous to list – they include beef and broccoli with oyster sauce, diced chicken with cashew nuts, barbecued pork, steamed lobster and the many kinds of *dim sum*.

Cantonese chefs like to mix fruit with meat or poultry, and lemon-roasted chicken and duck with pineapple are both typical. Another quintessential dish is chicken strips dipped in egg white and cooked with fresh sweet peas. This delicate dish is typically Cantonese in character: mild, lightly spiced and full of subtle flavor.

Perhaps, as a result of their competitive

natures, the Cantonese repertoire also includes the most expensive, elaborate, and exotic foods of all the Chinese cuisines, including shark-fin soup, bird's-nest soup and sea slug.

Sichuanese, Taiwanese and Hakka

Sichuanese food, with its trademark flavorings of chili pepper and garlic, may be the most popular Chinese cuisine in Taiwan. While Sichuanese cooking is reputed for spiciness, it is quite mild compared with Thai or Indian food. Sichuan-style cuisine uses a variety of chili oils, hot sauces and dried chili peppers to season its foods, but the chilis are not strong, and the dishes

garlic, chili peppers and a vegetable, usually cabbage. As with the other cuisines, there are dozens of good Sichuanese dishes; *mapo dofu*, spicy bean curd with minced pork, is a staple, and so is *yinsi juan*, a delicate fried bread roll that sometimes serves as a substitute for rice.

In recent years, Taiwanese food has enjoyed a renaissance. This cuisine combines Fujianese and Japanese styles with local ingredients such as sweet potato and indigenous species of clam, mullet, oyster and freshwater shrimp.

Like many Chinese cuisines, the origins of Taiwanese cooking lie in scarcity. The most famous dish is probably *danzi mian*, or slack-

usually have a complementary sweet or sour flavor that provides balance.

Chicken or shrimp cooked with a hot and sweet sauce of peanuts and chili is a signature dish. Dried chilis are cut into long strips, fried in oil, then removed and cooked with the meat, and at the end a rich mixture of soy sauce, wine, vinegar and sesame oil is added.

Hui guo rou, or "twice-cooked" meat, is pork that is boiled with scallions (spring onions), wine and ginger, then removed and stir-fried with

LEFT: northern-style hot meat-filled dumplings are a favorite snack. **ABOVE:** the various cuisines of China are found in Taiwan, including this array of Sichuan-style dishes.

season noodles. *Danzi* noodles were invented in 1895 by a fisherman from the southern city of Tainan as a way to stretch meager food supplies through the non-fishing season. It is made by boiling fresh noodles and beansprouts in a bamboo cup, after which the toppings are added: coriander, pork sauce, shrimp broth, vinegar, garlic and two small shrimps. This might be the best bowl of noodles you could eat in Taiwan.

Taro cakes are also popular. The cooks slice and steam *taro*, a type of root vegetable, then douse it with a pork-based sauce. The *taro* cakes stay firm and chewy, and the sauce adds texture and flavor. Condiments include a mouthwatering choice of pungent garlic, tongue-searing *wasabi* and a smooth, sweet-chili sauce.

The Hakka people are originally from the central plains of north China, and many eventually settled in Taiwan via Guangdong. Traditionally poor, and often transient, their food features preserved meats and vegetables, sundried sausage and liver, bean curd, and plenty of cabbage and pork. The signature flavorings are vinegar, sliced ginger, pickle and chili pepper.

Hakka food has enjoyed a revival in Taiwan, as the Taiwanese rediscover the virtues of simple peasant cooking. Pork features heavily. *Dibang* is a thick leg of stewed ham, cooked with tangy vegetables and a rich, sweet sauce.

Stewed tofu with pork meatballs is typical, as is *mei gan kou rou*, or dry plum fatty bacon: thick slices of marbled pork in a salty, tangy sauce. The defining Hakka dish, shredded beef and ginger, is superb, and the thinly sliced ginger has a remarkable mildness. How cooks achieve this flavor remains a Hakka secret.

Shanghainese and Beijing

There is argument about whether Shanghai has a cuisine of its own, or whether it absorbed its food culture from surrounding territories. But who cares? In Taiwan, Shanghainese means a rich, sometimes oily cuisine featuring gravies and stews made mostly with fish and pork.

Deservedly or not, Shanghai also gets credit for one of the most delicious of Chinese foods, the dumpling. *Xiao long bao*, the most popular type, is a mouthwatering mixture of green onion, ginger, pork and sesame oil. Another delicacy is *tang bao*, or "steamed buns with soup," made from delicate dumplings that contain a warm and fragrant burst of gingery soup.

Shizi tou, or lion's head meatballs, are ground pork mixed with beaten egg, scallions (spring onions), ginger, minced mushrooms and bamboo shoots, braised on a bed of cabbage. The cabbage absorbs the flavor from the meatballs, making this a very tasty dish.

Among the other well-known Shanghainese dishes are bean curd with pickled snow vegetable, a cold dish made from custard-like tofu, covered with the delicate snow vegetable, and sprinkled with seasonings. Shanghainese also cook many types of fish, the most famous being sweet-and-sour, where fish is coated in batter, deep fried and served with a tomato-based sauce.

As the former seat of the imperial court, Beijing once had a reputation as a gastronomic center, where mandarins and other privileged people ate rich and unusual foods.

In northern cooking, wheat flour largely replaces rice, and many of the dishes are served on delicate wheat pancakes or in sesame seed-coated buns.

The most famous northern dish is Peking duck, which is one of the highlights of Chinese cuisine. It is sometimes called *yi ya san chi* (one duck three ways), because the crispy skin is served first, followed by the meat, and then the bones, which arrive last in a rich soup.

Peking duck takes days to prepare. The duck is boiled, brushed with wine and honey, hung

---

NOT FOR THE FAINT-HEARTED

One notable Sichuanese dish is called *mala huo guo* (numb-hot fire pot). This large bowl of pig blood and pork broth, bubbling with brown peppercorns, red chili seeds and chili oil is not a meal for the faint of heart – it's a tastebud-destroying blaze of pungent pepper flavor.

The vat of broth boils away on the table, while guests order items like tofu, congealed duck blood, pig and ox intestines, mushrooms, fatty beef, pork balls, cabbage, and egg and pork dumplings to plunge into the boiling soup to cook. For tourists, there is a choice: the white pot is without the peppers, but the red pot has all the wicked spices (or a pot is divided in half by a "firewall").

◁ **DRIVE-THROUGH**
A common sight on the outskirts of the city: a perky, platform-shoed "*binlang* beauty" fills a passing customer's order for a box of fresh betel nuts.

△ **HIGH IN THE HILLS**
In the perfect growing conditions of the tropical, mist-covered mountains of southern Taiwan, a Rukai man prepares *binlang* for sale.

BINLANG BEAUTY: SITTING PRETTY

Binlang's popularity is undoubtedly linked to the "betel-nut beauties" who sell the nuts. The girls, some as young as 15, perch at roadside stands encased behind glass and elevated to eye level for the benefit of passing traffic. The *binlang* beauty's "uniform" consists of clinging blouse, ultra-short skirt and often outrageous platform shoes. According to local expats, the conscientious young ladies always cross their legs (as proper ladies should) when they sit on their perches. Outsiders may be forgiven for wondering if the sale of betel nuts is linked to the world's oldest trade. Indeed, Taiwanese realize that sex sells, and the girls flaunt it to full advantage. Among *binlang*'s biggest fans are passing taxi, bus and lorry drivers. Chewing *binlang* alleviates boredom and keeps drivers alert by releasing arecoline – without blowing smoke in anyone's face.

▷ **IN THE BOX**
Photos of scantily clad women on the side of betel-nut boxes are an added bonus for passing drivers who stop at roadside stands to replenish their pre-prepared *binlang* supply.

◁ **THE BIG PICTURE**
Betel nuts can be wrapped in the leaf of a Piper betel, or simply cut open and filled with lime ash and spices. The latter is popular with young people.

▷ **QUITE A HANDFUL**
A *binlang* girl shows off her stuff. Betel nuts are the island nation's second-largest cash crop after rice.

SHOPPING IN TAIPEI

The Taipei shopping experience is both international and parochial, ranging from famous haute couture and electronic gadgetry to local arts and crafts

In Taiwan, as in much of Asia, shopping is a national pastime. As in Hong Kong and Singapore, shopping malls have now taken over the island's large cities. Hotel arcades with high-end retail shops can be found in most of the top five-star hotels, and there are also occasional boutique arcades near department stores. Japanese chains tend to dominate the department-store scene, the most notable being Mitsukoshi and Sogo.

Where do the Taipei locals shop? It depends on their age. The youngest and trendiest shoppers, sporting low-slung hip-hugging jeans and pink sweaters (if they're women) and projecting leather and attitude (if they're men), are in Ximending. Located near the Taipei Main Station in the older part of the city, Ximending (West Gate area) is extremely popular with teenagers.

College students and other young adults shop at Dinghao, in the eastern part of town, while office ladies and salarymen can be found toting their shopping bags through the designer boutiques along Zhongshan North Road, or around Renai Circle. On weekends and holidays, Taipei offers a more interesting local experience as lively temporary markets for jade, flowers, and other items open up.

However, Taipei's youngest and hottest shopping district is Xinyi district, centered around Taipei 101, temporarily the world's tallest building. Numerous large-scale department stores and malls have sprouted here in recent years, as have the outsized Vieshow Cinemas and retail outlets. The massive new four-floor Taipei 101 Mall is now the area's shopping core.

Gargantuan mall complexes now dot other neighborhoods in Taipei, including Breeze Center on Fuxing South Road, Core Pacific City Living Mall on Bade Road, Section 4, Miramar Entertainment Park in Neihu, and Dayeh Takashimaya in Tianmu.

LEFT: designer clothing in eastern Taipei's Xinyi shopping district. **RIGHT:** the section of Boai Rd, south of North Gate, is where Taipei's camera shops are located.

Ximending and Dinghao

Hundreds of clothing stores, tiny coffee shops, restaurants and small theaters dominate jam-packed Ximending, which is also home to several pedestrian-only streets – a rarity in this vehicle-crazy town. Amid the neon lights, thumping music and frosty air conditioning is

an energy associated with crowds of young and trendy people.

The Dinghao district lies along Zhongxiao East Road, near Fuxing North Road. Here, the shoppers are older, decidedly female, and often accompanied by their young families. Marked by Sogo department store at one end and the Starbucks coffee shop on Yanji Street at the other, Dinghao is filled with high-end to mid-range boutique clothing stores such as DKNY, Nine West, Benetton, Episode and Esprit.

Cosmetics stores are in abundance here as well, including MaSa and the Body Shop, and the city's second Tower Records is found on Zhongxiao East Road just east of Sogo. Street vendors also benefit – illegally – from the heavy foot traffic. Knock-off designer handbags, watches, shoes, and clothes are not only popular, but also fairly inexpensive – if you bargain.

Zhongshan North Road has a number of exclusive designer boutiques that cater to well-heeled Japanese tourists and the local jet set. Stores such as Fendi and Gucci are found here alongside local designers like Shiatzy. High-end stores such as Tiffany's, Mont Blanc and a large duty-free shop are found in the nearby Grand Formosa Regent's shopping arcade.

Close to Dinghao, at the intersection of Renai and Dunhua roads, is Renai Circle, a key area

the Jianguo elevated expressway where it passes over Renai Road. The Antique Market is at the corner of Bade and Xinsheng roads.

The Jade Market is a packed, busy bazaar full of all kinds of jade items of many different qualities and provenance. Jade dominates, but other items for sale include freshwater pearls, amethyst, tiger's eye and many other semi-precious stones and crystals.

Vendors at the Jade Market are fairly honest. They generally will tell you if a product is real jade or not. However, as when shopping for any expensive product, it's best to know what you're looking for and how to tell the genuine

for upscale designer boutiques. Polo Ralph Lauren lies on Renai east of the circle with Calvin Klein nearby, while the famous jeweler Cartier is found just south, and Emporio Armani is on the northwest corner of the circle. There are also a number of designer boutiques lining wide, tree-shaded Dunhua South Road south of Renai toward Xinyi Road, as well as on nearby Anhe Road.

Local markets

For a more authentic local experience, try the temporary markets. On weekends and national holidays, the Taipei Holiday Jade Market and Taipei Holiday Flower Market open up under

JOINING THE TEA SET

The Taiwanese love their tea, and it shows. Teashops are a common sight, filled with silver barrels of tea leaves and dozens of brown-clay tea sets.

Traditional brown-clay tea sets come in many shapes and qualities. A set usually includes a teapot, cups and a container with a lid, which is used to collect discarded tea leaves.

For those new to the Chinese tea tradition, selecting a tea set involves choosing a design that appeals to you. However, connoisseurs will look more closely at the quality of the clay, the thinness of the crockery and how long it will take for the tea to "flavor" the teapot.

product from a well-made imitation. If you don't trust your instincts or your knowledge, you can go to one of the thousands of jewelry stores that line the streets in Taipei, as they offer an authentication certificate with the sales slip, albeit adding slightly to the cost.

Bargaining isn't encouraged, but it's not out of the question. The general rule of thumb is to offer half the asking price and work your way to a compromise. However, don't make an offer if you're not interested. Vendors dislike having to go through the trouble of bargaining and coming to an agreement on price only to be met with the bargainer walking away.

profusion of orchids and other flowers.

The two markets are open 9am–6pm on Saturdays and Sundays, as well as national holidays. It is crowded in the afternoons; mornings are a little quieter. Food vendors sell Chinese sausages, barbecued squid, sweet bean cakes and other treats near the Renai and Xinyi entrances.

Trinkets and collectibles

Dusty collectibles can be found in abundance at the Antique Market, a curious assortment of tiny shops and street vendors at the corner of Xinsheng and Bade roads.

Sifting through the crowded and cluttered dis-

Plants sprout everywhere in Taipei in luxurious profusion: from balconies and rooftops, in alleys and streets. The Taiwanese love their plants, and many of them come from the Taipei Holiday Flower Market.

Vendors at this market sell every kind of plant life imaginable. Bamboo, miniature maple trees, Japanese bonsai, bushes, leafy house plants, exotic ferns, gourds and citrus trees form part of the endless variety that can be found among the

LEFT: Xinyi area's Shin Kong Mitsukoshi department store.
ABOVE LEFT: Taipei Holiday Flower Market.
ABOVE RIGHT: spoilt for choice at the Jade Market.

plays requires patience and a keen eye. Most of the valuable items are from the mainland. Interesting trinkets include 1940s-era Shanghai-style posters advertising soap or cigarettes, bronze statuettes, coins, jewelry, silk textiles, wooden ornaments, and porcelain vases and bowls. Vendors may seem indifferent at first glance, but once bargaining begins in earnest, they come to life.

Locals warn tourists to beware of unscrupulous sellers, as well as pickpockets, as it's often difficult to tell the genuine antique from the fake. On some of the bronze "antiques," what looks like a patina of dusty age is actually a handful of clay rubbed on two weeks ago in China. As with expensive jewelry, it's advisable to visit a legitimate licenced retailer, or bring along a knowledgeable friend when purchasing high-priced antiques.

Dihua Street

Northwest of the Taipei Main Station is one of Taipei's oldest areas, Dihua Street. This area is rich in traditional wares such as Chinese herbs, kitchen utensils and handmade crafts.

In its day, Dihua was a port street near the Danshui River, and the main conduit for trade in Taipei Basin. During the

West Road. Both deal in handmade crafts.

On Civil Boulevard at Xinsheng South Road is the New Guanghua Market. Hundreds of electronic-goods shops are found in this new six-floor facility. Taiwan is one of the world's largest producers of computers and peripherals, as one look at Guanghua Market immediately proves. Great deals can be found, but it's advisable to be armed with a knowledge of what you will require. Many shoppers end up spending more than they

> **BUDDHIST BRACELETS**
>
> Buddhist bracelets – yellow jade or amethyst beads on an elasticized band – are popular accessories for Taiwanese men and women, and reputedly have protective qualities.

annual run-up to the Chinese Lunar New Year, this classical building-lined street is overrun with vendors and shoppers. The shops specialize in traditional holiday treats and paraphernalia to ring in the new year.

North of Taipei Main Station on Chengde Road near Changan West Road is another area of interest for the adventurous shopper. This district has a mixture of stores, from those supplying industrial equipment to ones selling Christmas decorations. In this neighborhood, two worthwhile stops are the wooden bucket heritage shop on the corner of Zhongshan North Road and Changan West Road, and the Taiwan Handicraft Paper Manufacturing Company at 47–2 Changan

intended due to the enthusiasm of fast-talking salesmen. Pirate copies of games and computer programs are easily found here.

Located at the corner of Zhongshan South Road and Xuzhou Road, government-sponsored Chinese Handicraft Mart (9am–5.30pm daily; closed national holidays) offers four floors of Taiwan-made Chinese, Taiwanese, and aboriginal souvenirs. On the first three floors, the merchandise includes jewelry, porcelain, wall hangings, painted fans, silk, teapots and furniture, while the basement offers T-shirts, slippers, toys and novelty items.   ❏

ABOVE: dried food stores along Dihua Street, Taipei.

The Best Buys

Taiwan offers a range of traditional Chinese handicraft items. Carved jade jewelry, engraved chops and Chinese tea sets are popular with the locals, and are easy to find in great variety. Other items such as traditional silk fabric and fine china are a little more difficult to find, but are classic souvenirs to take home.

The Taiwanese love their jewelry. There are jewelry and gold shops in almost every neighborhood. Jade is a prized semi-precious stone, and is believed by many to bring good luck. It comes in a variety of shapes. Round pieces with a hole in the middle are called *bi* and were initially carved to honor the gods of heaven, while the elongated carved jade known as *cong* was made to honor more earthly spirits. As with many other stones, jade comes in a variety of different colors, some more valuable than others. The jade from Taiwan is dark green, while Burmese jade is a lighter green and is preferred by many Taiwanese. Unless you're an expert, simply buy within your budget, and to your taste.

Chops are nearly as common today in Taiwan as they were hundreds of years ago in China. Engraved with a person's name and stamped on documents with a pasty red ink, they are used in place of a signature when conducting business such as banking, posting registered mail and authorizing legal transactions, though use of signatures alone is now legally recognized.

Because they are so widely used, chops can be found in almost every neighborhood. Engravers are identified by their displays of different chops, made from wood, plastic, stone, metal and jade. The engraving style is as important as the composition of the characters. The traditional style of calligraphy used is called *zhuan shu*; others include the clerical script *li shu*, and regular script *kai shu*. There are also scripts unique to chop engraving such as the "bird," "insect," and "phoenix." Prices of chops can vary enormously and most engravers include a carrying case and red ink.

Some of the most beautiful pieces of pottery and porcelain ever made lie in Taipei's National Palace Museum. However, those wishing to bring home a piece of quality china should look beyond the museum's expensive gift shop.

RIGHT: jade, which ranges from white to dark green, has always been a favorite gemstone for the Chinese.

Yingge, a town southwest of Taipei, is famous for its fine ceramic works, including porcelain. Hundreds of small shops and numerous large factories line its streets, and its artisans pride themselves on reproducing hand-painted works of art from centuries ago. Worth collecting are the latticed vases in which craftsmen cut individual holes out of the clay to produce a basket effect.

Another source of pottery and porcelain is the Chinese Handicraft Mart. The selection is not as varied as those you may find in Yingge, but it is conveniently located in Taipei.

Classic Chinese silk is an excellent gift purchase. The Yongle Market at 21 Dihua Street sells

all kinds of materials and, if you don't find what you're looking for in the building's three floors, there are also boutiques in the neighborhood, particularly along Yanping North Road. These shops will also tailor-make articles of clothing.

Electronic goods and camera equipment are a reasonably good buy and, generally, new products from Japan make it to Taiwan's shores faster than to North America or Europe. The greatest concentration of camera shops is on Boai Road, south of Zhongxiao West Road, near Taipei Main Railway Station.

Prices here are slightly lower than in most outlets in the US and Europe, but comparable to the wholesale prices found on the internet. A little browsing will help you discover the right price. ❑

PLACES

*A detailed guide to the entire island, with principal sites
clearly cross-referenced by number to the maps*

Taiwan's reputation as a producer of computers, peripherals and semiconductor chips makes it easy to forget that when Portuguese sailors first clapped eyes on it more than four centuries ago they named it Ilha Formosa, the beautiful isle. Today, it is true, too much of that beauty has been obscured by the island's headlong rush into prosperity. For those who seek it out, however, the surprise is that so much of that beauty remains. Despite the fact Taiwan has modernized, perhaps faster and more recklessly than any of its Asian neighbors, an expedition out of the urban blight of its major cities and townships never fails to yield the lingering influences of old ways and spectacular natural vistas – all of which belie the fact that this small island is one of the most densely populated places on the planet.

Taiwan, after all, is an island with immense diversity in terrain and culture, not to mention a growing highway system that not only encircles the island, but also slithers through its interior mountains. Small it may be, but Taiwan never wants for fascinating extremes, from periodic snowfalls on high mountain peaks to wave-lashed rocky shores, from high-tech science parks to traditional Daoist rituals.

Northern Taiwan, a mix of flatland and foothills, is the upper terminus of the Central Mountain Range that bisects the long and narrow island. Being so close to Taipei, the northern sights are, of course, sometimes crowded, as city residents seek escape. The coastal route along the north shore, while lacking the tropical beaches of the south, skirts a sculpted sandstone seashore of haunting beauty.

Taipei is Taiwan's largest city. With its rich cultural offerings and new-found confidence, it is the key to understanding the sense of self-identity that has emerged in the island over the past two decades. Outside Taipei, landscapes along the west coast are at turns agricultural and industrial. The major cities – Taichung, Tainan, Kaohsiung – are a mix of ports, industry and history. Tainan is the Kyoto of Taiwan, albeit in a modest way, while Kaohsiung is a distinctly industrial port city. Taichung falls somewhere in between.

The traveler in search of Taiwan's raw beauty will choose the eastern seaboard — a tempestuous shoreline of steep cliffs and crashing ocean waves. Villages and towns along the coastal road move to rhythms long forgotten elsewhere in Taiwan. Most notable of sights is Taroko Gorge, a fantastic marble chasm with an equally remarkable road sliced right through the marble.

And, finally, standing between east and west are the mountains of the Central Range, with their rambling bamboo forests and the dizzy peaks of Yushan towering way above the Pacific. ❑

PRECEDING PAGES: fishing along the surf-lashed north coast; Taipei's National Concert Hall, part of National Taiwan Democracy Memorial; the golden roof arches of Wenwu Temple, Sun Moon Lake. **LEFT:** Taiwan's most irresistible natural beauty is found along the east coast.

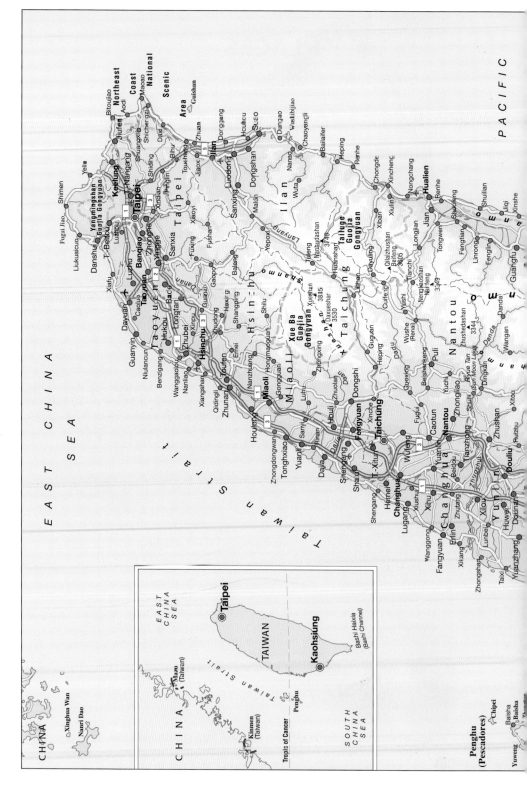

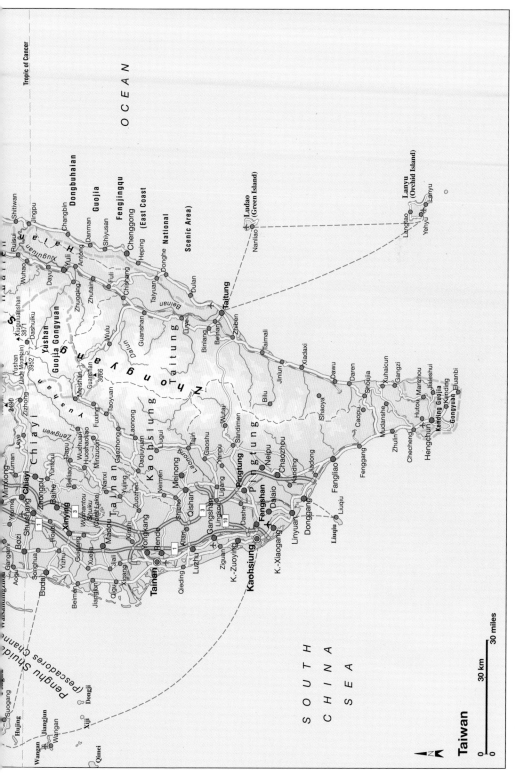

Taiwan

0   30 km

0   30 miles

TAIPEI AND ENVIRONS

*For a glimpse of where the rest of Taiwan is heading
tomorrow, take a close look at Taipei today*

For too many visitors to Taiwan, Taipei is little more than a jumping board to more interesting places. The major sights – such as the National Palace Museum, Longshan Temple, Taipei 101, and the Grand Hotel – are dutifully ticked off before people head down-country to destinations like Taroko Gorge and Alishan. Perhaps their stay is extended to include some of the city's lesser attractions, but rarely for long enough to get a proper feel for the place.

This is a pity because, while Taipei can hardly be described as beautiful, it is easily the most vibrant of the island's cities. And, while purists can be heard to complain that it is not the "real Taiwan," that it is a bureaucratic invention of the Japanese and the Nationalists, Taipei does give a fascinating insight into the Taiwan of the future.

If all major cities are melting pots of some description, the chief ingredients in Taipei's pot are tradition and modernity. Over the past two decades, a new generation of overseas-educated Taiwanese have been quietly transforming the city, and the process of transforming the rest of the island has begun.

The kind of traveler who sets off in search of "timeless rhythms" and the like may grumble that the future is less interesting than the past. But the truth is that, despite the overlay of Chinese culture, Taiwan is a young society, and there's no place better to observe where it's heading to than in Taipei. To witness that, however, it's essential to get off the tourist trail, if only for an afternoon. The National Palace Museum, as impressive as it is, says more about 21st-century cross-strait politics than it does about Taiwan.

To see the new Taiwan, spend an hour or so in Taipei's Ximending shopping district, with its Japanese pop fashions; take a stroll up fashionable Renai Road between Dunhua and Guangfu South roads, past the alfresco cafés serving latte and cappuccino; visit one of the city's night markets and watch the locals, both young and old, dine on the island's traditional *xiaochi*, or "little eats"; take an afternoon MRT jaunt out to Beitou to visit the young Beitou Hot Spring Museum and later have a refreshing soak; or take a combo MRT/gondola sojourn out to Muzha's tea plantations and spend a few hours sipping tea and gazing out onto the expansive city spread below.

Taipei and its environs are many things, but most of all they are a showcase for the new Taiwan that has evolved in the years since martial law was lifted in 1987 and a new wave of Taiwanese consciousness has sent locals to simultaneously explore their past and embrace a new future.

The visitor who gives Taipei short shrift will have to return one day to complete the jigsaw puzzle that is modern Taiwan. ❑

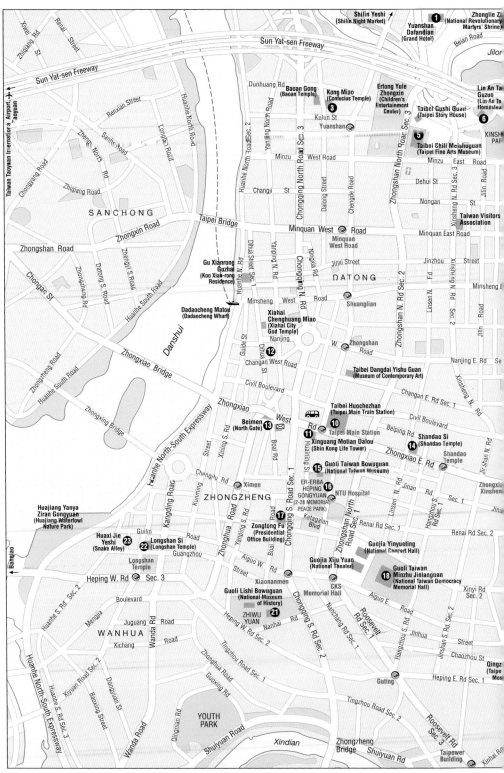

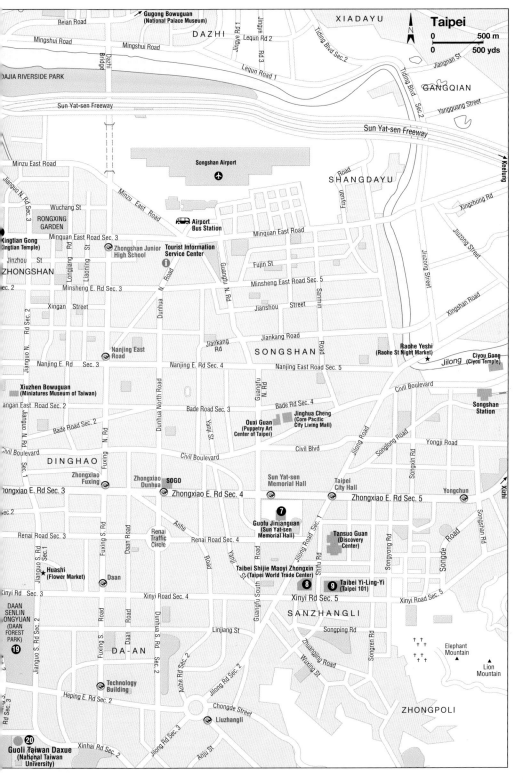

Taipei

0   500 m

0   500 yds

XIADAYU

GANGQIAN

DAZHI

Reian Road

Mingshui Road

Mingshui Road

Gugong Bowuguan
(National Palace Museum)

Jingye Rd 1

Lequn Rd 2

Jingye Rd 3

Lequn Road 1

Tiding Blvd Sec. 2

Jiangnan St

Tiding Blvd Sec. 2

Yangguang Street

Keelung

Sun Yat-sen Freeway

Sun Yat-sen Freeway

Xingzhong Rd

Jiuzong Street

SHANGDAYU

Road

Fuyuan

DAJIA RIVERSIDE PARK

Minzu East Road

Songshan Airport

Minzu East Road

Jianguo N. Rd Sec. 3

Wuchang St

RONGXING
GARDEN

Airport
Bus Station

Minquan East Road

Minquan East Road Sec. 3

Zhongshan Junior
High School

Tourist Information
Service Center

Fujin St

Jiuzong Street

Xingshan Road

Xingtian Gong
(Xingtian Temple)

Jinzhou St

ZHONGSHAN

Longjiang St

Liaoning St

Dunhua N. Road

Guangfu N. Road

Minsheng East Road Sec. 5

Sanmin

Sec. 2

Minsheng E. Rd Sec. 3

Xingan Street

Jianshou Street

Jiankang Road

Jianguo N. Rd Sec. 2

Jiankang Rd

SONGSHAN

Road

Raohe Yeshi
(Raohe St Night Market)

Ciyou Gong
(Ciyou Temple)

Jilong

Nanjing East
Road

Nanjing E. Rd Sec. 3

Nanjing E. Rd Sec. 4

Nanjing East Road Sec. 5

Guangfu N. Rd

Civil Boulevard

Songshan
Station

Xiuzhen Bowuguan
(Miniatures Museum of Taiwan)

angan East Road Sec. 2

Dunhua North Road

Bade Road Sec. 3

Bade Rd Sec. 4

Jinghua Cheng
(Core Pacific
City Living Mall)

Jianguo N. Rd Sec. 2

Bade Road Sec. 2

Fuxing N. Rd

Yanji St

Ouxi Guan
(Puppetry Art
Center of Taipei)

Civil Blvd

Jilong Road

Songlong Road

Songlong Rd

Yongji Road

Civil Boulevard

Civil Boulevard

DINGHAO

Zhongxiao
Fuxing

Zhongxiao
Dunhua

SOGO

Sun Yat-sen
Memorial Hall

Taipei
City Hall

Yongchun

Xizhi

Zhongxiao E. Rd Sec. 3

Zhongxiao E. Rd Sec. 4

Zhongxiao E. Rd Sec. 5

Songshan Rd

Sec.2

Fuxing S. Rd

Renai
Traffic
Circle

Anhe

7

Guofu Jinianguan
(Sun Yat-sen
Memorial Hall)

Jilong Road Sec. 1

Tansuo Guan
(Discovery
Center)

Songde Rd

Songren Rd

Renai Road Sec. 3

Daan Road

Renai Road Sec. 4

Yanji St

Shifu Rd

Huashi
(Flower Market)

Jianguo S. Rd Sec. 1

Daan

Taibei Shijie Maoyi Zhongxin
(Taipei World Trade Center)

8

9

Taibei Yi-Ling-Yi
(Taipei 101)

Xinyi Rd Sec. 3

Xinyi Road Sec. 4

Guangfu South Road

Xinyi Rd Sec. 5

Xinyi Road Sec. 5

DAAN
SENLIN
GONGYUAN
(DAAN
FOREST
PARK)

19

Jianguo S. Rd Sec. 2

Fuxing S. Road

Daan Road

Dunhua S. Rd Sec. 2

SANZHANGLI

Linjiang St

Songping Rd

Zhuangjing Road

Wuxing St

Elephant
Mountain

Lion
Mountain

DA-AN

Anhe Rd Sec. 2

Daan S. Rd

Jilong Rd Sec. 2

Heping E. Rd Sec. 2

Technology
Building

Chongde Street

Liuzhangli

ZHONGPOLI

Rd Sec. 3

20

Guoli Taiwan Daxue
(National Taiwan
University)

Xinhai Rd Sec. 2

Jianguo S. Rd Sec. 3

Jilong Rd Sec. 3

Anju St

TAIPEI

Map
on pages
124–25

The booming, vibrant capital is a cosmopolitan city that neverthe-less remains steeped in native Taiwanese, Chinese and Japanese cultures – a compelling combination for visitors

The capital of Taiwan is not an ancient city. Like Tokyo, Hong Kong and Singapore, it's a new arrival. Just 300 years ago, it was a place of swamps, its only inhabitants the indigenous Kaitagelan tribe, the only traces of whom today remain in the lingering influences of some of the old names for areas in the city. It was not until the first decade of the 18th century that Chinese immigrants from Quanzhou in Fujian province began to arrive. Over time they turned the area they called Mangka (renamed Wanhua by the Japanese), an elbow of land cradled by the Danshui and Xindian rivers, into a flourishing trading port.

By the late 19th century, the Chinese Qing dynasty had established most of its administrative agencies in Taipei, and the city center had moved from Wanhua to today's Zhongzheng district, now home to the Presidential Office Building and the National Taiwan Democracy Memorial Hall. And when the Japanese colonized Taiwan in 1895, they followed suit, making Taipei the capital. But even when the leaders of the Republic of China established their government in northern Taiwan in 1949, Taipei was still no more than a sleepy country town surrounded by rice fields and mud flats. As late as the mid-1960s, the city had few paved roads, and pedicabs were the primary means of public transport.

LEFT: new landmark – Taipei 101 tower.
BELOW: climbing high in Taipei.

Frenzy of growth

The changes that forever altered the face of Taipei during the 1970s were truly dramatic. All the blessings and evils of modernization gripped the city in a frenzy of growth, which, for better or worse, continues today. The clatter of pedicabs has given way to the clunk of pile-drivers, lumbering of heavy goods vehicles, and the click of taxi meters. Tens of thousands of taxis, buses, private cars and lorries – and hundreds of thousands of motorcycles and scooters – clog the underpasses, roundabouts and flyovers of modern roads and expressways, and a Mass Rapid Transit (MRT) system – some 10 years in the making and still expanding – now ferries Taipei residents around the city, both above ground and below. The drab, gray compartments of concrete that once characterized Taipei architecture now squat in the shadows of high-rise glass and metal.

The remarkable change that swept Taipei has also affected the city's three million or so residents. The utilitarian fashions of the 1950s were long ago mothballed in favor of the latest trends and designs from Paris, Hong Kong and New York. Youths patronize cafés that serve Starbucks coffee from Seattle, and dance in nightclubs to the latest sounds from Tokyo, London and New York.

Yet this veneer of 21st-century sophistication does not mask one implacable fact: Taipei remains one of the most staunchly traditional cities of Asia. Taipei

may look increasingly like Westernized Asian cities such as Singapore and Hong Kong, but far more than its chief Asian rivals, Taipei has not forgotten its heritage – the beating heart of Taipei is a unique mix of indigenous Taiwanese, Chinese and Japanese influences that makes the city ceaselessly fascinating for visitors.

Policy shifts

Taipei's stylish facade can be attributed, in part, to a pair of changes in governmental policy in the late 1970s. First, the government rescinded a long-standing ban on the construction of new hotels and other high-rises in Taiwan. Permits to build scores of high-rises were quickly issued. Hotels and office buildings mushroomed, and well-heeled residents donned the latest fashions to see and be seen in the new atrium lobbies, revolving bars and chic boutiques.

The second move that proved to be a catalyst for internationalism was a relaxation of restrictions on overseas travel. Prior to 1978, residents of Taiwan were prohibited from leaving the country, except to visit relatives, or for business or educational purposes. The change in policy permitted people to receive passports and exit visas purely for pleasure trips. Many Taipei residents had been saving for decades for the chance to taste foreign flavors firsthand and they flocked to Tokyo, Manila, Singapore and Seoul. (Many nowadays venture much farther – to Europe and the United States.) The new tastes in food, fashion and recreation they brought back have turned Taipei into a cosmopolitan city.

At the same time, there have been serious government efforts to improve the two side-effects of rapid modernization that have been a blight on the city's reputation: traffic congestion and pollution. Visitors to Taipei today who remember the mid-1990s are generally surprised to see how the establishment of bus lanes, addition

The ubiquitous scooter transports residents in and around Taipei.

BELOW: upscale shopping inside Taipei 101.

Map on pages 124–25

of expressways, opening of the MRT, and emissions controls on the city's innumerable motor scooters have combined to not only make Taipei's notorious traffic less frightening but also help lift the pollution that once hung over the city.

Yet, despite the rapid pace of change, the underlying currents of traditional Chinese culture continue to make Taipei an attractive destination for travelers. Not unexpectedly, the greatest source of visitors to Taiwan annually are the overseas Chinese and Taiwanese communities of the world. Taiwan also remains a magnet for Japanese, who have borrowed heavily from classical Chinese culture during the past 1,000 years. Visitors to Taiwan are always impressed by the hospitality of the Taiwanese people. In the end, *ren qingwei* – the flavor of human feelings – leaves many a visitor with thoughts of returning.

Administrative beginnings

Historically, Taipei's outskirts have attracted more interest than its center. When Koxinga drove the Dutch from Taiwan in 1662, he appointed General Huang An to command army and naval forces stationed at Danshui, at the mouth of the Danshui River, northwest of Taipei. New farming methods were introduced along the riverbanks, and soldiers were sent to reclaim land. Early in the 18th century, reclaimed lands were extended to the area of modern Wanhua, now the heart of old Taipei. Wanhua became a major port that reached its peak in the early 1850s, before port activity shifted to Dadaocheng because of silting and communal strife.

In 1875, the Qing emperor declared Taiwan a province, moving the capital from Taiwan Fu (today's Tainan) and establishing Taipei Fu ("Fu" meaning "administrative district"), at the site of modern Zhongzheng. A 5-km (3-mile) protective perimeter was constructed around the district. The Japanese expanded

As Taipei has developed physically, so too has its population increased dramatically, with Taiwanese from other parts flooding in to find work. The Taipei Greater Metropolitan Area alone has 6.5 million people, more than one quarter of Taiwan's population.

BELOW: Taipei street-sign assault.

BELOW:
window to Taipei, the Grand Hotel.

the area's physical boundaries when they took control of Taiwan in 1895. They changed the name Taipei Fu to Taipei Zhou, then merged suburban areas into a larger administrative district known as Taipei Ding.

In 1920, some 23 years after plans had been drawn, Taipei was formally recognized as a city. During the next dozen years, its population soared from 150,000 to 600,000 people, and the area it occupied expanded from 20 to 70 sq. km (7 to 27 sq. miles). In 1949, less than five years after China regained Taiwan from a defeated Japan, Taipei was made the focus of Nationalist government activities. It became a special municipality by decree in 1966, confirming it as Taiwan's political, cultural, economic and military center. The towns of Jingmei, Muzha, Neihu, Nangang, Beitou and Shilin were incorporated into Taipei in 1968. In 1990, the then 16 districts of Taipei City were reorganized into 12 districts.

Into the city

Modern visitors to Taipei, like the settlers of old, experience the city's outskirts first. Taiwan Taoyuan International Airport (CKS) is in Taoyuan, 40 km (25 miles) southwest of the capital. The airport – once one of Asia's largest and most modern – now looks down-at-heel compared to the gleaming new airports of Asian cities like Singapore, Kuala Lumpur, Osaka and Hong Kong, but a new terminal, opened in late 2000, goes some way to remedying this state of affairs. Buses and taxis whisk – traffic permitting – new arrivals along one of the two north-south freeways, linking the airport to Taipei in the north and to other destinations in the south.

Taipei was once described as the ugly duckling of Asian cities – an impression founded during the 1960s on the city's drab buildings, dusty streets, open gutters and battered pedicabs. And while Taipei can hardly be described today as "beautiful," it nevertheless has gone an enormous way toward banishing its previous reputation, transforming itself into a modern city that at its best rivals its Asian neighbors. Spacious six-lane boulevards shaded by islands of tropical trees have helped provide breathing space between the walls of new buildings, and a slew of young parks have given Taipei residents a green escape.

Street rambles

Wandering aimlessly through Taipei's streets is a good way of familiarizing oneself with the city and its people. It will uncover many surprises that could never be duplicated on guided tours around the main attractions. Bear in mind, though, that because of the city's size it would take weeks rather than days to explore all the city on foot. Therefore, concentrate on some of the city's more interesting districts for walking forays. For a broad-brush impression of Taipei, consider taking a trip on the MRT's Muzha line, which runs high above the traffic from the wooded hills of Muzha and into the heart of the city along fashionable Fuxing North/South Road.

One of the city's most visible landmarks for orientation is the **Grand Hotel ❶** (Yuanshan Dafandian). Located atop a ridge on the north side of the city core, this 530-room hotel looks somewhat like an ancient palace, built in the classical imperial style of old China and patterned specifically on Beijing's Forbidden City. The massive multi-story newest wing, finished in 1973, is crowned by the largest classical Chinese roof on earth. Once the most fashionable place to be seen in Taipei, the hotel had fallen into neglect by the 1990s, with a fire destroying the original roof in 1995. New management teams have since had some success in restoring the hotel's fortunes.

The Grand Hotel is as good a spot as any to begin touring Taipei. About half a kilometer (¼ mile) east of the Grand Hotel is the **Martyrs' Shrine ❷** (Zhonglie Zi; daily 9am–5pm), on Beian Road. The entire complex is built in the palace style of the Ming dynasty, each structure attempting to recreate a similar hall or pavilion in Beijing. Dedicated to the fallen heroes of the Republic of China's wars, the arched portals of the main gate open onto a vast courtyard, past guest pavilions and drums and bell towers. Two gigantic brass-studded doors stand before the main shrine, where the names of the heroes are inscribed beside murals depicting their feats. The late Chiang Kai-shek, Taiwan's first president, considered this a favorite retreat, often spending entire afternoons strolling through the grounds and halls. The changing of the guard on the hour (9am–4pm) is as much an attraction for visitors as the shrine itself.

Only a short taxi ride away in the opposite direction of the Grand Hotel, to the southwest, is the **Confucius Temple ❸** (Kong Miao; Tue–Sat 8.30am–9pm, Sun/holidays 8.30am–5pm), on Dalong Street. Built in 1925, it's a tranquil retreat. Absent are the throngs of worshipers supplicating their gods with prayer and offerings, the cacophony of gongs and drums, and the gaudy idols – unless you happen to visit on September 28, Teacher's Day (Confucius' birthday), when the temple is host to colorful dance performances by children. Absent, too, are images of Confucius. The tranquility is fitting – Confucius preached, among

Map on pages 124–25

Guard at Martyrs' Shrine looking as he should, straightfaced and straight ahead.

BELOW: changing of the guard at the Martyrs' Shrine, a fascinating spectacle.

Baoan Gong is one of the most important places of worship in Taipei, though it has not always been so – during the Japanese occupation it served as a language school and as a factory making bamboo mats.

other things, the virtues of peace and quiet. The temple's architecture is subtle yet exquisite in its simplicity, and highlighted by magnificent roofs.

Contrasting temples

By contrast, the 200-year-old Daoist **Baoan Temple** (Baoan Gong; daily), on Hami Street and next to the Confucius Temple, is a gaudy monument to Baosheng Dadi, the folk religion God of Medicine. Carved dragons decorate the main support columns, and the interior is crowded with the images of many deities. The main one of Baosheng Dadi was brought from Fujian province in China by early settlers in 1805.

Another temple of note is **Xingtian Temple** ❹ (Xingtian Gong; daily), on Min-quan East Road, Section 2, in the northeast quadrant of the city. Dedicated to the red-faced, black-bearded Guangong, the God of War and patron saint of merchants, the temple throngs with businesspeople praying for good fortune. The temple is unique for discouraging the burning of paper money and taking no donations. Built in the 1960s, it's a popular destination for those seeking advice from the spirit world. Freelance fortune-tellers line the pedestrian underpass outside.

Just south of the Grand Hotel is the **Taipei Fine Arts Museum** ❺ (Taipei Shili Meishuguan; Tue–Sun 9.30am–5.30pm, Sat until 8.30pm; charge), with 24 galleries of modern art, featuring local artists and sculptors, and changing exhibits from abroad. It claims to be the largest modern art museum in Asia and, if you're interested in the subject, is worth a visit for an overview of the local modern art scene. While you're there, call into the adjacent **Yuanshan Villa** (Taipei Story House; Tue–Sun 10am–6pm; charge; www.storyhouse.com.tw), a quaint mock Tudor-style building that reopened in 2003 after extensive renovation. Originally

BELOW: festivities at Baoan Temple.

BECOMING STREETWISE

Before setting out on a street ramble, it's worth remembering a couple of points about Taipei's street system, which invariably confuses newcomers.

The city has in the past moved decisively to standardize the English street names, but there remains significant confusion because there are many signs with street names put up by the central government's various bodies, indicating government sites, tourist sites, etc. These are less standardized. Thus, you may see the "Zhongshan" of "Zhongshan Road" also spelled Jungshan, Jhongshan, and Chungshan.

A second point of confusion is the habit of dividing roads into sections and then tagging them either "north," "south," "east" or "west," depending on what part of the city they happen to run through. Thus, an address on Zhongxiao Road, which effectively cuts Taipei into northern and southern districts, might, say, be 143 Zhongxiao East Road, Section 1. There could also very well be the following address: 143 Zhongxiao West Road, Section 1. Miss the "East/West" difference and you're lost.

Any addresses on Section 1 of a road will be close to the city center, while an address on Section 5 will be farther out. Addresses, therefore, provide a rough indication of where to find streets on the map.

built in 1913, it now houses an art showroom, history showroom, and a café.

Behind the museum is the **Lin An Tai Homestead** (Lin An Tai Guzuo; Tue–Sat 9am–9pm, Sun 9am–5pm; charge), an original 30-room family home of a wealthy merchant from the Qing-dynasty era. Built from 1783–1823, the graceful, somewhat minimalist structure was originally built entirely with materials brought from Fujian province in China. The buildings were moved and reconstructed at their current location after Dunhua South Road was widened in the late 1970s.

Opposite the museum is the venerable **Municipal Children's Entertainment Center** (Ertong Yule Zhongxin; Tue–Sun 9am–5pm; charge). It's only worth visiting if you have very young children – older children are likely to find the antiquated rides and tacky attractions less than thrilling.

Memorial to the National Father

In the eastern part of the city is an important memorial to the man known in both China and Taiwan as the "National Father," Dr Sun Yat-sen. Both PRC and ROC revere him as the founder of modern China. On Section 4 of Renai Road, and a long taxi ride away from the Taipei Fine Arts Museum (it's also possible to make the journey by subway if you change at Taipei Main Station), the main building of the **Sun Yat-sen Memorial Hall** (Guofu Jinianguan; daily 9am–5pm; www.yatsen.gov.tw) is distinguished by a sweeping Chinese roof of glazed yellow tiles. A 6-meter (20-ft) high bronze statue of Sun Yat-sen graces the main lobby. On exhibit are numerous photographs taken in mainland China during the early years of the 20th century. Perhaps the most interesting time to visit is at daybreak or dusk, when the extensive grounds fill with Taiwanese people flying kites, jogging, practicing martial arts and even disco dancing.

Map on pages 124–25

Ornate roof architecture of the Xingtian Temple, whose patron deity is Guangong, a god known for his physical strength.

BELOW: resident deities at the Xingtian Temple.

Taipei's MRT

Taipei has always been a notoriously difficult city to get around. But that all changed when the 7.7-km (4¾-mile) section of the Banqiao-Nangang MRT (Mass Rapid Transit) line from Longshan Temple to Taipei City Hall came on line at 1pm on December 24, 1999. Taipei was at last home to a mass rapid-transit system that allowed visitors to get to almost any part of the city without having to deal with choked traffic, confusing road signs and non-English-speaking taxi drivers.

Taipei residents were quick to embrace the system, which had been close to a decade in the making, with commuter numbers increasing from 470,000 to around 600,000 a day with the full opening of the new line, and now standing at more than 1.2 million.

Magnetic tickets are available at vending machines in the station concourses – press the button with the amount required for your destination and then feed the change into the slot. Transfers are allowed between all lines. "EasyCards," which are stored-value cards, can also be purchased. They permit bus transfers and use of an expanding network of parking garages and meters. Maps in the station concourses make it easy to choose the appropriate exit.

The best way to tackle the network is by starting at its hub, Taipei Main Station. From here, armed with a copy of the excellent free *Taipei Visitor's Map*, which clearly indicates both Taipei's attractions and all the MRT stops, the visitor can reach almost any of Taipei's major districts and tourist attractions on the color-coded system.

The blue line links Tucheng, Banqiao City, and nearby historic Wanhua (Longshan Temple station) with the Taipei World Trade Center (Taipei City Hall station) and Nangang, connecting with the elevated brown Muzha line (for the Taipei Zoo and Muzha's tea plantations) mid-route, while the green line (with a red-coded branch line in its southern section) connects the old sea port of Danshui with many of Taipei's major tourist attractions, moving south all the way.

Four stops north of Taipei Main Station, Yuanshan station provides easy access to the Taipei Fine Arts Museum and the Lin An Tai Homestead. Two stops south of Yuanshan station, it's a short taxi ride (or a 15-minute walk) from Shuanglian station to the historic market at Dihua Street.

At Taipei Main Station it's possible to either surface and explore some of the surrounding attractions (the panoramic view from the Shin Kong Life Tower for one), or take the blue line either southwest to Longshan Temple and Wanhua or east to the Sun Yat-sen Memorial Hall, Taipei World Trade Center, Taipei 101 Tower, and Warner Village complex. Continuing south on the Danshui-Xindian line, the NTU Hospital stop is next to the Taiwan Museum, Memorial Peace Park and the Presidential Office Building.

Guting station, south of Taipei Main Station, on the Danshui-Xindian line, is just a short walk from Taipei's student district, Shida – one of Taipei's most popular areas for a drink. Just one catch: stay out past midnight and you will be taking a taxi back to your hotel. ❑

LEFT: Taipei's modern MRT trains.

The Sun Yat-sen Memorial Hall is in the Xinyi district, an area in east Taipei that is one of the most vibrant parts of the city. Just over a block southeast of the memorial is the **Taipei World Trade Center ❽** (Taipei Shijie Maoyi Zhongxin; daily 9am–5pm; charge during exhibitions; www.twtc.org.tw), home to many of Taiwan's foreign "trade offices" (in diplomatically isolated Taiwan, an euphemism for "embassies"). East of the World Trade Center is the sprawling Warner Village complex, with restaurants, shopping, coffee shops and cinemas. Dominating the area is 508-meter (1,667-ft) **Taipei 101 ❾** (Taipei Yi-Ling-Yi), a financial center and retail hub in the world's tallest skyscraper. Its huge typhoon and earthquake motion-damper sphere on level 88 is visible from viewing decks (daily 10am–10pm; charge). The **Tapei 101 Observatory** (Taipei YiLing Yi Guanjing Tai) is located on floors 89–91 of the tower (daily 10am–10pm; charge), with panoramic views of the city and mountains.

Downtown walkabout

One place to begin a downtown walking tour is from **Taipei Main Railway Station ❿** (Taipei Huochezhan), though it's worth bearing in mind that this is now a tatty part of town. Still, it has two notable landmarks – the station itself and the soaring Shin Kong Life Tower. Taipei station is definitely old Taipei, but an underground mall associated with the MRT lifts the tone. Opposite the station and overlooking the Caesar Park Taipei (formerly the Taipei Hilton) is the 245-meter (800-ft) **Shin Kong Life Tower ⓫** (Xinguang Motian Dalou). High-speed elevators take visitors to the 49th-floor observatory (daily 11am–10pm; charge) in just 35 seconds, whose inner wall is adorned with monochrome lithographs depicting old Taipei.

Map on pages 124–25

TIP

Carry a card displaying your hotel's name in Chinese, just in case you get lost. When walking in Taipei, never take zebra crossings or even walk signals for granted: drivers reluctantly give right-of-way to pedestrians and frequently charge through red lights.

BELOW: Shin Kong Observatory.

Indulging your taste buds is one of the main attractions of a visit to Taiwan. The basement of Shin Kong Life Tower, where there is an air-conditioned hawker center, is a good stop.

BELOW: the North Gate.

Traditional shopping

The area around the tower is a bustling warren of boutiques, cafés and department stores. But, for a fascinating contrast, pay a visit to the traditional Taiwanese shopping district on **Dihua Street** (Dihua Jie). Taipei's most important historical street, Dihua Street parallels Yanping Road in Dadaocheng – after Wanhua, Taipei's oldest commercial district. The area has its origins in the mid-1800s when a power struggle among Fujian immigrants in Wanhua drove the losers here. Business prospered, first in the form of rice mills, and then later in the trade of tea, camphor, and other products. Most of the old buildings that can be seen in this area date from the late 1800s and early 1900s.

The construction is typical of early establishments in Taiwan: the shophouses look very small from the front, but extend quite a way back. Here, the merchant's family lived, inventory was stored, and often products were manufactured. Today, Dihua Street sells an unbelievable variety of Chinese products, from dried lotus nuts and shark fin to herbal remedies and fresh fish.

The air is thick with incense at the small and unpretentious **Xiahai City God Temple** (Xiahai Chenghuang Miao; daily), also on Dihua Street. Traditionally every Chinese city has its city god, and Xiahai is home to Taipei's. The temple, built in the 1850s, may be small, but it's never short of worshipers and on the 13th day of the fifth lunar month it becomes the focus of massive street celebrations, when the city god tours the surrounding streets in a palanquin.

West from the railway station and opposite the main post office (which offers a good philatelic section) stands the restored **North Gate** (Beimen), one of the four remaining city gates and the only one still fully intact. Built in 1884, it was once part of a system of walls and gates that were mostly torn down by the

Japanese. It may look like something of an anachronism, nestled against a major flyover at the intersection of Zhongxiao and Zhonghua roads, just before Zhongxiao crosses the river, but for some it is more impressive than the other imposing monuments around town. Many Taipei residents regard the Beimen as the spiritual heart of the city.

On the east side of the railway station, and definitely worth a visit, is the **Sun Yat-sen Historic Events Memorial Hall** (Guofu Lishi Jiniantang; Tue–Sun 9am–5pm) near the intersection of Zhongshan North Road and Beiping West Road. The modest exhibition is housed in a delightful Japanese-style building, once a luxury inn where Sun Yat-sen (Sun Yi-xian) stayed when he visited in 1913, and the grounds are a relaxing escape from the bustle of downtown Taipei.

Also a short walk from here, at 23 Zhongxiao East Road, Section 1, is **Shandao Temple** ⑭ (Shandao Si; Tue–Sun 9am–5pm), built by Japanese Buddhists early in the 20th century. It's not much to look at from the outside, but worth visiting for its museum's superb collection of Chinese Buddhist art.

Shopping Japan-style

Anyone who has spent time in Tokyo will find the area directly southwest of the North Gate, on the other side of the broad Zhonghua Road, particularly fascinating. **Ximending**, the shopping district most popular with Taipei youth along with the new **Xinyi** district, is the apotheosis of Taiwan youth's fascination with all things Japanese. Take a stroll around the area to soak up its bustling atmosphere and its bizarre fashions, and to take a look at its niche boutiques selling everything from *Hello Kitty* products to Japanese *manga*, or *manhua*, as comics are known in Mandarin. A number of streets are closed to vehicles on week nights and non-work days. It's perhaps fitting that Ximending should have a Japanese flavor, given that the Japanese jump-started the area's fortunes by building the Red House Theater, Taipei's first modern market and then movie theater, in 1908. The theater has now been converted into a café and live-performance venue, with regular weekend independent-brand markets in its plaza, and is found on Chengdu Road. Start your exploration of the area, as everyone else does, at the intersection of Chengdu Road and Zhonghua Road – the Ximen MRT station there is a popular rendezvous.

South of the train station, on Hsiangyang Road, stands the **National Taiwan Museum** ⑮ (Guoli Taiwan Bowuguan; Tue–Sun 10am–5pm; charge; www.ntm.gov.tw), eye-catching in Greek Revival style. It is noted for its collection of over 40,000 items related to Taiwan's natural history and also has displays of aboriginal handicrafts, clothes and artifacts.

Just behind the museum is **2-28 Memorial Peace Park** ⑯ (Er-Erba Heping Gongyuan; daily), known before 1996 as Taipei New Park, and renamed in memory of the Taiwanese who perished in an uprising against the mainland KMT forces that started on February 28, 1947. In keeping with its new name, the park is home to the 2-28 Memorial, a post-modern erection looking like two boxes mounted by a huge knitting needle, and the 2-28 Memorial Museum

Ximending is the most popular area in Taipei for youngsters called the "ha-ri-zu" – literally "want Japan tribe" – whose aping of Japanese fashions causes considerable hand-wringing amongst more conservative Taiwanese.

BELOW: the fashionable district of Ximending.

(Tue–Sun 10am–5pm; charge), an essential stop for anyone interested in the side of KMT rule that was kept quiet until recent years *(see page 34)*.

Oddities also featured in the park include a pair of old steam trains, seven cannons, and even a megalithic tomb. The best time to walk the grounds is at dawn, when thousands of city residents stretch, dance, exercise and practice *taiji*, *gongfu* and other Chinese disciplines. Visitors are welcome to join in.

Surrounding the park are most of the important government ministries and offices. From the park's southwestern end, it is only a short distance to the governmental center of Taiwan. Most prominent is the **Presidential Office Building** ⑰ (Zongtong Fu; free guided Chinese tours Mon–Fri 9am–noon, register before 11.30am), fronting an enormous plaza that is the site of colorful celebrations on Double Tenth: October 10, or National Day. The five-story complex, finished in 1919, has a central tower 60 meters (197 ft) high and is Taipei's most famous example of Japanese colonial architecture.

At the south end of Zhongshan Road is the impressive **East Gate** (Dongmen), the biggest of the original five gates of the 19th-century city wall. It was renovated in 1966, and its once very simple facade was ornately embellished.

Anachronistic memorial

A massive monument is the former **Chiang Kai-shek Memorial Hall** ⑱ (Zhongzheng Jiniantang; daily; memorial hall Tue–Sun 9am–6.30pm) now officially called the National Taiwan Democracy Memorial Hall (Guoli Taiwan Minzhu Jinianguan), on Zhongshan South Road, near the East Gate. Dedicated in 1980, the fifth anniversary of Chiang's death, the 76-meter (249-ft) high memorial hall dominates the landscaped grounds. Inside is an imposing bronze statue of the president,

whose KMT party lost the presidency in 2000. In years past, the memorial teemed with locals paying their respects as well as tourists; nowadays it's the park that attracts all the people. From morning until late evening, it's full of life – seniors chatting under a shady tree or feeding the beautiful fat carps in the placid ponds, mothers with children strolling the paths, and newlyweds taking wedding photos.

The main entrance to the memorial hall grounds is a magnificent arch, in traditional Ming style, that towers 30 meters (98 ft) high and stretches 75 meters (246 ft) across. Eighteen different styles of traditional Chinese windows run, at eye level, along the entire length of the memorial's perimeter wall. Forming part of the complex are the **National Theater**, built in Chinese palace style, and the **National Concert Hall**. The memorial hall itself closes at 6.30pm, but the grounds remain open for evening jaunts or jogs.

Not far southeast of the memorial is the residential Daan district, a minor attraction but in many ways a more interesting insight into Taipei than the tourist sights. Taipei's biggest park, **Daan Forest Park** ⓳ (Daan Senlin Gongyuan; daily), for instance, has become one of the most popular places to take a walk, jog, or, especially for young couples, to lounge in the sun.

Northeast of the park, under the Jianguo South Road elevated expressway, is where two of Taipei's most popular markets spring into life on weekends – the **Taipei Holiday Flower Market** (Taipei Jiari Huashi) and the **Taipei Holiday Jade Market** (Taipei Jiari Yushi). Both are open 9am to 6pm.

Opposite the park on Xinsheng South Road is Taiwan's only mosque, the **Taipei Grand Mosque** (Qingzhen Si; not open to non-Muslims), built in 1960 and the focus for Taiwan's 60,000 Muslims. The area behind the mosque, on Yongkang Street, is worth a visit mostly for a taste of urban, residential Taipei

Map
on pages
124–25

TIP

Take a stroll through the exhibition space underneath the National Taiwan Democracy Memorial Hall for a glimpse of 20th-century Chinese history and some fascinating relics of Chiang's rule.

BELOW: Taipei Grand Mosque.

that few visitors get to see. Take a stroll from Xinyi Road to Jinhua Street, taking time to detour down some of the alleys along the way, and you will pass everything from European-style coffee shops to Shanghai-style dumpling houses, Chinese antiques stores and toy shops. Yongkang Park, flanked by tea and coffee shops, is a perfect example of a neighborhood park.

Among the students

South of Yongkang Street, on the other side of Heping East Road, is the student district known colloquially after the Mandarin name of Guoli Taiwan Shifan Daxue (National Taiwan Normal University) – **Shida**. Shida Road is the focus of the area, though most of the action is on narrow Longquan Street that parallels Shida Road. By day, like much of Taipei, the area is somewhat nondescript, but at night Longquan Street becomes a bustling night market selling Taiwanese snacks and it is bordered by innumerable coffee shops, pubs and restaurants. Another lively student area can be found close by in Gongguan, the area south of **National Taiwan University** ⍟ (Guoli Taiwan Daxue), between Dingzhou Road and Roosevelt Road. It features outlets for discounted clothing, CDs and jewelry, budget Chinese and Southeast Asian ethnic restaurants, and a few cinema complexes.

A shrine statue in Taipei. The Chinese invariably give form and face to whomever they worship, save Confucius.

West of these areas, on the south side of Roosevelt Road is the **National Museum of History** ㉑ (Guoli Lishi Bowuguan; Tue–Sun 10am–6pm; charge; www.nmh.gov.tw), on Nanhai Road. The permanent display offers around 10,000 Chinese objects dating from 2000 BC to modern times, including a fine sampling of Chinese currency, but the museum is also frequently host to fascinating exhibitions from overseas. It is less crowded than its more famous counterpart, the National Palace Museum, and tours in English are conducted daily at 3pm. Local Taipei residents are known to visit the museum less for its historical exhibitions than for the coffee shop outside and the fourth-floor teashop, both of which are relaxing places in which to forget the bustle of the city.

The next stop is the adjacent **Botanical Garden** (Zhiwu Yuan; 4am–10pm), which has hundreds of species of trees, shrubs, palms and bamboo. Next door to the Museum of History is the National Taiwan Arts Education Institute. A short distance further south, on Chongqing Road, the **Postal Museum** (Youzheng Bowuguan; Tue–Sun 9am–5pm; charge) has an extensive stamp collection.

BELOW: Longshan Temple has intricate roofs embellished with dragons.

Dragon Mountain Temple

Continuing west along Heping West Road takes the visitor to the heart of old Taipei: **Wanhua**, now conveniently reached by subway. The focus of the area is the oldest and most famous of Taipei's myriad temples, **Longshan Temple** ㉒ (Longshan Si; daily), or Dragon Mountain Temple, a reference to a mountain and sacred temple in Fujian province where the area's immigrants originated. The temple is on Guangzhou Street, close to the Danshui River in the heart of old Taipei and southwest of the Taipei Main Railway Station. Owing its origins to a diverse community of Fujian immigrants, Longshan is unusually multi-denominational in character.

Originally constructed in 1738, the temple was

Map
on pages
124–25

inadvertently hit by an Allied air raid in 1945. So intense were the flames from the incendiary bomb that they melted the iron railings surrounding the large camphor-wood statue of Guanyin. The hall was totally destroyed – yet the wooden statue somehow withstood the searing flames, except for a bit of ash and debris around its feet. The main hall was rebuilt, in 1957, enveloping the statue that gazes with unceasing equanimity at worshipers from the main altar. Devotees attribute the survival of the statue to the supernatural powers of the deity herself, the Goddess of Mercy.

In addition to the miraculous carving of Guanyin, the temple is renowned for its fine stone sculpture, woodcarving and bronze work. Only the island's best craftsmen are permitted to perform maintenance and restoration work on the temple buildings. Especially striking are the 12 main support columns that hold up the central hall and which feature dragons hewn from solid stone.

Open until late, Longshan is usually packed with worshipers. The tables groan with gifts for the gods, who are partial to anything and everything, from oranges to potato chips, but mostly to cash, which is consecrated and then burnt in an urn at the rear of the complex. If you're wondering where all this religious paraphernalia comes from, take a stroll over to **Xiyuan Road** – which runs north-south along the western flank of the temple. This is where Wanhua's biggest collection of religious supplies shops is located. The oldest ones, which flank the temple, have been in business since the early 19th century, when many of the supplies had to be brought in from southern China's Guangdong province. The predominant colors are red and gold, although gleaming white porcelain (mainly used for images of Guanyin, the *bodhisattva* of compassion, and the Buddha) can be seen too under the bright glare of fluorescent lights. Aside from bundles

The Allied air raid was not the first calamity to strike Longshan Si. The statue of Guanyin also survived an earthquake that flattened the temple in 1815.

BELOW: worshipers making offerings of joss sticks, fruit and spirit money at Longshan Si.

Map on pages 124–25

of spirit money and incense, you could choose lotus-pod-shaped electric lamps, gaudy "protector gods," brass incense holders and votive plaques while somnolent Buddhist chant music plays in the background.

Second-hand goods, temples and markets

There are other interesting sights to see in Wanhua. On Lane 65 of Guilin Road, the **Second-Hand Goods Market** (Wanhua Ershou Shichang; daily), which started during the Japanese occupation but didn't begin to flourish until the Vietnam War, when US troops filled it with castoffs, makes for an interesting rummage. Farther up the same lane, just before Guiyang Road, the brown and somewhat monolithic **Mangka Church** (Wanhua Mengjia Jiaotang) stands on the site of what was once a fetching 1877 original of exotic Eastern inspiration. There are small street-corner temples, some enshrining religious statuary brought from Fujian by seafaring traders centuries ago. It's also worth strolling over to 179 Huanhe South Road, Section 1, next to the Danshui River, to take a look at one of Taipei's only remaining traditional Fujian-style merchants' homes.

Wanhua's most famous sight is known as **Snake Alley ㉓** (Huaxi Jie Yeshi; nightly). Only a few minutes' walk from Longshan Temple, the cramped arcade announces itself with a sign that reads "Taipei Hwahsi Tourist Night Market." Not so long ago, the alley heaved with shops stacked with cages of hissing snakes, whose blood and bile was mixed with spirits and herbs and drunk by men who believed the potion strengthened the eyes and spine and promoted male virility. Today, less than a handful of such shops remain, but the tourists still come.

If Snake Alley looks a little tired these days, head over to **Guangzhou Street**, which, with the onset of night, sets itself up as a push-and-shove night market. There are stalls selling swimwear, ersatz Italian fashions, Mickey Mouse masks, bootleg CDs, Buddhist chant tapes and multi-colored religious beads. Stands selling deep-fried squid and roast chicken jostle for attention with off-the-rack budget suits. Vendors here, armed with microphones, shout high-decibel race-track Taiwanese with the oratorical passion of someone out for a quick kill. You'll be lucky to hear any Mandarin in this neck of the woods.

However, top of the list of Taipei's night markets has to be **Shilin Night Market** (Shilin Yeshi; 5pm–1am) in the suburb of Shilin. With a history of around 100 years, it is known for the quality of its food, which represents Taiwanese snacks at their best. Another famous Taipei night market is **Raohe Night Market** (Raohe Yeshi; 5pm–midnight), on Raohe Street near Songshan Railway Station in the east of the city. It's easily accessible, although all the hustle there may be too much for some visitors. A huge, brightly lit gate inscribed with the words "Zau Ho Night Market of Tourist" stands at the entrance.

Not far from the Grand Hyatt, just southwest of Xinyi and Jilong roads, is **Tonghua Street**, a thoroughfare bustling with fun-seeking crowds looking for budget garments and cheap snacks. Alternatively, **Liaoning Street** offers a less crowded collection of open-air seafood restaurants, off Nanjing East Road, Sec. 3 just west of Fuxing North Road. ❏

The snake is much sought-after among locals for its medicinal properties.

BELOW: a snake handler.
RIGHT: Snake Alley Nightmarket.

NIGHT MARKETS: BURNING BRIGHT

Lit up like pinball machines and full of carnival atmosphere, the night markets of Taiwan are the brightest lights in town after the sun goes down

Night markets are an essential element of Taiwanese life and a top attraction for visitors. They burst into life every night in vivid color in towns and neighborhoods everywhere on the island. Every city in Taiwan has a number of night markets, but Taipei's Shilin Night Market (Shilin Yeshi) is the undisputed king of them all and is claimed to have started trading over 100 years ago. The market is a vast sprawl of aisles in a new multi-story complex. Fun-seekers surge into the market each night; in this good-humored chaos wafts the smells of a thousand delights while hawkers' cries entice customers to reach for their wallets.

Just about anything can be bought in a night market, from T-shirts to trousers to puppy dogs to shoes, but the main attraction is food, prepared in mobile carts, in street-side stalls, or in huge food halls. The night market vendors sell squid and pork, candied tomatoes, roast chestnuts, corn, juice and dumplings, and tables almost topple over with fruit and tofu and hundreds of other foods. Feeling adventurous? Try the duck's tongue or chicken's feet. Not feeling adventurous? Have a sandwich. There's something in a night market to suit every palate and pocket. Night markets are often the last stop on a late night out, faithful all-night eateries where revelers can down a hot bowl of noodles to soak up the night's excesses before going to bed. The markets often open at sundown, although they don't get crowded until 10pm or 11pm and sometimes remain open for business until dawn.

△ **FRUGAL FOOD**
Food is cheaper in the night markets because most of the vendors pay little rent. Many people do their grocery shopping at street stalls.

▷ **SOOTHSAYERS**
Palm reading, oracle-bone throwing, incense burning and other traditional forms of determining the future are popular.

▷ **FISHY SNACKS**
Barbecued fish is brushed in oil, painted with sweet chili sauce, and grilled over a hot charcoal fire. It is one of the most delicious street foods in Taiwan.

THE MAGIC OF SNAKE ALLEY

△ FAKE FINERY
Taiwan has made an effort to crack down on pirated goods, but a walk through any night market will yield a treasure trove of copycat products.

▽ SNACK SHOT
Shoot enough balloons and win some crackers or a beer. Prizes are also given for dart-throwing, ring-tossing, and sidewalk *pachinko* (pinball).

△ ANIMAL ARRAY
How much is that rabbit in the window? Besides the more common items, animals are often sold from cages at night-market stalls.

▽ TRADITIONAL HEALING
Snake soup and wine are popular in the winter. Despite a lack of medical evidence, many Chinese believe in the healing qualities of snake.

◁ BUYER BEWARE
Shoppers with an eye for quality can find many bargains. But once you buy something, there is no refund. You may not even find the vendor the next night.

Steamed snake meat and hot snake bile are not everyone's cup of tea, nor are freshly skinned cobras writhing on hooks, but Taipei's Snake Alley (Huaxi Jie Yeshi) does open a window into an older, less civilized side of Chinese culture, where snake was believed to have magical properties. There is an element of cruelty to Snake Alley, as the helpless cobras are hauled from their cages and skinned alive for the benefit of the spectators. The blood, bile and meat from the snakes is then used for soups and the carcasses hung out to dry. Snake Alley has been cleaned up for the benefit of tourists, some of whom may wonder about the supposed healing and virility-enhancing properties of the various snake concoctions. The brave of heart can drink a cup of steaming snake bile and find out for themselves. Along the narrow passageways are also fortune-tellers, vendors of herbal potions, and tattooists. The market is open from 7pm to midnight.

AROUND TAIPEI

The island's best museum, hot springs, tea plantations and stunning mountain views encourage visitors to leave the traffic jams behind and head for the suburbs

Map on page 148

At first glance, the district of Shilin, in the north of Taipei, seems to have little to offer the visitor, apart from the city's best night market, mentioned in the previous chapter. But it is also home to some of the city's best museums, including the island's most famous.

An imposing complex of beige-brick buildings, topped with green and imperial-yellow slate roofs, houses the **National Palace Museum ❶** (Guoli Gugong Bowuguan; Tue–Sun 9am–5pm; charge). The main building is impressive and the treasures within are unimaginable. Next to the museum is a small but perfectly styled recreation of a Song dynasty Chinese garden. Called **Zhishan Yuan** (Tue–Sun 7am–7pm; charge, free with NPM ticket stub), it's worth a stroll.

The Palace Museum which has been completely refurbished inside and out this decade, is home to some 6,000 works of art representing the zenith of 5,000 years of Chinese creativity. And these are just a fraction of the more than 700,000 paintings, porcelains, bronzes, rubbings, tapestries, books and other objects stored in nearly 4,000 crates located in vaults tunneled into the mountain behind the museum.

The museum opened in 1965. But the history of its treasures, which reads like a John le Carré thriller, can be traced back more than 1,000 years, to the beginning of the Song dynasty (AD 960–1279). The founder of that dynasty established the Hanlin Academy to encourage literature and the arts. The emperor's brother and successor later opened a gallery, where some of the items in the current collection were first housed. The gallery was then established as a government department for the preservation of rare books, old paintings and calligraphy. This imperial gallery became the prototype for Taipei's collection.

The Song collection was transported from Beijing to Nanjing during the Ming dynasty, then back again, foreshadowing the collection's many moves in the 20th century. The collection expanded considerably during the Qing dynasty (1644–1911), whose emperors were avid art collectors. The majority of items in the present collection are the result of their effort to seek out China's most important treasures.

Art on the run

But the real intrigues began in November 1924. Warlord Feng Yu-xiang, who had taken Beijing, gave the last surviving Manchu emperor, Puyi, and his entourage of 2,000 eunuchs and ladies two hours to evacuate the Forbidden City. Then the government had 30 young Chinese scholars and art experts identify and inventory the overwhelming collection of art treasures that had been hoarded within the palace for more than 500 years.

LEFT: Chiang Kai-shek honored at the entrance to the National Palace Museum. **BELOW:** friends gather at a carp pond, in NPM's Zhishan Yuan.

It took the scholars two years just to sort out and organize the collection. In the meantime, the government formally established the National Beijing Palace Museum and began displaying some of the treasures. By the time the task of identifying all the priceless objects was completed in 1931, the Japanese had attacked northwest China, and threatened Beijing. The art collection had, and still has, enormous symbolic value to whomever possesses it, bestowing a measure of political legitimacy upon its owners. To prevent the Japanese from seizing the collection, everything was carefully packed into 20,000 cases and shipped, in five trains, south to Nanjing.

Thus began a 16-year-long odyssey. The priceless treasures were shuttled back and forth across the war-torn face of China by rail, truck, ox cart, raft and foot, always a few steps ahead of pursuing Japanese and, later, Communist troops. Incredibly, not a single item was lost or damaged. A representative selection of the best items was shipped to London for a major art exhibition in 1936 – prompting an uproar among China's intellectuals, who feared the foreigners would never return the works. But all made it back to China. The following year, the Japanese occupied Beijing and threatened Nanjing. Once again, the precious collection was loaded aboard trucks and transported in three shipments over hills, rivers and streams to China's rugged western mountains.

Lion image at National Palace Museum. Those depicted in art bear little resemblance to the real animal.

BELOW: jade cup, Qing dynasty, 1782.

Safe in Taiwan

After the Japanese surrender in 1945, the Nationalist government brought the pieces back to Nanjing. But, when Communist control of the mainland appeared imminent in 1948, some 4,800 cases of the most valuable pieces were culled from the original 20,000 cases and sent for safekeeping to Taiwan. They were

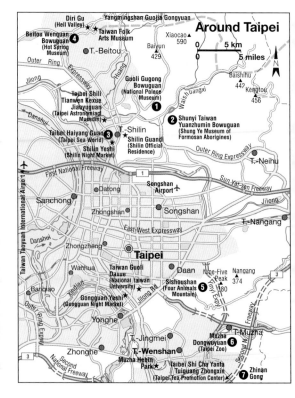

stored in a sugar warehouse in Taichung, where they remained hidden until the Zhongshan (Sun Yat-sen) Museum Building in Waishuangxi opened in 1965.

Among the items cached are 4,400 ancient bronzes, 24,000 pieces of porcelain, 13,000 paintings, 14,000 works of calligraphy, 4,600 pieces of jade, 153,000 rare books from the imperial library, and 390,000 documents, diaries and old palace records. Massive steel doors lead to the catacombs in the mountain behind, where the steel trunks are stacked one atop the other. One semicircular tunnel is 190 meters (620 ft) long, the other 150 meters (490 ft). The temperature is kept at a constant 18°C (64°F), and dehumidifiers line the corridors.

Little by little, the National Palace Museum has been revealing most of the secrets of its vaults. Paintings are rotated in special exhibitions every three months; other objects, like Hindustan jades and *ding* bronzes, are rotated at two-year intervals. It is said that it takes a full 12 years to display the entirety of the collection, which includes artifacts from tombs in Hunan province, along with bronzes, oracle bones, ceramics, porcelains and paintings. There are famous pieces such as the *feicui* (or *baicai*) jade cabbage – carved during the Qing dynasty, complete with camouflaged grasshopper – and a set of 79 wooden cups, carved paper-thin so that all can be held in a single large cup. There's also an amazing collection of miniatures carved from wood and ivory. One tiny cruising yacht, only 5 cm (2 inches) long and 3 cm (1¼ inches) high, has both crew and guests carved into its interior cabin. With its recent refurbishment, the museum has also moved to display its treasures according to historical dynastic period rather than artwork type. In addition, it is adding works specific to Taiwan's cultural experience as well as works from outside greater China showing the impact of Chinese culture in the region.

Map on page 148

On display at Taipei's National Palace Museum are bronze ding, *ceremonial cooking vessels with three legs and round bulbous bodies decorated with patterns and stylized animals. In China,* ding *were once symbols of power and sovereignty.*

BELOW: carved wooden cups, National Palace Museum.

View nature through a different light – stained-glass window at Beitou Hot Spring Museum.

BELOW: Shung Ye Museum of Formosan Aborigines.

Aboriginal collection

Close to the National Palace Museum is the **Shung Ye Museum of Formosan Aborigines ❷** (Shunyi Taiwan Yuanzhumin Bowuguan; Tue–Sun 9am–5pm, closed Jan 20–Feb 20; charge), a fascinating and tastefully presented introduction to the cultures of Taiwan's aboriginal tribes. The museum has exhibitions on the belief systems, artifacts and daily lives of the tribes who are thought to have settled the island more than 6,000 years ago, long predating the Han Chinese who now make up the vast majority of Taiwan's population.

Heading back toward central Shilin, on Lane 460 off Section 5 of Zhongshan North Road is the **Shilin Official Residence** (Shilin Guandi; Tue–Sun 9am–5pm), the second and main home of Chiang Kai-shek (Jiang Jie-shi). Long shrouded in mystery, the spacious grounds are now open to the public. The landscaped gardens – more in the European than Chinese style – are a popular location for wedding photographs, but it's possible to escape the crowds by taking a long flight of stairs to the top of a hill on the grounds for views of nearby Qixing Mountain.

Back in central Shilin, a worthwhile detour for those with children is the **Taipei Sea World ❸** (Taipei Haiyang Guan; Mon–Fri 9am–5pm, Sat–Sun 9am–9pm; charge), an in- and outdoor aquarium that took the city by storm when it was completed in the late 1990s, though tourists will be far less thrilled. A glass tunnel through the waters brings the visitor face to face with small sharks, stingrays, turtles and other underwater denizens. Close by, on Zhongzheng Road, the **Taipei Astronomical Museum** (Taipei Shili Tianwen Kexue Jiaoyuguan; Tue–Sun 9am–5pm; charge; www.tam.gov.tw) is another popular destination for children, with its golden dome planetarium and 3D IMAX shows.

Hot spring resort

North of Shilin, but easily reached by the MRT's Danshui line, is the suburb of Beitou (pronounced *bay tow*). It nestles snugly in lush green hills and is best approached not from Beitou station, but from **Xin Beitou station** (Xin Beitou Zhan), which has its own branch line, with connections approximately every 10 minutes. Beitou started out as a hot spring resort established by the Japanese administration, but the World War II and Vietnam War eras were its heydays, when its hot-spring hotels and drinking establishments made it a fully fledged R&R destination for troops. With the end of the Vietnam War, Beitou fell into neglect. Japanese tour groups would still arrive but, by the early 1990s, Beitou's hotels, which once numbered more than 70, had been reduced to little more than a dozen, most of them poorly maintained. Two things have changed Beitou's fortunes in recent years. One was the arrival of the MRT line, and the other was the recent revival of all things Taiwanese, which has led to a new hot spring boom across the island.

The best place to get a glimpse of the area's history and a feel for its recent revival of fortune is the **Beitou Hot Spring Museum ❹** (Beitou Wenquan Bowuguan; Tue–Sun 9am–5pm; closed national holidays), housed in what used to be the Beitou Public Baths, a Japanese building that dates from 1913. A 5-

minute walk from the monumental portals of the Xin Beitou MRT station, the museum is nothing if not educational. Exhibits feature the history of the area, and in a classic Japanese-style hall, complete with what looks like an acre of *tatami* matting, guides hold forth on the culture of hot-spring bathing. Downstairs, the original Beitou public bath is preserved in a cavernous room overlooked by stained-glass windows and Romanesque arches.

Almost all the hotels in the Beitou area feature hot sulfur spring water that runs directly from the taps into tiled tubs, either sunken or above ground. After a soak in these hot tubs, a professional massage completes the revival. (As in Japan, massaging people is one of the traditional occupations of blind people in China and Taiwan.) The best hotel in the area to have a soak also happens to be the oldest: **Hoshi no Yu**, Japanese for what translates literally as "bath of stars." The 100-plus-year-old hotel has been beautifully restored, and features a courtyard garden with a miniature pond swimming with delicate carp.

Beitou is easy to explore on foot. A street leads directly to **Hell Valley** (Diri Gu; Tue–Sun 9am–5pm; free), where the steamy, open sulfur pits offer a firsthand look at the natural activity responsible for the area's hot springs. The original settlers nearby called the valley "Patauw," meaning "sorceress," sure that dangerous magic-wielders caused the strange otherworldly phenomena. The Chinese came in the late 1600s to extract sulfur for munitions; there were once 27 sulfur mines in the area.

Rise of the Phoenix

After walking through the center of the hot-springs area, with its city park and Chinese pavilion, strollers will come to a traffic island. The right-hand fork off

Map on page 148

Beitou's hot springs were deemed especially beneficial to the health, a feature that still attracts large numbers of Japanese tourists. Taiwanese geologists think the reason may be the local rocks, which emit small amounts of radiation.

BELOW: steaming pool in Hell Valley.

Guangming Road proceeds past the New Angel Hotel, near to which Qiyan Road offers access to a challenging diversion: a climb up tranquil Phoenix Mountain. Those who venture up eventually come to a large double staircase guarded by two enormous lucky dogs. The stairs lead to the **Chen Memorial Garden**, whose chief attraction is its tranquility. The paved pathway behind the garden is the start of the exhausting mountain ascent. From the summit, there are sweeping views of Taipei, Beitou and the surrounding countryside. Trekkers find well-marked hiking paths heading in four directions from the top: all lead to main roads. Beyond the Chen Memorial Garden is the **Monastery of Central Harmony** (Zhonghe Chan Si), a Buddhist complex of pavilions, halls, arcades, shrines, statues and gardens.

Attractions within easy reach of Beitou include another impressive temple and mountain. **Xingtian Temple** (Xingtian Gong), which stands high on the road that runs between Beitou and the coastal town of Danshui, has the same name as its sister temple in downtown Taipei, but the setting is considerably more scenic, with a landscaped garden covering the entire hill behind. The main hall and subsidiary shrines are as lavishly decorated as any in Taiwan, but better maintained than most. The ruling deity here is the red-faced Guangong.

The route back to Taipei downtown, along Yangde Boulevard leading down Yangmingshan, passes the Zhongshan Building (Zhongshan Lou) complex, and the buildings of the Chinese Culture University, built in traditional Chinese style.

East of the city

The Taipei World Trade Center and the Warner Village cinema complex effectively mark the eastern extent of Taipei. Rising above them are the wooded hills of the Songshan Nature Reserve, which includes the **Four Animals Mountain ❺** (Sishoushan). The "animals" are a fanciful reference to the shapes of the four peaks here, which to those with a fertile imagination look like a tiger, an elephant, a lion and a panther.

Apart from stunning views of Taipei, the attraction of Songshan's hiking trails is their accessibility. Most of Taipei's nearby rural attractions require at least an hour of travel, most of which is spent sitting in choking traffic conditions. Songshan's trails, on the other hand, start less than a 5-minute taxi ride from the World Trade Center, at the end of Zhuangjing Road (which begins opposite the Trade Center). From here it's possible to warm up with a relatively untaxing ascent up the 180-meter (590-ft) Elephant Mountain.

Walkers looking for a slighty more strenuous workout and the best panoramas should follow the trail to Nine-Five Peak, named after a hardy 95-year-old Kuomintang (Guomindang) general who climbed to its 380-meter (1,247-ft) summit in 1915.

South of the city

The MRT's elevated Muzha line makes an excursion south of Taipei an easy feat nowadays. The first stop for most visitors is the MRT's last stop, **Taipei Zoo ❻** (Taipei Muzha Dongwuyuan; daily 9am–5pm; charge). As zoos go, it's not world class, but the animals for the most part do have spacious enclosures,

BELOW: the region's low elevation supports a luxuriant growth of bamboo.

and it's a good place to take children. It also represents a rare opportunity to see Taiwan's black bear, an animal that is seldom seen in the wild these days, as well as other indigenous Taiwanese species of animals.

For most visitors, however, the real attraction of Muzha is not its zoo but its surrounding hills studded with tea plantations. But, before venturing out to the plantations, make a stop at **Zhinan Temple ❼** (Zhinan Gong; daily) which, nestled in wooded hills, is easily the most stately and photogenic of Taipei's many temples. Dedicated to Lu Dong-bin, one of the eight immortals of Chinese mythology and figuring in both the Daoist and Buddhist pantheons, legend has it that lovers should never visit the temple together, as Lu, an immortal of amorous disposition, has been known to snatch beautiful women from the men who love them. The temple is approached by a long flight of steps; for those not in the mood for a climb, the temple, viewed from below, is an impressive sight in itself.

The tea plantations, in what is called the Maokong area, have become a popular escape for people from Taipei over the past 20 years. Not so long ago, they restricted their business to growing tea. Today, many have opened atmospheric teahouses that usually offer entrancing views of the surrounding countryside, with the rich smell of tea in the air. The **Taipei Tea Promotion Center** (Taipei Shi Cha Yanfa Tuiguang Zhongxin; Tue–Sun 9am–5pm; tours in English are provided with two days' notice) for example has a teahouse and offers demonstrations of the tea production and brewing process. The famous local variety is known as *tieguanyin* (Iron Goddess), a variety of *oolong*. Most of the teahouses are on Zhinan Road, Section 3. The area is best reached by backtracking on the Muzha MRT line to Wanfang station and taking a No. 10 or 11 minibus from there, or by taking a taxi from the zoo. ❏

Map on page 148

TIP

The new Maokong Gondola whisks visitors from Taipei Zoo up to Zhinan Temple and then on to the Maokong tea plantations (http://gondola.trtc.com.tw; charge).

BELOW: perched on a mountainside is the Zhinan Temple complex.

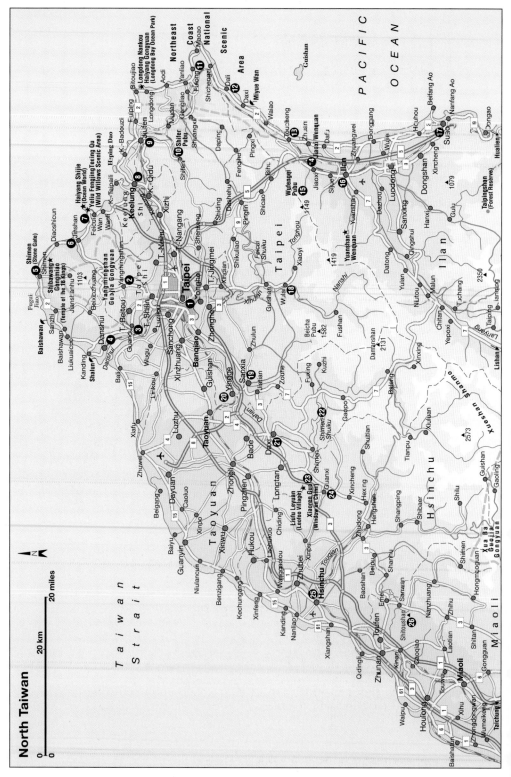

North Taiwan

NORTH TAIWAN

While other parts of the island trumpet high-profile attractions, this region offers uncrowded beaches and hiking trails

Northern Taiwan tends to get short shrift with many Taiwan visitors, due to the fact that its attractions are overshadowed by the island's more famous sights like the Taroko Gorge, Sun Moon Lake and Alishan. This is a pity because, for those who make the effort, there is much natural beauty and history to be found within easy striking distance of Taipei's city limits.

Although the bustle of downtown Taipei may be somewhat over-whelming, it is worth bearing in mind that in less than an hour it is possible to reach destinations that move to far more traditional rhythms. The nearby ports, for example, of Danshui and Keelung are home to forts and ruins, remnants of the island's modern colonial history, and superb seafood dining, while the coastline that stretches between them is an eerie landscape of weathered rock formations.

Meanwhile, closer to Taipei city center, Yangmingshan National Park offers hiking trails, steaming fumaroles, hot springs and bird-watching. East of the city is the village of Jiufen, a former gold-rush town with laddered streets and interesting arts and crafts, and which provides both a pleasant escape from Taipei and a fascinating insight into small-town Taiwan. Jiufen is near Fulong Bay, which has a beach that is rated among the best in northern Taiwan and which, outside of summer holidays, is usually deserted on weekdays.

South of Fulong begins Taiwan's dramatically beautiful eastern coast, and even for those not planning to follow it as far as Taitung, it's worth traveling at least to Suao, renowned for its cold springs – the perfect antidote to the stifling heat of the summer months. Head-ing back in the direction of Taipei, the hot-spring resort of Wulai is also one of the few places in northern Taiwan where it is possible to get an insight into Taiwan's aboriginal cultures.

The area immediately southwest of Taipei is less compelling than the northern coastline, but it is still not without attractions. In the vicinity of the Shimen Reservoir, a popular escape for Taipei resi-dents, are the theme parks of Window on China, which presents the architectural triumphs of China, Taiwan and, nowadays, some of the Western world, in miniature, and the sprawling Leofoo Village. Also situated close by are the fascinating compounds of Taiwan's Hakka minority at Guanxi, one of the few places in Taiwan, along with Meinong in the deep south, where it is possible to get a glimpse of traditional Hakka culture.

Meanwhile, farther south again, past the city of Hsinchu, with its world-famous Hsinchu Science Park, is the Buddhist retreat of Shi-toushan, a mountain cluster of temples where it is possible to stay overnight in a Buddhist monastery. ❏

PRECEDING PAGES: serene lakeside scene in northern Taiwan.

YANGMINGSHAN AND DANSHUI

Map on page 156

A tour of Taiwan's northern coast, or even just a day trip out of bustling Taipei, provides an insight into both the natural glory of the island and its colonial past

The sights and traffic in **Taipei ❶** monopolize most of a traveler's time in northern Taiwan, but an excursion beyond the city and its suburbs will offer another side of life on the island. The closest northern attraction is **Yangmingshan ❷**, about 40 minutes' drive along winding roads. Large numbers of wealthy industrial tycoons, movie stars and entrepreneurs, as well as expatriate businesspeople, live here in luxurious villas clinging to the slopes in the cool climes above Taipei, while artists seek out the abandoned farmsteads that dot the area as subjects for their work. Originally called Grass Mountain, the name was changed to honor a philosopher, Wang Yangming (1472–1529). For visitors to Taipei, however, the attraction is less the mountain's residential prospects than the sprawling **Yangmingshan National Park** (Yangmingshan Guojia Gongyuan), which comprises not only the park's crowning Yangming Park, but Datun Nature Park and a host of other natural features. Yangmingshan is far more than just a pleasant park with landscaped walks sitting at the summits of Taipei's most famous nearby peaks, and it's worth making the time to visit it.

Comprising the westernmost peaks of the Datun mountain range, Yangmingshan came into existence through volcanic activity around 2 million years ago. The lingering evidence of the mountains' volcanic origins is one of the chief draws for Taipei residents today, especially in winter, when they flock to Yangmingshan's many hot-spring resorts.

LEFT: a bird's eye-view from Yangmingshan.
BELOW: hot spring at Yangmingshan.

Walkways and flowers

Those with limited time should restrict their excursion to Yangming Park, rather than venture farther afield within the much larger national park. This well-maintained park features walkways that wind through colorful gardens of trees, bushes, fragrant flowers and grottos. From the middle of February until the end of March, an annual spring-flower festival is held in the park, with the entire mountainside awash with cherry blossoms and carpeted with bright, flowering azaleas. Just north of the park is the **Yangmingshan National Park Visitors' Center** (Youke Fuwu Zhongxin; daily 9am–4.30pm), which has a display room on the area's geology, computer information consoles and tourist information – a useful stop for those planning a hike in the area.

Deeper into the national park, popular walks include the "Bird Watching Trail" and the "Butterfly Corridor" (around two hours' walk, round-trip), though keen lepidopterists will probably be disappointed unless they visit during the top butterfly months of May and June. The latter walk terminates on the outskirts of the

TIP

Yangmingshan
National Park gets
very busy on
weekends and
holidays, particularly
in spring and summer.
Winter weekend
evenings also see the
roads in the area
chock-a-block with
traffic, as Taipei
residents head into the
hills for a hot-spring
soak.

BELOW: on the trail in
Datun Nature Park.

350-hectare (860-acre) **Datun Nature Park**, which also features hiking trails and observation decks, and lies to the northwest of Yangming Park.

Northeast of the Yangmingshan Visitors' Center is the striking volcanic landscape of **Lengshuikeng Walking Area** (best avoided on weekends), and a little farther east **Qingtiangang**, which pulls in the crowds with its Alpine-like meadow and encircling ridge (which features a hiking trail), something of a novelty in Taiwan. To the northwest is the **Xiaoyoukeng Fumarole Nature Preserve**, with its dense stands of bamboo and wafting sulfurous clouds. The highest point here is **Seven Stars Mountain** (Qixingshan), at 1,200 meters (4,000 ft). A steep, but not dangerous, path leads to the top, where the view is remarkable – but check the condition of the trail at the Yangmingshan National Park Visitors' Center before setting out.

Northern routes

There are a number of ways to approach the north shore of Taiwan, the extent of which is marked by the natural boundaries of the Danshui River to the west and Keelung Harbor to the east. It's possible, for example, to drive to Danshui on the northwest coast and then follow the northern coastline, which is dotted with picturesque farming towns, fishing villages and some stunning coastal vistas, to Keelung where it is then possible to double back to Taipei. If just headed to Danshui, however, fewer people drive nowadays, because the new Danshui MRT line makes it possible to avoid traffic and save a lot of time by taking a train to Danshui in around 25 minutes.

Nevertheless, even for those who take the easier MRT option for the journey out, it's still worth considering following the northern coastline, either by bus

Map
on page
156

or taxi. From Danshui, Shengdao 2 (No. 2 Provincial Highway) proceeds eastward through Baishawan, Jinshan, Yeliu and Wanli, then to Keelung. From this harbor town, travelers have the option of taking the Sun Yat-sen Freeway back to Taipei. From Keelung, it is also possible to continue on a southeast coastal course to Bitoujiao, Fulong and its excellent beach, and Toucheng, then return north to Taipei past waterfalls and through Xindian via Shengdao 9 or much more quickly via the much-tunneled new National Highway No. 5.

On the way to Danshui, alongside the Danshui River, is **Guandu ❸**, with an eye-catching 550-meter (1,700-ft) long red bridge. Directly on the river and close to a cliff is an extremely large temple complex, **Guandu Temple** (Guandu Gong), one of Taiwan's three oldest and most important Mazu temples (along with Lugang's Tianhou Temple and Beigang's Chaotian Temple). Built in 1712, the temple is a 15-minute walk from the Guandu MRT station, and also features a small adjacent Buddhist temple dedicated to Guanyin, the Goddess of Mercy. It's also worth taking a stroll around the vicinity of the temple – a viewpoint high above the river can be accessed via a tunnel through the cliff.

A short walk south of the temple is the **Guandu Nature Park** (Guandu Daziran Gongyuan; Tue–Fri 9am–5pm, Sat–Sun 9am–6pm; charge), which, occupying the confluence of the Danshui and Jilong rivers, is a haven for migratory birds. Those visiting the nature center or taking any of the park's walking trails should make as little noise as possible; viewing shelters are provided along the trails for wildlife observation. Two stops on by the MRT is Hongshulin station, jumping off point for the **Hongshulin Mangrove Conservation Area** (Hongshulin Baohu Qu). Like Guandu Nature Park, this is another good place for bird-watching. Bike paths (with rentals) move along both sides of the Danshui from Taipei past Guandu and on toward the coast.

Stonework on the walls of the Hongmao Cheng, the fort at Danshui.

BELOW:
ROC flag flies high over Hongmao Cheng (Fort San Domingo), Danshui.

Danshui

The terminus of the MRT is in a town with a rich historical heritage: **Danshui ❹** – together with Guandu, a popular day trip from Taipei. The town was the main point of contact in northern Taiwan between the Chinese and foreign traders during its heyday as the island's major port in the 19th century. Even before that, the Spanish – who had occupied Keelung – extended their claim to Danshui, where, in 1629, they built a fort, **Fort San Domingo** (Hongmao Cheng; Tue–Sun 9am–4.30pm; charge), on one of the hills close to the river. After the Spanish were booted out, Danshui was occupied by the Dutch until 1662, bombarded by French warships in 1884, and claimed by the Japanese in 1895. Before they left, the Japanese built the island's first golf course in Danshui, now known as the Taiwan Golf and Country Club. Opened in 1919, the club remains popular among visitors and residents alike.

Today, the fort is a primary Danshui attraction. It may be a relatively modest affair, but the red-brick structure atop a small hill overlooking the mouth of the Danshui River encapsulates much of Taiwan's history: first built by the Spanish, rebuilt by the Dutch, taken over by Chinese Ming and Qing dynasty administrations, before serving as part of the British consulate in the late 19th and early 20th centuries. It's known locally

*A tribute to George
Lesley Mackay.*

as the Hongmao Cheng, the "fort of the red-haired barbarians," a name that dates back to the Dutch. How much it resembles the original, however, is difficult to say after the Dutch rebuilt it. It's also difficult to ascertain whether it even started out red, or whether later Taiwanese renovations took a lead from the fort's popular name. But, idle musings aside, it's not without its charm. Displays inside the fort feature old maps of Danshui and reproductions of trade treaties.

Expatriate coziness

Also on the grounds is the **former British Consulate** (Yingguo Lingshiguan; Tuc Sun 9am–4.30pm), which was built as an annex in 1867, when the British took out a lease on the fort from the Qing dynasty government. It is a splendid two-story colonnaded structure, cooled by sea breezes that flow from one flung-open bay window to the next, the empty fireplaces hinting at an insulated ex-patriate coziness through the brief winter months. Gazing at the dining room and the well-preserved bedrooms, it's easy to imagine the lives of the consular staff who were posted here in the days when there were no quick flights to more exotic destinations, and a journey home took many weeks.

The town the consular staff were surrounded by, a busy Taiwanese trading port in which the locals regarded the residents on the hill as "red-haired barbarians," can be seen pictured in black and white photographs labeled only in Chinese in various rooms around the building.

Although Danshui nowadays is a bustling, fairly modern town, it is still worth taking a stroll in search of the atmosphere of old Danshui. The small section of town locals call Laojie, or "old streets," can be found a short walk southwest from the fort, next to the ferry pier. From here it is possible to take a waterside

BELOW: the former
British Consulate.

stroll (popular at sunset) or to strike north up to the **Danshui Presbyterian Church** (Danshui Jiaotang), a legacy of the famous foreigner whose name, for many Taiwanese, is almost synonymous with Danshui – George Leslie Mackay.

Mackay's legacy

A Canadian missionary, Mackay's efforts to improve health and education in Danshui from 1872 until his death in 1901 have left Danshui with a number of Western-inspired buildings. Opposite the church is the **Mackay Hospital**, Taiwan's first modern hospital, now converted into a memorial to Mackay. Just to the north of the fort is the **Bajiao Ta**, or the Octagonal Tower, which looks like a Renaissance-inspired pagoda and is the pride of the Danjiang (sometimes spelled Tamkang) High School. Opposite the school, on the grounds of the Aletheia University, is **Oxford College**, designed by Mackay and Taiwan's first venue for Western-style education.

Near Hongmao Cheng, at the mouth of the Danshui, is one of the town's most popular attractions, **Fisherman's Wharf** (Yuren Matou; daily 8am–6pm). The wharf is a 20-minute direct bus ride (Red No. 26) from the Danshui MRT terminus, and houses traditional eateries and a coffee shop with grand views of the river and Yangmingshan behind. Perhaps the main attraction for tourists, however, is the chance to get on one of the **Blue Highway** (Lanse Gonglu; charge; 50-minute sea/river rides) cruise boats. There are hourly cruises (look for stands on the dock beside the boats) of the river mouth and along the nearby coast, making it obvious why the Portuguese called Taiwan the "beautiful island" when passing by in the late 1500s. There is a ferry service from below the MRT terminus to the wharf, and from the terminus across the river to the town of Bali. ❑

Map on page 156

TIP

At the ferry pier below Hongmao Cheng, a number of cafés and restaurants offer alfresco seating with views of Taiwan's most celebrated sunset.

BELOW: an evening on Danshui waterfront.

THE NORTH COAST

The north coast is characterized by bathing beaches, unusual rock formations and the occasional temple and museum, while its only city is home to possibly the best night market in Taiwan

Map on page 156

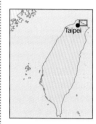
Taipei

The immediate stretch of the North Coast Highway (Shengdao 2) that travels north of Danshui is limited in attractions, most being swimming beaches that are geared to summer crowds fleeing the heat of downtown Taipei. However, in recent years the Tourism Bureau has put in place many new seaside parking facilities and viewing platforms, and licensed numerous coffee and snack kiosks featuring cool, umbrella-shaded seating. The roadway has also been widened, making cycling safer. The most popular beach is **Baishawan Beach** (Baishawan Haishui Yuchang; daily 8am–sundown; charge). Because of its proximity to Taipei, it pulls huge crowds on summer weekends. Otherwise, it is a convenient spot to swim and sunbathe. The beach has snack bars, changing rooms and a nearby hotel. Baishawan is also known for windsurfing.

From Baishawan, the North Coast Highway rounds the northernmost nib of Taiwan at **Fugui Cape** (Fugui Jiao), which is marked by a lighthouse. The latter is part of a military installation and is off-limits. Here, the Taiwan Strait is on the left, Pacific Ocean on the right, and the East China Sea to the north.

Natural wonder

About 4 km (2½ miles) on from Fugui Cape, a natural wonder appears: **Stone Gate ❺** (Shimen), an impressive stone arch formed by tidal erosion, with an 8-meter (26-ft) high opening. Tidal erosion may have created it, but it's now far removed from the tides, tectonic forces having pushed the land here beyond the reach of the waves. Locals say the name derives from the fact that, from a distance, the arch looks like the gates of a vast stone city. On top of the arch are seats affording splendid views of the coastline and the sea, while a stroll around the area of the arch is a good introduction to the wind- and tide-eroded geology of Taiwan's northern coast. Walkways, bridges and viewing platforms make exploration easy.

Not far away, on a side road 31 km (19 miles) along the North Coast Highway, is the **Temple of the 18 Kings** (Shibawang Gongmiao; 24 hours; accompanying games arcade and night-market). It's a small affair, but almost always bustling with crowds, with incense thick in the air. Legend has it that 17 merchants and a dog were killed in a rough crossing from China during the Qing dynasty, and, when this temple was founded in their memory, the dog, who died trying to save his master, was made a god, too.

As the highway turns southeast, it follows the stretch of coast that in Chinese is poetically known as Diaoshi Haian, "the thrown rock coast," on account of the fact that the beaches are made up of jumbled rocks.

The next point of interest is **Jinshan ❻**, which is worth pausing at for several reasons. For one, Jinbaoli

LEFT: a rocky path at Yeliu Scenic Area.
BELOW: sandstone formations at Yeliu.

Street, in the old town of Jinshan, is one of the few places in all of Taiwan where it is still possible to see some lingering Qing-era architecture. There is also a viewing area where all Taiwanese tourists stop to admire the **Candlestick Islands** (Lazhu Yu), a cluster of coral outcrops that lie around 400 meters (440 yards) offshore. Another interesting site is the **Jinshan Youth Activity Center** (Qingnian Huodong Zhongxin), which – unpromising though it sounds – has excellent swimming facilities and a superb hot spring.

TIP

Shuttle buses run directly to the Ju Ming Museum from next to the Jinshan Township Office, 257 Zhongshan Road, Jinshan (Tue–Fri 10.30am, 2pm; Sat–Sun and holidays 10.30am, 12.30pm, 4pm).

Sculpture detour

Those with their own transport might consider making a very worthwhile detour just before reaching Jinshan. Just past the 39-km mark on the North Coast Highway, a signposted side road turns inland and, after a 15-minute drive uphill, passes the **Ju Ming Museum** (Ju Ming Meishuguan; Tue–Sun 10am–6pm, Nov–Apr until 5pm; charge, children free; www.juming.org.tw). The museum is a celebration of the work of Ju Ming, Taiwan's most celebrated sculptor and features around 500 of Ju Ming's works. The landscaped grounds host works by other sculptors, too.

Inland along the same road, the road passes the **Jinbaoshan Cemetery** (Jinbaoshan Fenchang; 24 hours), a site of pilgrimage for local music lovers, as Teresa Deng, Taiwan's most famous musical export (in Asia at least), who died in 1995, is buried here. Vistas of the valley below, and coast, are stunning.

Farther down the coast, the wave-buffeted geology of Taiwan's northern coastline finds one of its most unique manifestations at **Wild Willows Scenic Area ❼** (Yeliu Fengjing Teding Qu; daily 8am–5pm; charge), formally Yeliu Geological Park. The white, yellow and brownish sandstone promontory here,

BELOW: Jinbaoshan's neat row of tombs.

directly in front of the pounding ocean, has been etched into all manner of artistic shapes by the weather and erosion. The terrain is other-worldly, attracting crowds of curious onlookers from Taipei.

As is so often the case, the Taiwanese have provided most of the rock formations with fanciful names, and for Taiwanese visitors half the fun of visiting is identifying them. The Queen's Head Rock could pass for the profile of the ancient Egyptian sovereign Nefertiti, while other rocks are variously dinosaurs, griffins, fish and even, in one case, the famous lost shoe of Cinderella.

To cope with the crush of visitors and to attract more, **Ocean World** (Haiyang Shijie; daily 8.30am–5pm, Sat–Sun until 5.30pm; charge) was opened near the entrance to Yeliu Scenic Area. Here, the usual contingent of dolphins, seals and other aquatic animals perform as at any sea park around the world. There is also an interesting 100-meter underwater aqarium tunnel.

Just a short distance south of Yeliu is the beach resort of **Feicui Bay** (Feicui Wan), which goes by the English name of Green Bay Seashore Recreation Club (clubhouse: daily 8am–11pm; beach: May–Oct daily 8am–11pm). Unfortunately, even for those who just want to promenade along the sands and perhaps take a paddle, an entry charge is exacted. In the height of summer, it is worth paying if only for a glimpse of the hurly-burly of Taiwanese beach culture – a little like Taipei-by-the-sea.

The bay itself offers parasailing, hang-gliding and sailing. Equipment for these activities can be rented. The Green Bay Club also provides an amusement park for children and several dozen beach-side bungalows. This expensive, overnight accommodation should be booked well in advance. Another upscale place to stay is the Howard Beach Resort Pacific Green Bay.

Map on page 156

The much-revered "King of Beasts" is, quite literally, found everywhere as guardian of important buildings and temples.

BELOW: seascape at Yeliu.

Map on page 156

Some of the stalls operating in Keelung's Miaokou Night Market have been serving up snacks for close to a century. The famous long-running stalls are marked with the Chinese characters meaning "old shop."

BELOW: Keelung night market.
RIGHT: fishing boats at Keelung port.

Keelung

From Green Bay, the highway runs through Wanli and on to the port of Keelung, Taiwan's northernmost city and second-largest port. **Keelung ❽** is the junction for the North Coast and Northeast Coast highways, and the northern terminus of the North-South Freeway (formally called the Sun Yat-sen Freeway). Its natural harbor has 57 deep-water piers and three mooring buoys that can handle vessels up to the 27,000-metric ton (30,000-ton) class. The port has excellent facilities for the loading and unloading of container ships; the container depots are massive. About 100 million metric tons (110 million tons) of freight are handled here annually. Only Kaohsiung, in the south, has more extensive port facilities.

Keelung's 390,000 inhabitants are basically wedded to the port trade and its offspring industries, but its setting and history make it an interesting stop. Like Danshui, Keelung has long been a center for Taiwan's contacts with the rest of the world. Japanese pirates, Spanish conquistadors, Dutch soldiers, American traders, French marines and Japanese imperialists have all made Keelung their base over the past three centuries.

Keelung's most famous landmark is an enormous white statue of Guanyin, the Goddess of Mercy. The 22.5-meter (74-ft) statue is propped up on a 4-meter (13-ft) high pedestal that enables the deity to watch over the entire city. Her stature is increased by the statue's position high on a hill in Zhongzheng Park (daily 9am–5pm). Two finely proportioned pavilions grace a knoll next to the statue, inside which stairs lead to a viewing perch. Farther up the hill from the park is Keelung's most important historical attraction: the remains of **Ershawan Fort** (Haimen Tianxian; daily 9am–5pm). Built in 1840, the only intact segment of the fort today is the restored fort gate, but the grounds, with replica cannon emplacements, make for an interesting stroll.

Peace Island, Lover's Lake

On the southern edge of the harbor mouth is **Peace Island** (Heping Dao), connected to Keelung proper by Peace Bridge. Its chief attraction is the dramatic coastline in Heping Dao Gongyuan (Heping Island Park; daily 6am–midnight; entrance and parking charge) on the seaward side of the island, which features more of the oddly weathered rock formations that distinguish the northeast coast.

Farther afield, next to the scenic **Qingren Lake** (Qingren Hu), to the north of Keelung, are the remains of the **Dawulun Fort** (Dawulun Baotai; daily 9am–5pm), another 19th-century cannon emplacement. It gets few tourists and is an atmospheric place to visit, though the fort's remains are in imminent danger of disappearing under the plant life that has sprouted over it.

For Taiwanese visitors, however, Keelung's chief attraction is not its historical sights but its bustling main night market, universally lauded as the best in northern Taiwan. Located in the center of town, in front of the Dianji Temple, it's known as the **Miaokou Yeshi**, or the "temple mouth night market" (24 hours; most vendors dusk–3am). With more than 300 food stalls, all the varieties of Taiwanese snacks are represented. A day in Keelung is not complete without a visit to the night market, if only to soak up the atmosphere. ❑

THE NORTHEAST COAST

Map on page 156

The nostalgic town of Jiufen is just the start of the attractions along the northeast coast, an area with impressive waterfalls, fine beaches, hot springs and peaceful countryside

Not far south of Keelung is the small inland town of Ruifang, the jumping-off point for one of northern Taiwan's most picturesque getaways. Its name meaning literally "nine parts," **Jiufen ⑨** is an arts and crafts mountain retreat that began life as a gold-rush town. Today, it might be little more than a ghost town if nostalgia hadn't reclaimed it.

Before the 1890s, locals claim that just nine families lived up in these hills northeast of Taipei – hence the name, which is a reference to provisions being brought by boat and divided into nine portions for the climb up from the shore. It was the discovery of gold dust in the sand by local women, who used the sediment that washed down from the hills to scour their cooking woks, that kick-started the tiny town's fortunes. By the mid-1930s, Jiufen was known as "little Shanghai," a place of bright lights, windfalls, and desperate toil. A decade later, the gold was gone and so were the bright lights.

Down memory lane

Locals claim that Jiufen first captured urban Taiwan's attention when it was featured in a television advertisement in the 1980s. Movie makers also had their eye on the place, with its picturesque laddered streets and antique homes, at around the same time. Finally it was Hou Xiao-xian, then Taiwan's pre-eminent film director, who, in 1989, clinched Jiufen's status as one of Taiwan's top-billed memory-lane travel destinations when he filmed his groundbreaking art-house portrayal of Taiwan's tragic 2-28 Incident *(see page 34)*, *City of Sadness*, there.

Today, the chief attraction of Jiufen is its narrow streets lined with teahouses, souvenir shops and snacks. Being a popular retreat for artists, it is also a good place to buy pottery – the **Jiufen Folk Art Gallery** (Jiufen Minsuguan; daily 10am–midnight) has items for sale. Most of the sights are of minor interest – the **Shengping Theater** (Shengping Juchang), once the focal point of Jiufen's bustling nightlife, the City of Sadness Restaurant (24 hours), used as a movie set – but cumulatively they evoke a charm that is second to none in Taiwan.

Follow the narrow streets up to the look-out that offers views of the wooded hills, an occasional temple or pagoda peeking out of the greenery, and, in the distance, the sparkling waters of Shenao Bay, with an ant-size fishing boat chugging out of the harbor, a faint chalk line of spume following in its wake. For a more strenuous workout, there's a steep walk up the path that snakes along the shoulder of Mt Keelung offering superlative views of the northeast coast.

It's also worth taking some time out to visit the interesting **Jiufen Gold Mining Museum** (Jiufen Kuang-

LEFT: an image of the lion stands guard at the Mazu temple in Suao. **BELOW:** Jishan Road, Jiufen is lined with interesting stalls.

Taiwan's biggest rock festival, the Ho-Hai-Yan Music Festival, is held over three days at Fulong Beach each summer. Some 20,000 revelers attend at any one time. Admission is free and trains run hourly between Taipei and Fulong.

BELOW: panning for gold at the Jiufen Gold Mining Museum.

shi Bowuguan; daily 10am–6pm; charge). Unfortunately, there are no English signs on the exhibits, which are mostly rock specimens. The museum curator gives a half-hour demonstration to all visitors of how Jiufen laborers once extracted gold from the sediment in the nearby hills; the demonstration needs no English translation. Many visitors like to stay overnight here; locals rent rooms for about NT$300 per night – watch for signs along Jishan and Qingbian roads – and some teahouses stay open all night the night before a holiday.

Train to Niagara

Ruifang is not only a staging post for Jiufen: it also sits at the head of the picturesque Pingxi railway line, which was originally built to carry coal to Keelung. The line now ferries nostalgic tourists on its narrow-gauge tracks about once an hour between 7am and 11.15pm (day passes available). Apart from the pleasures of a rustic train journey, the main reason to take a ride is to visit **Shifen Waterfall** ⑩ (Shifen Pubu; daily 8am–5.30pm; charge), a short trip from Ruifang and around 10 minutes' walk from Shifen station. Shifen Pubu is known locally as the "Niagara Falls of Taiwan," and, while there's obviously more than a trace of hyperbole in such an appellation, the falls are nevertheless impressive.

Back on the coast, the Northeast Coast Highway (Shengdao 2) moves out eastward from Keelung to coastal enclaves like Ruiping and Bitoujiao, a stone bluff overlooking the Pacific Ocean. Like Yeliu, to the northwest of Keelung, its rock formations make for a spectacular blend of land and sea. The area has a camping ground and walkways for viewing these rock formations. Next to Bitoujiao are the cliffs of Longdong – one of northern Taiwan's most popular destinations for serious climbing enthusiasts – and the **Longdong Bay Ocean Park** (Longdong

GOLD IN THE HILLS

Jiufen may once have been a gold-rush town, but the only gold nowadays is in the tourist industry. According to Zeng Shui-chi, the curator and owner of Jiufen Gold Mining Museum, the old methods by which gold was extracted from the sediment that washed down from the hills are forgotten by all but one man – Mr Zeng himself.

Mr Zeng recreates the gold extraction process in his small museum, reliving the skills he first learned at the age of 14. He first grinds sediment with a huge pestle and mortar, adding water and grinding again with a pedal-powered serrated metal wheel, transferring the results to a wooden slat that he splashes with water, allowing the chaff to flow away into a large pot.

After a while, the occasional sparkle begins to appear in the grit. Not long after that his work will have reduced a bucketful of sediment to half a small bowl of black mud, a miniature night sky twinkling with golden stars.

Jiufen may have forgotten its past in its quest for the tourist dollar, but Mr Zeng is determined to do his bit to make sure that at least the occasional visitor who strays from the gift shops and teahouses gets a glimpse of the days when hopefuls toiled under the sharp-eyed gaze of overseers to extract gold from the sand.

Nankou Haiyang Gongyuan; daily 8am–6pm; entrance and parking charge), with sea-water swimming pools, an aquarium and tourist boats that cruise the bay.

A few minutes' drive south of Bitoujiao lies Yanliao, though no self-respecting Taiwanese tourist would make the drive without stopping at the small town of Aodi, which lies midway and is famous for seafood that can be sampled at any of the many local restaurants. In Yanliao, a memorial stele honors Taiwan's soldiers and civilians who died resisting Japan's 1895 colonial occupation of Taiwan; Japanese forces came ashore here. The area has also been developed as yet another seaside resort and can get very crowded on summer weekends.

Fulong ⓫, the next stop on the Northeast Coast Highway, belies the notion that Taiwan's best beaches lie only in the southern reaches of the island. The white-sand beach here hugs the northern shore of a cape that juts into the Pacific Ocean. Because of its location, the sun rises on the right and sets on the left as one looks out to sea. To further enhance the setting, the cove is entirely surrounded by rolling green hills. Enthusiastic strollers will find that accessible shoreline stretches for kilometers in both directions. About 100 meters (110 yards) inland, a stream runs parallel to **Fulong Beach** (Fulong Haishui Yuchang; facilities: May–Oct daily 8am–6pm; charge), in effect forming a secondary beach. A bridge leads to the seashore, and sailing boats and windsurfing boards can be rented.

Historic trail

A little south of Fulong, at **Dali ⓬**, look out for the wonderfully ornate Daoist temple known as **Tiangong Miao**, or the Jade Emperor Temple. The temple is worth a stop in its own right, but it's also significant in that it marks the trailhead of the **Caoling Historic Trail** (Caoling Gudao), a meandering, and in parts flag-

 Map on page 156

 TIP

Trains run directly to Fulong from Taipei, via Ruifang, before continuing down the east coast, making it possible to visit Fulong as a full day's outing. The new National Highway No. 5 from Taipei to Ilan also makes road access much easier.

BELOW: the rocky cliffs of Cape Bitou.

TIP

On weekdays, the Caoling Historic Trail presents a rare opportunity to peacefully enjoy the countryside, but be warned that there are none of the usual amenities associated with tourism – bring plenty of water and possibly a picnic lunch.

stoned, path that was cleared in 1807 to facilitate the migration of Chinese immigrants from Taipei Basin to the fertile Lanyang Plain of Ilan County.

In its time, this was a pioneering route that enabled passage through the mountains that separate north and northeast Taiwan, thereby obviating the need for a dangerous sea journey along the windswept northern coastline. Most of the trail has now been abandoned, but the rustic section between Fulong and Dali has been restored, and takes around 3–4 hours on foot. Stone markers engraved with Chinese characters mark the way, and there are several pavilions en route to rest.

There is little to see between Dali and **Toucheng** ⓭, a tiny coastal village with a modest beach resort that is usually less crowded than Fulong or other northern beaches. Before reaching Toucheng, however, the coastal road does pass Miyue Wan, or Honeymoon Bay, a pleasant strip of beach that is popular with surfers. Also, as the road skirts the shore, travelers get a look at an offshore island called Guishan Dao (Turtle Island), so named for obvious reasons. Formerly a military garrison, the island is now open to tourists (May–Oct; apply to Tourism Bureau one month in advance).

One of the area's attractions lies in the hills behind Toucheng. About 5 km (3 miles) behind the village is **New Peak Falls** (Xinfeng Pubu). The falls are found 500 meters (550 yards) beyond the main entrance to the complex, inside a canyon. By stepping carefully down the rocky ledge, swimmers can slide into the refreshing water that cascades 50 meters (165 ft) down a stone chute.

Time for a soak

BELOW: hot-spring resort at Jiaoxi Wenquan.

The other chief attraction of this lovely region is the **Jiaoxi Hot Springs** ⓮ (Jiaoxi Wenquan), located around 7 km (4½ miles) north of Ilan, and in its hey-

Map on page 156

day – like many hot-spring resorts in the past – an infamous red-light district. Today, the small town has cleaned up its act and numerous hotels offer the opportunity for a refreshing soak in the area's health-bestowing waters. Small restaurants scattered about the town specialize in tasty and fresh seafood. For the faithful, there are two temples in Jiaoxi; farther down the main road is the **Temple of Heavenly Accord** (Xietian Miao).

Less than 10 minutes' drive into the hills behind the Jiaoxi Wenquan is **Five Peaks Flag Scenic Area** (Wufengqi Fengjingqu). Vendors around the parking lot sell the area's sought-after products of dried mushrooms, preserved plums and other fruits, fresh ginger and medicinal herbs. Among the last is a furry little doll with four "legs" formed by roots, and two "eyes" made with buttons. The vendors call it *jingoumao* (Golden Dog Fur). It's actually a fern-plant that roots in stone and grows from remote cliff sides. When rubbed into cuts, scrapes, lacerations and other festering skin wounds, it stops the bleeding immediately and promotes rapid healing with a minimum of unsightly scarring.

The trail from the parking lot leads to **Wufengqi Falls** ⓯ (Wufengqi Pubu), a vine-and-fern-spangled waterfall that cascades musically in sprays and sheets down a 60-meter (200-ft) cliff. A viewing spot faces the falls from across the stream. Cement steps lead up along a side of the canyon, enabling one to get close enough to cool off in its stinging spray.

Shengdao 9 continues south from Jiaoxi to the bright little city of **Ilan** ⓰. Although this is the county seat, and a good place to stop for lunch or perhaps overnight at one of the many hotels, Ilan has little to hold the visitor for long. Taiwanese visitors generally descend on the town to pick up supplies of the local specialities known as "Ilan's four treasures." Of these only *yashang* – duck cured in brine and smoked in bamboo cane – is likely to be of interest to the foreign palate.

Temple guardian at a Daoist temple dedicated to Mazu, Goddess of the Sea. There are some 500 temples dedicated to Mazu in Taiwan.

BELOW: bobbing fishing boats at Suao port.

On to Suao

Fifteen minutes south of Ilan lies the international seaport of **Suao** ⓱, though by no means on the same scale as Keelung or Kaohsiung. It's worth a stop for two reasons: its famous cold springs and the nearby fishing port of Nanfang Ao.

Suao's cold springs (daily 8am–10pm; charge) were discovered by the Japanese in 1928. Rich in bubbling carbon dioxide, locals compare it to soaking in natural "soda water" and have even taken to bottling the stuff as a drink. Definitely only an experience for the hardy in the cold winter months, a dip in the cold springs is a perfect antidote to the heat of summer – once the initial shock wears off. Unusually for Taiwan, outdoor communal pools are available (the sexes are segregated). It's expected that you wear swimwear; you will be required to rent some if you don't have your own.

Suao's international harbor is a dull affair, but that's all the more reason to head approximately 3 km (2 miles) south of town to the small fishing port of **Nanfang Ao**. It is famous mostly for its seafood, which is cooked fresh in innumerable restaurants, but foreign visitors are inevitably charmed by the town's timeless and bustling harbor crowded with gaily colored, high-prowed fishing boats. ❑

SOUTH OF TAIPEI

Close to the capital can be found a surprising mix of attractions, from displays of aboriginal culture and fascinating cave temples to a ceramics town filled with kilns and shops

Map on page 156

A lovely ride back to Taipei is in store for travelers who double back up the Northeast Coast Highway from Suao, then head inland along Shengdao 9 (Provincial Highway No. 9) towards Pinglin and beyond to Xindian, just south of Taipei. The highway twists and turns through the spectacular Central Mountain Range, revealing vistas of spellbinding beauty as it zigzags back to Taipei, taking in the tea-growing area of Pinglin en route.

South from Xindian, in the opposite direction from Taipei, the mountainous retreat of **Wulai** ⑱ is popular for its Atayal aboriginal performances and for its hot springs. Displays of aboriginal culture in Taiwan are sometimes rather tacky, and the performances here at the **Wulai Aboriginal Culture Village** (Wulai Yuanzhumin Wenhua Cun; daily 9am–7pm) are an example. Nevertheless, given that few visitors get the opportunity to travel into the remotest parts of mountainous Taiwan that sustain some pockets of traditional aboriginal culture, a visit to one of the island's aboriginal "theme parks" is a worthwhile outing. Atayal dance performances are held four times a day (charge for theater), and admission to a small folk art museum is included in the charge.

A cable car (daily 7.30am–10pm; charge) carries visitors across the gorge to a place in the mountains appropriately called **Dreamland** (Yunxian Leyuan; daily 8.30am–5pm; charge), which has additional ethnic performances, a pond for rowing and fishing, a small amusement park for children, restaurant/coffee shop (open until 10 or 11pm), spa, swimming pool and hotel. Traditional tribal arts and crafts, wild mountain mushrooms, Taiwan-grown Chinese herbs and souvenirs are available in stores and many restaurants offer exotic fare like snake and freshwater eel and, intermittently, wild boar and deer.

During the chilly winter months, Wulai is favored for its outdoor hot springs. In the popular hot-spring resort areas of Yangmingshan and Beitou, hot-spring water is piped into hotels. Here in Wulai it's possible to soak in an outdoor pool of piping hot water and commune with nature. The hot springs can be found on the north side of town after crossing the suspension bridge. There are also a number of quality hot-spring hotels.

Another Wulai activity, though more popular with Taipei residents than with overseas visitors, is the hiking trail that leads out from the town into **Doll Valley** (Wawa Gu; mountain pass from village police station; charge) for a round trip of about 5 km (3 miles). Apart from its mountain views, its chief draw is its abundance of bird life and genuine Atayal hamlets.

Temple restoration

Southwest of Taipei are several other places well worth a stop. Only 20 km (12 miles) away from Taipei

LEFT: the Wulai cable car.
BELOW: a performance at Wulai Aboriginal Cultural Village.

Taiwanese not only enjoy eating papaya, but also drink its juice, blended with milk and called "mugua niunai."

is the busy old town of **Sanxia** . The town's old center is worth exploring, based around Minquan Street, Heping Street, Renai Street and Zhongshan Road. Many of the old buildings on these streets rate among the best-preserved examples of late Qing architecture on the island. Nevertheless, Sanxia's chief claim to fame is the **Sanxia Temple of the Divine Progenitor** (Sanxia Zushi Miao; daily 4am–10pm), originally built in 1769.

The temple is among Taiwan's most renowned, due to the efforts of Li Mei-shu, a master craftsman who dedicated 36 years of his life to restoring it after its destruction by a fire in 1948. It is said that each of the celebrated 122 stone columns took 1,000 days to complete. Today, long after Li's death, the restoration work continues under the supervision of Li's son, and the results are commonly lauded as the best example of temple art in Taiwan and amongst the best in the Chinese world. The Li Mei-shu Memorial Gallery (Li Mei-shu Jinian Guan ; Sat–Sun 10am–5pm; groups by arrangement Mon–Fri; charge; www.limei shu.org) can be found at 10, Lane 43, Zhonghua Road in Sanxia.

Potter's haven

A short hop away is **Yingge** town, a potter's haven. Some of the factories allow tours, providing a chance to watch how "muddy" clay is transformed into a beautifully painted Chinese vase, treasured in the Ming or Qing courts of old. Many shops line pedestrian-only Taoci Laojie (Old Pottery Street), selling everything from simple earthenware to the finest porcelain, and from ordinary teapots to delicate figures – some of which are predictable while others exquisite.

The town's newest artistic masterpiece is a rather large one – the **Yingge Ceramics Museum** (Yingge Taoci Bowuguan; Tue–Fri 9.30am–5pm, Sat–Sun until 6pm; charge; www.ceramics.tpc.gov.tw), opened in late 2000. Located at 200 Wenhua Road, the large, airy structure, itself a work of spatial art, is part of an impressive display on the story of Taiwan ceramics, surrounded by a 14-hectare (35-acre) park filled with displays of ceramics. Audio guidance is provided in English.

Several other attractions within hailing distance of Taipei – and all to the south – beckon travelers. To the southwest, past Yingge on Shengdao 3 (Provincial Highway No. 3) is the old town of **Daxi** . On the Dahan River, main tributary to the Danshui River that flows through Taipei and out to sea, Daxi is a history buff's delight. Up until the days of Japan's colonial rule of Taiwan the waters were navigable this far upstream. Trade was brisk, camphor the main draw. The main dock was by today's Heping Road. In the old commercial area formed by Heping and Zhongshan roads, old baroque-facade commercial establishments stand shoulder to shoulder, many built by Western trading firms and later by Japanese. Facades bear the names of the business concerns and wonderful carvings of birds, animals, flowers, and plants.

Today the narrow-front, deep shophouse-style locations house traditional businesses producing dried beancurd, religious-worship items, and old-style wooden furniture, and also engaged in ironmongering and stone working, the goings-on visible from the street. Tourists are welcome to come in and watch.

BELOW: pottery found on Yingge Old Street.

The entire district has been refurbished, street-wiring put underground, making for a stimulating step back into the past. Local tourists snap up the dried bean-curd, for which Daxi is renowned. The secret is said to be in the mineral-rich waters of the surrounding hills.

Map on page 156

Theme parks

The **Shimen Reservoir** ㉒ (Shimen Shuiku; Mon–Fri 8am–5pm, Sat–Sun 7.30am–6pm; charge) nearby offers pathways, gardens, viewing pavilions, eco-tours from the visitor centre (Chinese), displays, motorboat rides, and restaurants that specialize in fish caught by the Shimen Dam, completed in 1964 with American aid. It's more of an attraction for locals than it is for foreign visitors.

More quirky, but in a similar vein, is **Window on China** ㉓ (Xiaoren Guo; Mon–Fri 9am–5pm, Sat–Sun and holidays 9am–6pm, July–Aug Mon–Fri until 8pm, Sat–Sun until 9pm, seasonal time variations; charge), near the town of Long-tan. On a site covering 25 hectares (67.5 acres), the most important buildings and temples in Taiwan, as well as many notable buildings in mainland China, not to mention the Sphinx and the Leaning Tower of Pisa (among other international architectural triumphs), have been erected in miniature. Vegetation is provided by countless bonsai trees grown to proportionally correct sizes.

Reactions to the park tend to be mixed. Some visitors come away enchanted, others find it all somewhat tacky.

If Xiaoren Guo is not enough fun, close by is the **Leofoo Village** (Liufu Leyuan; daily 9am–5pm; charge), which manages to somehow pack in the Wild West, Arabia, Southeast Asia, assorted carnival rides and even a wild-game safari into one place.

One of Sanxia Zushi Temple's (see page 178) *122 intricate stone columns – each carved from a single slab of stone – depicts a plum tree, with 50 different kinds of birds on its branches.*

BELOW: Window on China, an outdoor park that contains replicas of world-famous architectural wonders.

Map
on page
156

The sanheyuan –
literally "three-box
courtyard" – served
as a miniature
fortress for an
extended Hakka
family, with a central
building and two
smaller structures
flanking a garden
protected by a front
wall. Such houses are
found in Hakka
villages like Guanxi.

BELOW: pagoda
below Shitoushan.

A more traditional experience can be found just off Shengdao 3, south of Leofoo, at the village of **Guanxi** ㉔. After Meinong *(see pages 246–7)* in the south of Taiwan, Guanxi is Taiwan's best-preserved Hakka village, having a number of impressive ancestral homes built in the Hakka courtyard style the Chinese call *sanheyuan*. The oldest, the **Fan Family Home**, at 47 Pinglin Village, dates from 1700.

East of Guanxi and Shimen Shuiku is **Hsinchu** ㉕, more famous for its Science Park *(see opposite page)* than as a tourist attraction. That said, Hsinchu is not without its attractions, though none compelling enough to rate the city a special visit. In the center of town (at the intersection of Zhongzheng and Dongmen roads) look out for the Qing dynasty Yingximen Gate, which like Taipei's city gates stands as a reminder of the days when Hsinchu was walled. On either side of the gate can be seen what was formerly the city moat. In the south of town is the uninspiring Zhongshan Park, which is home to a small zoo and next to Hsinchu's small Gongmiao, or Confucius Temple.

On the Lion's Head

Not far south of Hsinchu – on Shengdao 3, about halfway between Taipei and Taichung – is **Lion's Head Mountain** ㉖ (Shitoushan; daily; parking charge), some 20 km (12 miles) east of both north-south freeways. It is a pleasant excursion for travelers bound for central Taiwan. When viewed from the proper angle, the peak does bear a resemblance to the king of beasts. But the mountain's main significance is its role as a center of Buddhism during the past 75 years; a number of the temples here were built directly in natural caves found in the mountain. There are also a number of small shrines and pagodas.

From the arched entrance above the parking lot, it is possible to hike up the lion's head, then down along its spine, visiting the temples and other sites along the way. From the old stone arch at the entrance, 1,500 steps lead up to the top. From there, a path leads down to the tail of the lion. The round-trip walk takes about three hours, with the last part a stroll through flower-scented forests and bamboo patches.

The first main temple on the path is the Zhonghua Tang. Healthy vegetarian meals cooked by Buddhist nuns are available in several of the temples on the route. The main shrine hall of the first temple, just above the dining room, rises on beautifully sculpted stone columns that depict celestial animals and ancient Buddhist legends. The massive multi-storied structure just beyond the temple is the **Kaishan Monastery**, a different kind of study and activities center for resident monks and nuns. Feel free to inspect the ornate temples, observe monks and nuns at their daily duties, and listen to the sounds of the forest.

The steep path winds up around the lion's "mane" to the **Moon-Gazing Pavilion**, serving well its purpose on moonlit nights. From there, the paved trail cuts past several more cave-temples, the Pagoda of Inspiration, monastic quarters, bridge and viewing terraces. The rustic cave-shrines of the **Water Screen Convent** are the last major sights on the trail, which deposits hikers back near the parking lot. ❑

Silicon Valley of the East

Whenever Taiwan is referred to as the Republic of Computers, it's mostly due to a large plot of land that was, as late as the 1970s, home to a tea plantation. At that time, Taiwan had no high-tech industry, and the government was looking for ways to stem the flow of the island's best brains from migrating overseas. The answer was the Hsinchu Science Park (www.sipa.gov.tw), an experiment that aimed to incubate a breed of entrepreneurs who would hopefully launch Taiwan into a new era.

The results speak for themselves. Today, Taiwan is one of the world's foremost producers of everything from sound cards to scanners. With more than 390 companies employing over 117,000 people, the park is already so crowded that additional science parks are now operating in Tainan, Taichung and Miaoli counties.

However, in 1981, when the park was first founded, there were no signs that its present fortunes were headed this way. The former tea plantations had to be converted into an environment that would attract the best Taiwanese brains, who had become accustomed to high salaries and living conditions overseas, many of them in California. Developments included an international school, medical facilities, luxury housing and landscaped gardens. Returnees were offered tax breaks and low-cost facilities, and, by the late 1980s, Taiwanese venture-capital financing was available to anyone peddling a convincing high-tech start-up.

The miracle did not happen overnight, however. Initially, it was the producers of computer peripherals and PC clones that seized the opportunity to set up in Hsinchu. Commentators are quick to point out that the park's initial success was due to its luck of being in the right place at the right time: just as IBM PC clones became big business in the US, Hsinchu was able to offer itself as a low-cost manufacturing base. Initially producing components for international names, it

wasn't very long before Hsinchu companies began launching their own-brand computers.

But it was government initiatives to spur the development of integrated circuits (IC), or semiconductors – the "brains" of computers – that really put Hsinchu on the map. Research had commenced in 1974, when Taiwan's state-run Industrial Technology Research Institute established the island's first semiconductor foundry with licensed US technology. By 1985, it had evolved into Taiwan Semiconductor Manufacturing Corp. (TSMC), now the world's largest contract manufacturer of semiconductors.

It has not all been plain sailing, however. Worldwide price wars have resulted in limited pricing traction for both PC hardware and semiconductors in recent years. Companies which were once spoilt by seemingly unending expansion now face greater competition and tighter margins on their profits. Still, Taiwan's IT sector continues to grow, and, with companies branching out into telecommunications and opto-electronics, there are clear signs that the park is by no means content to rest on its laurels. ❑

RIGHT: a technician at Hsinchu.

WEST-CENTRAL TAIWAN

While most people live on the fertile plains, the real attractions of this region lie in the mountains and offshore

Central Taiwan, roughly covering the region from Miaoli to Chiayi, west of the Central Mountain Range, is many things. On the one hand, it boasts the most varied terrain on the island. From the summit of snow-capped Yushan, or Jade Mountain, the landscape drops 3,952 meters (12,800 ft) to the harbor at Taichung.

The alluvial plain that divides the highlands from the Taiwan Strait is filled by vast green rice fields and plantations of bananas, pineapples, papayas, sugar cane, tea and other crops. Yet the same alluvial plain is one of Taiwan's key urban heartlands. Picturesque scenes of rural idyll are wont to give way with surprising rapidity to sprawling towns and cities, smoke-belching factories and ugly garbage dumps.

In truth, while the low-lying plains are home to some important cultural attractions, the traveler is best rewarded by concentrating on the island's surprisingly underrated Central Mountain Range. The most famous attraction is Alishan, the object of pilgrimage for its sunrises over what the Taiwanese refer to poetically as the *yunhai*, or "sea of clouds." In fact, as Alishan abuts Yushan National Park, many of the mountain's sunrise tours end up straying into the park.

Central Taiwan was hit by a devastating earthquake on September 21, 1999, and although complete recovery has been impossible, great strides have been made. The celebrated tourist area of Riyue Tan, or Sun Moon Lake, was made a national scenic area and is enjoying a renaissance. With much of the mountain region's topsoil rendered unstable by the terrific shaking it received and by later typhoons, landslides can be expected to occasionally shut down roads during the wet summer months from May through September.

Visited by relatively few foreign tourists, the islands that lie off Taiwan proper in the Taiwan Strait remain among Taiwan's best-kept secrets. Until the 1990s, Kinmen and Mazu were off-limits military outposts, but those who have visited after they opened to tourism in 1992 have discovered them to be fascinating museums of antique Hokkien fishing villages, with the added interest of military history. More barren are the low-lying Penghu Islands, formerly known as the Pescadores. Blasted by cruel winds in winter, in summer they become a haven for seekers of surf and sun, though for foreign visitors the prime attraction, as at Kinmen and Mazu, is likely to be the islands' perfectly preserved villages, which can be explored in traffic-free leisure on rented motorcycles. ❏

PRECEDING PAGES: Mazu island coastline at dawn.
LEFT: farmer in Central Taiwan transplanting wet-rice seedlings.

TAICHUNG AND ENVIRONS

With cosmopolitan Taichung as a convenient base, the visitor can explore the arts and crafts of a region that has its fair share of striking temples, shrines and museums

Map on page 188

Less than an hour out of Taipei, travelers on the main southbound highway begin to see dramatic changes in the surrounding countryside. Factories are fewer, and lush farmland more prevalent. The gray tones of the capital give way to green patchworks of ripening rice, fruit plantations and vegetable plots.

Taichung

The urban center of central Taiwan is **Taichung ❶**, whose name means, not coincidentally, Taiwan Central. As Taiwanese cities go, Taichung may be a long way from rivaling Tainan in terms of cultural attractions, but it is a far more leisurely paced city than, say, Taipei. Comparisons to Taipei before the big boom of the 1970s are to a certain extent inevitable but, as any Taichungite will be quick to point out, Taichung has its own style and flavor. Taiwanese is spoken here far more than in the capital, and, with more space to spread out, Taichung tends to do things on a grander scale than Taipei does – offering some of the island's biggest restaurants, nightclubs and karaoke parlors.

Taiwan's third-largest city, Taichung has a population of around 1 million people. Located in a shallow basin about 20 km (12 miles) from the coast and 150 km (93 miles) south of Taipei, Taichung enjoys the island's best year-round climate, without the seasonal extremes of heat and cold that mark the north and south.

Taichung was founded in 1721 by immigrants from the Chinese mainland. They originally named it Datun, or "Big Mound." The city's current name was adopted by the Japanese after they took possession of Taiwan in 1895. Today, 20-hectare (49-acre) **Zhongshan Park** occupies the hillock upon which the original settlement was built. The two pavilions rising above the lotus-filled lake are a Taichung landmark.

Although Taichung is a pleasant enough city, for the visitor its chief assets are in its dining and nightlife, making it a good place to be based while exploring more interesting scenic and cultural destinations around the region. The city itself has only a few attractions worth taking time to visit.

The **Martyrs' Shrine** (Zhonglie Zi; Tue–Sun 9am–4.30pm) on Lixing Road northeast of Zhongshan Park was erected in 1970. Its design provides a superb example of the harmony and balance inherent in classical Chinese architecture. Many locals claim that it is even more outstanding than the famous martyrs' shrines in Hualien and Taipei. Protected by two bronze guardian lions, the shrine commemorates the 72 Chinese who were beheaded in 1911 by the Manchu court, on the eve of the republican revolution.

Next to the Zhonglie Zi, on Shuangshi Road, is Taichung's tranquil **Confucius Temple** (Kong Miao;

LEFT: parade joy at Taichung.
BELOW: Taichung's Martyrs' Shrine.

The Chinese words meaning "goldfish" are phonetically identical with the two words meaning "gold in abundance."

Tue–Sun 8.30am–5pm), notable for the constrained design of its roof. In this shrine, the eaves curve gently downward, cleaving close to the earth rather than flaring audaciously heavenward. And indeed, Earth, not Heaven, was the sage's prime concern. On the altar is a simple black stone stele with Confucius's name engraved in gold on its smooth unadorned surface. Although he believed in spirits and deities, Confucius insisted that people should steer clear of them. Every year on 28 September (Teacher's Day), the birthday of Confucius, the temple hosts a colorful spectacle of ancient rituals and archaic costumes.

Happy Buddhas

The **Baojue Temple** (Baojue Si; daily), on the northern edge of the city on Jianxing Road, contains one of the largest and fattest Buddha images in all Taiwan. This is the proverbial happy Buddha, the golden shimmering Milefo, who sits laughing on a massive pedestal in one corner of the temple compound, towering 30 meters (100 ft) above the ground. Smaller statues of the same Bud-

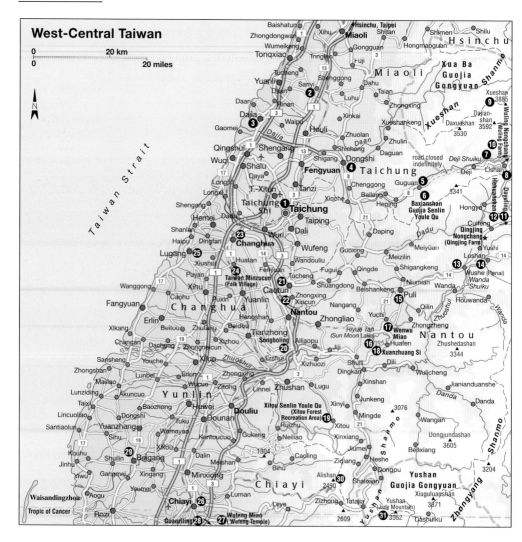

dha are also scattered around the complex. Within the hollow pedestal of the giant pot-bellied Milefo is a room used for meetings, while in the adjacent building are several thousand cremation urns.

Also worth visiting is the **Taichung Folk Park** (Taichung Minsu Gongyuan; Tue–Sun 8.30am–10pm; charge; www.folkpark.org.tw) on Luxun Road. Established in 1979, it features traditional Minnan, or Hokkien, architecture and arts and crafts exhibits. The buildings, with their sweeping needle-pointed roofs, are exquisite, and the works of folk art inside number over 3,000. Of particular interest are the exhibitions of Taiwanese crafts presented by artists in residence.

The **Taichung Museum of Natural Science** (Taichung Ziran Kexue Bowuguan; Tue–Sun 9am–5pm; charge; www.nmns.edu.tw) on Guanqian Road, northwest of Zhongshan Park and off Taichung Harbor Road, is aimed at young children as is the adjoining Space Theater. The **National Taiwan Museum of Fine Arts** (Guoli Taiwan Meishuguan; Tue–Fri 9am–5pm, Sat–Sun until 6pm, English tours daily at 10.30am and 2.30pm; free; www.tmoa.gov.tw), west of Zhongshan Park on Wuquan West Road, is an ugly brick building, but has 24 galleries devoted to modern Taiwanese and foreign art in mostly changing exhibits.

Those with children should take a look at **Ocean World Education Hall** (Taichung Shengwu Jiaoyuguan; daily 9am–7pm; charge) on Wenxin South 7th Road. An aquarium of the sort that can be found all over Asia these days, it has a shark pool and a section devoted to jellyfish, among other attractions.

The shopping scene

Taichung's main shopping district is located along Zhongzheng Road, west of Zhongshan Park and between the railway station and Wuquan Road. Along with the usual department stores, 7-Eleven outlets and fast-food restaurants are silk fabric shops, fresh-produce markets and interesting herbal shops, redolent with the pungent aromas of medicinal plants. Taichung residents are particularly proud of Jingming 1st Street, in the center of town, which was Taiwan's first genuine pedestrian mall, complete with alfresco cafés, restaurants and even a bar or two, along with some boutiques. It's a highly popular place for Taichung's chic set to promenade, and a recommended spot to relax over a drink and people-watch.

In the evening, Taichung's most famous night market **Zhonghua Night Market** (Zhonghua Yeshi) comes into action on Zhonghua Road. It stays open until the early-morning hours and features numerous long-established food stalls that can usually be picked out by their large numbers of diners. Elsewhere, Taichung's nightlife is less cosmopolitan than Taipei's, but no less lively.

A 20-minute drive northwest of downtown Taichung, on Taichung Harbor Road, is **Donghai University** (Donghai Daxue). The entire wooded 139-hectare (343-acre) campus was built according to the architectural style of the Tang dynasty, the period regarded as China's golden age of culture and the arts. This subtle and restrained style differs radically from the sometimes garish style that prevailed in China after the Ming period. Almost all campus buildings are constructed in the square, squat, colonnaded Tang style, with plain

Map on page 188

TIP

The weekend editions of the local English-language newspapers have listings of nightlife venues that are popular with foreigners and Taiwanese alike.

BELOW: getting around Taichung.

Map on page 188

tiled roofs. A modern departure is the abstract Christian Chapel, designed by Sino-American architect I.M. Pei to symbolize a pair of hands touching in prayer.

Just 10 km (6 miles) northeast of Taichung lies an interesting example of landscape gardening, the **Encore Gardens** (Yage Huayuan; Mon–Fri 8.30am–10.30pm, Sat 8.30am–midnight, Sun 8am–midnight; charge). The colorful flower gardens are decorated with copies of famous European statues and a fountain, lit by colored lights, dances to an odd mix of Western and South American rhythms.

Carving a reputation

Birthday celebration of Mazu, Goddess of the Sea.

BELOW: ruins of the Lin family home.
RIGHT: celebrants at the Mazu festival in Dajia.

Some 40 km (25 miles) north of Taichung is **Sanyi ❷**, a small town stretched along one main road that parallels National Freeway No. 1. The town is famous throughout Taiwan as the island's woodcarving center, and indeed this is such a booming business here that it is estimated that around half the local population support themselves through the craft. Quality varies, as do prices, and much of what is produced here, mainly big and heavy pieces, is aimed at the Taiwanese market. It is fascinating to stroll around the shops, and perhaps to stop and watch a local craftsman transform a large tree root, for example, into a masterpiece.

On Shengdao 17 (Provincial Highway No. 17), 25 km (16 miles) southwest of Sanyi, is the small town of **Dajia ❸**. It is significant for its **Zhenlan Temple** (Zhenlan Gong; daily 3.30am–11pm), which houses one of Taiwan's most revered images of Mazu *(see pages 66–7)*, the Holy Mother, protectress of fishermen and the island's patron saint. The image was brought to Taiwan centuries ago by fishermen from Fujian province, and before her birthday on the 23rd day of the third lunar month the image sets off on an eight-day pilgrimage around central Taiwan in a palanquin accompanied by thousands of pilgrims. ❑

LOST LIN HISTORY

While the tragedy of the 9-21 Earthquake – so-called because it took place on September 21, 1999 – was overwhelmingly human, it also caused an important cultural loss. Reconstruction in the aftermath of the earthquake was understandably focused on rebuilding lives, and certain cultural relics have almost disappeared for good.

Chief among them is the 200-year old Lin Family Gardens in Wufeng, just a 10-minute drive from downtown Taichung. The Lins were one of Taiwan's wealthiest aristocratic families. Most of them emigrated after the Nationalists took over the island, leaving behind their sprawling, classically designed home, complete with ponds and gardens. In the two years before the earthquake struck, NT$100 million had been spent restoring the mansions to their former splendor, and they were poised to open to the public. In less than a minute, the earthquake practically leveled them. Tragically, two members of the Lin family were also killed when their home collapsed.

Restoration work on the national historic site has long been underway, but for the foreseeable future, for reasons of safety, the complex is closed to the public.

THE CENTRAL CROSS-ISLAND HIGHWAY

Map on page 188

Mountain resorts, farms and hot springs punctuate the spectacular Central Cross-Island Highway, which weaves its way past the island's rich geographical features

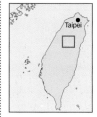

North and then east of Taichung, the Central Cross-Island Highway stretches for 200 km (120 miles) from Dongshi through Taroko Gorge to the east coast. The islanders claim no visit to Taiwan is complete without a trip across this road, for it displays – with striking beauty – the full gamut of the island's natural attractions: lush subtropical valleys and snow-capped peaks, alpine forests and rocky ravines, steamy hot springs and roaring rivers, mountain lakes and the shimmering sea.

The highway was completed in 1960 at great human cost. Ten thousand laborers, most of them retired servicemen who had fought on the mainland in the 1940s, struggled for four years to complete the road and hundreds either lost their lives or were injured on the project.

In two places, the highway forks. At Lishan, the north route traverses the upper spine of the Central Mountain Range to reach Ilan and the Northeast Coast Highway, 110 km (68 miles) away; the south route heads to Dayuling. At Dayuling, the location of the second fork, one route moves east through Taroko Gorge; the other cuts south 40 km (25 miles) around Hehuanshan, the Mountain of Harmonious Happiness, to Wushe and Lushan hot-springs resort, leading back to Taichung or on to Sun Moon Lake.

After the 9-21 Earthquake, the highway was blocked off by landslides and structural damage for quite some time. Not long after reopening further weakening from typhoons caused another collapse. The government has closed, indefinitely, the section from just east of Guguan to just east of Deji. All sites listed in this chapter are still open and accessible, however, with a detour via Shengdao 14 through Puli, also called the New Central Cross-Island Highway.

The western half of the Central Mountain Range, between Guguan and Lishan, sometimes resembles Switzerland more than a subtropical country. Visitors should let the terrain guide their choice of clothes: a sweater or jacket is often welcome at these altitudes.

Earthquake devastation

The first 20 km (12 miles) from **Dongshi ❹**, the most devastated town in Taiwan's 1999 earthquake, lead past a series of alternating rice fields and vineyards. The first notable village is **Guguan ❺**, or Valley Pass, a hot-springs resort that is located approximately 1,000 meters (3,280 ft) above sea level. Guguan has undergone major tourist development, and features numerous hotels and inns with piped hot-spring water, restaurants and handicraft shops. Despite concern on the part of geologists that the area is unstable as a result of the earthquake,

LEFT: the Central Cross-Island Highway cuts across steep mountains.
BELOW: rice seedlings.

Crunchy rose apple, or "lotus in the mist," is a fruit enjoyed by the Taiwanese.

BELOW: terraced fruit orchards, Fushoushan Nongchang.

the tourists are back. At Guguan, a side road leads to the **Eight Immortals Mountain National Forest Recreation Area** (Baxianshan Guojia Senlin Youle Qu; daily 7am–5pm). The virgin forest here is a popular destination for bird-watchers. Beyond Guguan, the highway climbs steeply for a few kilometers into the Central Mountain Range. At the **Deji Reservoir** ❼ (Deji Shuiku), Taiwan's highest, a torrent of water gushes beneath the impressive hydroelectric plant.

Lishan

East of Guguan is **Pear Mountain** ❽ (Lishan) on the crest of the Central Mountain Range, near the Central Cross-Island Highway's halfway point. Shengdao 7, to Ilan in the northeast, begins here.

Swept by alpine breezes and drifting mists, lodges and restaurants dot the slopes of this mountain village, settled by decommissioned soldiers and Atayal aborigines after the highway was pushed through. The **Lishan Guest House**, an alpine version of Taipei's Grand Hotel, features terraces, pavilions and sculpted shrubbery in its spacious grounds. This was one of Chiang Kai-shek's scores of villas, like most others rarely visited but with staff always at the ready. Lishan is enchanting in spring (February to April), with apple, pear and peach trees in full blossom.

An interesting side trip from Lishan is **Fortunate Life Mountain Farm** (Fushoushan Nongchang; daily 6.30am–9pm; guided tours daily 8.30am, 4pm; entrance and parking charge; www.fushoushan.com.tw). Essentially a large fruit orchard spread across a hilltop, Fushoushan appears more European than Asian. The entrance is through an arched gate less than 1 km (1,100 yards) south of Lishan village. From there, a pine-lined drive leads past a church and steeple in a 5-km (3-mile) ascent. Terraced acres of apple and pear orchards surround West-

ern-style farmhouses. Trees are braced against the stiff mountain wind by elaborate bamboo scaffolding; individual fruits are protected in bags from insects and birds. When in season, these fruits are on sale here. At the entrance of the farm is a small museum of local artifacts and illustrations.

Along the Fushoushan drive is **Huagong Tianjin**, a small café where Chiang Kai-shek kept a private holiday bungalow. The road ends at Huagong, a knoll guarded by giant wind-torn trees.

Mountain resort

Lishan is the staging point for mountaineering expeditions to **Snow Mountain** ❾ (Xueshan), Taiwan's second-highest peak at 3,885 meters (12,746 ft). The climbing season is October to December and March to April. January and February on occasion see snowfalls, which make the trails impassable, and at other times of the year rain, winds and the risk of landslides make an ascent too dangerous.

Apart from spectacular mountain views, for many climbers, one of the reasons to visit this remote part is to see some of Taiwan's native flora and fauna. This, after all, is the habitat of the Formosan black bear, though sightings are extremely rare these days even for those who know where to look. Lucky hikers, however, may see deer and white-faced flying squirrels.

The ascent of the mountain begins at **Wuling Recreational Farm** ❿ (Wuling Nongchang; daily; entrance and parking charge; www.wuling-farm.com.tw), a popular mountain resort – originally founded by the government for retired servicemen – offering spectacular views of the surrounding peaks. A 2½-hour hike from the farm is a hostel at 2,440 meters (8,000 ft), which climbers use as an overnight staging post for the final 2½-hour assault on the summit.

Map on page 188

The four-day, round-trip expedition up Xueshan requires a special permit (for three people minimum) and prior permission from the National Police Administration, 7 Zhongxiao East Road, Section 1, Taipei; tel: (02) 2357-7377; www.npa.gov.tw

BELOW: autumn colors at Wuling Nongchang.

Map on page 188

TIP

Adventurous travelers should ook for a guide in Wushe to take them to nearby Hongxiang village. Approachable only on foot, Hongxiang has a non-commercial hot spring where bathers can bask in natural surroundings.

BELOW: Lushan hot-spring inns.
RIGHT: view from the Central Cross-Island Highway.

Still on Shengdao 8 and 30 km (19 miles) beyond Lishan, **Dayuling ⓫** village straddles the highest point of the highway, at an elevation of 2,600 meters (8,530 ft). East of here, the highway descends rapidly past Wenshan Wenquan (Wenshan Hot Springs) and through the Taroko Gorge to the east coast.

Dayuling is the junction for Shengdao 14, which heads southward from **Hehuanshan ⓬**, the Mountain of Harmonious Happiness, and continues to the Lushan Hot Springs and Wushe (Renai). Hehuanshan, looming 3,420 meters (11,220 ft) above sea level, is just 9 km (6 miles) south of Dayuling. From January to early March, slushy snowfalls sometimes turn the mountain white temporarily. This is Taiwan's only vehicle-accessible site where snow can be enjoyed, and locals flock here whenever there are reports of a coming downfall. Needless to say, the driving is treacherous. Even in the heat of summer, temperatures up here rarely rise above 15°C (59°F). Hiking, mountain climbing and hot-spring bathing are the most attractive activities at that time of year.

Further on, the settlement of **Renai ⓭** (Wushe) is embraced by the tall peaks of the Central Mountain Range. Although its name means "foggy community," it is renowned for its crystal-clear alpine air, as well as a profusion of wild cherry and plum blossoms in early spring. Far below, the green mirror of **Wanda Reservoir** (Wanda Shuiku) is surrounded by abrupt mountain escarpments. The Chinese word for landscape is *shanshui* – literally, mountains and water – and this lake is a perfect example of that expression. A trail leads from the village to the lake, where only shore fishing is permitted. In Wushe village are a few local inns and ethnic-minority handicraft shops.

Wushe made its mark on Taiwan's history in 1930, when the Atayal minority tribal group residing there staged a bloody but futile uprising against Japanese occupation forces. The Japanese, with modern weaponry, killed more than 1,000 of the tribesmen, but not before losing 200 of their own people. A memorial plaque in the village commemorates the massacre. About 3 km (2 miles) before Wushe, on Shengdao 14, is **Qingjing Recreational Farm** (Qingjing Nongchang; Mon–Fri 8am–4pm, Sat–Sun 8am–5pm; charge), a major attraction giving Taiwanese a rare opportunity to see cows grazing in green fields and even to hug sheep.

Hot springs and more

Lushan ⓮ village straddles a turbulent stream traversed by a suspension footbridge. Hot-spring inns lie along both banks of the river. On the far side of the river, just beyond the last hotel, a trail leads past a pair of waterfalls to the smoldering source of the area's hot springs. The simmering puddles that have formed in crevices around the source are hot enough to boil eggs, and many visitors do just that. The water lends flavor and vital minerals to the eggs, making them highly nutritional.

Lushan village is famous for its tea, medicinal herbs, petrified-wood canes, wild-blossom honey and dried mushrooms. Potent medicinal deer-horn shavings and tanned deer skins, very expensive or unavailable in Taipei, can be seen here. These are illegal, and not easy to find at all, unless you know certain locals very well. ❑

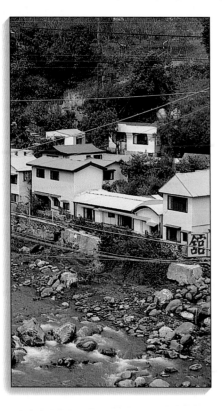

NANTOU COUNTY

Romantic Sun Moon Lake, shrines housing miraculous relics, experimental forests and leafy tea plantations are major features of Nantou County, home to the geographical center of the island

Map on page 188

Nantou County hogs the middle of Taiwan. More precisely, its sprawling town of **Puli** ⓯ is known as the exact geographical center of the island. A monument (Taiwan Dili Zhongxi Bei), approached by a flight of stairs to the northeast of town, marks the actual point.

Puli is famous throughout Taiwan for the quality of its water and the beauty of its women. Despite this, there's precious little of note in the town itself, which was badly damaged in the 9-21 Earthquake in 1999. On the outskirts of town are a large number of temples, however, including **City God Temple** (Chenghuang Miao), a monastery founded in 1924, standing in a grove of palms. Nearby, a marked turnoff leads 3 km (2 miles) up a pretty valley to **Carp Lake** (Liyutan), a pleasant picnic spot devoid of people, except straw-hatted farmers. These horticulturists specialize in growing edible and medicinal fungi on wooden planks and shaded arbors.

Sun Moon Lake

It's a short drive from Puli to Taiwan's most enduringly popular honeymoon resort – **Sun Moon Lake** ⓰ (Riyue Tan; vehicle charge; www.sunmoonlake.gov.tw), 750 meters (2,460 ft) above sea level and in the western foothills of the Central Range. Entirely enfolded in mountains and dense tropical foliage, there were actually two lakes here – the Sun and Moon – before the Japanese built a hydroelectric dam and raised the basin's water level. Under sunny skies, the dreamy landscape of turquoise waters, jade-green hills and drifting mountain mists lends itself well to the moods and passions of honeymooners and other amorous couples flocking to the lake's shores.

Before the Japanese built the hydroelectric dam, the aboriginal tribe that once flourished here, the Thao, or Shao in Mandarin Chinese, had their major village on the slopes of the hill between Sun and Moon lakes. After the basin was flooded, only the upper reaches of the hill, where the Thao sacred burial grounds are located, still showed. The village was moved to the south shore, and was later moved again to higher ground – the present site – when the Nationalists decided to raise the water level.

Needless to say, none of this has sat very well with the Thao. Adding insult was the fact that the government refused to recognize them as one of the "official" tribes of Taiwan. Thankfully, their numbers have risen to about 500 – after dropping below 200 at one stage. The Thao are now one of Taiwan's 13 officially recognized tribes, and have gained control of their village lands and the tip of their sacred mountain (with a name change from Guanghua Island to Lalu Island). Today, the Tourism Bureau includes the tribe

LEFT: Pagoda of Filial Virtue, Sun Moon Lake. **BELOW:** poinsettia, Sun Moon Lake.

Wall engraving of monk at Xuanzhuang Si, a temple named after the Buddhist pilgrim who made the legendary "Journey to the West" to retrieve Buddhist scripts.

BELOW: lion-guardian at Wenwu Miao.

in the planning for the Sun Moon Lake National Scenic Area, set up to help revive the area's fortunes after the 9-21 Earthquake pummeled the region and almost sank a local economy that was heavily dependent on tourism.

Daoist shrine

A good starting point for an exploration of the lake is the Chinatrust Sun Moon Lake Hotel, perched on a high embankment overlooking the lake. Heading east and south, the road leads first to the majestic **Wenwu Temple** ⑰ (Wenwu Miao; use side entrance after 8pm), a temple of martial and literary arts. This Daoist shrine, dedicated to Confucius and the two great warrior deities Guangong and Yue Fei, is built into the hillside in three ascending levels. The two largest stone lions in Asia stand sentry at the entrance, and the portico is graced by two full-relief windows of carved stone, depicting the celestial dragon and tiger. A viewing terrace at the rear allows unimpeded vistas of the lake. The temple, like everything in the area, which was close to the epicenter of the quake, was badly damaged in September 1999, but has been fully restored.

The shrine to Confucius occupies the upper rear hall, with decorative motifs drawn from Chinese folklore predating by centuries the arrival of Buddhism in China. Symbolic of the ultimate subservience of the sword to the pen, the temple's martial shrine sits slightly lower than the literary shrine. Contained within are the red-faced Guangong, the God of War, but more likely to be worshipped by practical businesspeople on account of the god's legendary mathematical skills, and the white-faced Yue Fei, a Sung-dynasty patriot and military hero who attempted, without success, to recover the empire from the barbarian Mongol nomads.

The temple complex is interesting for its complicated layout, with various

pavilions and side halls connected by ornate passages and stairways. Throughout the grounds stand potted bonsai trees, tropical flowers, and shrubs sculpted to resemble animals. The pair of 4.5-meter (15-ft) tall gods at the entrance, carved from solid wood and colorfully painted, rank among the best in Taiwan.

Further along the road, a bronze statue of Chiang Kai-shek (Jiang Jie-shi) gazes across the lake to the Cien Ta (Pagoda of Filial Virtue). Still further on, what was once the drab and commercial Dehuashe Aboriginal Village has now been reclaimed by the small Thao tribe as ancestral land and turned into a housing community designed by volunteer architects to reflect the traditional lifestyle of the Thao people. There is a tourist center here with handicrafts and aboriginal song/dance performances.

Preserved relics

High on a hill near the southern end of the lake, the **Xuanzhuang Temple** (Xuanzhuang Si; daily 5am–6pm) houses some of Asia's most precious Buddhist relics. This temple was built for the safekeeping and preservation of the relics, known as *si-li-zi*.

Devout Buddhists believe that the small kernel-shaped stones – found among the ashes of highly accomplished Buddhist monks and Taoist adepts after their cremations – are formed by the forging of spirit and energy after a lifetime of intensive meditation and other spiritual disciplines. The ashes of the historical Buddha, Sakyamuni, yielded 12 cups of these tiny black-and-white pebbles, some of which are enshrined in the Xuanzhuang Si. Flames will not consume them, it is said, nor will steel sledgehammers crack them. Of course, Western science thumbs its nose at the Buddhist explanation, insisting that they are kidney- or gall-stones.

TIP

Riyue Tan is at its best just after daybreak, the perfect time to drive around its circumference – it is too big to walk. However, taxis and public buses are scarce, so unless you have your own transport, it is a good idea to book a taxi the night before. Bicycles can be rented at the Youth Activity Center.

BELOW: burning incense at a temple.

Lying on the western edge of the Pacific Rim of Fire, where the tectonic plates frequently collide, earthquakes are a common phenomenon in Taiwan.

BELOW: wall embellishment from the Xuanzhuang Si.

Unusual properties

The *si-li-zi* nuggets are said to have other unusual properties. The two that were carried to this site by monks during the Nationalist retreat of 1949 have not remained static over the centuries. It is claimed that they have expanded, contracted, or even generated new kernels, depending upon how much prayer and offering is performed.

There are now seven little nuggets enshrined at the temple. The relics are kept within a miniature jewel-encrusted pagoda of solid gold on the altar of the main shrine hall. A tiny light illuminates the nuggets inside the pagoda. (An attendant reports that one of the kernels is beginning to shrink and disappear due to insufficient visits by the faithful.)

Also in the main shrine hall are a gilded reclining Buddha and a handsome statue of Xuanzhuang himself. This Tang-dynasty monk made a pilgrimage to India that was immortalized in the classical Chinese novel *Journey to the West*. After 17 years of Buddhist study, lecturing and travel in India, Xuanzhuang returned to the imperial Chinese capital of Changan (now Xian) in 645. Over the next two decades, he translated 1,335 *sutras* from the Sanskrit language into classical Chinese, thus playing a major part in bringing the Buddhist religion to China.

On the second floor of the Xuanzhuang Si stands a shrine to Guanyin, the Goddess of Mercy who is universally venerated in Taiwan.

On the third floor, another small golden pagoda protects a shard of what is believed to be Xuanzhuang's skull, looted from China by the Japanese during World War II. In 1955, a Japanese monk was dispatched to return the bone – both its age and authenticity have been verified – at Chiang Kai-shek's request.

9-21 EARTHQUAKE

At 1.47am on September 21, 1999, the sleeping population of Taiwan was jolted awake. An earthquake measuring 7.3 on the Richter scale had struck on the Chelungpu fault-line, close to Nantou County's tourist playground of Sun Moon Lake.

The earthquake was so severe that it even toppled buildings in Taipei, 150 km (93 miles) away. Thousands of aftershocks, some measuring more than 6 on the Richter scale, later rumbled across the island. The aftermath left 2,405 dead, 10,718 injured, more than 30,000 homes leveled and more than 25,000 damaged. The number of homeless was uncertain, but news reports generally quoted more than 100,000.

Years after the quake occurred, many areas remain unstable, impairing tourism and economic recovery. Some residents are still suffering psychological problems.

According to geologists, the earthquake resulted in major topographical changes in the mountains of central Taiwan – a crunch of 1.4–7 meters (4½–23 ft) horizontally and 1.3–3 meters (4½–10 ft) vertically. The resulting instability means heavy rains can cause collapses and mudslides, temporarily closing high mountain roads.

Upon handing over the relic, the monk-messenger died. His ashes are now kept in a wooden pagoda nearby.

Atop a hill beyond the Xuanzhuang Si stands the ornate, nine-tiered **Pagoda of Filial Virtue**, Cien Ta. It was erected by Chiang Kai-shek in memory of his mother, and hence the name. An uphill walk through cool glades of bamboo, fern, maple and pine leads to the foot of the pagoda. From here, there are spectacular views of the entire lake.

Glories of mystery and China

The last stop on this lake-side jaunt is the **Xuanguang Temple or Glory of Mystery Temple** (Xuanguang Si; daily 5am–9pm), a minor shore-side shrine. Below this is a dock from which rowboats or motor launches can be hired for short cruises around **Lalu Island** (previously named Guanghua or Glory of China Island by the homesick Nationalists). The restful pavilion on the island was shattered in the earthquake. The island itself, sitting smack on a major fault line, almost sank beneath the waves. The Thao aborigines no longer allow tourists on the island, its shores now surrounded by a floating aquaculture garden on rafts whose bounty can be enjoyed in local restaurants.

The specialty of restaurants on Riyue Tan is fresh carp which can be eaten braised, steamed or highly spiced. The lake is home to a unique species of carp called the president fish, because Chiang Kai-shek took a liking to them. Although bony, fresh president fish is very delicious. Along with the aforementioned carp, most restaurants specialize in what the Chinese call *yewei*, or literally "wild flavor", which in the past meant freshly killed or picked in the wild, but these days almost always meaning just "fresh."

Map on page 188

One interesting exhibit is in a separate shrine hall at Xuanguang Si. A monk's body refused to decay after his death and his hair continued to grow; he was encased in solid gold and placed in his own hall.

BELOW: the arresting colors of dawn at Sun Moon Lake.

An exquisite tea set is a nice memento of your visit. Shops all over the island overflow with tea-brewing paraphernalia of all sorts.

BELOW: Xitou Bamboo Forest.

Forest heights

There are three important experimental forests in the mountains of central Taiwan. The Huisun Forest (daily 7am–8pm; charge), with towering trees and flowering shrubs, managed by Zhongxing University, is found in the highlands north of Puli. The Alishan forest of cypress, cedar and pine is accessible from Chiayi. However, the **Xitou Forest Recreation Area** ⓳ (Xitou Senlin Youle Qu; daily 7am–10pm; entrance and parking charge) within the Xitou Bamboo Forest, a side trip off Shengdao 3 (Provincial Highway No. 3) between Taichung and Chiayi, is the most famous and easily the most interesting of the three forested areas.

Forty percent of Taiwan's supply of raw bamboo and bamboo products comes from this 2,485-hectare (6,140-acre) forest research station, operated by the National Taiwan University; the forest recreation area is open to tourists. There are many varieties of bamboo in this green forest, along with vast tracts of cypress, cedar and pine. The station cultivates and distributes more than one million tree shoots annually for Taiwan's extensive reforestation projects.

Visitors to Xitou can stroll along paved footpaths shaded by leafy canopies. At 1,150 meters (3,773 ft) above sea level, this is a favorite spot for hikers and campers. Motor vehicles are strictly prohibited within the recreation area.

One of the most popular walks leads to the remains of a sacred tree, 3,800 years old and 46 meters (150 ft) high. University Pond features a bamboo bridge arching gracefully over carp-filled water, there is a very popular new raised boardwalk (charge) stretching 180 meters (590 ft) through the treetops, 22.6 meters (74 ft) at its highest, and a 7-km (4-mile) trek leads to a remote ravine with a waterfall. For the hardy, the resort of Alishan, to the south, is a full day away by foot, but this excursion requires a permit and equipment.

Souvenir shops in Xitou village, which is a popular honeymoon retreat, sell bamboo products and other mountain goods – mushrooms, tea and herbs. There are two guesthouses, operated by the government forestry bureau, and an alpine hostel managed by the China Youth Corps, built of bamboo and local wood, along with a clutch of newer hotels just outside the village. Bamboo shoots are, of course, the specialty of the resort's restaurants.

Leaves of tea

Returning toward Taichung, and just before the town of Nantou, at the village of Mingqian, Shengdao 16 meets Shengdao 3. About 10 km (6 miles) further, the **Pine Bluff** ⓴ (Songboling) tea-production region spreads across a hilly plateau. Despite the name, there aren't many pines on this bluff. Instead, groves of areca palm and giant bamboo shelter large tea plantations.

At most times of the day, women wearing straw hats and bandannas can be seen plucking the tender leaves from these green shrubs, dropping them into huge baskets carried on their backs. Between the tea plantations are fields of pineapple and banana trees.

The main street of Songboling village is lined with teashops offering a service known locally as Old Folks' Tea, as only old folks (and presumably idle travelers) seem to have the time to enjoy this leisurely pursuit. Samples of many varieties of tea are brewed in tiny clay

Map on page 188

pots and poured into thimble-sized cups; the first infusion in the pots is always poured away, the tea too coarse. A variety of fragrant loose teas as well as teabags are available for purchase.*

Dongding (Frozen Peak), a young Oolong leaf from the highest plantations above Songboling, is regarded by many as Taiwan's best tea. It has a superb flavor, subtle fragrance and practically no bite. Those who buy bulk tea in Songboling get the same wholesale price as major Taipei retailers, which varies a great deal, depending on quality. The more expensive the blend, the better the bargain.

In addition to its famous tea, Songboling has one other attraction: a Daoist temple known as the **Palace of the Celestial Mandate** (Shoutian Gong). Some of the most exquisite stone sculptures in Central Taiwan, depicting Daoist legends and Chinese folklore, comprise the portico.

Of special interest, carved in full relief from solid stone, are two huge, round windows that brace the temple. One depicts the celestial dragon and the other the tiger, a duo found in all Daoist temples. The intricate ceiling inside the hall and the finely painted 4.5-meter (15-ft) solid wood doors are impressive. The temple comes with an attached guesthouse, should you be tempted to spend a meditative night there.

South of Songboling is Yuanquan, a station on the famous Jiji Railway Line. Named after the picturesque small town of **Jiji** to the east, trains on this line take 50 minutes to travel the less than 30 km (19 miles) of narrow gauge that span the rustic countryside between Changhua and Nantou counties, making it the island's most popular tourist railway line. Though Jiji was the epicenter of the 9-21 Earthquake, and was nearly leveled, the railway line has been restored, the colonial-style station rebuilt, and the town is thriving. ❏

As a popular tea amongst old-timers (it was also former president Chiang Ching-kuo's favorite), Songboling's tea is also known colloquially – and somewhat hopefully – as changqing cha, or the "tea of eternal youth."

BELOW: picking tea near Songboling.

SOUTH OF TAICHUNG

Map on page 188

To visit some particularly ornate temples, witness how Taiwan life used to be, and enjoy some of the most extravagant religious celebrations, make the journey south of Taichung

The area south of Taichung is not short of attractions. About 20 km (12 miles) from the city is **Caotun ㉑**, where the **Crafts Exhibition Center** (Minyi Zhanlanguan; Tue–Sun 9am–5pm; www.ntcri.gov.tw) contains an extensive display of local handicrafts and modern manufactured goods. The four-story, air-conditioned building houses bamboo and rattan furniture, Chinese lanterns, lacquerware, ceramics, stonecraft, woodcraft, curios, jewelry, cloisonné and textiles. All items on display are for sale at fixed prices.

Just 2 km (1½ miles) from Caotun is **Zhongxing Village ㉒** (Zhongxing Xincun), the former seat of Taiwan's now defunct provincial government (the central government absorbed provincial affairs in the 1990s). Given its past importance, Zhongxing was designed as a model "new" village, built along US lines, with detached houses surrounded by gardens and tidy suburban-looking streets. With the dismantling of the provincial government in 1998, however, the area fell on hard times, and this was compounded by the 9-21 Earthquake, which did enormous damage to the community. Today, it's a pleasant place to pass through, but not worth more than a brief stop.

Impressive Buddha

Thirty minutes by road southwest of Taichung is the typical country town of **Changhua ㉓**, notable for the impressive Buddha image atop **Eight-Trigram Mountain** (Baguashan; www.trimt-nsa.gov.tw), which, really more a hill than a mountain, sits on the immediate outskirts of town. The rather sterile-sounding name derives from the combinations of broken and unbroken sticks used by the Chinese in traditional divining procedures.

The 30-meter (100-ft) high concrete Buddha image meditates serenely atop a 5-meter (16-ft) high lotus dais. It took five years to complete and required 270 metric tons (300 tons) of concrete. The Buddha itself is hollow, with life-size dioramas of Sakyamuni Buddha's life built into the walls. The second floor features the story of his birth, the third his enlightenment under the bodhi tree, the fourth his discourses and teachings, and the fifth his death and entry into nirvana.

Behind the Buddha image is a palatial three-story temple, one of the largest in Taiwan. Within it is an impressive collection of gilded icons. In the shrine hall on the top floor is a large golden statue of the Buddha, attended by two disciples. Beside this main hall are a traditional octagonal pagoda of eight tiers and an ornate three-tiered pavilion of classical design.

Back in town is Changhua's **Confucius Temple** (Kong Miao; daily), which has some historical value, dating back to the early 18th century. Constructed by a

LEFT: a buddhist monastery in the Nantou district.
BELOW: Buddha statue at Baguashan.

county magistrate, in its time it has gone through eight major renovations. The temple retains many original Qing architectural features despite being sacked by the Japanese during their occupation of the island. Such is the temple's importance, the road it sits on takes its name – Kongmen (Confucius Door) Road.

Not far east of the temple, back towards Baguashan, on the northern side of Zhongshan Park, is an interesting relic of the brief Dutch occupation of the island. **Hongmao Jing** means literally the "Red-Hair Well," but it's also known locally as the Barbarian Well, a reference to the fact that the Dutch dug and used it some 350 years ago.

Changhua is also famous as the penultimate destination of Taiwan's biggest Mazu pilgrimage, which on the last day, before returning to Dajia in Taichung County, passes through Changhua in a mock fireworks battle between pilgrims and Changhua residents who make a big show of trying to force Mazu to stay in Changhua rather than return home.

Close to the town of **Huatan**, south of Changhua and about 15 km (9 miles) from the Changhua exit on the Sun Yat-sen Freeway, is an interesting place to explore the island's indigenous mysteries. Founded in 1990, the **Taiwan Folk Village** ㉔ (Taiwan Minzucun; daily 9am–5pm, Sat–Sun until 8.30pm; charge; www.tfv.com.tw) has several original structures of traditional architecture, dismantled at their original sites and rebuilt on its present grounds. There are nearly 100 reconstructions of various styles of building. A visit here offers probably the best introduction to traditional crafts. A full day is needed to see and enjoy the activities, which also include a children's theme park with rides and games. Buses depart regularly from Changhua bus station, located just next to the railway station.

BELOW: street food.

Lugang

West beyond Changhua, the ancient inland port of **Lugang** ㉕ lies sleepily near the shores of the Taiwan Strait. A main port of entry during the Qing dynasty (1644–1911) for waves of Chinese immigrants from Fujian province, Lugang was abruptly closed down by the Japanese in 1895. Thereafter, silt and sand rendered the port useless for commercial shipping; fishing is now the major maritime activity. The town is a day excursion from Taichung.

Lugang is interesting for its insight into old Taiwan. Along with some impressive temple architecture, it is an area where traditions live on. Although most of the town is recognizably modern, many of the narrow residential lanes have changed little since the Qing dynasty days. Artisans can still be seen fashioning furniture with ancient tools and techniques in open-front shops, and here and there are shops specializing in forgotten crafts such as Chinese lantern making.

Altar tables, shelves, ornaments, beams, eaves and other furnishings and fixtures are hewn into shape, then finished with elaborate detail at numerous workshops lining the main street. The fragrance of freshly sawn camphor and wet lacquer drifts everywhere. Incense is also produced in Lugang, and it is interesting to see how the enormous coils that hang from temple ceilings and burn for days are produced by hand.

The oldest temple in Lugang, and one of the oldest in Taiwan, is **Longshan or Dragon Mountain Temple** (Longshan Si; daily), dating from the 18th century. Located on Sanmin Road, just off the main avenue of Zhongshan Road, the temple was constructed by early Chinese settlers as an expression of gratitude to Guanyin, the Goddess of Mercy, for their safe passage from the mainland. Guanyin is enshrined in the main hall of the temple.

Longshan may not be quite the oldest temple on the island, but it is regarded as the most artistically significant, earning it the appellation "Taiwan's Forbidden Palace." Of particular note is the circular, carved ceiling over the main altar. Appearing on postcards and in brochures, it is as close as Taiwan gets to having a Sistine Chapel. The wall murals are the work of master artist Guo Xin-lin. The benches beneath them are usually occupied by lolling groups of elderly men – often the subject of photographic portraits, both professional and amateur. Also worth noting are the elaborately carved stone-dragon pillars.

A 200-meter (218-yd) stroll through quaint lanes leads to the **Phoenix Mountain Temple** (Fengtian Gong; daily), a small structure built in the early 19th century by immigrants from Fujian province. The painted guardians on the main doors are particularly well executed.

The first Mazu center?

Down Zhongshan Road from the Longshan Si is the impressive, and old, **Tianhou Temple** (Tianhou Gong; daily). The image of Mazu, Goddess of the Sea, on the main altar, is said to have been brought here in 1684 from the original Mazu shrine on Meichou Island by Admiral Shi, who captured Taiwan for the Qing emperor. If true, this story substantiates the claim of Lugang's people that this was the first center

Map on page 188

Incense sticks are lighted and placed in a censer before the image of the god to whom the offering is being made.

BELOW: "spirit money" for the afterworld.

TIP

The entrance to Tianhou Gong is clustered with stalls serving famous local snacks. The specialty in this part of town is *e-a-jian* – oyster omelette – which is available all over the island, but nowhere is it quite like Lugang's, say locals.

BELOW: incense shop in Lugang.

of the Mazu cult in Taiwan. There are numerous other exotic icons here. Among them is the magnificent Jade Emperor in a temple of his own, in the same compound. At the rear of the temple is a small Mazu Culture Museum. Signs to many more temples and shrines are posted throughout the residential maze.

Also worth a visit is the **Lugang Folk Arts Museum** (Lugang Minsu Wenwuguan; daily 9am–5pm; charge) a 30-room European-style villa that couldn't look more out of place in Lugang if it tried. Designed as a private residence in 1919 for a wealthy landowner by a Japanese architect in Orientalized Edwardian style, it is one of the most unusual mansions on the island. Inside is an interesting collection of old furniture and household fixtures, vintage photos, paintings, personal effects, costumes, books and musical instruments, and other items reflecting the lifestyle of Taiwan's people.

Triple attraction

West of the Lugang Minsu Wenwuguan, on Qingyun Street, is the unusual triumvirate of the **Wenkai Academy** (Wenkai Shuyuan), **Civil Shrine** (Wen Zi) and **Martial Temple** (Wu Miao). Together they form a compound that brings together an academy that, in its day, produced a large number of Taiwan's cultural elite, a shrine that once served as a meeting place for one of the island's first literary associations, and a temple dedicated to Guangong, who is worshiped both as the God of War and as the God of Commerce.

Turn right out of the Wenkai Shuyuan, continue straight ahead, and the first intersection is at **Zhongshan Road**, Lugang's main thoroughfare. This is where most of the town's longest established shops can be found. Highlights include the **Wanneng Tin Shop** (Wanneng Xipu), where the Chen family has been

creating traditional Taiwanese crafts out of tin for generations. Also famous is the **Shi Chin-yu Incense Shop** (Shi Chin-yu Xiangpu), which has been making and selling incense for more than 200 years. Just past the incense shop is **Old Market Street** (Gushi Street), a fascinating alley lined with traditional red-tile-roofed shophouses. Here you can find the **Wu Dunhou Lantern Shop** (Wu Dunhou Denglongpu), where the old master can be seen most days hand-painting traditional Chinese lanterns that he has made himself. And farther still along Zhongshan Road, not far from the Tianhou Gong, is a collection of handicrafts shops selling everything from hand-crafted wooden furniture to delicate fans.

For a glimpse of the maze-like, traditional back alleys for which Lugang is so famous, visit the **Nine-Turns Lane** (Jiugu Xiang), which is approached from Zhongshan Road by taking Xinsheng Street (close to the Wanneng Xipu) and turning into Jinsheng Street. The twisting lane was once protected by a gun tower, still in place, and is said to have been built this way to simultaneously protect it from the strong summer winds and from attack by pirates and bandits.

Map on page 188

Lanterns are so important they have an entire festival dedicated to them. These are from Wu Dun-hou Lantern Shop in Lugang.

On to Chiayi

Chiayi ㉖ straddles Zhongshan Gaosu Gonglu (Sun Yat-sen Freeway), about halfway between Taichung and Tainan, lying slightly north of the Tropic of Cancer. While mostly serving as a springboard to nearby attractions, Chiayi itself is a pleasant city, more relaxed than either Taichung or Changhua, and with a smattering of sights to keep the visitor occupied for a few hours while waiting for connecting transportation.

The city's most significant cultural attraction is the **Beiyu Temple** (Beiyu Dian; daily) – literally the "North Hell Temple," close to the center of town on Minquan Road. The temple was built in 1697 to house an image of the God of Hell, which originates from the late Ming dynasty in China. The current temple is, for the most part, a restoration completed in the late 1970s, but the seven-story main tower still contains the original image. The traditional Chinese vision of hell is not so different from the sinning Christian's – a place of imaginative and ever-lasting tortures – with the difference that the Chinese God of Hell can be bought off ahead of time with incense, spirit money and even Pringles.

On the eastern outskirts of town, a kilometer from the railway station, is **Chiayi Park** (Chiayi Gongyuan), which has a small Confucius temple dating from the late Qing and restored in 1961, and a botanical garden. It's the latter, with its shaded walks through groves of exotic plant life and trees, that makes the park worth a visit. In contrast, the **Chiayi Night Market** (Chiayi Yeshi; daily 5pm–midnight) is in the center of town, close to the railway station on Wenhua Road. Chiayi is famed for its snack food, and eating here is considered a special treat by out-of-town Taiwanese visitors.

BELOW: temple icon, Lugang.

Doubly revered

Seven km (4 miles) east of Chiayi is an unassuming cultural attraction of immense historical significance: the **Wufeng Temple** ㉗ (Wufeng Miao; Tue–Sun 9am–5pm; charge). Wufeng is perhaps the only historical personage revered by both the non-indigenous and indigenous Taiwanese. An 18th-century Chinese official born in 1699 to a merchant family in mainland Fujian province, he emigrated to Taiwan as a youth and studied the customs and dialects of the indigenous peoples. Appointed as official interpreter and contact between Chinese settlers on the plains and recalcitrant tribes in the mountains, he worked tirelessly to end feuding between the two camps.

The tribes followed the disturbing practice of invading the plains to harvest Chinese heads as sacrifices to their gods. Folklore, which the aborigines themselves vehemently contest, has it that Wufeng, wise at the age of 71, devised a courageous scheme to end the practice. On a certain day and at a certain place, he told his tribal friends, they would see "a man wearing a red hood and cape, and riding a white horse. Take his head. It will appease your gods." The tribal warriors followed his instructions, lopping off the head of the mysterious rider. Only after removing the red cowl did the warriors discover that the man they had killed was none other than their old friend, Wufeng. This act of self-sacrifice so moved and terrified the local chief that he called a meeting of all 48 of the tribal headmen in the Alishan region. They agreed to end the practice of head-hunting.

This story is forwarded as truth at Wufeng's former home, a simple but traditional Chinese house built around a courtyard. Out front is a statue of Wufeng on his horse, being pulled down for decapitation, while within the house is a small museum of artifacts and a series of large oil paintings, with English-language captions, recalling the life and times of Wufeng. Nineteenth-century aborigine lifestyles are depicted in a collection of vintage photographs.

An enormous memorial garden, commemorating the peace established between Chinese and minority groups through Wufeng's efforts, was built in

BELOW: *doufu* (bean curd) stall, Chiayi night market.

1984. The garden contains clusters of traditional dwellings, grottoes and an artificial lake. Wufeng's grave can be found on the hill behind his house. His birthday is celebrated with elaborate ceremonies on November 12 each year.

Map on page 188

Therapeutic waters

About 15 km (9 miles) south of the Wufeng Temple, a short distance off Shengdao 3 to Pingtung, is the rustic hot-spring spa of **Guanziling ㉘**. Resting in a low mountain pass between Chiayi and Wushantou Reservoir, it is renowned for its therapeutic mineral waters. Skin ailments are believed to find rapid relief in the water, which is also said to relieve chronic gastro-intestinal problems.

Also of note, next door to Wufeng Miao, is the Deyuan Chan Si (Deyuan Zen Temple), a small but delightful one-story structure framed by tree-studded hills.

The road that runs around the mountains behind Guanziling village has a number of interesting sights. About 5 km (3 miles) from the hot springs, in close proximity to one another, are the **Exotic Rock** and the **Water-Fire Crevice** (Shuihuo Tongyuan). The rock is an enormous fossilized boulder the size of a house, part of a prehistoric landslide frozen in place at this spot. Bizarre fossil skeletons are etched into its sides. The crevice is more astonishing. Boiling-hot mineral water bubbles like a cauldron in concert with a constant flickering fire, actually escaping natural gas, the flames of which have licked the grotto black. Fire and water seem to pour together from the earth.

Also in the Guanziling area are the **Blue Cloud Temple** (Biyun Si), built in 1701, the more modern **Monastery of the Great Immortals** (Daxian Si), and the small, highly ornate **Temple of the Immortal Ancestor**. It is a short drive to a medicinal herb farm, the **White River Reservoir** (Baihe Shuiku) and the Pillow Mountain Cable Car. Taxis cover the entire circuit around Guanziling.

BELOW: Monastery of the Great Immortals, Guanziling.

Map on page 188

TIP

If visiting Beigang during the Mazu celebrations, remember to bring earplugs: the staccato bursts of firecrackers, gongs and drums are ear splitting.

BELOW: Chaotian Temple, Beigang.
RIGHT: image cone, Chaotian Temple.

Beigang

Northwest of Chiayi, via **Xingang** (with its elaborate Daoist temple **Fengtian Gong**) is the town of **Beigang** ㉙, on Shengdao 19, a 23-km (14-mile) drive from the Sun Yat-sen Freeway. Beigang's chief claim to fame is **Chaotian Gong** (daily 4am–midnight), a temple dedicated to Mazu, Goddess of the Sea. It is probably the most extravagant of Taiwan's over 500 temples dedicated to the island's patron deity. Koxinga (Guoxingye) attributed the safe passage of his war fleet across the Taiwan Strait to the divine protection of Mazu; ever since then, she has been highly revered in Taiwan.

More than 3 million pilgrims visit Chaotian Gong, the Palace Facing Heaven, every year, leaving large sums of cash in annual donations. During the April or May festival week commemorating Mazu's birth, the town is the site of a fascinating display of ancient folk religion and traditional customs.

Beigang is not as lively as it once was during Mazu's birthday celebrations, as a dispute between temples has resulted in Beigang being taken off the Dajia Mazu's annual pilgrimage circuit. Nevertheless, it is still an exciting time to visit, and the crowds are not nearly as overwhelming as in Xingang. Religious rites are performed with a pomp and ceremony that has not changed significantly in 1,000 years. One particularly colorful (and frequent) ritual involves the parading of a holy icon in a gilded, silk-tasseled palanquin. When the procession returns to the temple gates, the deity is welcomed back amid thick clouds of incense, exploding firecrackers and a cacophonous din of gongs, cymbals, drums and flutes.

Four stone lions and the four Immortals mounted on dragons guard the front gate of the temple, but it is the roof that demands study. There may not be a livelier, more colorful set of eaves and gables on the island. Hundreds of glazed ceramic figures cavort among miniature mountains, palaces, pagodas and trees, depicting tale after tale from folklore. On the central roof are the Three Star Gods of Longevity, Prosperity and Posterity – the three cherished goals of the Chinese people in this life. The pagoda on the main beam of the central shrine hall symbolizes the communion of Heaven and Earth. The roof beams on the side halls have pairs of gamboling dragons pursuing the elusive Pearl of Wisdom.

Within the temple courtyard stands a three-tiered pagoda, where paper offerings are burned. Pilgrims pay real money to temple vendors for ersatz paper money, incense and other gifts for the gods. Thus, the temple fills its coffers with legal tender, the gods benefit from the symbolic offerings, and the pilgrim is blessed by both.

There are many tall image-cones (known as Buddha mountains) bearing the names of the temple's financial patrons. Lit up like Christmas trees, they stand in pairs at the temple's altars. Most temples have only two such cones, but the Beigang temple has no fewer than 12, clear evidence of its immense following and generous patronage. Offering tables are heaped high with meat, fish, poultry, fruit, candy, incense, wine, real cash and even bottles of soft drinks, left conveniently uncapped so that their essence might reach the gods. An open-air market occupies the streets that surround the temple, selling everything imaginable. ❑

ALISHAN AND ENVIRONS

Alishan is the gateway to Taiwan's highest peaks, providing the opportunity for viewing spectacular sunrises, catching a glimpse of abundant wildlife, and enjoying a relaxing soak in a hot spring

Map on page 188

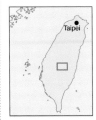

C hiayi's fame in Taiwan is due less to its indigenous sights than to the fact it is the gateway to one of the island's most famous sights: **Alishan** ③⓪, home of Alishan Forest Recreation Area (daily 24 hours; charge; www.ali. org.tw) which, abutting Yushan National Park, also provides easy access to Taiwan's loftiest peak, Yushan, or Jade Mountain as it is sometimes called.

Alishan's popularity is due primarily to the famous sunrise view from the summit of nearby **Celebration Mountain** (Zhushan). Indeed, it is a spectacular event. As visitors stand shivering in their jackets 2,490 meters (8,170 ft) above sea level, gazing into the graying mist, the sun suddenly peers over the horizon. Golden shafts of light pierce the dawn, skipping across the thick carpet of clouds that cover the valleys to the east. This sea of clouds springs to life like a silver screen the moment the sun glances across it, undulating in vivid hues of gold and silver, red and orange. On holidays and weekends, the summit is overcrowded with thousands of excited and noisy visitors. These are not the days to witness an idyllic sunrise. On any given day, nonetheless, hundreds of people make the pre-dawn ascent, usually by tour bus. By 7am, most will be back at the hotel for breakfast.

The mystique of the weather

More often than not, however, fog and mist are so thick atop the peak that sunrise watchers find themselves floating within the clouds rather than gazing at clear skies above them. But, even if the weather in Alishan is terrible, most visitors will depart quite delighted. There are two explanations, both founded in legend, for this appreciation of less-than-clear conditions.

In ancient times, clouds and rain symbolized the mating of Heaven and Earth. It is said that a king of Sichuan made an excursion to Wushan, or Sorcery Mountain, where he grew tired in the middle of the day and fell asleep. He dreamed that a woman approached him and identified herself as the Lady of Wushan, saying, "Having heard that you have come here, I wish to share pillow and couch with you."

When the lovers later parted, the woman told the king: "I live on the southern slope of Wushan, on top of a high hill. At dawn I am the morning clouds; in the evening I am the pouring rain. Every morning and night I hover about these hills."

The legend established a standard for Chinese writers, who have used clouds and rain as a poetic metaphor for sexual intercourse. Clouds symbolize the essence of the woman, rain that of the man. Colorful thematic variations have enriched centuries of Chinese literature, with phrases like "After the rain had come, the clouds dispersed," and "The clouds grew thick but the rain never came."

LEFT: the verdant Alishan forest.
BELOW: it is best to see Alishan on foot.

Morning at the parks sheds light on the social traditions and rituals of the local people. Qigong is a form of exercise involving coordination of the mind, breathing pace, and soft slowing movements, performed to help lower tension.

BELOW: sunrise breaks over Alishan.

But there is one reason, even more compelling than the sensual imagery, that draws Chinese to mountain retreats several times a year, regardless of the weather. Drifting mountain mists are regarded as possessing extraordinary curative powers, due to their high concentration of *qi* (pronounced "chee"), or vital energy, the most fundamental of all Chinese physical and spiritual concepts. *Qi* is considered the basic force that animates all forms of life. The most potent *qi*, it is believed, rises in the atmosphere and clings as mist to the mountains, like cream rising to the top of milk. The legend of Wushan further reinforces this concept, suggesting that mists are the vital essence emitted during the mating of Heaven and Earth on high mountain peaks.

From time immemorial, the Chinese have cultivated the custom of *deng-gao* – ascending high places. They believe the *qi* found in the mist strengthens their longevity and virtue. One of the most ancient of all Chinese characters – *xian*, for "immortal" – combines the symbols for man and mountain. And while the practical and urban Chinese are unlikely to become mountain-top ascetics, they are convinced of the restorative powers of high-altitude mists.

Petrified forest

Rain and mist, however, may not hold the same delight for foreign visitors, but there are other reasons to visit the Alishan area. The region is blanketed with thick forests of red cypress, cedar and pine, some of them thousands of years old. When these ancient plants finally fall to rest, the Taiwanese let sleeping logs lie. The great gnarled stumps and petrified logs form some of Alishan's most exotic sights. The walking paths and grottoes behind Alishan House incorporate several of these formations, and there are many more on the trails. One of the park

highlights is a huge tree called the Three-Generation Tree. This may indeed be a natural wonder: a tree growing in a tree, growing in yet another tree.

Perhaps Alishan's greatest attraction for Western travelers is the three-hour train ride (you will need to stay overnight) on the Alishan Forest Railway to the mountain resort from Chiayi Beimen Station. Antique narrow-gauge diesels and steam locomotives, specially restored for this route, chug along the zigzagging 70 km (44 miles) of narrow-gauge, crossing 114 bridges and passing through 49 tunnels, one of them 770 meters (2,530 ft) long. Unless you happen to be visiting on the weekend (not recommended if avoidable), there is no need to book ahead, either for the trains (which on weekends leave at 9am and 1.30pm, with return journeys at 1.20pm and 1.40pm, Mon–Fri leave 1.30pm and return 1.20pm) or for a hotel room. A wide range of accommodation to suit different budgets is available, but for a treat, Alishan House, under the aegis of the Taiwan Forestry Tourism Corporation office, is the oldest and the most charming and picturesque. Its Shanghai-cuisine dining room serves the best food in the area.

Ascent of Jade Mountain

Alishan is the billeting post of mountaineering expeditions to **Jade Mountain** ❸ (Yushan; www.ysnp.gov.tw). At 3,950 meters (12,960 ft) in altitude, Yushan is the highest peak in Asia east of the Himalayas, south of Russia's Kamchatka Peninsula and north of Borneo's Mt Kinabalu. Even higher than Japan's majestic Mt Fuji, this peak was called New High Mountain during the 50 years of Japanese occupation. Its original name was restored by the Chinese in 1945. Yushan is far more visited than the others, however, and physically fit individuals will find their endurance challenged by the overnight expedition to ascend Yushan's summit.

Map on page 188

Travelers arriving in Alishan by train will be met by professional "sunrise hunters," who organize tours for the next morning. It's best to use their services: they know the best places to see the sunrise given the mercurial weather conditions.

BELOW: take a train to the mountains.

Map on page 188

It is not necessary to climb Yushan in order to have a hot-spring soak at Dongpu. From Alishan village, there are roads leading 20 km (12 miles) to the hot springs.

Wildlife galore

Yushan actually has 11 peaks, of which the highest is Main Peak. Climbing to the top is no afternoon stroll. For a start, the rock face is often crumbly, and rockfalls are not unknown. It's also a long way up. But, even for those who do not attempt the summit, walks at lower altitudes in Yushan National Park can be rewarding. Wildlife is abundant, with more than 150 species of birds and 220 species of butterflies recorded. There is also a strong likelihood that visitors will catch a glimpse of wild monkeys, not to mention wild boar, mountain goats and flying squirrels – the park is home to 34 different kinds of mammals.

At Tatajia (also spelt "Tataka"), on the Jade Mountain Scenic Highway section of the New Central Cross-Island Highway, there is a visitor center (daily 9am– 4.30pm, closed 2nd and 4th Tue each month). This is also the staging post for assaults on the mountain (permits are required, obtained at the park headquarters in the nearby town of Shuili, north on Shengdao 21) or walks farther afield into the national park. The center presents multimedia exhibitions on the park daily.

From here it is a 9-km (5½-mile) uphill trudge to the Paiyun Cottage (a hostel with campsite), where climbers spend the night before tackling the main summit of the mountain, leaving the hostel at around 3am in order to reach the summit in time for the sunrise.

The ascent from Paiyun follows the west face of the peak, and, for those who decide not to return the way they came, a treat is in store. Down the east face of the mountain winds the **Batongguan Historic Trail**, which after around 6 km (4 miles) joins up with another trail leading down to the hot-spring town of Dongpu at 2,600 meters (8,530 ft). What better way could there be to finish up a climb of east Asia's highest peak than with a soak in a hot spring? ❑

BELOW: hostel near the peaks of Yushan.

Taiwan's Top Hikes

To most people, Taiwan means hot coastal cities and smoke-belching factories. But two-thirds of the island is covered with remote and beautiful peaks, which are laced with good hiking trails.

Taiwan is home to the highest mountain in East Asia – Yushan (Jade Mountain) – while scores of peaks soar above 3,000 meters (9,800 ft). Protected by national parks, and home to rare Formosan black bears, landlocked salmon and other wildlife, the mountains are among Taiwan's top attractions.

Trekking in Taiwan is not for the fainthearted. The Central Mountain Range is steep and wild, and much of it is covered with thick forest. Summer thunderstorms rise unseen, and facilities are few and far between. But, for those willing to carry their own gear, the mountains are among the most beautiful in Asia. The trails, though steep, are generally well-kept.

There are some easy walks to do in Taiwan. Yangmingshan National Park, for instance, is on Taipei's doorstep, and daytime hikes through its sulfur fumaroles and thick forests can end with a hot dinner and a cold drink in the suburb of Tianmu.

Taroko National Park (see page 271) is also full of trails. These lead to alpine lakes, Atayal tribal villages, peach and pear orchards, and hidden swimming holes. The trails wind across high suspension bridges, along sheer cliffs, up and down steep switchbacks, and sometimes through tunnels. Here, too, a hiker can finish the day by soaking in a hot spring, or relaxing in a five-star hotel or a comfortable hostel.

But the top hikes in Taiwan – Qilai Ridge and Yushan – require a strong back, some experience and proper equipment, which includes a tent and stove, food and water, a sleeping bag, good boots and warm clothes.

Yushan is one of the most popular hikes in the country. The trail starts near the top of the new section of the Central Cross-Island Highway, and winds steadily upward through magnificent forests of fir and cedar. The first day's trek is a long one – 1,000 meters

(3,300 ft) to Paiyun Cottage, a couple of hours below the summit. Most trekkers spend the night in or near the hostel, and leave before daylight to catch the sunrise from the main summit of Yushan. The view from the top is amazing, though you're likely to have lots of company.

To really get away from it all, try the Qilai Ridge trail, a lovely, treacherous meander straight down the rocky spine of Taiwan's rugged Central Mountain Range.

It takes four hours and a lot of legwork to hike to the top of Qilai Ridge from Hehuanshan on the Central Cross-Island Highway section to the north. The ridge trail then goes up and over a succession of rocky peaks, and is regarded as the most dangerous trek in Taiwan, but one that is unrivaled in beauty.

From Qilai Ridge, much of Taiwan is on display: to the east are Taroko Gorge and the broad blue Pacific, and to the west are the rolling green foothills and the city of Taichung. In the north is the famous rock spike of Dabajian shan, and far to the south, barely visible, is Yushan. ❑

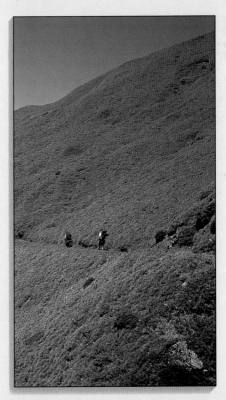

RIGHT: trekking Qilai Ridge is a journey off the beaten track.

Map on page 224

THE TAIWAN STRAIT ISLANDS

If you ever need evidence of the friction that exists between Taiwan and mainland China, visit the islands of the Taiwan Strait, which are also home to unspoilt fishing communities and fine beaches

BELOW:
war memorial at
Guningtou Military
History Museum,
Kinmen Island.

Taiwan has administrative control of a number of surrounding islands. Rarely visited by foreign travelers, some, like Kinmen and Mazu in the Taiwan Strait, are fascinating for their Hokkien-style fishing villages and their place in the stand-off with mainland China.

Both Mazu and Kinmen (formerly known as Quemoy) lie just kilometers off the coast of China's Fujian province. Heavily fortified, they were long considered by Taiwanese a hardship posting for young men doing their compulsory military service. All that changed in 1992, when the islands suddenly opened to tourism after nearly 50 years as an off-limits military secret.

Few travelers, either Taiwanese or foreign, visit **Mazu**, the northernmost of the islands. Flights to the young main airport are now regular, though often cancelled by fog. Amenities are scarce, though improving, and English barely spoken at all. Of more interest to foreign travelers are the southern islands of **Kinmen ❶**, which lie 280 km (174 miles) from the coast of central Taiwan and just 2 km (1¼ miles) off the coast of China's Fujian port city of Xiamen.

Kinmen is actually an archipelago of 15 islands. Three of them, however, are controlled by China, and only two of the Taiwan-controlled islands – Kinmen main island and **Little Kinmen** (Xiao Kinmen) – are open to tourism. Kinmen's main town is **Jincheng**, little more than a sprawling village in the southwest corner of the main island. It has a large number of hotels – though accommodation is usually two-star – restaurants and souvenir shops, making it a good base for an exploration of the island, either by taxi, hired car/motorcycle, or bicycle (Kinmen has little traffic, making it perfect for such a trip).

Under attack

The most famous attractions on the island are **Guningtou Military History Museum** (Guningtou Zhanshiguan; daily 8.30am–5pm) and **Guningtou Battlefield** (Guningtou Zhanchang; daily) to the north of Jincheng. Propaganda rules the day, but the story is compelling all the same. Mainland Chinese troops – 12,000–17,000 of them, nobody is absolutely sure – sailed across from Fujian to Guningtou in fishing boats around 2am on October 25, 1949. By 8am the next day, the Chinese troops had dug in, and a Taiwanese counter-attack by the 14th, 18th and 114th divisions was underway, as Taiwanese aircraft bombed artillery positions on the Chinese shore.

At 2pm on October 26, Chinese troops took the village of Beishan. Some of the buildings there still stand, riddled with bullet holes, weeds sprouting among the rubble inside. The village soon became the site of heavy fighting and was recaptured in the night.

The conflict resulted in some 15,000 dead, around 3,000 of them Kuomintang (Guomindang) troops (though the figures are impossible to verify), and around 6,000 Chinese prisoners of war.

Under fire

Another military site is the **August 23rd Artillery Battle Museum** (Baersan Zhanshiguan; daily 8.30am–5pm), in the far east of the island. Established in 1988, the museum commemorates the 1958 artillery war between China and Kinmen. It started on August 23 with a sudden burst of artillery fire from Fujian, and within two hours the mainland artillery had rained more than 57,000 shells on the small island. The bombardment continued until October 6, by which time the Chinese had fired nearly 500,000 shells at Kinmen. Meanwhile, the Taiwanese military replied in kind, forcing – according to the Taiwanese view of things – the Chinese to call a cease-fire. The museum itself, a collection of tanks, artillery emplacements and fighter aircraft in a grassy field, is a fascinating reminder of the simmering stand-off between China and Taiwan.

North of here is another interesting military sight: **Mashan Observation Station** (Mashan Guancezhan; daily 8–11.30am, 1.30–5pm, closed Thur am). Kinmen's closest point to China is still a military outpost, and visitors are required to relinquish their passport before entering. A winding tunnel, dank and narrow, leads to a pillbox with telescopes, from where it is possible to view the pale hills of China in the distance, and, on a good day, the outline of the city of Xiamen.

Easily the island's most fascinating military sight is an obligatory stop for Taiwanese tour buses. **Zhaishan** (not far from Guningtou Zhanchang) is a hollowed-out small mountain offering a glimpse of just how fortified Kinmen is –

Despite the military garrison that it still is and the undeniably militaristic bent of most of its tourist sites, Kinmen Island throws up charming surprises such as this traditional village.

BELOW: soldiers train on the beach at Kinmen Island.

underground. Inside, two 360-meter (1,180 ft) waterways (together called Zhaishan Tunnel; daily 8am–5pm) leak out into the sea, providing a safe haven for naval boats.

After the military sights, Kinmen's most winning attraction is its old Hokkien-style fishing villages. For a look at one in immaculate condition, visit **Shanhou Folk Culture Village** (Shanhou Minsu Wenhuacun; daily 8am–5pm; charge), a picturesque settlement that, despite the fact it has been turned into a tourist attraction, has little of the tackiness found in similar "cultural villages" on the Taiwan mainland. The village originally dates from the turn of the 20th century, and many of the houses here are still lived in by their owners, who eke out a living selling souvenirs and local snacks to tourists. The houses, with their sweeping eaves and courtyards, are extremely photogenic.

Penghu

One of Taiwan's best-kept secrets, the **Pescadores Islands ❷** (Penghu) are far enough off the beaten trail that it is unlikely you will see another foreign face while you are there. During the winter, ferocious winds scour the archipelago's 64 islands, but, with the onset of summer, Penghu becomes a subtropical island getaway, with pristine beaches, tiny, picturesque fishing villages and superb seafood.

Penghu has a long history. Nearly every army that has ever attacked Taiwan has used it as a springboard, including the Dutch, Koxinga (Guoxingye), the Manchu Qing and the Japanese, who took control of the archipelago as part of their annexation of mainland Taiwan.

Over the years, treacherous coastal shoals surrounding Penghu have claimed countless ships. These shipwrecks help to account for the nearly 150 temples and

An interesting feature of Kinmen, which is blasted by strong winds for much of the winter, are the so-called protective Wind Lions that stand at the edge of every village. They come in all shapes and sizes, looking like Tolkienesque trolls, some of them "dressed" in red bibs.

BELOW: sorting out a good catch, Penghu Island.

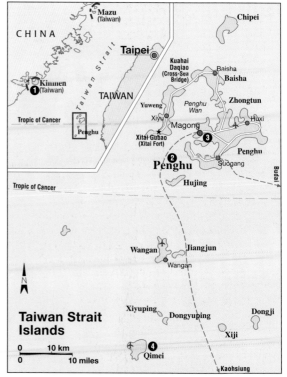

Map on page 224

assorted monuments dotting the otherwise barren islands. Half the archipelago's population of around 150,000 live in Magong, the Penghu county seat, on the main island of Penghu. Fishing is the primary source of income; the only crops that grow here are peanuts, sweet potatoes and sorghum, used for making potent Kaoliang (Gaoliang) liquor.

Magong

TIP

The Penghu Youth Activity Center lays out tables on its patio overlooking the sea and serves drinks – the perfect place to watch the sun sink over the horizon. Liquid Sports now also has a popular bay-view café.

Magong ❸, which is close to the islands' main airport, makes a convenient base for explorations farther afield. Hotels and restaurants are plentiful, and the small town even has a surprisingly active nightlife. The town also has a smattering of sights to fill a leisurely afternoon. In the south of town are the remains of the Qing dynasty **City Walls** (Magong Cheng), which are in surprisingly good shape. Close by, on Chenyi Street, is the **Tianhou Temple** (Tianhou Gong; daily), Taiwan's oldest temple. Built in 1592, it is dedicated to Mazu. Its interior stone carvings are more impressive than its unassuming exterior lets on. Close by the small temple (just follow the crowds), on Zhongyang Street, are a pair of ancient wells. The one farthest up the street, the **Four-Eye Well** (Siyan Jing), so named because it has four openings, is the oldest on the island, and Taiwanese tourists line up here for photo-shoots.

On the beachfront western part of town, the modern white building is the **Penghu Youth Activity Center** (Penghu Qingnian Huodong Zhongxin). Brochures about the island's attractions are available at the front desk, and tastefully-appointed rooms are available for those who book ahead (http://penghu.cyh.org.tw). Beneath the center, on the waterfront, is the small **Guanyin Temple** (Guanyin Ting; daily), from which haunting chants can be heard at dusk. There is good windsurfing in the bay here; look for the Liquid Sports Shop (www.liquidsport.com.tw), where English is spoken.

From Magong, the best way to explore the main island of Penghu, nearby **White Sand** (Baisha) Island, and **West Island** (Xiyu; also known as Yuweng Dao – Old Fisherman Island), which are attached to each other by bridges, is to hire a motorcycle or rent a taxi and follow the coastline. The islands are blessed with some stunning and usually deserted beaches which are often fronted by traditional fishing villages where little seems to have changed since the 19th century.

Xiyu is reached by the 5.5-km (3½-mile) **Cross-Sea Bridge** (Kuahai Daqiao). Close to the southernmost extent of the island is **Western Fort** (Xitai Gubao; 24 hours). Built in 1887, all that remains are its sturdy walls, which provide a fine view of the coastline.

If Penghu's main island is not quite remote enough, regular flights and tour boats depart from Magong to the tiny **Isle of Seven Beauties** ❹ (Qimei Yu). According to local lore, seven virtuous Ming dynasty beauties were said to have drowned themselves in a well on this island to protect their chastity from marauding pirates.

The even more remote Penghu island of **Wangan Island** (Wangan Dao) can be approached by air and boat. It is famous for its turtles, but is also home to some quaint fishing villages, and features an impressive, craggy coastline. ❏

BELOW: ploughman and his ox, Kinmen Island.

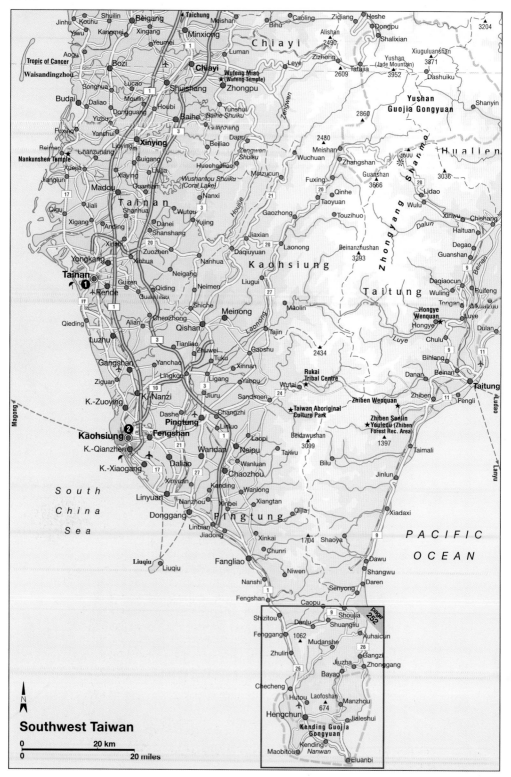

Southwest Taiwan

page 252

SOUTHWEST TAIWAN

This fertile land of big skies and open spaces is the cradle of the island's culture and traditions

Stretching from north of Tainan to the island's southernmost tip at Eluanbi, southwest Taiwan is a world far removed from the crowded north and the heavily cultivated central plains area. The pace of life slows down and space opens up in this sunny, flat and fertile region. This is Taiwan's "Big Sky" country, where travelers have more opportunity than elsewhere, save perhaps the isolated east coast, to find themselves completely alone and to discover absolute quiet.

Apart from the cultured sophistication of Tainan, and the raw entrepreneurial vigor of the island's second city, Kaohsiung, this is a land of smaller towns and big vistas. Though in the past southwest Taiwan was home to the majority of the population, the island's political and economic focus – deeply and sometimes darkly intertwined – has shifted to the north over the past century and a half. This caused a certain degree of resentment with Taiwanese southerners, who felt neglected and left to fend for themselves by what they have perceived as a mainlander-dominated central government. Yet the resulting shift in population has left them with a greater reserve of land to work with than their northern and central neighbors, with a stronger sense of their traditional Taiwanese culture and roots, and with a better-developed sense of love for the outdoors. The elections of Taiwanese-dominated central governments in recent years have also resulted in more balanced economic development.

Each of Taiwan's regions possesses its own enchantments. Taiwan's southwest is recognized – even in the self-confident north – as the cradle of the island's culture and traditions. Old Tainan was the first capital. This is where Koxinga (Guoxingye) accepted the surrender of the Dutch in 1662 and this is where he died within the year, at the site of the Dutch-built fort (Fort Zeelandia). Here in the south, Taiwanese, rather than Mandarin Chinese, is the language of choice.

Many of the island's oldest temples and shrines dot the region, especially in Tainan. Here is where you'll find Taiwan's largest and most graceful places of worship, and where you'll also find many of the island's newest and tallest temples – in the form of skyscrapers that reach for the heavens. And within sight of these monsters of economic achievement are the endless expanses of sugar cane, and fruit and betel-nut trees, which serve as evidence of a traditional culture that revels in its agricultural roots as it meshes with the "progressive" 21st century.

If it is open spaces and sun that you need, while still being within range of the city, the southwest is the place for you. ❏

PRECEDING PAGES: Lianchitan, or Lotus Lake, north of Kaohsiung, has pretty pavilions, temples and pagodas built around it.

TAINAN

Maps:
Area 228
City 232

The island's fourth-largest city is clean and cultured, combining a modern social scene with a deep respect for tradition in a maze of narrow lanes and an abundance of historic temples

Tainan is to Taiwan what Kyoto is to Japan, and Kyongju to Korea. The city was capital of the island from 1683 to 1885, and its history, and thus its modern flavor, is inextricably linked with the exploits of Koxinga.

Known in Taiwan by his given name, Zheng Cheng-gong, Koxinga (Guoxingye; Lord of the Imperial Surname) was a Ming loyalist who was at odds with the new Qing court. He fled to Taiwan, landing near Tainan in 1661 with 25,000 troops in 400 war junks. He besieged the Dutch fort at Anping, eventually driving the *hongmao fan* (red-haired barbarians) from the island. The Ming stronghold that he established lasted through two more generations of Zheng leadership, until his grandson finally capitulated to the Qing court in 1683.

Koxinga brought more than troops to Taiwan. He carried a camphor-wood icon of Mazu, which still sits in the shrine to this goddess at Luermen (Deer Ear Gate), where Koxinga first landed. Moreover, his entourage included about 1,000 writers, artists, musicians, craftsmen and master chefs, whose function was to launch a Chinese cultural renaissance in Taiwan. (A similar group of scholars and artisans followed Chiang Kai-shek (Jiang Jie-shi) to Taiwan in 1949.)

Today, Tainan remains highly conscious of its rich cultural legacy. For decades a sleepy town of temples and pleasant memories, Tainan is currently attempting to restore its former glory. Taiwan's fourth-largest city of just over 750,000 people is focusing into a tourist attraction. Light industry, agriculture, fishing and tourism are all encouraged in the area, and a sci-tech park has been launched, but large industrial plants and their accompanying pollution are kept at arm's length. The goal is to maintain a clean and cultured city, a showcase for visitors.

LEFT: Taiwanese, a young-at-heart lot.
BELOW: Koxinga statue at a Tainan temple.

Traditional and civilized

While Tainan is perhaps Taiwan's most socially progressive city, it is also its most traditional. A maze of narrow lanes, courtyards and garden walls are tucked around hundreds of shrines and temples. Native *bai-bai* religious worship festivals are observed far more frequently and extravagantly than in the north, and most residents prefer to speak the native Taiwanese dialect instead of Mandarin.

As the most "civilized" city in Taiwan, Tainan naturally excels in that most civilized of all Chinese pursuits – food. After dinner, many Tainanese retire to sip coffee at the cozy, chic cafés found all over the city, or relish a cup of tea in one of Tainan's unique teahouses. Overall, Tainan is far more sedate at night than Taipei or Taichung.

Tainan is a pleasant city to explore by foot, day or night. Most of its chief points of interest are concentrated in the old downtown section and temples are

the city's hallmark. There are 220 major temples and countless minor shrines scattered throughout the town and surrounding countryside.

Shrine to a national hero

It is perhaps appropriate to begin at **Koxinga Shrine** Ⓐ (Yanping Zhengwangsi; daily 8.30am–3.30pm; charge). Set in a garden compound of tropical trees and breezy pavilions on Kaishan Road, the shrine was built in 1875 by imperial edict from the Qing court in Beijing – the former Ming resistance leader had been forgiven – and now has been deified as a national hero. The building housing the shrine went up in 1662.

A statue of Koxinga stands in the central shrine hall, flanked by those of his two most trusted generals. In the colonnades are enshrined the 114 loyal officers who followed him to Taiwan. An adjoining museum displays antiques, pottery, paintings, documents and costumes reflecting the great man's life and times. Left in ruins following the Japanese occupation, the shrine was restored after World War II, and again in 1962. Major festivities for this father of modern Taiwan are held three times a year – on 12 February (the Dutch surrender to Koxinga), 29 April (Memorial Day) and 27 August (Koxinga's birthday).

Three blocks from the shrine, on Nanmen Road, is Tainan's **Confucius Temple** Ⓑ (Kong Miao; daily 8.30am–5.30pm; charge), the oldest temple dedicated to the sage in Taiwan. Also serving as the first – and long the premier – educational institution in Taiwan, it was built in 1665 by Zheng Jing, Koxinga's son, as a center for the Chinese cultural renaissance in Taiwan. Restored 16 times since it was built, it still stands out as Taiwan's foremost shrine to the great teacher, reflecting a classical architectural style otherwise seldom seen on the island.

TIP

Try these Tainan specialty dishes: *duxiaoyue danzi mian* (passing-the-lean-months noodles); *guancai ban* (coffin cakes); *dingbiancuo* (pot-side pancake soup); or *shuijing jiao* (crystal pork dumplings). Intrigued?

BELOW:
Buddhist monks, downtown Tainan.

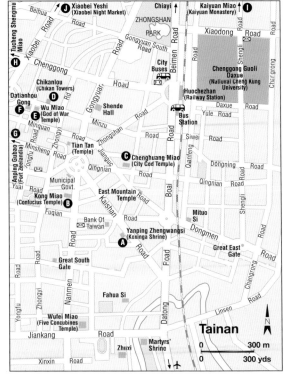

The temple is set in a garden compound, divided by arched gates and corniced walls into a series of courtyards, each with its own halls. Originally, these court-yards served as schools for the branches of classical Chinese studies. Confucius is enshrined in the central Dachengtian (Hall of Great Success), with a simple gilded stele of stone, adorned with flowers and incense. Plaques bearing hon-orific inscriptions to Confucius from various Qing-dynasty emperors also hang here. Ancient costumes, books and musical instruments – used in formal cere-monies marking Confucius's birthday each year – are displayed in the temple.

Map on page 232

The city god

Tainan's residents believe that their behavior is reported to the emperors of heaven and hell by Chenghuang, the city deity (each prefecture has its own separate city god, who is something like a government official). His small, old, and very original temple, the **City God Temple ⓒ** (Chenghuang Miao; daily 6am–9pm), is located on Qingnian Road, between Jianguo and Boai roads. The main shrine is a fascinating jumble of smoke-stained icons, antique hardwood fixtures and intricately hewn beams. Within is a solemn bearded statue of the deity, with life-sized statues of a warrior and a scholar standing guard on either side. In the side-wall niches are two dozen smaller icons of smooth camphor-wood, clothed in silk brocade.

The open beam-work on the temple ceiling is noteworthy. Unlike other ceil-ings, this one is varnished rather than painted, its surface etched with fine fili-gree. Relics and ritual objects hang everywhere, among them two giant abaci with hardwood beads the size of melons, used to tally the merits and faults of each citizen for Chenghuang's "annual reports". By the front door a sign with

Dragons – frequently found on temple roofs – rank top in the Chinese almanac of creatures and are a symbol of natural male vigor.

BELOW: Datianhou Gong, Tainan.

Qianli Yan, "Eyes that See A Thousand Miles," is a temple guardian found at most temples dedicated to Mazu, the Goddess of the Sea.

BELOW:
young boy in Tainan.

a gold inscription reads *Erlaile* ("So you have finally come"), for this is also the place where your spirit has its final judgment day.

Chikan Towers

The **Chikan Towers ⑩** (Chikanlou) were built in Chinese-pavilion style during the Qing Dynasty, on the site of Fort Provintia, an old Dutch fort. Located on Minzu Road, Section 2 (daily 8.30am–9pm; charge), little remains today of the original fortification, once known to local Taiwanese as Hongmaolou (Tower of the Red-haired Barbarians). It was built in 1653 as a Dutch stronghold, then taken over as Koxinga's initial administrative headquarters in 1661.

The towers house visual displays of Koxinga sailing across the Taiwan Strait and ousting the Dutch. Bronze statues in the adjoining park depict the surrender. Nine stone turtles in the park, bearing memorial steles, were inscribed by imperial edict in 1786 and presented to a Chinese magistrate in Taiwan for successfully suppressing an uprising.

An indispensable stop on any Tainan temple tour is **God of War Temple ⑭** (Wu Miao; daily 5am–9pm), one of the oldest and most authentic Daoist temples in Taiwan. Located almost directly across Minzu from the towers – the main entrance is off Yongfu Road, Section 2 – a highly detailed facade of stone, carved in deep relief, graces the entrance to the central hall of this gaudy complex. Inside, an elevated shrine is dedicated to the red-faced warrior-god, Guangong. It is an exquisite shrine with finely painted door gods and attendant dragons, side panels of sculpted stone depicting animals and Daoist immortals, a large center pagoda for burning offerings, and a circular ceiling featuring hundreds of carved, gilded gods. Wu Miao is one of the most ritually active temples on the island. Exorcisms and other rites are frequently held. On some days you can follow the sound of drums, gongs, cymbals and loud incantations to the rear courtyard to find trance mediums trying to contact the spirits of the deceased friends and relatives of anxious supplicants.

Temple of the patron saint

Great Queen of Heaven Temple ⑯ (Datianhou Gong; daily 5am–9pm), Tainan's downtown Mazu shrine on Yongfu Street, is just past Wu Miao down Ererqi Xiang (Lane 227). Fortune-tellers line the lane. It was opened in 1683 to enshrine Taiwan's patron saint. This temple claims to be the oldest Mazu shrine on Taiwan proper, a boast disputed by another temple in Lugang. Tall, well-wrought and smoke-stained statues of Mazu and her two bodyguards grace the shrine hall. Worshiped by unmarried men and women, Yuexia Laoren (Old Man Under the Moon) is a secondary deity in the temple; it is believed that a prayer to this god will help to find a mate.

In **Fort Zeelandia ⑰** (Anping Gubao; daily 8.30am–5pm; charge), on Guosheng Road, a 15-minute taxi ride from downtown, are more reminders of Tainan's military past. Fort Zeelandia was built by the Dutch in 1624, then heavily reinforced between 1627 and 1634. Bricks were held in place with a mixture of sugarcane syrup, glutinous rice and crushed

oyster shells and a large section of one wall, covered with banyan roots, is still intact. After Koxinga took possession of Fort Provintia he laid siege to this bastion, with the Dutch surrendering only after nine months. Over the centuries various additions have been made to the fort. During the Opium Wars of the 1840s–1850s cannons were installed by the Chinese. In the 1970s, an observation tower was erected. From the top of the tower, there once was a good view of the coast (silting has moved the coastline several kilometers to the west). In a small museum, paintings, maps and relics of Tainan's colonial past are on display.

Koxinga landed at Luermen (Deer Ear Gate), a shallow bay north of Fort Zeelandia and out of range of its guns. The spot is consecrated by an elaborate Mazu temple, **Queen of Heaven Temple at Deer Ear Gate** (Luermen Tianhou Gong; daily 8am–9pm), built upon the site of an older structure erected to thank the goddess for safe passage from China. Mazu's shrine, within the main hall, is protected by enough writhing dragons to frighten away an army of devils. Her two fierce guardians, one red and one green, stand fully armed in classical martial-arts postures. Sitting before the large central icon of Mazu is a row of smaller, black camphor-wood icons bedecked with finery. The one in the center is said to be over 1,000 years old, brought from the Chinese mainland by Koxinga.

Largest in the region

A few kilometers north of Luermen Tianhou Gong is what Tainan bills as the largest temple structure in this part of Asia: **Tucheng Temple of the Holy Mother** (Tucheng Shengmu Miao; daily 8am–9.30pm). The entry is formed by an immense two-story facade braced by a pair of large pagodas. The sculpted-

Map on page 232

TIP

Lonely hearts, take this advice when visiting Datianhou Gong *(see page 234)*. Pluck a red thread from the Old Man Under the Moon's sleeve, wrap it in the auspicious red paper provided and thereafter carry it at all times. Your mate will, in time, come cooing.

BELOW: festival time at Luermen Tianhou Gong.

YANSHUI "ROCKET HIVES"

The Yanshui "Rocket Hives" Festival certainly ranks as one of the island's more unusual celebrations. The madness takes place each year in the rural town of Yanshui, between Chiayi and Tainan, on the 15th day of the lunar new year. Hundreds of thousands of people converge on the town's streets. Large platforms laced with honeycombs stuffed with thousands of rockets – the rocket hives – are fired, then all hell breaks loose and the town is taken over by a Dantesque fervor.

Why? Early in the 1800s plague hit Yanshui. Townsfolk called on Guangong, the God of War, to drive off the demons causing the trouble. People set off fireworks to help him wage battle, and when the plague disappeared they decided to continue the practice.

The fireworks begin at dusk and continue until 4am. Smart folk wear motorcycle helmets and gloves (sold on the street), along with layers of old clothing (there are sparks and minor injuries galore).

It's impossible to book accommodation at this time of the year, so take the train to the nearest stop at Xinying (7 km/4 miles away), switch to taxi or bus to Yanshui, rock(et) the night away, and head home next morning a bona-fide "Taiwan hand."

Map
on page
232

TIP

A *Milefo* is a fat-bellied, jolly fellow. Whenever you see one, if possible, give the smiling deity's belly a good rub. It is believed this will bring happiness and good fortune.

BELOW: the classic lines of Tainan's Tucheng Temple of the Holy Mother.

dragon columns that support the portico were hewn from solid stone by Taiwan's finest temple artisans. An equally magnificent shrine hall stands behind the first, with six major shrines in the walls. The small black wooden icons are paraded about town on elaborate palanquins during festivals. Both temples at Luermen can be reached by following Chenggong Road west from the rail station, then bearing right onto Anming Road, which becomes Shengdao 17 (Provincial Highway No. 17). The temples are on the left, on the city's outskirts.

One of Taiwan's oldest Buddhist monasteries is **Kaiyuan Monastery** ❶ (Kaiyuan Miao; daily 8.30am–9pm), built during the 17th century by Koxinga's son and successor, Zheng Jing, in memory of his mother. It is on Kaiyuan Road, 10 minutes northeast of the city center by taxi. Sitting within the central shrine hall is a smiling, pot-bellied *Milefo*, the Happy Buddha, guarded by four enormous celestial sentries in fierce poses. The altar table boasts a very old, intricately carved panel with coiling dragon motifs. Numerous side shrines dedicated to attendant deities contain traditional Chinese temple furnishings of sculpted hardwood. Another shrine hall with altars and image-cones sits behind the main hall. This is a functioning monastery as well as a public temple and at one corner visitors may peek into a fully equipped Buddhist vegetarian kitchen, where all the monks' meals are prepared.

The famous **Xiaobei Night Market** ❷ (Xiaobei Yeshi; daily approximately 5pm–3am), located some 10 minutes northwest of downtown by taxi on Ximen Road, Section 3, features numerous stalls offering clothing and scores of tiny, open-air eateries. Take the opportunity to crowd in together with half the city's populace on a warm, sultry Tainan night to quaff draft beer and feast on the city's many renowned *xiaochi* (snack-food) selections. ❑

Plague God Boats

A rare experience awaits travelers to Taiwan's south, who will be rewarded with vivid and lifelong memories. This is Shao Wangchuan (Burning of the Plague God Boats), an event that happens just once every three years, in the Chinese zodiac years of the Ox, Dragon, Goat and Dog.

The largest of such celebrations occurs in Donggang, one of Taiwan's three biggest fishing ports, a half-hour's drive south of Kaohsiung. It is centered on Donglong Gong (Donglong Temple), dedicated to the plague gods – called Wangye, or kings in Chinese – who have been worshiped for as long as 2,000 years as protectors against pestilence and disease. The week-long festival leading up to the burning of the boats, filled with the parading of Wangye images, takes place in the ninth lunar month (October or November).

A nearly full-size mock-up of a junk is constructed for the festival, outfitted with masts and sails. Life-size icons of the Wangye are placed aboard the extravagantly decorated craft, which is then heaped high with sacrificial offerings that range from tasty foods to practical things such as televisions and fancy cars. In Chinese culture it is believed the world beyond is much like our own, and folk there need practical necessities as well; when burned, the essence of the offerings is transported and can then be used on the other side – in this case, by the helpful gods.

Prior to being burned, the boat, with the gods aboard, is paraded around town to drive out pestilence. On the final day it is brought from the temple to the shoreline, surrounded by a mountain of spirit money, and, after elaborate ceremonies conducted by the Daoist temple's six high priests, is set alight at 3 or 4 o'clock in the morning. The ship's varnish cracks, the cloth of the sails snaps, a whirlwind of firecrackers is set off, and the temple complex is lit up as bright as day by the flames. *Tongqi*, or spirit mediums, flagellate themselves and go into trances, indicating that the plague gods are indeed present. Smoke and ash drift skyward, to the other world, and revelers slowly drift home,

feeling protected. Those who have not worshiped at the boat at least once that day, it is believed, are sure to suffer illness.

Taiwan's southwestern coast is home to almost all of the island's 700-plus plague god temples. In the old days, when people in disease- and pestilence-racked southern China set Wangye boats adrift, the currents would bring them, if they did not sink, to the Penghu Islands or to southwestern Taiwan. Locals, filled with both fear and reverence, would build temples to the gods. This being an expensive game, and the people being exceedingly practical as well as religious, the practice arose of burning the boats on shore rather than setting them off at sea to deliver their cargo of misery elsewhere.

Several legends relate the origins of the plague gods. In each story, the gods begin life as scholars. In one, several scholars throw themselves down a well poisoned by plague demons in order to save a town; in others they are wrongfully killed by an emperor, who deifies them after their ghosts begin wreaking vengeful havoc. ❑

RIGHT: offerings for the spirits of the "plague gods."

KAOHSIUNG

Although smog remains a problem, Kaohsiung and its hinterland are still intriguing, with some remarkable temples, interesting colonial relics, decent beaches and raucous nightlife

Maps:
Area 228
City 240

Kaohsiung ❷ is Taiwan's industrial showcase and a city of superlatives. It is Taiwan's largest international seaport, its major industrial center, and the only city on the island besides Taipei with a true international airport. Kaohsiung is also Taiwan's largest container port and one of the largest in the world, with an extremely large dry dock for ship repairs and maintenance. With well over 1 million inhabitants, the city is Taiwan's second largest, and the only one besides Taipei to enjoy the status of a special municipality – equal to a province.

Kaohsiung is the southern terminus of the Zhongshan Gaosu Gonglu (Sun Yat-sen Freeway), the first north-south artery, about a six-hour drive from Taipei. It can be reached from Taipei by train, express bus or plane. Visitors from abroad can also fly direct to Kaohsiung from Hong Kong and many other destinations. For most travelers, however, Kaohsiung is an overnight stop on the way to see the other attractions of southwest Taiwan.

A city of humble origins, Kaohsiung has experienced meteoric economic growth, but the concentration of heavy industry has caused considerable pollution. The local government is trying to attract high-technology and other service industries in its central districts, moving smokestack factories out to suburban industrial zones. For now, unfortunately, the city is still often shrouded with smog. Fishing remains a major enterprise, with over 1,500 vessels registered here plying waters as far as South Africa. Agriculture, however, is glaringly absent in the immediate vicinity, another indication of the city's industrial orientation.

LEFT: Buddhist scholars in the shrine hall at Foguangshan.
BELOW: the looming 85 Sky Tower.

Long live the mountain

The city center is dominated by modern tower blocks, including the magnificent rocket-shaped 85 Sky Tower, formerly the tallest building in Taiwan, whose 85 stories house a major international hotel in the upper half (viewing deck on 75F; 11am–11pm; charge). **Longevity Mountain** ❹ (Shoushan) overlooks Kaohsiung harbor and the oldest section of the city. Unfortunately, on most days the views are disappointing; only when the smog clears can they be described as impressive. Early-morning photo shoots are generally the only way to overcome this problem.

On top of Shoushan, which serves as a park and a nature reserve with hiking trails, is **Martyrs' Shrine** (Zhonglie Zi; daily 8.30am–6pm), and next to it a series of other temples, pavilions, historical monuments and terraces. Among these is **Yuanheng Temple** ❺ (Yuanhengsi; daily 4am–9pm), found on the eastern slopes of Shoushan. This grand and solemn temple, originally built in 1679, was rebuilt in 1926. It is an important religious center and is dedicated to the Goddess 0f Mercy. Besides providing an insight

TIP

Avoid traveling on the two national freeways on long weekends and holidays. They become heavily backed up, with reckless drivers placing others in peril. Normal travel times can triple. The extra expense of a short plane/high-speed train ride is worth it.

into modern Chinese Buddhism, a visit to Yuanhengsi reveals a dazzling array of golden Buddha statues in the imposing main hall.

Temple addicts may also want to include two other complexes on their rounds in Kaohsiung. The **Three Phoenix Palace** ⓒ (Sanfeng Gong; daily 4.30am–9pm), on Hebei Road, is the largest temple in Taiwan devoted to the demon suppressor, Nacha Taizi. Stone lions stand sentry at the foot of the steps, which lead up to an elaborately carved stone facade. The central hall contains three major icons, exquisite altar tables and 10 large image-cones that glow warmly, bearing the names of the temple's financial patrons.

Three Mountain Kings

At the corner of Taren and Yancheng roads is the **Temple of the Three Mountain Kings** ⓓ (Sanshan Guowang Miao; daily 5am–9pm). This 300-year-old Buddhist temple is dedicated to three brothers, private tutors to a man who saved the life of a Chinese emperor. When the emperor rewarded the man, he

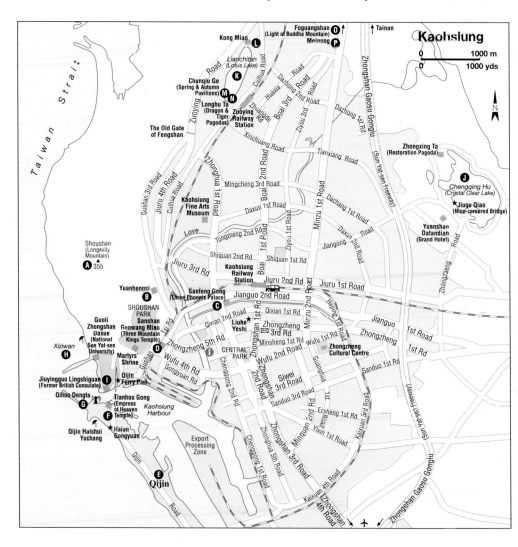

gave credit to his three teachers, consequently making each brother "King of the Mountain" in three mountainous regions of Fujian province. The exquisite shrine hall houses a dozen deities in a complex panoply of ornamentation.

Beach life

There are two beaches within the Kaohsiung city limits. One, **Qijin Beach** (Qijin Haishui Yuchang), has a black-sand beach that is insulated not only from the bustle of downtown Kaohsiung, but also from the murky waters of the harbor, being located on the seaward side of a long island that forms a breakwater for the harbor. This is **Qijin** island, one of the city's oldest and most popular tourist areas, which the increasingly tourism-savvy government has done much to spruce up and make presentable in recent years. A four-minute ferry ride, from a small dock next to the entrance of the Binhai fishing wharf, takes visitors to the north end. The island can also be reached by car, via the harbor tunnel, at the south end.

The island is 11 km (7 miles) long, but only 200 meters (660 ft) wide. There are a number of attractions besides the beach. At the foot of the ferry landing lies raucous **Qijin Seafood Street** (Qijin Haiyangjie), which provides a quick glimpse (and taste and smell) of Taiwan's seagoing past and present. As Taiwan's number-one fishing port, Kaohsiung naturally offers excellent fresh seafood. Dozens of seafood restaurants stand cheek-by-jowl on Qijin. Whether kept on ice or alive in tanks waiting for customers to make their choice, the sheer variety of seafood is unbelievable.

Nearby the seafood area is **Empress of Heaven Temple** (Tianhou Gong; daily 5am–9.30pm), one of the oldest architectural structures in the city. Erected in 1691 and dedicated to the protector of mariners and fishermen, this is a lively temple that is in constant use by Qijin islanders who are often obliged to risk the sea's moods. Up the small mount behind the temple is **Qihou Lighthouse** (Qihou Dengta; Tue–Sun 9am–4pm), a pristine 11-meter (36-ft) high structure that guards the harbor's exceedingly narrow north-end mouth. Constructed in 1883, riveting views of the tightly packed harbor can be enjoyed as ships squeeze by below. Other experiences to be savored on the island are **Seashore Park** (Haian Gongyuan) and a ride in a traditional *sanlunche*. These rickety three-wheeled carts, which wait by the ferry, were the main form of wheeled transport in Taiwan until the 1960s, and are now rarely seen elsewhere.

Beyond Shoushan, back on the mainland near the northern entrance to the harbor, lies **Xizi Bay** (Xiziwan; daily 10am–7pm) beach. The water is not as clean as that of Qijin's, but it is still a pleasant enough place for seaside strolls. It is located near **National Sun Yat-sen University** (Guoli Zhongshan Daxue), with its modern buildings: sports grounds and other facilities have been developed on reclaimed land. Pedestrians can reach the university grounds through a 230-meter (755-ft) long foot tunnel, a cool but windy retreat during hot summer days.

On the steep hill overlooking the harbor entrance stands the **Former British Consulate** (Jiuyingguo Lingshiguan), the oldest example of colonial architecture extant in Taiwan. After the Treaty of Tianjin

Map on page 240

TIP

Qijin meal prices are often not listed, or are unclear. There will be little or no English, so bring a local friend if possible, and be sure to confirm the price of each individual dish before it is served.

BELOW:
seafood kebabs for sale at Qijin.

Hong zhi, or red paper, is said to usher in good fortune. Hung up in homes and offices, it is adorned with good-luck phrases rendered in calligraphic style and in gold ink.

BELOW: Liuhe Night Market.

(1858), the first British vice-consul to Taiwan arrived here in 1861. Five years later, the official British consulate was built on the 30-meter (100-ft) high hill guarding the small entrance to the harbor. Today, the British colonial-style, red-brick building houses a café (daily 11am–midnight), with a museum gallery featuring photographs, relics, maps and models (almost all labeled in English) that give a fascinating insight into the city, past and present. The view from above, looking out over the harbor to the lighthouse on Qijin, is worth mentioning. Nothing remains of the fortifications that once guarded the harbor. The building itself has been fully restored, after having become an uninhabitable ruin by the 1980s after suffering a number of Taiwan's infamous devastating typhoons.

Shop till you drop

As Taiwan's leading industrial and export city, Kaohsiung is naturally a good place for shopping. Best buys are modern manufactured goods, clothing and other contemporary items, rather than arts and crafts. Most of the older shopping areas are located within walking distance of the major hotels. A good street for window shopping and absorbing local color is narrow Xinle Street, which runs parallel to Wufu 4th Road, between Ai He (Love River) and the harbor area. The street is packed with every imaginable type of contemporary Chinese good. Side lanes lead to more colorful markets.

In recent years, numerous local and international business conglomerates have gone on a building spree in Kaohsiung, erecting an impressive number of five-star international hotels, department stores, and malls. This is because Kaohsiung expects, and is strenuously seeking, to be the main beneficiary from Hong Kong's slow economic decline and the long-anticipated opening of direct

trade between mainland China and Taiwan (Kaohsiung sits close to the most heavily used regional sea lanes). The local dining and shopping experience has quickly become more sophisticated. Among the numerous top-flight department stores one can visit are spacious Japanese-style concerns such as Hanshin (266-1 Chenggong 1st Road), Shin Kong Mitsukoshi (213 Sanduo 3rd Road), Tali Ishihtan (59 Wufu 3rd Road), and the massive new Dream Mall (153 Zhonghua 5th Road), with its giant rooftop ferris wheel.

When darkness falls

After Taipei, Kaohsiung has Taiwan's most active nightlife. The busy but pleasant **Liuhe Night Market** (Liuhe Yeshi; daily dusk–approx 2am) on Liuhe 2nd Road, some blocks south of the railway station, offers plenty of food stalls and many bargains. Here you can savor a few of the numerous local culinary specialties famous around the island. The Love Canal, which runs east from the harbour through the downtown core, has boardwalks on both sides and offers cafés and river cruises plus live music and busker-type fun on weekends

A 25-minute drive northeast of downtown Kaohsiung is **Crystal Clear Lake** ❸ (Chengqing Hu). This is the largest lake in the Kaohsiung area (and a very important source of its drinking water – Kaohsiung is prone to shortages). Similarities have been drawn between the lake and Hangzhou's renowned Xihu (West Lake), on the Chinese mainland. A broad tree-lined esplanade leads to the Ming-style entry arch of the lake's park (6am–5pm). The entrance fee gives access to a 7-km (4-mile) long road sweeping the lake's circumference.

A leading attraction at Chengqing Hu is the tall and stately **Restoration Pagoda** (Zhongxing Ta; daily). The winding staircase takes you to the top of the

TIP

When at Liuhe Yeshi, ask where *mugua niunai* (papaya milk), *Fengshan Qishangao* (Fengshan Qishan cake), and *apo mian* (old woman/grandma noodles) are served. You'll be amply rewarded for your linguistic efforts.

BELOW: Chengqing Hu, or Crystal Clear Lake.

Map on page 240

One of the many gods from the Daoist pantheon graces the Spring and Autumn Pavilions at the southern end of Lotus Lake.

seven-story tower, which at 43 meters (141 ft) is the tallest structure in sight. Lovely panoramic views of the entire district, and especially the expanse of the emerald-green lake, can be slowly taken in at the summit.

There are also islands, towers, bridges, pavilions, an orchid collection and an aquarium, along with boating, fishing, hiking, horse riding, golf and swimming. Amble along the **Nine-cornered Bridge** (Jiuqu Qiao), which for its 230 confusing meters (755 ft) meanders along in a most eccentric manner across the lake's waters – ghosts can't move at right angles, and thus fall into the waters. Just outside the entrance gate to Chengqing Hu, a driveway leads uphill to the massive **Grand Hotel – Cheng Ching Lake** (Kaohsiung Chengqing Hu Yuanshan Dafandian), built in classical Chinese-palace style.

Confucius Temple

Thirty minutes' drive north of downtown Kaohsiung, in Zuoying, lies another lovely body of water called **Lotus Lake ⓚ** (Lianchitan; daily 8am–5pm). The architectural attractions here include Kaohsiung's **Confucius Temple ⓛ** (Kong Miao; daily 8.30am–5.20pm).

Divided by corniced walls and "moon gates" into various courtyards and garden grottoes, the complex is enclosed within a long wall, enameled in brilliant red and fringed with gold tiles. The temple's design was inspired by a style common during the Song dynasty, and rarely seen in Taiwan. The most interesting time to be here is September 28 each year, when solemn and majestic (and amply attended) Teacher's Day celebrations are held in honor of Confucius, the great teacher, on his birthday. Festivities begin at the crack of dawn, the same time any good teacher rises for the day.

BELOW: Wuli Pagoda, on Lotus Lake.

The **Spring and Autumn Pavilions** (Chunqiu Ge; daily 8am–5pm) stand on an islet connected to the south shore of Lianchitan by a short causeway. Though the main pavilions are dedicated to Guanyin, Goddess of Mercy, a Daoist temple dedicated to Guangong is located directly opposite the entrance to the pavilions. Legend has it that Guanyin appeared above the clouds here riding a dragon. She commanded that believers construct an image depicting the event between the "pavilions of summer and autumn." And so it came to be; the complex was completed and opened in 1951.

A goddess' stone's throw away stand the twin, seven-tiered **Dragon and Tiger Pagodas** (Longhu Ta; daily 8am–5pm), which also sit over the water and are connected to shore by a nine-cornered bridge. Entry is down the dragon's throat, exit via the lion's, symbolizing the transformation of bad luck to good fortune. The Chinese consider filial piety a cardinal virtue, and inside are paintings of 24 scenes from traditional tales used to inspire obedience and good deeds. In one painting, a son sits on his parents' bed to allow the mosquitoes to sate themselves on him before his parents retire; another shows a son thawing a hole in a frozen lake with the heat from his body, to catch a carp for his hungry mother.

Buddha Mountain

No visitor should miss **Light of Buddha Mountain**  (Foguangshan; daily 9am–5pm; www.fgs.org.tw), at least an hour's drive northeast of Kaohsiung (off Shengdao 21 a few kilometers before it meets Shengdao 22) in lush rolling hills. This is the center of Buddhist scholarship in Taiwan. The complex consists of several shrine halls surrounded by cool colonnades, pavilions and pagodas, bridges and footpaths, libraries and meditation halls, ponds and grottoes, and exquisite Buddhist statuary. Near the entrance, the tallest Buddha image on the island – 32 meters (105 ft) high – is surrounded by 480 life-sized images of disciples that loom into view long before you reach the complex. The major shrine hall is known as the Daxiong Baodian (Precious Hall of Great Heroes). The size of a large theater, this hall has no artificial lighting. Sunlight enters through windows running the entire circumference of the hall, along the tops of the walls.

Enshrined within are three 20-meter (66-ft) tall Buddha images, seated in meditation and displaying various *mudra* (hand gestures). Every inch of wall space is neatly compartmentalized into thousands of tiny niches, each containing a small Buddha illuminated by a tiny light bulb – over 14,000 in total.

Other items in this cavernous hall are a huge drum and bell hanging in the corners from wooden frames, and a pair of towering 10-meter (33-ft) image-cones bearing the names of the temple's donors.

North beyond Foguangshan is an old village of deep and sturdy character called **Meinong** , known for the hand-crafting of lovely oil-paper umbrellas decorated with calligraphy and colorful paintings *(see picture story on pages 246–7)*. The skills needed to produce these items are increasingly rare these days, making Meinong's umbrellas collectors' items. Prices are reasonable, and the local craftsmen are proud to explain and demonstrate their skills. ❑

Map on page 240

TIP

Foguangshan offers tours of the complex in English as well as meditation classes and retreats with English instruction.

BELOW: Dragon and Tiger Pagodas on Lotus Lake.

THE UMBRELLAS OF MEINONG VILLAGE

A remnant of last century, the paper umbrellas of Meinong provide a fascinating look at a once flourishing Hakka culture in southern Taiwan

The tradition of making bamboo and paper umbrellas persists to this day in Meinong, a small town in northeastern Kaohsiung county which is well known for its traditional Hakka community. According to local folklore, a Meinong businessman visiting Chaozhou, Guangdong (in mainland China), discovered a small shop selling the umbrellas. Impressed by what he saw, the businessman urged the master craftsman to return to southern Taiwan with him but he refused. Undeterred, the businessman purchased the umbrella shop, tools and contract, giving the umbrella-maker little choice but to move to Meinong to teach his trade. Here, since 1924, the Hakka people have been engaged in the crafting of bamboo and paper umbrellas, waterproofed with oil to make them both practical and decorative. Though paper umbrellas are less popular than they once were, the tourists keep the artisans in business.

Local Hakka tradition once involved giving two paper umbrellas – seen as auspicious – to each new bride as a wedding gift. The round shape suggests a special union, as *yuan*, the Chinese word for circle, sounds like the words for "fate" and "satisfaction," thereby uniting the couple in love forever. *Zhi*, meaning paper, sounds auspiciously similar to *zi* – son – wishing sons on the family. Finally, the character for umbrella, *san*, connotes the granting of blessings of abundant children and grandchildren on the couple.

▷ **MOVING MOUNTAINS**
Freshly painted and oiled paper umbrellas drying in the sun. The craggy topography in the courtyard reflects the mountainous landscape surrounding Meinong.

△ **TIED TO FORTUNE**
Paper umbrellas once made wedding gifts for Hakka girls. The five strings wound around the bamboo frame bestowed "five fortunes" upon the new family.

△ **OIL PAINTING**
At Meinong's Yuan Xiang Yuan Cultural Village is a museum of traditional Hakka culture with demonstrations of umbrella painting.

◁ **COOL SHADE**
Meinong residents relied on paper umbrellas until commercially made ones debuted in 1963. Today, they are largely produced for tourists as souvenirs.

▽ **IN THE FOLD**
Once the exclusive domain of men, umbrella workshops now rely on both sexes to keep tradition alive. Here, a young woman ensures that an umbrella folds properly.

MEINONG'S TOBACCO CROPS

Aside from the locally made paper umbrellas and Hakka culture, Meinong was also known as the center of the most important tobacco-producing region in Taiwan. Local plantations grew about 30 percent of the nation's tobacco. Planted in late September, tobacco leaves were harvested from late January to early February. Men and women alike joined in the harvest, slinging heavy loads onto trucks for delivery to buyers.

With Taiwan accepted into the WTO in 2002, tobacco production and farm-gate prices were set by the market. Farmers could not compete, and the industry was shut down in 2007. Old abandoned red-brick curing sheds still dot the landscape and are now being used as garages or chicken pens; learn more of this local history at the Meinong Hakka Cultural Museum in town.

▷ **BAMBOO AND PAPER**
A thick bamboo that grows only in the mountains of central Taiwan is used for umbrella frames. The bamboo is soaked in water to remove insect-attracting sugars.

◁ **BRUSH STROKES**
A highly skilled umbrella painter deftly wields a calligraphy brush in his right hand, while turning the umbrella with his left hand.

▷ **UP IN SMOKE**
Just opposite the paper-umbrella workshops sprawl the valuable tobacco fields which provide employment for locals.

KENDING

The attractions of this largely unspoiled, sun-kissed natural playground include exotic flora and fauna, stunning views, dramatic geographical formations, and fine beaches

Map on page 252

The coastal crescent that occupies Taiwan's southern reaches is known as the Hengchun Peninsula (Hengchun Bandao). The peninsula is most often referred to simply as Kending, a rather vague term that, generally, is meant as a specific reference to Kenting National Park (Kending Guojia Gongyuan), which takes up a large part of the landmass of the area. There is also the town of Kending near the middle of the peninsula in the south, adding a bit of initial confusion for those visiting the area for the first time.

The peninsula is surrounded on three sides by water; the Pacific Ocean lies off the east coast, the Bashi Channel (Bashi Haixia) to the south, and the Taiwan Strait (Taiwan Haixia), separating Taiwan from southern China, to the west. The merging of the waters creates a pastel tapestry of green and blue swirls. Lumbering down the middle of the peninsula is the great tail of the Central Mountain Range (Zhongyang Shanmo). Two arms reach into the sea: Goose Bell Beak (Eluanbi), longer and to the east; and Cat's Nose Cape (Maobitou), stubbier and more westerly. The broad bay between the two points harbor some of the island's best swimming beaches and many scenic attractions.

Tropical playground

The Kending area is Taiwan's tropical playground. The sun shines on more days here than in the north. When it does rain, the skies darken quickly and the clouds drop their load and move on without delay; the sun comes out again and play continues.

The peninsula is home to some of the island's best fishing. Relentless wind and water erosion has made for some spectacularly rugged coastal scenery. Offshore, coral reefs beckon snorkelers and scuba divers with schools of colorful fish. After splashing about in the surf off one of the many sand or shell-sand beaches, a leisurely stroll or hike through dense tropical forest or open, hilly rangeland – among stately palm trees, richly flowering bougainvillea, and wide expanses of sisal plants – is just minutes away. When the sun goes down, the night heats up; the abundance of seaside bars, discos, restaurants and resort hotels act as a honeypot for the island's nighthawks.

Wildlife spotting in the protected Kending area will bring ample reward to the nature-lover. On land there are small mammals, lizards, snakes, butterflies and 184 species of bird. In the autumn, migratory birds, headed for warmer nesting sites in the Philippines, swarm in on their way from Korea, Japan, mainland China and as far away as Siberia.

The town of **Hengchun ❶** is the usual point of entry into Kending. It is situated midway between the towns of Checheng and Kending, about 9 km (5

LEFT: unusual coastline at Cat's Nose Cape (Maobitou). **BELOW:** lone fisherman at Kending.

A domestic airport opened In Hengchun in early 2004, with bus and shuttle-bus connections to Kending. From Taipei, this cuts travel time, about eight hours by rail and/or vehicle, to just two hours.

BELOW: beach fun at Kending; Sail Rock in background.

miles) from each other. It is reached by Provincial Highway No. 26 (Shengdao 26), which is the access road from Kaohsiung. The highway heads south to the coast, moves down toward the tip of Eluanbi, then snakes back up the east side of the peninsula, serving as the main route for moving around the district.

In Hengchun is the impressive Chinese clock tower and the ancient **East Gate** (Dongmen), along with remains of the town wall. This is the only town in Taiwan with all four of its original gates remaining intact, the East Gate being the most complete. The gates formed part of extensive fortifications raised in the late 19th century to ward off attack from foreign colonial powers and to intimidate rebellious local aborigines.

Moving about 100 meters (330 ft) or so from the East Gate, you'll witness a renowned local geological phenomenon – the *chuhuo* ("fire coming out"). The earth here literally burns, the sprouting blue-orange flames eternally fed by a reservoir of natural gas within the earth.

Kenting National Park

Beyond a few outlying areas, **Kenting National Park** ❷ (Kending Guojia Gongyuan; www.ktnp.gov.tw) takes up most of the southern end of the peninsula. Formally established in January 1982, this is Taiwan's sole tropical national park, with a strong emphasis on conservation. The park encompasses both land and maritime environments, totaling 33,631 hectares (83,104 acres) and divided between the two environments. A surprise to most visitors is how densely populated the park area is; many a soul was here before the park came into being, and residents have been permitted to stay on and make a living, though new residential buildings are prohibited. Many locals have drifted into the tourism

service trade, but there are still significant stretches of agricultural land that preserve a welcome element of traditional Taiwanese rural culture amid the fast-paced world spawned by the steady growth of the park's resort and recreational facilities. There are aboriginal farming hamlets in the northern area of the park that are mostly hidden away. Beyond Hengchun, all sites listed in this section lie within the boundaries of the national park.

Map
on page
252

On the beach

The roadside resort valley of Kending, in which the town of **Kending ❸** sits, lies between the hilly bulk of the national park in the hills to the north and the beaches fronting **Kending Bay** (Kendingwan) and **Small Bay** (Xiaowan) on the shore directly south and southeast. Xiaowan features an unspoiled white-sand beach that stretches for about 200 meters (660 ft), with a boardwalk fronted by a café/bar and small snack bars. The clear azure waters at the two beaches are warm and gentle, perfect for swimming from April to October. (Note that, although swimming areas are marked at Xiaowan, there are no lifeguards.) There is a wide choice of accommodations in the area, from five-star resort hotels to family-run hostels and several good campgrounds; the national park headquarters can give prices and advice on these. Close by is one of the three nuclear power stations owned and operated by the Taiwan Power Company (Taiwan Dianli Gongsi).

In Kending and Xiaowan (as well as Nanwan, or South Bay, *see page 255*) you can rent all the toys needed for recreation in the area. Shops offer equipment and advice on snorkeling, scuba diving and cruises of various sorts. The majority of shops also provide basic instruction for surfing, snorkeling and diving. In Kending you'll also find outlets hiring out jeeps, scooters and bicycles for exploring the park on land. There's no better way to search out the peninsula's countless nooks and crannies, wind blowing through your hair, than by using open-air transportation.

TIP

A visit to the Kenting National Park's visitors' center, on Shengdao 26 (Highway 26), a few kilometers west of the town of Kending, is by far the best way to get your bearings.

BELOW:
Kenting Forest Recreation Area.

Exotic flora

In the low hills above the two-pronged peninsula sprawls **Kenting Forest Recreation Area ❹** (Kending Senlin Youlequ; daily 8am–5pm, Sept–Nov 6am–5pm; parking and entrance charge), a lovely haven for exotic flora and strange formations of coral rock exposed by tectonic activity. This area, the progenitor of the national park, was first established as a preserve by the Japanese in 1906, who combed the Earth to find exotic species of plants and transplanted here all that could thrive in the climate. The Taiwanese have continued to expand the collection: currently there are more than 1,200 species growing in the giant 50-sq. km (19-sq. mile) research station. Paved paths and marked scenic routes interlace the recreation area, and most trees and shrubs are identified in Latin and English, as well as in Chinese. There are different areas for separate categories of plants: medicinal plants, tropical fruits, rubber trees and so on.

Scenic points to be taken in along the paths include the 137-meter (449-ft) long tunnel through contorted limestone called **Fairy Cave** (Xiandong). Here is an ethereal world of stalactites and stalagmites, eerily

The sun and the luxurious warmth in Kending provide a favorable climate for tropical growth. The old trees and buttress roots found here are unique to the area.

illuminated by lamp, that serves as home to bats. There is also **Yixiantian** (One Line Sky), a deep gorge which was opened up like a sandwich by an ancient earthquake.

In **Chuironggu** (Valley of Hanging Banyan Roots), visitors enter a preternatural world where thick banyan roots stretch 20 meters (66 ft) through cliffs of solid stone to reach the earth, their green canopies whistling in the wind high above. Visitors can also marvel at the famous **Looking-glass Tree** (Jietong Jumu; the formal English name does not match the Chinese), estimated to be more than 400 years old. The tree's thick roots, resembling supporting buttresses, grow above the ground.

From a 27-meter (89 ft) high observation tower in the district, visitors can take in the entire breadth of the long, lazy bay that stretches from Maobitou to Eluanbi. On a clear day, if you get up to the top early enough, distant Lanyu (Orchid Island) can be spotted, as well as – some claim – the northernmost island of the Philippines.

From Diyixia (First Gorge), confirmed trekkers can enter the dense groves of the adjacent **Sheding Nature Park** (Sheding Ziran Gongyuan; daily 8am–8pm), located uphill and slightly eastward from the forest recreation area. Here, in contrast to the area just left, visitors find the riches of nature existing in their natural condition. It takes a little over an hour to walk through a wild jungle world of ancient trees, dark ravines, coral-rock formations and shrieking birds. The section near the front entrance of the park, toward the south and the highway, is laced with walkways that are punctuated with bird-watching pavilions.

To the west of the forest recreation area is **Mt Big Point ❺** (Dajianshishan), the symbol and premier landmark of the national park. Though designated a mountain, it is in fact just 318 meters (1,043 ft) high.

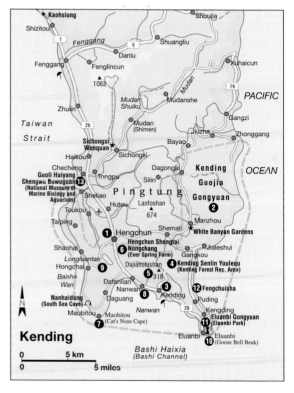

Dajianshishan provides the opportunity for good exercise and grand vistas. There are two routes to the top, both beginning at the entrance to Kending Senlin Youlequ. The first is a comparatively gentle path that meanders along the slopes to the north. The southern trail first takes the adventurous visitor past the tourist-jaded cattle, goats and sheep of **Kending Farm** (Kending Muchang; daily 8am–5pm; charge), a large livestock research facility. Then, as the "big" and "point" features of the mountain's name become more self-evident, the footpath narrows and steepens, with roots, stone handholds and ropes all lending a hand. This last section is not long, and the intrepid are rewarded with exhilarating views of green pastureland and the surf-washed coast surrounding Nanwan off to the right.

Eco-farming

Those looking for a nice change of pace might make their way up to **Ever Spring Farm** (Hengchun Shengtai Nongchang; daily 8am–10pm; charge), located between the forest recreation area and Hengchun. Access is off Sheng-dao 26 not far from Hengchun's grand Nanmen (South Gate). This is a large, private eco-farm engaged in natural, chemical-free farming. Incongruously, within the farmlands, is a rather luxurious hotel with floors of Turkish marble and saunas made of aromatic Chinese cypress, but in keeping with the spirit of things, there are also rustic "farmhouses" for rent and a good camp ground. Share a little quiet time with the 700 Nubian goats or forests of fireflies (from the eco-viewing platforms), ride horses, enjoy the owner's private stock of spirits distilled from honey, and dine on the farm's organically grown starfruit, mangoes, sugar apples and other savory delights.

Map on page 252

TIP

Though they conduct business within a national park, the district's hotels, shops and restaurants are privately run, and not directly supervised by park authorities. Most are trustworthy, but make sure you always get (and compare) prices first.

BELOW: performing at the Spring Scream Music Festival.

SPRING SCREAM MUSIC FESTIVAL

The annual Spring Scream music festival, started in the early 1990s, has become one of the rites of spring for Taiwan's rock 'n' roll-loving expatriate crowd, who come from the far-flung corners of the island to frolic for four fun-filled, music-frenzied days in Kending.

Held in early April, the Spring Scream bash sees about 300 bands from Taiwan, Japan, the US, Australia and elsewhere performing almost non-stop. The venues are located throughout the park and at Hengchun Airport (free shuttle-buses take people back and forth from Kending town. Charter buses also travel to and from major cities). For many, this is *the* party of the year. Indie rock, hip-hop, old-time rock and roll, punk... whatever stimulates you, musically, is to be found here.

Rooms throughout the park are booked well in advance, and rates spike skyward, but since many of the revelers have little intention of sleeping anyway, this seems not to matter. Campsites are filled with people catching a few winks; cars and vans become temporary sleeping quarters. Many come in by chartered bus, party a day or two without break, then head back home to resume their normal lives.

Find out more about the music fest, and about booking bus and festival tickets, at www.springscream.com.

TIP

Kending overflows with people during the hottest months (May–October), especially on weekends/holidays. Visit during November–April, when temperatures drop, room and gear-rental rates fall, and, although foreigners still feel warm enough, locals become scarce.

BELOW: jet-skis for rent at Nanwan beach (South Bay).

The Cat's Nose

Eight km (5 miles) west and south of the town of Kending, **Cat's Nose Cape** ❼ (Maobitou; Apr–Oct 8.30am–6.30pm, Nov–Mar until 5pm) pokes into the sea in a jumble of contorted coral-rock formations. To get there, turn south on Xiandao 153 (County Road No. 153) where it meets Shengdao 26, about 3 km (2 miles) south of Hengchun town. This promontory is stubbier than Eluanbi, its rival across the southern bay, and does not reach out so far. Those who named it claim the massive rocks here, which have come crashing down unseen and unheard with the sea eating out the cliffsides over the years, make the cape resemble a crouching cat when seen from afar. The sea shimmers a deep sapphire-blue, and the cape provides superb views of the sun-swept peninsular crescent. A rocky path cuts through the craggy formations. This is a relaxing place for picnics, or for solitary walks along extremely rugged coastline.

Among the main points of interest are the bizarre geological formations found along what is informally called **Skirt Coast** (Qunjiao Haian Jingguan), which stretches from the tip of the Maobitou peninsula to Houbihu Yugang (Houbihu Fishing Harbor) on the east side. Offshore boat tours offer the best views of the magnificent scenic tableaux here, made up of flat-top bluffs, rocky cliffs, rugged coastline strewn with giant boulders, and massive coral reefs sticking up and then sinking below the pounding waves. Be sure, as well, to search out soothing, inspirational **South Sea Cave** (Nanhaidong). A small shrine is maintained here, and elevated sea-viewing terraces make this a fruitful stop to take in the scenery and for landscape photographers.

In the corner on the east where Maobitou meets the main body of the peninsula is **South Bay** ❽ (Nanwan). Shengdao 26 rolls right by it. The beach here,

about 1 km (1,100 yards) long, is just as popular as those at Kending (beach facilities daily 8.30am–5.30pm; parking charge). Nanwan is also sometimes called Lanwan, or Blue Bay, for its deep blue waters. It is actually a fishing village, and local fisherman can often be seen hauling in the day's catch.

As in Kending, quality accommodations are available (after these two spots pickings become slim), as well as a clutch of gear-rental shops that cater to enthusiasts hell-bent on water sports. In addition, matching its sister town down the coast to the east, one finds a healthy dose of restaurants, coffee shops, bars and discos behind the beach, making this the second of the peninsula's party spots after day-time recreational activities cease. The beach has marked swimming areas, lifeguards and shower/changing room facilities.

Map on page 252

Watching the birds

Above Maobitou on the western side of the peninsula, about 3 km (2 miles) southwest of Hengchun, is **Longluan Lake ❾** (Longluantan), the best place in the national park – if not the entire island – to watch tropical and migratory water birds. Taiwan sits smack in the middle of many an Asian feathered migrant's flight path, and this protected lake is a prime spot for their seasonal recuperation. Surrounded by lush wetlands, the lake is off-limits to bird-watchers. However, a fine bird-watching center (daily 8.30am–5pm; charge) has been set up at a spot that overlooks the thriving mini eco-environment. Telescopes allow close-up observations, with a supply of on-site reference materials (in English) encouraging intelligent observation. Prime time for viewing is between October and May. Ducks, wild geese, snipes and plover are just some of the birds to be enjoyed. The eagle-eyed might even spot the magisterial, and elusive, gray-faced buzzard.

An egret stops to rest at Longluan Lake, possibly the best area in all of Taiwan to bird-watch.

BELOW:
Kending beach.

Map
on page
252

TIP

Kending offers good scuba diving. A basic three-day, open-water training course with internationally recognized accreditation can be had for as little as NT$5,000. Most park rental shops have qualified instructors.

BELOW: Eluanbi lighthouse, Kending.
RIGHT: rocky shoreline, southern coast.

Taiwan's tail

Opposite Maobitou, **Goose Bell Beak** ❿ (Eluanbi) extends for several kilometers beyond Kending like a giant tanker plowing out to sea. Often referred to as Taiwan's tail, the promontory has Taiwan's best white sand beaches. The seascapes here are riveting. Of special note is hulking **Sail Rock** (Chuanfanshi), just off the shore on the west side of Eluanbi, near the town of Kending. This is a towering slab of coral rock that juts 18 meters (60 ft) straight up from the sea's rocky bottom. With the waves rippling by, those with a historical bent and an active imagination will see what others have seen – the huge sail of a Chinese imperial war junk moving toward the horizon. Facing the rock on the coast is a quiet little bay with a sandy beach.

Eluanbi Park ⓫ (Eluanbi Gongyuan; daily 7am–5.30pm; entrance and parking charge), covering 65 hectares (160 acres) and taking up the bottom section of the promontory, features a 3-km (2-mile) long paved path that winds through ancient coral heads of fantastic shapes and through a maze of manicured lawns.

It is believed that the first aboriginal inhabitants of Taiwan – likely to have been of Malayan origin, probably sailing in from the northernmost islands of the Philippines – settled in the wide bay of Kending between the two promontories. On Eluanbi and elsewhere around the Kending coast there is ample archeological evidence of the early settlers' culture.

Some 15 minutes by car from Kending is **Eluanbi Lighthouse** (Eluanbi Dengta) – the central attraction of the promontory park – a landmark erected at the tip of the cape in the 1880s. The lantern atop the 22-meter (72-ft) tower – said to be the brightest in all of Asia – has saved countless vessels from certain peril on the notorious coral shoals that reach into the sea. A tacky tourist complex at the foot of the lighthouse houses restaurants, a car park, and countless stalls selling food and souvenirs.

Outside the park, Eluanbi's rocky eastern side ends in dramatic cliffs. Interesting here is the sand dune at **Windblown Sand** ⓬ (Fengchuisha). This romantic, blustery spot is the site of a unique natural phenomenon. During the rainy season (May–October), sand and a type of reddish soil are carried down together from a distant plateau, forming what appears to be a river of red sand running into the sea. When winter arrives powerful monsoon winds force the red-sand river – 1,500 meters (5,000 ft) long and 200 meters (660 ft) wide – back up off the shore and over the lip of the cliffside, to a height of over 70 meters (230 ft).

After Kending, most people head back via Kaohsiung. On the way, past Hengchun just outside the national park at Checheng Village, a visit to the immense **National Museum of Marine Biology and Aquarium** ⓭ (Guoli Haiyang Shengwu Bowuguan; July–Aug daily 8am–8pm, hours vary other seasons; charge; www.nmmba.gov.lw) is guaranteed to leave a powerful impression.

The shark tank has a number of varieties, but the big show occurs in the colossal one-million-gallon Open Ocean Tank at feeding time. The coastal and inland waterways section is also well designed, and the kids enjoy the Hands-On Pond. Six beluga whales from Russia also took up residence in 2002. ❏

EAST COAST

Steeped in tradition, the beautiful east coast remains untarnished by developments seen elsewhere in Taiwan

On the Pacific side of the great Zhongyang Shanmo (Central Mountain Range), which bisects Taiwan from north to south, lies the island's rugged east coast, unsurpassed for its contours of land, sea and sky. Parts of the eastern seaboard look much like California's Big Sur coastline. Insulated by a wall of mountains from the industrial and commercial developments of the western plains and the north, eastern Taiwan remains an enclave of old-fashioned island culture, a refuge where the flavor of human feelings retains its natural taste.

"East is East, and West is West," wrote Rudyard Kipling, and in Taiwan seldom do the twain meet. Everything about the east coast is different from the west and north. As if to emphasize this difference, the sun rises over the ocean at around 5am, awakening the east while the west side slumbers in darkness. Then the sun abruptly disappears over the Central Range in the late afternoon, plunging the east coast into dusk while the rest of the island still basks in sunlight.

The sun and sea have shaped the eastern coastal lifestyle. People here are early-to-bed and early-to-rise sorts, their skins burnished brown by constant exposure to the strong sun, their cheeks rosy from steady ocean winds and mountain mists. Farming and fishing remain the pillars of the east coast economy, though tourism is fast becoming a third support, adding some much-needed stability. Eastern Taiwan's rugged mountains, deep inland valleys, and narrow plains are home to many of the island's ethnic minorities. The raw beauty and wild terrain here appeal to their senses, much as the coast's beauty appeals to travelers attracted by remote and unspoiled places.

Because of the slower pace of economic development, the tribespeople in this area have managed to retain some of their traditional habits and customs, a solid sense of historical and cultural continuity, and a strong sense of community and solidarity. However, as the east side of Taiwan and the offshore islands are slowly opened to the outside world, and to a tidal flow of new socio-cultural influences, the ways of existence that make the Ami, the Dao and other tribes unique have come under threat. Visitors to the area should not miss the opportunity to witness authentic aboriginal rites and ceremonies, and to explore the abundance of archeological treasures that have been taken from the earth.

On the east coast, the weather is far less predictable, seas are rougher, hot springs are hotter, mountains higher, butterflies bigger, and the people more robust than in the tamer regions of Taiwan. Travelers here are welcomed with hospitality – and curiosity. ❑

PRECEDING PAGES: Ami harvest dance, Hualien – stronghold of the Ami minority.
LEFT: rocky eastern coastline, just south of Suao.

HUALIEN

Eastern Taiwan's largest city and its rugged environs provide a home for the ancient Ami people and a temporary base for travelers seeking natural splendor and exciting river sports

Map on page 264

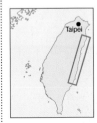

The roller coaster, 110-km (68-mile) long route between Suao and Hualien is literally a cliffhanger, with the crashing breakers of the Pacific Ocean eroding the rocks 300–450 meters (980–1,500 ft) below the highway. Chiseled into sheer stone cliffs that rise in continual ridges, the road was built in 1920, along the route of the original footpath that was hewn out of rock in 1875. At first there was only one lane to cope with the convoys of cars, taxis, buses and trucks. Now, however, with continual widening, traffic can move freely in both directions. The journey takes two hours or so, but the traveler is rewarded with magnificent views and a rush of adrenaline.

Travelers who forego the vehicular routes to this region have two other options to consider. A railway links Hualien with Taipei, using 90 km (56 miles) of track that crosses 22 bridges and passes through 16 tunnels, one of them 8 km (5 miles) long. The trip takes three hours and is usually heavily booked on weekends and around holidays, so tickets should be purchased in advance. The domestic airlines fly to Hualien several times a day from the three major centers. It is perfectly possible to leave any of these cities early in the morning, tour Hualien and all of Tailuge (Taroko Gorge, Taiwan's premier natural attraction – *see page 271*) by bus or car, and return to base by nightfall.

Those who are queasy about flying should be aware that the short, inverted V-shaped flights over the sharp central mountain hump to Hualien and Taitung, though perfectly safe, are known for being turbulent.

LEFT: Ami beauties, Hualien.
BELOW: Hualien marble products for sale.

Cheerful city of marble

Those who visit **Hualien ❶**, which serves more as a jumping-off point for trips to the famous gorge to the north and to the national scenic areas to the south than as a destination in itself, will find it a pleasant and cheerful small city. With 90 percent of the Hualien County area dominated by mountains, the city itself – the largest settlement on Taiwan's east coast, with 110,000 people – fills the narrow strip of flat land separating the mountains from the sea. Hualien's greatest claim to fame is marble. Uncountable tons of pure marble are contained in the craggy cliffs and crevices of nearby Tailuge. The marble is mined by engineers headquartered in Hualien, and processed both in large factories and small workshops. Local bargains include marble lamps, ashtrays, bookends, vases, goblets and just about everything else. Hualien's finer hotels are notable for their solid-marble waste bins, marble bathrooms, and marble coffee tables; the city for entire sidewalks of marble. Travelers visiting Hualien by air for the first time are startled by the heavy use of marble in the new airport terminal. Hualien even boasts marble temples. **Temple of Eastern Purity** (Dongjing Chansi;

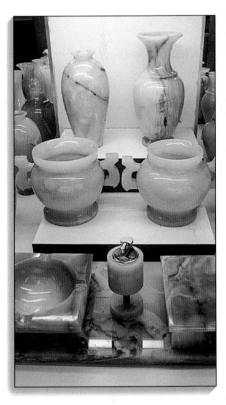

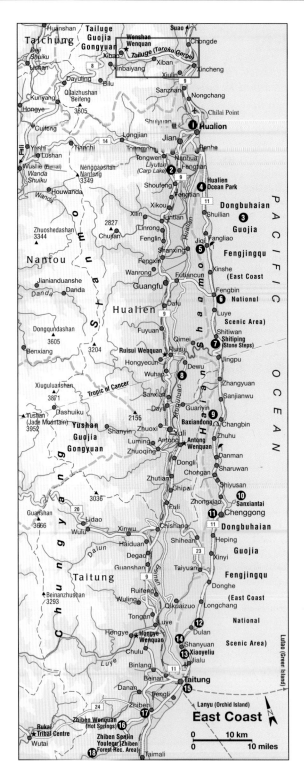

daily dawn–9pm), located on a hill downtown on Huagang Road, has floors, walls, columns and shrines all constructed of local marble. Within the main hall sit three gilded Buddhas. Behind the hall stands a modest pagoda, with a small shrine at ground level,

Shrines and temples

Hualien's most renowned temple – and one of its oldest – predates the discovery of marble here, and thus is constructed of traditional materials. This is the Daoist **Hall of Motherly Love** (Cihui-tang; daily 6.30am–9pm), near the end of Zhonghua Road, just before it crosses a small canal en route to Liyutan (Carp Lake). The sculpted stonework on its facade and columns, and its painted door gods, are its most impressive elements, as in other major Daoist temples.

A very ornate shrine, **Regal Mother of the West Temple** (Wangmu Niang-niang Miao; daily 7am–9.30pm), is on the left side of the complex. Prior to a renovation in 1983, it was braced by two of the biggest image-cones on the east side of Taiwan, indicating that this temple is bankrolled by big wheels from the wealthier west, in addition to more frugal east-coast donors. Two old and authentic shrines are built into alcoves on either side of the central altar, each with its own set of carved dragon columns and a pair of guardian lions.

Behind stands a four-story annex called the **Palace of the Jade Emperor** (Yuhuang Dadi Dian; daily 7am–approx 10pm). Here, there is extensive use of marble. This remarkable build-ing can house 2,000 pilgrims in three floors of dormitories, and can feed them in a huge ground-floor dining room. A top-floor shrine to Yuhuang Dadi is surrounded by carved and cast icons representing every major reli-gious tradition of China. Major festiv-ities occur here on the 18th day of the second lunar month, about six weeks after the lunar new year. At this time, thousands of pilgrims from throughout Taiwan and elsewhere in East Asia con-verge on the temple to have their chronic ills cured through faith, receive the blessings of the priests, and leave donations for the temple's maintenance and expansion.

Map on page 264

The **Martyrs' Shrine** (Zhonglie Zi; daily 8.30am–5pm), built into a hillside on the northern outskirts of Hualien in Zhongzheng Gongyuan (Zhongzheng Park), is an impressive architectural complex that reflects classical Chinese concepts of balance and proportion.

One of Hualien's favorite recreational resorts is **Carp Lake** ➋ (Liyutan), a 30-minute drive by car southwest of the city. Taiwan's largest natural inland lake, Liyutan is a pleasant destination for a leisurely half-day excursion. Set amidst tropical fruit plantations in the foothills of the towering Central Mountain Range (Zhongyang Shanmo), this fish-shaped lake resort hosts colorful dragon boat races in June. Boating and fishing are popular here, but visitors must bring their own fishing gear. Rowboats, paddleboats and sailcraft are all available for rent. Anglers who manage to reel in one of the lake's famous carp can have it cooked at one of the numerous roadside restaurants. A foot/bicycle path circles the lake (bike rentals available), providing for a nice stroll. There are also a number of well-marked hiking trails that move off from the lake to the tops of the hills nearby. The hikes are not too demanding, and trailblazers are rewarded with calming vistas. Campsites and paragliding facilities are also available.

A young Ami woman all decked up in an elaborate headdress of beads and pom-poms.

Home to the Ami

The alluvial plain on which Hualien sits is home to Taiwan's largest ethnic minority, the Ami, numbering about 150,000. About 80,000 live in the city itself, giving the place a laid-back, unhurried pace; time slows down here, especially in comparison to Taiwan's other Han Chinese-dominated urban centers. During

BELOW:
Liyutan (Carp Lake).

A farmer inspects a paddy field, eastern Taiwan. Rice planting remains one of the economic pillars of this region.

the annual Ami harvest celebration, in late August and/or early September, the town is particularly festive. At other times, performances of traditional tribal dances are staged for visitors in the **Ami Culture Village** (Amei Wenhua Cun; daily 9am–5pm; charge), about a 15-minute drive south from downtown off Shengdao 11. There are also various displays of cultural relics and artifacts here. Visitors being escorted around on guided tours probably will be taken also to marble factories on the way to Tailuge, to "look around," with aboriginal song and dance shows sometimes put on to get you in the souvenir-buying mood.

South from Hualien

Scenery along the coastal highway heading south from Hualien grows more gentle and pastoral. On one side, the deep-blue waters of the Pacific either crash frothily against rocky capes or nuzzle the beaches of quiet coves. Inland, the Coastal Mountain Range forms a massive windscreen, sheltering brilliant green plantations and terraced paddies that cover arable land.

There are two routes connecting Hualien with Taitung. The foothill route, Shengdao 9 (Provincial Highway No. 9), features three rustic hot springs: **Ruisui**, **Antong** and **Hongye**. It follows the railway and runs parallel to the coast, 15 km (10 miles) inland. Most people, however, prefer the coastal route of Shengdao 11 (often called Haian Gonglu, the East Coast Highway) for its greater scenic attractions.

Much of the land on either side of this route, running from the coast back to the coastal mountains, falls within the boundaries of the **East Coast National Scenic Area** ❸ (Dongbuhaian Guojia Fengjingqu; www.eastcoast-nsa.gov.tw), perhaps Taiwan's most spectacular, pristine and ruggedly beautiful public park area, which was set up in 1988 and is run by the Tourism Bureau. Encompassing 41,500 hectares (102,500 acres), the scenic area runs from the mouth of the Hualien He (Hualien River) in the north, on the southeast outskirts of Hualien itself, to Xiaoyeliu (Little Wild Willows) near Taitung. The island of Ludao (Green Island) is currently included within the park *(see page 284)*. All sites described in the rest of this chapter are within Dongbuhaian Guojia Fengjingqu, off Shengdao 11.

Just inside the scenic area's northern boundary, and past the visitors' center, is the 51-hectare (126-acre) **Hualien Ocean Park** ❹ (Mon–Fri 9am–5pm, Sat–Sun 8.30am–5.30pm; charge; www.hualienoceanpark.com.tw). This is Taiwan's first international-standard ocean park designed by renowned international firms. Within the eight theme areas is a whale and dolphin aquarium, sea lion habitat park, sea lion theater, the Main Street, Water Fun Park, Crystal Palace, Underwater Kingdom, and more. The park is a first-class facility, facing the surf and with a superb hotel overlooking it. A visit could take up two full days. Shuttle buses make runs to major hotels in Hualien.

Not far south of Ocean Park is **Jiqi Seaside Resort** ❺ (Jiqi Haishui Yuchang; May–Sept daily 8.30am–6pm), the first good swimming beach south of Hualien. The small bay here, surrounded on three sides by mountains, has clear water, and sometimes the waves break perfectly for bodysurfing. There is an impressive range of activities on offer, including

BELOW: breathtaking view from the Suao–Hualien Highway.

paragliding and sailing. Behind the beachside resort is a recreation area where forest walks, picnic areas and a lovely lookout over the entire area can be enjoyed.

Just south of the bay at **Jiqi**, the interested visitor can discover incredible rock formations and a tribal village. This stretch of coast is inhabited by the Ami, who have been left much to themselves over the years in this isolated area. Visitors to this area can still have a glimpse of the Ami's traditional way of life.

Those seeking authentic glimpses of Ami life should visit the little coastal town of **Fengbin** ❻, a short drive south of Jiqi. The harvest festival's opening ceremonies are especially exciting here. (The Ami welcome visitors to these traditional rites and ceremonies.)

Thirty km (19 miles) past Jiqi is the **Stone Steps** ❼ (Shitiping). This area of coastline was formed from eroded volcanic conglomerate, creating intriguing formations. In some areas the rock has been worn and polished, creating a natural staircase – hence the site's name. The rock's grayish-white color contrasts markedly with the changing blue shades of the sky and ocean. The effect is most dramatic with the deep, shifting hues and tones of daybreak and sunset.

River pleasures

Not far beyond Shitiping, the **Xiuguluan River** ❽ (Xiuguluan He) offers year-round white-water rafting in a four-hour trip (Class 1–3 rapids), originating in the coastal mountain foothills next to Ruisui, one of the hot springs areas on the inland Shengdao 9 route to Taitung. Visit the Ruisui Rafting Service Center (daily 9am–5pm) at 215 Zhongshan Road, Section 3, Ruisui Township, if you are keen on this activity. Most of the rafting companies now have offices in Hualien City, and arrange transportation.

Map on page 264

BELOW: Ami harvest festival, near Hualien.

The Xiuguluan He offers exciting white-water rafting trips. In summer each year, an international rafting competition takes place on the river, organized by the ROC Tourism Bureau (www.rafting.url.tw).

BELOW: campers' tug-of-war on an east-coast beach.

The Xiuguluan is the longest river on the island's east coast, and one of the few with enough year-round water volume to allow recreational boating and rafting. The often breathtaking scenery surrounding the gorge-pressed waters of the river is one of the primary reasons for the popularity of rafting here. The waterway begins in the inhospitable mountains of Taiwan's central reaches, making its way seaward – sometimes meandering, often roaring – along a twisting and turning concourse that snakes 108 km (67 miles) before its waters push out into the Pacific. The 22-km (14 mile) rafting course takes up the lower stretch of the river's route, ending just before the river mouth at the coast. The best time to test the waters is about two weeks after a typhoon, when they are at their angriest.

The highway that follows the river's course, **Ruigang Highway** (Ruigang Gonglu), is in itself worth a trip. As well as offering dramatic views of rolling white waters and sheer cliff faces, it takes visitors by the Ami village of Qimei.

Traces of cave life

About 40 km (25 miles) south of the mouth of the Xiuguluan, near Changbin, a tall and craggy cliff borders the ocean. This cliff shelters **Caves of the Eight Immortals** ❾ (Baxiandong; daily 8.30am–5pm; charge), and at the same time provides superb panoramic views of the east coast.

The caves were inhabited intermittently by different prehistoric peoples; this region is prime turf for archeologists, and artifacts are common enough that you'll see them used as markers or decorations on roadsides, in fields and in the courtyards of local farmsteads. Many have been recovered from the caves, particularly Chaoyindong (Sound of the Tide Cave), but most of the caves are now used as temples, inhibiting any appreciation of the historical importance

of the place. The visitor center houses some of the artifacts, plus dioramas.

Steps from the parking lot lead to where a shrine hall is built into the mouth of a large cavern facing the ocean; in an adjacent cave sit three garish pink Buddha images. The final ascent leads through bamboo thickets close to the top of the bluff. Here, the trail splits. The right fork leads to the Haileidong (Sea Thunder Cave), a stone grotto where ascetics once lived and meditated. The left fork ascends to the topmost cave, containing a crude shrine with several icons. On a clear day, sharp-eyed observers can almost see the southern tip of Taiwan. After the exertion from the climb, the black sand beach at the foot of the cliffs is a refreshing place for a dip. There is another beach at **Bamboo Lake** (Zhuhu), 10 km (6 miles) further south.

Map on page 264

Immortal island

Between Zhuhu and Chenggong there is an island outcropping of contorted coral known as **Platform of the Three Immortals** ❿ (Sanxiantai; daily 9am–5pm; charge). A multispan, dragon-like bridge traverses the knee-deep water separating it from the mainland, and wooden walkways wind through a maze of bizarre coral formations, stone-rimmed pools, exotic plants and a cute little lighthouse, with pavilions and picnic tables set up along the way.

According to legend, three of the Eight Immortals stopped here to rest while en route to Penglai, their island abode somewhere in the Pacific. Early imperial explorers sent out to find Penglai brought back descriptions of an island paradise that have led some later historians to believe that paradise was Taiwan – unknown to the Chinese at the time.

A few kilometers further south is the old fishing town of **Chenggong** ⓫, the largest town in the area. A large, intense fish market takes places at the docks each day at 3–4pm. Zooming quickly along the coastal route another 30 km (19 miles), one arrives at **Dulan** ⓬, a bay area renowned for its strange "upward flowing water." A large irrigation canal, dug by hand by local farmers to water their crops, lies west off the highway. Environmental factors combine to create magic, for the water in the channel here (rainy seasons only) really does seem to flow uphill – an optical illusion, of course.

Just 8 km (5 miles) to the north of Taitung is **Little Wild Willows** ⓭ (Xiaoyeliu; daily 8.30am–5pm; charge), a place where contorted abstract sculptures have been created by the hand of nature. Countless seasons of erosion by wind and tides have turned the rock and exposed coral into otherworldly forms that compete well with the natural art carved at the place's better-known cousin, the original Yeliu (Wild Willows), on the north shore near Taipei *(see page 166)*.

Just north of Xiaoyeliu is **Shanyuan Seaside Resort** ⓮ (Shanyuan Haishui Yuchang; daily May–Sept 8.30am–6pm; charge). This popular destination – avoid weekends and holidays if possible – possesses a wonderful 1.5-km (1-mile) stretch of fine yellow sand. Watersports including windsurfing are available, and the resort is the region's yachting center. The beach tapers into picturesque coral reefs at either end, making for enjoyable snorkeling expeditions. ❑

BELOW: windsurfer at Shanyuan beach.

TAROKO GORGE

Spectacular Taroko Gorge enthralls visitors with its dramatic landscapes and is home to an abundance of wildlife, but memories of human tragedy here temper the traveler's excitement

Map on page 272

N ine out of 10 people who visit Hualien tour **Taroko Gorge** (Tailuge), one of the most spectacular natural wonders of the world and Taiwan's foremost scenic attraction.

By car, cab or bus, the route from Hualien heads north for 15 km (9 miles), through vast and green plantations of papaya, banana and sugar cane. When the road reaches **Xincheng** it cuts westward, straight into the cavernous, marble-rich gorge of Tailuge (24 hours; free). *Tailuge* means "beautiful" in the Ami dialect, though it is in fact the Atayal people, who inhabit the north end of the island, that have been the most recent aboriginal residents. Visitors at once realize that the people who named the site were not exaggerating. A gorge of marble cliffs, through which flows the torrential Liwu He (Liwu River), Taroko Gorge winds sinuously for 19 km (12 miles) from Tianxiang to the coast.

From mountain to sea

The gorge is part of **Taroko National Park** (Tailuge Guojia Gongyuan; 24 hours; www.taroko.gov.tw), which stretches 36 km (22 miles) from east to west, and 42 km (26 miles) north to south. Covering an expanse of 92,000 hectares (37,000 acres) in the central mountains, altitudes range from the tip of the highest mountain, Nanhutashan (Mt Nanhuta) at 3,700 meters (12,100 ft), to sea level where the giant slumbering hulks drop into the pounding surf. The area is renowned for its lofty mountains, deep canyons cutting off from the main gorge, head-spinning precipices, elegant waterfalls and raw, wild rapids. Wildlife is plentiful: naturelovers paying close attention are sure to be rewarded with sightings of some of the 108 species of butterflies, 122 species of birds, 14 species of amphibians, 25 species of reptiles and 24 species of large mammals that enjoy the run of the park, where the capture of such living beings is prohibited by law.

Over 200 million years ago, coral reefs dominated the shallow tropical waters where Taiwan now sits. As layer upon layer was built up and pressed down on layers below, limestone formed. The intense heat of powerful geotectonic movements transformed the limestone into massive deposits of marble.

The origins of the gorge lie four million years past, when the Eurasian tectonic plate began to crush against the Philippines plate, pushing up the island's mighty Central Mountain Range. The colossal pressure created by the plates as they struggled against each other threw up the huge blocks of marble lying deep beneath the surface. As time ticked slowly by, the Liwu He worked its wonders, grain by grain, etching the marble away and leaving cliffs of solid marble that stand over 300 meters (984 ft) high in places. It is

LEFT: spectacular Taroko Gorge, arguably Taiwan's most famous attraction. **BELOW:** aboriginal child at Taroko.

The road through Taroko Gorge winds in and out of tunnels which splice through the thickly marbled mountains. Not surprisingly, lives were lost in its construction.

estimated that Taiwan's heavy annual rainfall, along with the fact that the island is still being heaved higher out of the sea, is helping to deepen the gorge by about 5 mm (⅕ inch) a year.

Impressive but tragic road

The road that slices through the gorge, Zhongheng (the Central Cross-Island High-way), is in many ways just as impressive as the gorge itself. Spanning the chasm and the high mountains to connect the east side of Taiwan to the west, the highway was hacked out by hand in sections. The road, started in 1956, was initially con-ceived as a military route, enabling quick troop movements should mainland China attack and the coastal routes be cut off. Demobilized servicemen, most of whom had grown up on the mainland, had little education, were unable to speak Tai-wanese and therefore had little prospect of civilian employment in Taiwan, were given the job of cutting out the one-lane highway from the mountains. More than 450 of these men lost their lives in the great engineering project, which was com-pleted in four years. The eastern section of the highway, ending at Dayuling, 78 km (48 miles) from the ocean, winds through 38 tunnels cut from solid rock.

The first scenic points along the route are **Light of Zen Temple ⑧** (Changuangsi) and **Eternal Spring Shrine** (Changchunsi), in the first 3 km (2 miles) past the visitors center at the eastern entrance to the park off Shengdao 9 (Provincial Highway No. 9). Changuangsi is a sombre four-story Zen Buddhist monastery styled along classical Chinese lines. The mountainous *mise-en-scènes* here are invigorating. Nearby Changchunsi is a memorial to the retired service-men who lost their lives constructing Zhongheng, still sometimes called the Bao-dao Caihong (Rainbow of Treasure Island) by members of the older generation

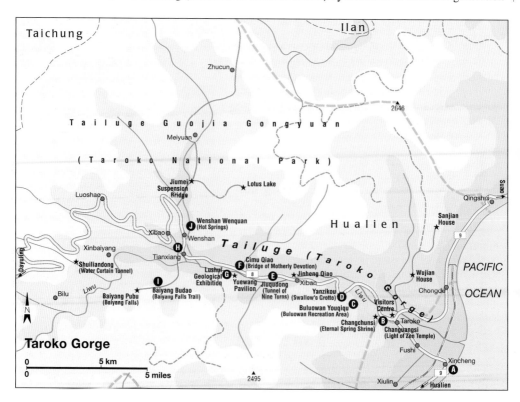

living along the route. The shrine is perched on a cliff overlooking the boulder-strewn valley. Moving westward, it is found off the highway to the left after emerging from the first long tunnel. An underground spring emerges and rushes beneath the structure, floating past a graceful moon bridge that forms part of the small complex. The spring has come to symbolize the dedication, sacrifice and undying spirit of the rough and ready men in whose honor the shrine was erected. Appropriately, worshipers light cigarettes rather than incense in their memory.

Atayal homeland

Between Changchunsi and Yanzikuo, just off the highway to the south, is **Buluowan Recreation Area** (Buluowan Youqiqu; daily 8.30am–4.30pm, closed 1st and 3rd Mon each month; charge). The gorge and surrounding area were home for generations to the Taroko tribe, an offshoot of the Atayal people, Taiwan's second-largest tribe. Most have now moved away from the gorge, but Buluowan has been designated a scenic spot by the national parks administration, and members of the tribe live and work here. The small village has a theater where traditional tribal dances are staged for visitors, a museum with displays of Taroko arts and crafts (with an adjoining gift shop), and over 20 recreations of traditional Taroko wooden huts that visitors can rent. Food is provided at the resort; accommodations must be booked in advance. A stay of a day or two is a good opportunity to learn more of the customs and everyday life of this proud and noble people.

More genuine and undisturbed Taroko villages can be accessed by a number of trails that start off from the gorge. Many of the trails are in fact the traditional paths that connected the remote and almost inaccessible Taroko settlements scattered around the gorge and the tight canyons of the Liwu He's tributaries. Before

Map on page 272

TIP

In Taroko Gorge there are three small campsites (free; first come first served), the Taroko-style huts at Buluowan, church guesthouses, and two international hotels; try to book well in advance.

BELOW:
the Eternal Spring Shrine, Taroko Gorge.

coming to the area, the Taroko lived further off in the mountains, away from the coast. Between 1680 and 1740, internal conflicts rented the Atayal people, and many on the losing side – the Taroko – crossed hunting trails over the Central Mountain Range, moving down the Liwu He. In the process, the aborigines already living here, from the *pingpu* (plains) tribes, were decimated and scattered.

Detailed information and advice on the area's trails can be obtained from the park's visitors center located at the eastern entrance to the gorge (daily 8.30am–4.45pm, closed 2nd Mon of each month), where there is a leisure information center as well as special displays on Atayal culture and the district's ecology. Many staff members speak excellent English.

Swallow's Grotto

At **Swallow's Grotto** (Yanzikou), a series of magnificent cliffs tower so tall on either side of the road that direct sunlight hits the floor of the gorge only around noon time. A little further up the road, **Fuji Cliff** (Fuji Duanyai) sets visitors' heads reeling as they look up its sheer stone face, with the roar of the river below.

Swallows' nests hang precariously from holes in the sharp precipices on the opposite side of the road at Yanzikou. These nesting places were in fact etched out of the limestone by natural erosion; many may, long ago, have been the exit points for powerful underground streams. With the increase in visitors in recent decades, the tiny birds have left the area.

Over countless years erosion has also created grotesque formations in the immense marble outcroppings that seem to hang from the cliffs. Walking along this stretch of road is pleasant; the tunnel cut into the face of one cliff has separate paths for vehicles and walkers.

BELOW: a Taroko village woman.

Walk: don't ride

Wherever possible, visitors should walk the gorge instead of riding in enclosed vehicles. From Yanzikou one can walk to **Jinheng Bridge** (Jinheng Qiao), where the gorge's famous Yindianren ("Indian") rock looms solemnly into view. Nature's mysterious forces have worked to hew the stone of the cliff face on the north bank of the river into the likeness of a native North American chief's head. The image is even crowned with a giant headdress made of vegetation that clings on top of the craggy rock.

  Tunnel of Nine Turns ❻ (Jiuqudong) is a remarkable feat of engineering – it cuts a twisting, crooked road of short tunnels and half tunnels through solid marble cliffs (now pedestrian-only). Located about 1 km (⅝ mile) past Jinheng Qiao, one can see the exposed faces of some of the thickest deposits of marble in the area. Many of the unfortunate souls who fell to their deaths in the building of the road did so here; to get at the stone, workers would be suspended from flimsy, makeshift bamboo contraptions, dangling in mid-air above the rocks and water far below.

  In this section the sheer perpendicular walls framing the slicing river's course press in to within just a few dozen feet. The effect is awesome; the vision fantastic. In some places the sky disappears from view. **The Bridge of Motherly Devotion ❼** (Cimu Qiao), just up from the Tunnel of Nine Turns, is worth a stop to explore the rocky riverbed, a jumble of huge marble boulders tossed carelessly down the gully by some ancient convulsion. A small marble pavilion stands on a hillock.

  Just beyond the bridge, on the road's south side, is the **Lushui Geological Exhibition ❽** (daily 9am–4pm, closed 2nd and 4th Mon each month). The

Map on page 272

TIP

If possible, try to hike the many trails around the gorge in the quiet of early morning – when monkeys and other small mammals venture down into the area to feed on wild fruits and plants.

BELOW: a tunnel cut through marble in Taroko Gorge.

Chinese lanterns are a throwback to Taiwan's ancient past.

facility is a superb way to get your geo-historic bearings of the gorge, Taiwan's towering mountain ranges, and the rugged east coast, and offers a plentiful supply of information in English. The first-floor exhibit expounds on fundamental geological principles and processes. The second floor explores the special landscapes and geological characteristics of Taroko National Park.

The next stop on the Tailuge tour is **Tianxiang ⓗ**. During the Chinese New Year holidays only buses may enter the gorge between 7am and 4pm. The park's shuttle buses, with guides, run from Xincheng Railway Station (charge per person).

A suspension bridge just before Tianxiang leads across the river to an exquisite seven-story pagoda perched on a peak. The vistas here, especially in the mornings when the slumbering mountains are wrapped in a quilt of mist, are enough to inspire religious conviction. From the pagoda a short, refreshing walk will lead you to a small temple nearby.

Not far up the road from Tianxiang, on the left side moving inland, visitors will come to the entrance of the most popular of Tailuge's many trails, **Baiyang Falls Trail ❶** (Baiyang Budao). The trail does not demand great exertion, and is clearly marked. A 380-meter (1,247-ft) tunnel begins the 3.6-km (2¼-mile) round-trip trek, which opens directly onto a red railed bridge over a small cascading river.

The goal is to reach **Water Curtain Tunnel** (Shuiliandong). To get there, six more tunnels must be navigated. The longer ones have solar-powered lamps, turned on at the entrances, which go off automatically after two-and-a-half minutes – so don't dawdle if you don't like the dark.

BELOW: Tianxiang village, Taroko Gorge.

Along the way, the park's panoply of rich flora and fauna comes in closer than on the main highway. Try to differentiate the juniper from the dwarf bamboo,

the spruce from the pine; enjoy the Chinese photinia, the orchids, the alpine flowers, and the lithophytes (stone plants). Lucky sojourners will hear, and may even be able to spy, the now rare Formosan rock monkey (Formosan macaque), the Formosan pangolin, the Formosan long-nosed tree squirrel, the Formosan serow, and perhaps even the Formosan black bear. Wild boars, goats, hares and snakes are also frequently seen in the gorge. Keep your eyes peeled and cameras at the ready.

Map on page 272

Picnic at the falls

Upon making your way through the fourth tunnel, you will arrive at **Baiyang Falls Bridge** (Baiyang Pubu Qiao). Directly across this bridge is a suspension bridge that leads to a viewing platform on the far side. From this vantage point you can enjoy some marvellous scenery of the gushing, hurtling Baiyang Pubu and the snaking river valley. The air tends to be somewhat damp here, so an extra layer of clothing might come in handy for those prone to chills. This is a memorable spot for a light picnic and a session of photo-taking with the roaring of the waterfall pounding down into a deep pool.

The falls are one of the better-known scenic spots in the park. Another one, Shuiliandong (Water Curtain Tunnel), is located just 300 meters (990 ft) further up the trail. Leaving the falls, two more tunnels are passed through. The next, Shuiliandong, streams with a curtain of water, end to end, that gushes from the low ceiling. Unfortunately, due to the effects of the 9-21 and later earthquakes, the tunnel is currently closed indefinitely because of concern regarding its stability. The Baiyang Pubu walk should take a leisurely two hours.

TIP

Local snack foods and canned drinks can be bought at the Tianxiang bus station, but hikers should bring their own food supplies. Also, since not all tunnels have lights, a flashlight is advised.

Wenshan Hot Springs

Just a few minutes' drive beyond Tianxiang – approximately 3 km (2 miles) – a series of steps at the mouth of the third tunnel from the town leads down to the dramatic setting of the **Wenshan Hot Springs ❺** (Wenshan Wenquan).

The magnificent walk to the bottom of the gorge is an appetizer for the hot springs themselves. After a swaying suspension bridge crosses the Dasha Xi (Dasha River), steps carved into the cliff side lead along a small tributary to a large hot pool lying in an open cave of solid marble, which is immediately adjacent to the sparkling fresh water tumbling along the rocky riverbed. However, note that access has been indefinitely restricted due to rock-face instability.

The water in the hot pool is crystal-clear, despite heavy concentrations of sulfur and other minerals, which stain the rocks and whose pungent aroma wafts through the air. A bubbling spring lets the hot water seep through a crack in the cave wall, and a drain hole spills the pool into the river. Bathers can enjoy the sensation of hot spring and cold river water rushing simultaneously over their limbs; the hot waters are around 46–48°C (115–118°F). There are no showers or vendors to spoil the beauty of this spot, and large boulders provide the only cover to bathers changing their clothes. From here, Zhongheng continues towards Dayuling. ❑

BELOW: scenic Wenshan Hot Springs.

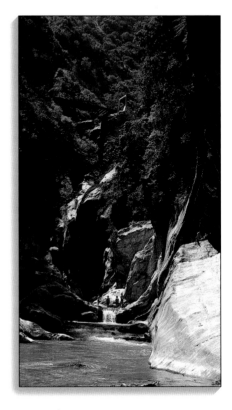

TAITUNG

Map on page 264

The area around Taitung is home to a soothing mix of invigorating hot springs, refreshingly unspoiled forests and harmonious temples that inspire meditation

Reached from the north by both Shengdao 9 (Provincial Highway No. 9) and Shengdao 11, the sleepy seaside city of **Taitung ⑮** is pleasant and airy. At about the same latitude as Kaohsiung on the opposite coast, Taitung is the economic hub for the lower portion of the east coast.

The city is not much of a traveler's destination in itself, but is a convenient springboard for excursions to nearby places such as Zhiben Wenquan (Zhiben Hot Springs), Ludao (Green Island) and Lanyu (Orchid Island), Huadong Zonggu Guojia Fengjingqu (East Rift Valley National Scenic Area; www.erv-nsa.gov.tw) and the Dongbuhaian Guojia Fengjingqu (East Coast National Scenic Area; www.eastcoast-nsa.gov.tw), whose south entrance lies just north along Shengdao 11. Taitung can be reached directly by air from Taipei and Kaohsiung. There are also regular train and bus services from Kaohsiung and Hualien.

Within the city limits are a few sites worth visiting. The most popular is **Carp Hill** (Liyushan), in the western section of the city, with its **Dragon and Phoenix Temple** (Longfeng Fotang; daily 8am–9pm) providing fine views of the city and sea. The temple itself, tucked into the lower east side of the hill, is not particularly noteworthy, except for some interesting icons and a small collection of 3,000–5,000-year-old archeological artifacts unearthed in the area. These stone implements include coffin slabs and hand tools, proving that people lived on Taiwan long before the dawn of written history.

Smiling gods

On Zhonghua Road near Renai Road stands a modest Mazu temple, **Palace of the Empress of Heaven** (Tianhou Gong; daily 7am–9pm), with its ornately enameled and gilded facade. The Sanxingshen (Three Star Gods) of Longevity, Prosperity and Posterity smile down from the central roof beam.

Taitung's beach is located at the end of Taitung Road off the main avenue. The beach, however, is unsuitable for swimming, as the entire Taitung shoreline froths and churns with rough breakers. As for dining, there is good seafood in the eateries found along Zhengqi Road, and traditional Taiwanese snack foods can be purchased along Zhonghua Road.

On the outskirts of the city, at 1 Bowuguan (Museum) Road, is one of Taitung's finest treasures, the **National Museum of Prehistory** (Guoli Taiwan Shiqian Wenhua Bowuguan; Tue–Sun 9am–5pm; charge; www.nmp.gov.tw). It is dedicated to increasing understanding of the island's original peoples. The museum is also in charge of Taitung's **Beinan Culture Park** (Beinan Wenhua Gongyuan; Tue–Sun 9am–5pm), one of the richest archeological finds in Taiwan in the past few decades, located behind the train station.

LEFT: spread of Chinese dim sum, literally, "heart bits." **BELOW:** local fruit produce at a market near Taitung.

All for a good soak. The mineral-rich waters and the clean air are the main reasons why visitors flock to the Zhiben Hot Springs.

BELOW: Zhiben Hot Springs was developed by the Japanese.

South from Taitung

Tucked against the mountainside at the mouth of a rugged canyon, along the rocky Zhiben River, is **Zhiben Hot Springs ⓰** (Zhiben Wenquan), one of Taiwan's oldest and most remote hot-spring resorts. Dubbed "Zhiben" (Source of Wisdom) by the Japanese, it was developed as a resort by the Japanese around the beginning of the 20th century. It was, in fact, the Japanese who brought a love of hot-spring soaking to the Taiwanese during their 50-year uninvited stay (1895–1945) as colonial masters on the island.

The village of **Zhiben ⓱** lies on the coast 12 km (7 miles) south of Taitung. The hot-springs area is another 2 km (1¼ miles) inland; all hotels and inns are either directly beside the river's south bank or in the hills behind. This is almost as far away as one can get from big, bustling Taipei – in spirit and in distance – and yet still be in Taiwan.

The Zhiben Xiagu (Zhiben Valley), which cuts into the steep mountains beyond the spa, is reminiscent of the lovely wild gorges hidden deep within the remote mountain ranges of western Sichuan province, on the mainland, and is well worth exploring. Here are thick forests and clear streams, steep cliffs and waterfalls, bamboo groves and fruit orchards, robust mountain-dwellers, and exotic flora and fauna.

The resort area can be divided into three primary districts. The first district is the first reached from Taitung – a concentration primarily of older hotels, with more and more new being built, where mineral waters are piped in from the hills. The second district, before the mouth of the valley, is home to a clutch of newer hotels and downscale retail outlets that sits directly across Zhiben He from Zhiben Senlin Youlequ (Zhiben Forest Recreation Area), which also happens to be the third district.

The retail establishments in the second district have sprung up, in large part, in direct response to the slowly growing popularity of the forest park. The **Jyhbeen Hotel** (Zhiben Dafandian), in the first area, is the site of the biggest outdoor mineral pools in all of Taiwan.

Set against the tangled mountain behind the hotel, the triple pool is canopied by cliff-hanging banyans and swaying palms. It is constructed entirely of smooth cobblestones and oddly shaped rocks. The hottest pool is unbearable for those with tender toes. But the medium one is just right for long, soothing soaks. The hot pools are about 5 meters (16 ft) wide and 2 meters (6½ ft) deep, and are fed directly by springs bubbling up from the low mountains. The adjacent cool pool, fed by a waterfall contrived to drop from an overhanging tree, is big enough for swimming laps. Use of these pools is free to hotel guests, but anyone may enter and soak in them for a nominal fee.

The hot-pool regime

The Zhiben mineral water is said to be good for therapeutic bathing. Six soaks of 15–20 minutes each over a period of two days are said to alleviate the following ailments: skin irritations and festering sores, rheumatic inflammations, arthritis, lower spine and sciatic pain, weak limbs, poor circulation and sluggish digestion. Non-believers are urged to try the following regimen:

soak in one of the hot pools for at least 15 minutes, then slide into the cool pool and swim slowly around the rim, using breaststroke or sidestroke. Free-style swimming is too splashy here; the idea is to reach long and stretch the muscles slowly, rather than pump them full of adrenaline. If you are at the Zhiben Dafandian, stand beneath the waterfall and feel a thousand leathery palms pound your back with a water massage, guaranteed to iron out the kinks from the most tightly knotted necks, and to loosen the stiffest shoulders. Then drift back to the hot pools and slip in for another long soak, repeating the process at least twice. It makes a new person out of the weariest wayfarer.

Zhiben Xiagu is worth a thorough exploration by foot. A few hundred meters beyond the first section of the resort village, a sign points left towards **White Jade Waterfall** (Baiyu Pubu), which lies about a kilometer up a winding paved path that echoes loudly with the chorus calls of birds and insects. The waters of the unhurried, timeless falls tumble down a jumble of strewn boulders, dense growths of fern, bamboo and gnarled roots. The biggest treat in Zhiben Xiagu is **Clear Awakening Temple** (Qingjuesi; daily 7.30am–9pm), located up a steep hill off the main road about a kilometer from the lower hot-spring area. The narrow road to the temple begins just before the second resort district (look for the red arch), moving south from the river.

A brace of big elephants in white plaster stands at the foot of the steps to the elegant shrine hall. While Daoist temples display the dragon and tiger, the elephant is strictly a Buddhist motif. Inside the hall are two of the most exquisite, tranquil and beautifully crafted Buddha images in all of Taiwan. The two statues sit together, one behind the other, gazing in meditative serenity through half-closed eyes, exuding feelings of sublime harmony, if such a thing were possible.

Map on page 264

TIP

The best times to enjoy the hot pools are at daybreak, when, under a rising sun, wild monkeys chatter as they gather breakfast from the trees above. Avoid weekends and holidays if possible – when locals pack families into cars and head for the hills.

BELOW: sleeping capsules at Zhiben Hot Springs resort.

The bronze Buddha, 3 meters (10 ft) tall and weighing 1 metric ton (2,200 lbs), was made in Thailand and occupies the rear of the shrine. The priceless jade Buddha, 2.5 meters (8 ft) tall and weighing more than 4.5 metric tons (9,900 lbs), is seated in the meditative lotus position in the foreground. This Buddha image was a gift from Buddhists in Burma (Myanmar), and, while some say it is made of solid white jade, seeing is believing. It is, nevertheless, a movingly impressive piece of religious art.

Mysterious relics

To the left of the altar is a small, solid-gold, jewel-encrusted pagoda encased in glass. This houses two of the mysterious relics of the Buddha known as *silizi*, tiny nuggets said to have been extracted from the Buddha's ashes after his cremation over 2,500 years ago. A series of graphic color prints from India are arranged along the upper walls. Captioned in Sanskrit, these illustrate milestone events in the life of the Enlightened One.

On the ground floor is a study hall and lecture room, where the monastic community meets to study the sutras. Next to the shrine hall is a dormitory, with communal and private rooms for visitors who wish to stay a night or two, and a dining room that serves good vegetarian cuisine. Banyan trees and lush green mountains surround the monastery, and silence – despite the spirited resort-hotel neighbor to the left – still manages to reign supreme.

Though justly maligned because of the incongruity of its location beside a sacred place of worship, by far the nicest place to stay at Zhiben Wenquan is the luxurious **Hotel Royal Chihpen** (Zhiben Laoye Dajiudian), one of the most amenable hot-spring inns on the entire island. Still among the best

BELOW:
an early-morning soak at Zhiben.

accommodations available in the second spa district, its bronze fountain and neatly sculpted hedges make it easily distinguishable from the other hotels lining the roadside.

Zhiben Forest Recreation Area

Just across the river from the second spa district is the **Zhiben Forest Recreation Area** ⑱ (Zhiben Senlin Youlequ; 7am–5pm, July–Sept until 6pm; charge; http://trail.forest.gov.tw). The main entrance, across a newly built bridge, is 10 minutes up the road; the suspension bridge here is meant to serve as an exit only. The bridge provides quite a thrill, swaying freely when walked across. The forest recreation area is a wooded world of walking trails, greenhouses, streams and waterfalls, and ancient "holy" trees. Thankfully, it still has comparatively few visitors: most come here to soak the days away in the hot springs, and to party the nights away in the karaokes and nightclubs. Zhiben is largely free of the unsightly litter that blights many of Taiwan's other resorts, and people take extra care of the forest area.

There is also a picnic area, a designated bonfire area and a well-marked hiking trail that is a joy to walk – you'll have a better than even chance of finding yourself completely on your own. The trail circuit takes about three hours to complete.

Perhaps no stretch of major road in Taiwan is as untrammeled as Shengdao 24, which cuts inland and westward from Zhiben to cross the mountains toward Kaohsiung. Note that the road beyond Zhiben to the aboriginal village of Wutai is narrow and often one lane only, with traffic strictly controlled due to rockfalls and other nature-induced disruptions. There is also the train, but this spends a lot of its time in tunnels. ❏

TIP

Adventurous types should soak themselves in sandy riverbeds instead of the spas. Dig a hole, let it fill, and slide in. The area's aborigines have been coming down from the hills for centuries to do just that in winter.

BELOW: kids have it best at Zhiben.

Map on page 264

Map
on page
285

LUDAO AND LANYU

Off the southeast coast of Taiwan are two small islands;
the first is worth visiting for its stunning natural scenery, and
the second for its unyieldingly traditional way of life

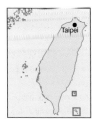

F or the traveler with a taste for offbeat destinations, two islands easily reached from Taitung offer worlds far removed from the mainstream of Chinese civilization. Within sight of Taitung, about 30 km (18 miles) due east, is **Ludao** (Green Island). Originally known as Huoshaodao (Fire-burning Island) – beacons once burned there to prevent fishing vessels from being wrecked on its coral shoals, and to help local boats find their way home – it inherited its new name in 1949. The island was formed long ago by an enormous volcanic explosion, which pushed up the central peak. A tiny speck in a huge rolling sea, at 16 sq km (6 sq miles), Ludao has begun only recently to be systematically developed for tourism; it wasn't so long ago that a holiday here meant sitting out a long prison sentence at poorly run government-owned lodgings. Said lodgings are now part of the Human Rights Memorial Park (visior center/prison Tue–Sun 9am 5pm).

Green Island

Ludao's human history began in 1804, when a group of fishermen from Liuqiuyu, an island off the southwest coast of Taiwan, was blown off course. Liking the place where they had been washed up, one man persuaded his family and friends to move to the then uninhabited island a year after they had returned to their homes. Today, there are about 2,000 permanent residents.

The waters and reefs around Ludao are excellent for swimming, scuba diving, fishing and shell collecting. Glass-bottom boats out of **Nanliao Fishing Harbor ❶** (Nanliao Yugang), on the northwest coast, offer otherworldly views of reefs home to 203 species of coral and more than 300 varieties of multicolored fish. Trails lead into the hills for hikers, and a paved 17-km (11-mile) long road circles the island's rim.

In the north, about half way to the east side, is **Gongguan Village ❷** (Gongguan), a lovely fishing village anchoring a timeless natural setting that looks as though it might be part of a movie-set tableau. Though the village cannot be recommended for its lively nightlife – there are no karaokes or nightclubs on the island – a leisurely saunter around the colorful pastel homes will cause an afternoon to float by pleasantly.

At the northeast corner of Ludao, just past Gongguan, is **Guanyin Cave ❸** (Guanyindong). According to legend, in the later 1800s an old fisherman lost his way at sea in a terrible storm. A fireball suddenly appeared in the sky and guided him safely back to shore, where he found safe haven in this underground cave, formed from eroded coral. Within it he saw a stone that resembled Guanyin, the Goddess of Mercy. Taking this as a divine sign, he prostrated himself before the stone and gave thanks for his safe return. Ever since, the cave has been sacred to island

BELOW: picturesque Green Island, also known as Ludao.

inhabitants, who have constructed a miniature temple inside. Visitors must first climb down a tree-lined trail to the entrance. The goddess is represented by a stalagmite – perhaps the very "stone" the fisherman saw – adorned with a red cape.

Saltwater spring

Perhaps the island's main attraction is a natural phenomenon seen almost nowhere else on earth – a saltwater hot spring. **Zhaori Hot Springs ❹** (Zhaori Wenquan; pools daily 7am–10pm, trails daily 9am–3pm; charge for pools and sighseeing trails) is located very near the island's southeast tip. "Zhaori" means "facing the sun" – lucky soakers can watch the sun rise over the Pacific. The spot is also called Xu Wenquan (Rising Sun Hot Springs).

Seawater washes gently into three large, circular pools at high tide. The pools are thermal springs, and the cooler seawater acts to control the temperature, making the spot just right for soaking. As the saltwater permeates down into the earth it is heated and pressurized, then gushes back out to make soothing bubbling mini-geysers. Only two other saltwater hot springs are known – on Japan's Kyushu and in Italy near Mt Vesuvius. On quiet Ludao, there is no better fun than to head over to Zhaori Wenquan on a warm, breezy evening, slip into a steamy, slightly frothy pool, and watch the day fade slowly away. The Tourism Bureau has built facilities around the open-air pools, and created a "spa" pool behind the beach.

Ludao is accessible by air or sea, with regular flights, taking between 12 and 15 minutes from Taitung. Four boat companies service the island, on infrequent schedules, from Taitung. If a ferry is overcrowded wait for the next one to come. Visitors wishing to stay overnight on Ludao can choose from about 10 comfortable hotels and hostels; there is also a campground near the hot springs

TIP

Ludao's visitors' center at Nanliao (daily 8.30am–5.30pm) offers a good multi-media island orientation. Whatever you need – bike and scooter rentals, campsite information, snorkeling and diving information or, accommodation – help is here.

BELOW:
Orchid Island (Lanyu).

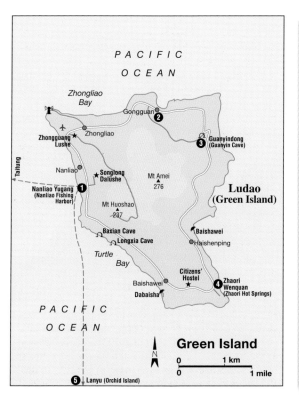

that can accommodate 1,000 people. A tour-bus service takes visitors to ten scenic sites (Apr–Sept; NT$100, tickets valid one day, hop on/off service), allowing users to hop on or off buses, which come at 1-hour intervals.

Traditional Dao canoe – the pride of every Dao man who crafts it by hand and without the aid of any nails.

Orchid Island

Orchid Island ❺ (Lanyu) is the most unlikely jewel in the waters surrounding Taiwan. An island of steep mountains soaring high above valleys and rocky, rugged shores, this emerald isle covers an area of 45 sq km (17 sq miles). It is 60 km (37 miles) east of Taiwan's southern tip, 80 km (50 miles) southeast of Taitung and is home to more than 2,800 Dao (also called Yami).

With colorful costumes and a strongly matriarchal society, the Dao are often regarded as the northernmost extent of Polynesian ancestry. These people live simply from the fruits of the sea, supplementing their daily catch with taro, sweet potatoes, yams, millet, paddy rice grown using Chinese techniques and a few fruits. Goats and pigs are also raised, with many wandering the roads.

Current government plans are to make Lanyu a national park. The master plan is now on hold, because, although the concentration of financial and planning resources is sure to be a boon to the island's economy, which has fallen far behind the Taiwan mainland, the Dao have put up fierce opposition. They are well aware that an uncontrolled influx of tourists is likely to spell the end of their culture, and want a greater say in determining their future.

The government has constructed typhoon-proof concrete housing blocks on Lanyu island, but some of the Dao people still prefer to live in their traditional homes, adapted by centuries of use to their indigenous environment. Indigenous Dao houses are built partly below ground with only the roof showing up against

hillsides or embankments as protection from the fierce typhoons that often rip across the island. These dwellings provide rooms for weaving, ceramics-making, storage and other practical functions, as well as for eating and sleeping. Open pavilions are built on stilts outside the main house for use on sultry summer days.

The relatively pristine condition of Dao culture is a result of Japanese non-interference in the first half of the 20th century. During their occupation of Taiwan, the Japanese isolated the island as a living anthropological museum. Modern appliances were not permitted, and the ancient culture was preserved as much as possible in its original form. Since that time, however, the combination of Chinese business acumen and Christian missionary zeal has had a profound impact on the Dao. The building of a nuclear-waste disposal site on the island, foisted on the Dao under suspect circumstances, still engenders conflict today, making the islanders ever suspicious of the motivations of mainlanders.

The grand tour

The entire island can be driven around, following the 50-km (31-mile) paved road, in a little over two hours. Hotels can arrange mini-bus tours, scooters can be rented, or taxis can be hired. Six villages dot the island; the traditional dwellings can now only be seen in two, on the east coast. The coastal rock formations, eroded by weather and water, are particularly impressive with rocks shaped like lions, dragons and turtles. One thing missing, given the island's name, are wild butterfly orchids. Almost all the plants have been dug up and sold, but, if you're very lucky, you might come across one on a hike into the more remote mountain areas. There are adequate accommodations and meals at a number of hotels on the island, and regular flights from Taitung (about 25 minutes). ❏

Map on page 285

TIP

As the Dao have long been treated by visitors almost as if they are zoo exhibits on display, many demand fees if photographed. Cultural sensitivity will help avoid misunderstandings. A telephoto lens wouldn't hurt either.

BELOW: Dao woman.

TRADITIONAL DAO CULTURE

The best time to visit Lanyu is in spring, a festive season when new boats are launched with much fanfare, and the favorite delicacy of the Dao – flying fish – literally leaps into their boats.

Every Dao man dreams of building at least one boat in his life. The ingeniously constructed canoes are the pride of each household that can afford to make one (and a vital economic tool). Adorned with intricate decorations, they are made with traditional tools, constructed of 27 pieces of wood cut from living trees and held together with pegs.

During the spring Feiyu Jie (Flying Fish Festival), the launch of a new boat and a few other occasions, Dao men wear traditional loincloths and sport traditional "armor" during ceremonies. Some still insist on wearing loincloths year-round; the armor is now merely ceremonial, consisting of a rattan vest, helmet, and perhaps a spear.

Beyond his boat, the helmet is the most prized possession of a proud Dao man, and is brought out of storage on only the most special of occasions. Conical in shape, and made of silver, it covers the head completely, with small slits left for the eyes. To make one, strips of silver are pounded from coins (previously metal from shipwrecks and raids was used, as the Dao do not smelt metal).

INSIGHT GUIDES

TRAVEL TIPS

TAIWAN

TRAVEL TIPS

T RANSPORTATION

GETTING THERE AND GETTING AROUND

GETTING THERE

By Air

Taiwan lies along one of the busiest air routes in Asia, and stopovers on the island may be included on any round-the-world or regional air ticket at no extra cost. Many international airlines currently provide regular air service to Taiwan. It is a good idea to make flight reservations as early as possible; this is especially true when trying to get off the island, particularly after the week-long Chinese New Year holiday period in January or February.

International Airports

Most of the international air traffic to and from Taiwan goes through **Taiwan Taoyuan International Airport**, which is in Taoyuan, a 45-minute drive from downtown Taipei.
Tourist Service Center:
Terminal 1, tel: (03) 383-4631;
Terminal 2, tel: (03) 398-3341;
fax: (03) 383-4250;
e-mail: cks@tbroc.gov.tw.
In the south of Taiwan is **Kaohsiung International Airport**. Regular air services connect this city to numerous Asian destinations.
Tourist Service Center:
tel: (07) 805-7888;
fax: (07) 803-3043;
e-mail: khtsc@tbroc.msa.hinet.net.

Sea

It is only possible to enter Taiwan by sea from the southern Japanese island of Okinawa. Entry ports are at Keelung in the north and Kaohsiung in the south.

GETTING AROUND

By Air

Scheduled domestic flights in Taiwan are provided by **Mandarin Airlines** (subsidiary of China Airlines), **UNI Air** (subsidiary of EVA Airways) and two others.
Prices are low; for example, it costs only about NT$2,200 to fly from Taipei to Kaohsiung (one way). The airlines tend to have the same pricing schemes, similar schedules and similar quality of service. To buy tickets, it is normal to show up at the domestic airline counters and simply book the first flight out (except during three-day weekends and the Chinese New Year season).
Strict security measures are enforced on all domestic flights within Taiwan, and all foreign passengers need to show their passports or ARCs (Alien Resident Certificates) prior to boarding domestic flights.
For further information on flight timetables, contact numbers, etc, visit www.caa.gov.tw/en.

Domestic Airline Offices

Taipei
Far Eastern Air Transport
5, Alley 123, Lane 405,
Dunhua N. Rd
Tel: (02) 4066-6789
Fax: (02) 2514-8522
www.fat.com.tw
Mandarin Airlines
14F, 134 Minsheng E. Rd, Sec. 3
Tel: (02) 2717-1230
Fax: (02) 2545-1812
www.mandarin-airlines.com
TransAsia Airways
9F, 139 Zhengzhou Rd

Tel: (02) 2449-8123
Fax: (02) 2557-0840
www.tna.com.tw
UNI Airways
38 Renai Rd, Sec. 1
Tel: (02) 2518-5166
Fax: (02) 2322-3578
www.uniair.com.tw

Kaohsiung
Far Eastern Air Transport
12F, 385 Minquan 2nd Rd
Tel: (07) 335-3351
Fax: (07) 335-5001
Mandarin Airlines
9F-2, 380 Minquan 2nd Rd
Tel: (07) 802-6868
Fax: (07) 336-4039
TransAsia Airways
2F, 148 Zhonghua 3rd Rd
Tel: (07) 335-9355
Fax: (07) 211-4043
UNI Airways
2-6 Zhongshan 4th Rd
Tel: (07) 791-1000
Fax: (07) 791-8088

To and From Airports

Taipei
The **Taiwan Taoyuan International Airport** (www.taoyuanairport.gov.tw) is about 45 km (28 miles) southwest of Taipei. The traveling time to/from downtown is 45 to 60 minutes. Major hotels offer shuttle-bus services. Four major bus companies provide a frequent service as well from the airport and from designated downtown spots, including major hotels: Evergreen, Toward You, Fe Go and Taiwan Bus. Buses run from 5am to 2am. The one-way fare for adults is NT$75 (Taiwan Bus) to NT$100/NT$145 for the other lines. If you need assistance on arrival, proceed to the information center at the airport.

Beyond Taipei, a bus service is also provided from the airport to Taichung, Banqiao, Taoyuan, and Zhongli.

There is a limo service (the cars are Mercedes and Volvos) from the international airport; the service counters can be found near the hotel service counters. A taxi from the airport to downtown Taipei will cost around NT$1,200 at current prices. Taxi fares include a 50 percent surcharge added to the fare showing on the meter, plus one freeway toll. For the trip from Taipei to the Taiwan Taoyuan International Airport the fare is supposed to be what is displayed on the meter, but few drivers will agree to the trip for a fixed fee less than NT$1,000.

Songshan Domestic Airport
(www.tsa.gov.tw) is right in the city: from the bus terminal here you are only 10 to 20 minutes (depending on traffic) by cab from most major downtown hotels. The bus fare to/from Taiwan Taoyuan International Airport is NT$75 one-way (Taiwan Bus service).

Kaohsiung
The easiest and best transport is a taxi to the downtown hotels.
Kaohsiung International Airport
(www.kia.gov.tw), located to the south of Kaohsiung, is very close to the city center. The taxi fare should be about

NT$300. The city's spanking-new mass rapid transit system also has services to and from the airport. Most major hotels are close to a station, though a short taxi ride station-to-hotel will still be necessary in most cases.

Taichung
Taichung's new **Taichung Qing Quan Gang International Airport**
(www.tca.gov.tw), at present, only operates charter flights to regional destinations, plus some regular domestic flights. International flights are expected in the future. The taxi fare to downtown Taichung is about NT$180. There are now three regular city bus route services, with fares according to distance.

By Long-Distance Bus

Fleets of private-company deluxe express buses serve Taiwan's major towns and cities. There are frequent scheduled buses to all major destinations except those on the east coast, which enjoy less frequent service and rely more on trains. By departure time, almost all buses are fully booked, especially on weekends and holidays.

The best way to purchase reserved-seat bus tickets in advance is to go directly to the appropriate

bus station and buy them one or two days prior to departure. Most hotel travel desks and local travel agencies can make arrangements.

By Train

The Taiwan Railway Administration maintains an extensive network that runs around the island and connects all major cities and towns. The trains are often full, and if you do not like to stand, a seat reservation is necessary. There is an almost unbelievable crush on long weekends and holidays, as much of the population of the north drains into the center and south to visit families. However, without a travel agent, getting a seat reservation on the train is quite complicated and time-consuming. These problems have been eased slightly with the Taiwan High Speed Rail (THSR; www.thsrc.com.tw) connecting the north and south of Taiwan along the west coast, now operational (operated as a separate system, not by the TRA).

The Railway Administration offers different types of service:
Putong – slowest, most basic, and very cheap
Pingkuai – cheap, slow, no reserved seats, no air conditioning
Fuxing – limited stops, air-conditioned express

BELOW: transport for the whole family.

TRANSPORTATION

ACCOMMODATIONS

EATING OUT

ACTIVITIES

A – Z

LANGUAGE

Juguang – first-class, air-conditioned express
Ziqiang – speedy air-conditioned express

Reservations for express trains in Taiwan can be made up to seven days before your travel date; tickets can be collected up to three days in advance – have your passport with you. Although you may purchase round-trip tickets in advance, the booking for the return trip must be confirmed upon arrival at your destination. It is highly advisable to purchase tickets at least several hours in advance, and preferably a full day prior to departure. In all cities and towns, advance train tickets may be purchased directly at the main railway station by lining up at the appropriate counter. Most hotels and travel agencies can arrange advance train reservations.

If you are planning to travel around Taiwan by train, go to counter No. 1 at the **Taipei Main Train Station** service desk (Service Hotline 081-231919). Show them your itinerary. The staff will provide a quote for the total fare, which will be quite cheap compared to buying tickets individually. Tickets must be purchased three days before departure. For details, call (02) 2371-3558 (English spoken). The **Taiwan Railway Administration** website is www.railway.gov.tw.

Do not expect to see too much on a train ride. Most locals close the curtains to get some sleep, and may express annoyance if your curtain remains open.

By Car

It's best to rely on public transport such as the subways (Taipei and Kaohsiung), buses, taxis and tour buses to get around Taiwanese cities and towns. Trying to drive yourself around a congested city is a needless risk. However, if you plan an extended tour down-island or along the northern coastline, renting a car is a good way to go as you'll see many more sights and enjoy the freedom to stop whenever and wherever you wish.

Car rental agencies that place ads in the English-language dailies are reputable and have representatives who speak English. You can also call an Avis, Budget or Hertz reservation center before your trip to Taiwan, who have associations with local companies.

If you would like to splurge a bit and see the island in true comfort and convenience, the best way is to hire an air-conditioned limousine,

driven by a chauffeur who also acts as a personal guide and interpreter. Any hotel travel desk or local travel agency can arrange this. The cost varies according to the type of car and, of course, the length of the trip.

Motoring Tips

No matter how well you drive, Taiwan traffic demands great attention. The locals have a strong belief in fate and a big appetite for "face," leading them to take incredible chances and to respond to even the slightest challenge from other drivers. The roads themselves are well maintained, however, and give relatively easy access to all of Taiwan's major sights.

Following are some helpful points worth bearing in mind:
● There are millions of motor scooters on the roads, and they constitute the single greatest hazard to car drivers.
● Also steer clear of all military vehicles. Military drivers are notorious for their careless driving. Regardless of the circumstances, military vehicles always have the right of way, and they know it. This same rule applies to buses, gravel trucks, and all other oversized vehicles. The "system" used is the larger the vehicle, the more "rights" are assumed; pedestrians are at the bottom of the ladder.
● Though roads down south are well marked, unlike in areas to the north, the instructions are often in Chinese only. So look for route numbers instead of place names, and match them with those on your maps. Route

numbers are also inscribed on the stone mileage indicators set along the roadsides.
● Taiwan's "freeways" are in fact tolled. Lanes at toll stations are marked in Chinese and English (for cars with toll tickets, cars paying cash/buying toll tickets, trucks, etc), with lane violations strictly punished with hefty fines. If renting a car, ask the agency for a familiarization drive before setting out
● Keep your fuel tank at least a third full at all times. In the more remote mountainous and coastal regions, fuel (gas) stations are rare.

Rules of the Road

● Seat belts are mandatory on all roads for drivers and front-seat passengers; all fines will be given to the driver/owner of the vehicle.
● Safety seats are obligatory for children four years and under, or under 18 kg.
● There is no right turn on a red light.
● Speed limits on freeways and provincial highways are generally 90 or 100 kph (60 or 62 mph).
● Yield signs are frequently ignored; the rule-of-thumb is whoever gets the nose of his vehicle in a space first owns that space.
● Signal lights are inconsistently used, so beware.

Parking

Double-parking is permitted if emergency flashers are on and the engine is left running; most local drivers forget about the flashers and engine parts of this law. Sidewalk curbs have been painted different

BELOW: commuters lining up at an MRT station

ABOVE: Taipei train station, with Shin Kong Life Tower behind.

colors in Taipei. If red, no parking is allowed, day or night. If yellow, parking is only allowed five minutes during the day (though the time limit is frequently ignored). If left unpainted or a white line, parking is permitted any time.

Taipei City Transport

Taxis

Taxi fares are calculated according to meter. If you wish to retain a taxi for a full day, or for a long, round-trip excursion, ask a hotel concierge to negotiate either a set fee or a discount on the meter fare.

Taiwan taxi meters calculate both time and distance to determine the fare. The meters have three windows. The top-left window shows the time consumed, when not moving, in minutes and seconds. The top-right indicator is the distance in kilometers. The largest window meter shows the fare in NT dollars. The rate in Taipei (closely followed elsewhere) is NT$70 for the first 1.5 kilometers, an additional NT$5 for each 300 meters, and NT$5 for each two minutes the taxi is stationary. From 11pm to 6am there is a 20 percent surcharge, and during Chinese New Year there is an additional charge. Give an NT$10 tip for cabs dispatched by phone, and for luggage placed in the trunk (boot).

Small towns and villages have fixed rates for the use of a taxi within a certain area, generally ranging from NT$50 to $70. It is best to ask locals for the correct rate; even Taiwanese travelers have to do this to avoid being overcharged.

Note: Although Taiwan's taxi drivers are almost uniformly friendly and polite, too many tend to drive recklessly. Especially outside Taipei, tourists are sometimes scared out of

their wits as their taxi drivers weave carelessly between speeding buses and trucks, narrowly miss pedestrians, run through red lights, careen through swarms of buzzing motorcycles, and screech blindly around corners.

Very few taxi drivers in Taiwan speak or read English sufficiently well to follow directions given in English. Have your destination written out in Chinese before venturing out by cab. Hotel name cards, local advertisements, even restaurant matchboxes will prove useful in getting you around town by taxi.

Mass Rapid Transit

The construction of Taipei's Mass Rapid Transit (MRT) System began in 1988. Six lines are now operational, making travel to most areas of the city fast and convenient. In any station, you can buy individual tokens or buy a day pass for NT$200 (includes NT$50 deposit). This allows you to use the system as you please for that one day. You may transfer to different lines; and there are also same-day transfers that can be used on the city bus routes. The system runs from 6am to midnight.

There are charts with clear English on the ticket machines. Check the amount indicated for the station you

Easycard

Stored-value EasyCards (machines not available in all stations) allow transfers between the MRT and city/county bus lines as well as use of city parking garages, street-side meters, and the Maokong Gondola in Muzha. The Easycard can be topped up at dedicated machines in all stations.

want to go to (your own station is marked in yellow, others in white). Fares range from NT$20 to NT$65, depending on distance. The Metro Taipei Service Hotline number is 2181-2345 (24 hours).

Bicycles are permitted on the end carriages of trains on weekends and holidays at NT$80 per trip (no access during 4–7pm heavy travel period). Access to the stations when with a bike is via the street-level elevators at each station designed for use by the disabled. Access is permitted at a steadily increasing number of stations; designated stations are clearly marked on boards within the system, as well as online (www.trtc.com.tw).

Work on an MRT system in Kaohsiung began in mid 2002. The two main lines became operational in 2008, running through the city north-south and east-west. The north-south line connects Kaohsiung's international airport, main train station, and its high-speed rail station with downtown. For more info, go to www.krtco.com.tw.

City Buses

For budget travelers in Taipei, buses provide frequent and inexpensive means of transport to points within or outside the city limits. Bus services in other cities are poor.

It is advisable to avoid the buses in Taipei during the 7.30–9.30am and 5–7pm rush hours. All buses are air-conditioned. The fare is NT$15 (adults) for each leg of a route (some long routes are broken up into separate legs; most journeys that do not cross into suburban areas involve just one leg). Fares can be paid in cash by dropping correct change in a box beside the driver. Most locals nowadays use the EasyCard, swiping the card against a digital-sensor pad beside the driver.

City bus services run continuously from about 6am until 11.30pm. To tell the driver to stop at the next stop, push one of the large colored buttons mounted on the sides. There are so many buses and bus routes within metropolitan Taipei that it is best to ask a hotel clerk or local acquaintance for directions before venturing out. All buses are designated by code numbers, which indicate their routes; starting and ending points are written in Chinese at either side of the number. Buses to/from MRT stations will also have start and end points written in English. More information on the bus system, including downloadable maps, can be found at www.taipeibus.taipei.gov.tw.

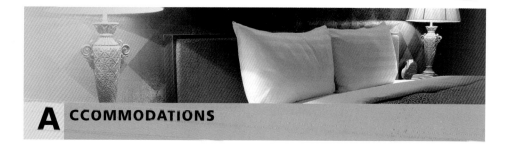

A CCOMMODATIONS

HOTELS, YOUTH HOSTELS AND GUESTHOUSES

HOTELS

Luxury hotels in Taiwan are renowned for their attentive, gracious service rendered with a spirit of pride and a genuine desire to please. Visitors are treated as personal guests rather than anonymous patrons, and hospitality is approached more as an art than as an industry.

However, Western travelers will occasionally encounter frustrations. One reason is the language barrier. Although trained in English, many local hotel staff understand little, but will avoid losing face by pretending to understand, and then promptly forget about it.

Another reason is cultural: Taiwanese priorities often differ from Westerners', and what seems of vital importance to you, such

as punctuality, may seem trivial to the locals.

Tourist hotels in Taiwan are generally ranked into two categories: International Tourist and Regular Tourist hotels. The former will offer greater luxury and more varied facilities, while the latter provide more basic accommodations. Ranked below these are budget hotels and guesthouses/hostels.

Hotels in Taipei are quite expensive. Singles or twin rooms will cost, in international tourist hotels, anything between NT$6,000–10,000. In Kaohsiung, the cost per room drops to between NT$4,000–6,500. Other quality places with some business, recreational, and dining facilities are considerably cheaper and you can expect to pay between NT$2,500–4,000 per night. Taiwan's hotels accept all major credit cards.

YOUTH HOSTELS AND GUESTHOUSES

By sleeping in dormitories, eating in cafeterias, and traveling by bus, you can see Taiwan for around US$100 per day – especially if using the facilities of the China Youth Corps (CYC). CYC operates a series of youth activity centers and youth hostels. Reservations may be arranged online or by writing or calling CYC headquarters at 219 Songjiang Road, Taipei, tel: (02) 2502-5858, fax: (02) 2502-1924; e-mail: cychq@cyc.org.tw; www.cyc.org.tw; limited English beyond website. Facilities may also be contacted directly. For an address list, go to the CYC website or contact tourism bureau offices overseas or in Taiwan.

Due to their popularity, groups and individuals from overseas should make reservations at CYC and other facilities well in advance. They are usually fully booked from July to September, and from January to February (holiday time for local students). If you haven't booked, call ahead to make sure there is room. Rates vary, but on average three meals a day can be had for about NT$500. The average price is NT$1,000 to NT$1,500 per person a night. Most places have private rooms at higher rates, and some have large bungalows.

Other non-CYC guesthouses and hostels provide inexpensive accommodations, clean rooms with basic furnishings, shared shower facilities, and simple cooking facilities. Ask at the domestic tourism bureau centers for details; the bureau is also now coordinating numerous youth travel packages (www.taiwan.net.tw).

BELOW: Taipei 101 and the Miramar ferris wheel light up Taipei.

TAIPEI

ABOVE: The Grand Hotel, Taipei.

Baguio Hotel
367 Bade Rd, Sec. 2
Tel: (02) 2781-3121
Fax: (02) 2771-8796
www.baguio-hotel.com.tw
A small business hotel of 100 rooms in the center of the main business and shopping district. Offers standard business and other services and amenities, as well as a decent Western restaurant. **$$**

Brother Hotel
255 Nanjing E. Rd, Sec. 3
Tel: (02) 2712-3456
Fax: (02) 2717-3334
www.brotherhotel.com.tw
Offers an excellent Cantonese dim-sum restaurant, and sits in a popular bar/restaurant district. However, the rooms are old and tired, and staff often seem distracted. **$$$**

Caesar Park Taipei
38 Zhongxiao West Rd, Sec. 1
Tel: (02) 2311-5151
Fax: (02) 2331-9944
www.caesarpark.com.tw

Formerly the Taipei Hilton, now run by a quality Taiwan-based group, the entire Hilton staff decided to stay on when management changed, testament to the good service you'll find here. The facility is getting somewhat old, however, and is stuck in a crowded old section of town by the main railway station. **$$$$**

Cosmos Hotel
43 Zhongxiao W. Rd, Sec. 1
Tel: (02) 2361-7856
Fax: (02) 2311-8921
www.cosmos-hotel.com.tw
Rooms are rather small in this hotel located in a noisy, but convenient, area near main Taipei railway station. **$$$**

Far Eastern Plaza Hotel Taipei
201 Dunhua S. Rd, Sec. 2
Tel: (02) 2378-8888
Fax: (02) 2377-7777
www.shangri-la.com
Superb selection of restaurants; Marco Polo on 38th floor has superb cityscapes; good meeting

and conference facilities. **$$$$**

First Hotel
63 Nanjing E. Rd, Sec. 2
Tel: (02) 2541-8234
Fax: (02) 2581-2411
www.firsthotel.com.tw
A mid-sized business hotel (200 rooms) in the heart of the eastern commercial district. The restaurants are quite good considering the hotel's price range (the Hunanese, Shanghainese, and Teppanyaki restaurants are recommended). Standard business services: business center, internet, and airport transport. **$$**

Gloria Prince Hotel Taipei
369 Linsen N. Rd
Tel: (02) 2581-8111, ext. 1350
Fax: (02) 2581-5811
www.gloriahotel.com
Known for its expansive health club, this hotel offers a fine business center, and has a good location near the center of Taipei. It suffers somewhat from being in a slightly crowded area lacking quality shopping and entertainment establishments. **$$$**

Golden China Hotel
306 Songjiang Rd
Tel: (02) 2521-5151
Fax: (02) 2531-2914
www.golden-china.com.tw
Located just northwest of main business district. Has three good restaurants (Taiwanese, Cantonese, and European). **$$$**

Grand Formosa Regent Taipei
41 Zhongshan N. Rd, Sec. 2
Tel: (02) 2523-8000
Fax: (02) 2523-2828
www.regenthotels.com
Great rooftop swimming pool with food and beverage service. Other main attractions are the extra large and comfortable atrium area plus health club and sauna. Offers above-average meeting and banquet facilities. **$$$$**

The Grand Hotel Taipei
1 Zhongshan N. Rd, Sec 4

Tel: (02) 2886-8888
Fax: (02) 2885-2885
www.grand-hotel.org
One of Taipei's architectural landmarks with facilities including pool, health club, and tennis courts; located on a hill, with superb night-time views of the city; received an extensive facelift in the late 1990s. **$$$$**

Grand Hyatt Taipei
2 Songshou Rd
Tel: (02) 2720-1234
Fax: (02) 2720-1111
www.taipei.hyatt.com
Located next to the Taipei World Trade Center and Taipei 101 in Taiwan's newest business/shopping district, this is considered Taiwan's best hotel. It wears a grandiose atmosphere; Ziga Ziga, with live music and dancing, is extremely popular, and the weekly night-time poolside barbecue is a treat. **$$$$**

Howard Plaza Hotel Taipei
160 Renai Rd, Sec. 3
Tel: (02) 2700-2323
Fax: (02) 2700-0729
www.howard-hotels.com
Elegant décor with a continental ambiance; the grand, leafy atrium area is popular for regular buffets and afternoon tea. The hotel's boutique arcade (four levels) carries many high-quality brand-name import goods. **$$$$**

Imperial Hotel Taipei
600 Linsen N. Rd
Tel: (02) 2596-5111
Fax: (02) 2592-7506
www.imperialhotel.com.tw
This older hotel, overhauled internally in the mid-2000s, is located in the busy SoHo area. The Front Page Bar's happy hour draws a regular

long-term expat crowd with its generous free food servings. **$$$$**

The Landis Taipei
41 Minquan E. Rd, Sec. 2
Tel: (02) 2597-1234
Fax: (02) 2596-9223
www.landistpe.com.tw
Though small and away from the new east-end business district, the superb personalized service and top-of-the-line European restaurants here compensate. The French Paris 1930 restaurant is perhaps Taiwan's best. **$$$$**

The Leofoo
168 Changchun Rd
Tel: (02) 2507-3211
Fax: (02) 2508-2070
www.leofoo.com.tw/hotel
Located in a slightly older, crowded section of town working itself upmarket. Has nice coffee shop, as well as a combo-cuisine Asian/Western buffet restaurant and a Cantonese restaurant. **$$**

Miramar Garden Taipei
83 Civil Blvd, Sec. 3
Tel: (02) 8772-8800
Fax: (02) 8772-1010
www.miramargarden.com.tw
One of Taipei's newest hotels. Good dining and business facilities. The alfresco Garden Terrace café and outdoor swimming pool are especially popular. **$$$**

Hotel Riverview Taipei
77 Huanhe S. Rd, Sec. 1
Tel: (02) 2311-3131

Fax: (02) 2361-3737
www.riverview.com.tw
Situated near the Danshui River in Taipei's oldest district, filled with traditional old shops and eateries. Has a business center and health center. The glass enclosed top-floor restaurant is known for its steaks. **$$$**

Royal Palace Hotel Taipei
81-1 Daan Rd, Sec. 1
Tel: (02) 2776-6599
Fax: (02) 2752-7388
www.royalpalace.com.tw
A small hotel, with just 90 rooms, the staff here are more polite, courteous, and professional than local establishments of this size. Offers standard services and basic amenities, but no more. **$$**

San Want Hotel
172 Zhongxiao E. Rd, Sec. 4
Tel: (02) 2772-2121
Fax: (02) 2731-0302
www.sanwant.com
Known for its good Cantonese dim-sum and Chaozhou restaurants, this hotel caters specially to business travelers, offering private meeting rooms, a non-smoking floor, airport transfer service, IDD, business center, and more. In the heart of the main upscale shopping and business district. **$$$**

Sheraton Taipei Hotel
12 Zhongxiao E. Rd, Sec. 1
Tel: (02) 2321-5511/080-231-666/7 (islandwide toll-free)
Fax: (02) 2394-4240

BELOW: The Sherwood Taipei.

www.starwoodhotels.com
One of the older five-star properties, a thorough upgrading both inside and out in the early 2000s has restored much of the grande dame's "star" quality. The hotel houses numerous quality restaurants, and has an extensive boutique arcade in the basement **$$$$**

The Sherwood Taipei
111 Minsheng E. Rd, Sec. 3
Tel: (02) 2718-1188
Fax: (02) 2713-0707
www.sherwood.com.tw
Considered number two in Taipei by many, this hotel has the best dining establishments and take-out services. The business facilities are good, but the meeting and banquet facilities sometimes fall short of expectations. **$$$$**

Sunworld Dynasty Hotel
100 Dunhua N. Rd
Tel: (02) 2719-7199
Fax: (02) 2545-9288
www.sunworlddynasty.com
Great location near upscale shopping, bars, and restaurants, and has an outdoor heated swimming pool. Among international travelers, it is frequented mainly by Japanese and airline crews. **$$$**

Taipei Fortuna Hotel
122 Zhongshan N. Rd, Sec. 2
Tel: (02) 2563-1111
Fax: (02) 2561-9777
www.taipei-fortuna.com.tw
Located in an upscale shopping area, about 15 minutes by taxi from the main business district. There are limited meeting and business facilities, but the hotel offers a fair-sized health club and three good restaurants. **$$$**

Taipei Fullerton 41
41 Fuxing S. Rd, Sec. 2
Tel: (02) 2703-1234
Fax: (02) 2705-6161
www.taipeifullerton.com.tw
In the same style as Fullerton 315 listed below, rooms (100) are slightly more elegant and decorated in earth tones. This is reflected in slightly higher rates. All other amenities are the same. Also close to Muzha MRT line station. **$$$**

Taipei Fullerton 315
315 Fuxing N. Rd
Tel: (02) 2713-8181
Fax: (02) 2713-6199
www.taipeifullerton.com.tw
A stylish facility located right off Muzha line MRT station and close to domestic airport. Known for relaxed, refined service, has good business center (24 hours), conference room, sauna, fitness center, and outdoor garden. ADSL access each room. **$$$**

The Westin Taipei
133 Nanjing E. Rd, Sec. 3
Tel: (02) 8770-6565
Fax: (02) 8770-6555
www.westin.com.tw
One of Taipei's younger (though surprisingly small at 288 rooms) international hotels, located in the heart of the business and bar/restaurant district. The hotel concentrates on business travelers who prefer to be right downtown; it has numerous restaurants, most quite good, but the quality tends not to match the steep prices. Piano bar and indoor pool. **$$$$**

Whispering Pines Inn
21 Youya Rd, Beitou
Tel: (02) 2891-2063
Fax: (02) 2891-2037
A cozy 20-room Japanese-style inn built in the Japanese colonial era, with in-room hot-spring tubs and located in the Beitou hot-spring resort area. Featuring lots of original woodwork, this is the perfect romantic weekend getaway. The perfect place for soaking and relaxing, although the facility is in need of some restoration. **$$**

Y Hotel Taipei
19 Xuchang St
Tel: (02) 2311-3201
Fax: (02) 2311-3209
www.ymcataipei.org.tw
Just south of Taipei Railway Station and main MRT, train, and bus lines, the YMCA offers clean, simple rooms. Self-service launderette and good ground-floor coffee shop/diner. Friendly staff, English-speaking, accustomed to foreigners. **$$**

NORTH TAIWAN

Zhongli

Hotel Kuva Chateau
398 Minquan Rd, Taoyuan County
Tel: (03) 281-1818
Fax: (03) 281-1616
www.kuva-chateau.com.tw
Only 15 minutes from CKS International Airport, 25 minutes from Taipei, and thus popular with the business crowd. First, and only, deluxe hotel in the area, with 246 rooms, all with internet access, a non-smoking floor, spa, and airport shuttle service. **$$$**

Hsinchu

Ambassador Hotel Hsinchu
188 Zhonghua Rd, Sec. 2
Tel: (03) 555-1111
Fax: (03) 555-1112
www.ambassadorhotel.com.tw
Within minutes of Hsinchu train station and science park. Has a good fitness center, indoor heated swimming pool, sauna, and business center. The fashionable Shinkong Mitsukoshi Department Store is within the same complex. **$$$$**

Caesar Park Hotel Hsinchu
75 Zhonghua Rd, Sec. 2
Tel: (03) 532-6622
Fax: (03) 542-3232
www.caesarpark.com.tw
This is the oldest of a limited number of international-quality hotels in this city; all are located close to the science-based industrial park, the primary draw for overseas travelers. The hotel has a good combination of recreational and business facilities; there are three restaurants, the food and service merely adequate. **$$$**

Royal Hsinchu
227 Guangfu Rd, Sec. 1
Tel: (03) 563-1122
Fax: (03) 563-1899
www.royal-hsinchu.com.tw
A comfortable and stylish hotel, perhaps the pick of the limited Hsinchu lot. It sits right by the science park, close to the main north-south highway. The hotel offers good business facilities. **$$$**

Ilan

Art Spa Hotel
6 Deyang Rd, Jiaoxi Township
Tel: (03) 988-2011
Fax: (03) 988-3838
www.art-spa-hotel.com.tw
A luxurious newer hotel in the hot-springs village of Jiaoxi. Japanese- and Western-style rooms, soaking tubs with piped-in waters in each. Good on-site combo-cuisine restaurant, café, and outdoor BBQ (flat fee, food for 10). **$$$**

Landis Inn Lotung
14-19F, 511 Gongzheng Rd, Luodong, Ilan County
Tel: (03) 961-3799
Fax: (03) 961-3800
http://lotung.landishotelsresorts.com
Managed by a subsidiary of the Ritz Taipei group, this small hotel of just 68 rooms has superior service. Most guests in the hotel head for the extensive outdoor recreational facilities in the area. The hotel provides good but limited restaurant and meeting and banquet facilities. **$$$**

Lion Hotel
222 Zhongshan Rd, Sec. 3, Luodong, Ilan County
Tel: (039) 551-111
Fax: (039) 576-954
www.lion-hotel.com.tw
This is a small, clean hotel with limited amenities and business services. It is mostly frequented by local travelers, with plenty of families. It is close to an expansive complex of outdoor recreational facilities and a theme park, the main local draws. **$$**

Keelung

Evergreen Laurel Hotel Keelung
62-1 Zhongzheng Rd
Tel: (02) 2427-9988
Fax: (02) 2422-8642
www.evergreen-hotels.com
Right on the tightly packed harbor, this hotel is in a crowded, traditional shopping and night-market district. It offers good business facilities, fair-sized rooms, sauna and

ABOVE: Spring City Resort.

aerobics studio, and good views at the front. Most local sights are within walking distance. Four non-smoking floors. **$$$$**

Howard Beach Resort Pacific Green Bay
1-1 Feicui Rd
Wanli Township, Taipei County
Tel: (02) 2492-6565
Fax: (02) 2492-6588
www.howard-hotels.com.tw
Located on the north coast not far outside Jilong, this is the closest upscale hotel resort to Taipei. Indoor and outdoor swimming pools, jacuzzi, gymnasium, sauna, beach volleyball court on a private beach, yachting, and much more. Food and drink facilities. **$$$**

Hua Shuai Hotel
108 Xiao 2nd Rd
Tel: (02) 422-3131
Fax: (02) 422-3140
This is a tiny, no-frills place that offers basic recreational, dining, and business facilities. Its primary attraction is its location downtown near the harbor district. **$$**

Taoyuan

Evergreen Transit Hotel, Taiwan Taoyuan International Airport
4F, Terminal 2, Taiwan Taoyuan International Airport, Taoyuan County

Tel: (03) 383-4510
Fax: (03) 383-4610
www.evergreen-hotels.com
Opened in April 2003. Small range of recreational facilities in this 21-room complex managed by Evergreen International Hotels. Rooms are spacious and comfortably appointed. Inside security zone. **$$**

Howard Lake Resort Shihmen Dam
176 Minfu St
Longtan Township, Taoyuan County
Tel: (03) 411-1234
Fax: (03) 411-1212
www.howard-hotels.com.tw
The best hotel by Shimen Dam, a popular destination with locals one hour south of Taipei in the mountains. The area offers good hiking and boat cruises around the lake. The hotel provides fair to good restaurants, a health center, and swimming pool. **$$$$**

Westin Resort Ta Shee
166 Rexin Rd
Daxi Township, Taoyuan County
Tel: (03) 387-6688
Fax: (03) 387-5288
www.tasheeresort.com.tw
A steadily improving hotel, with the Westin chain now handling management, located in the foothills 40 minutes south of Taipei. This is home to Taiwan's best golf course, and has great recreational facilities, including outdoor tennis courts and a swimming pool with superb mountain views. **$$$$**

Yangmingshan/ Danshui

Landis Resort Yangmingshan
237 Gezhi Rd
Tel: (02) 2861-6661
Fax: (02) 2861-3885
www.landisresort.com.tw

PRICE CATEGORIES
Price range indicated is for two people, including breakfast:
$$$$ more than NT$6,000
$$$ NT$3,500–6,000
$$ NT$1,500–3,500
$ NT$2/300–1,500

High in the hills, all rooms and other facilities here, featuring contemporary styling, offer great views down to Danshui River. Enjoyable soaking pools fed from nearby hot springs, mountain spring-fed swimming pool, and recreation/fitness room all have large windows offering fine mountain views. **$$$$**
Spring City Resort
18 Youya Rd, Beitou District, Taipei
Tel: (02) 2897-5555
Fax: (02) 2897-7245

www.springresort.com.tw
The newest hotel in the rejuvenated Beitou hot-springs area, each of the rooms and each restaurant is done in a completely different architectural style (Japanese, Art Deco, and so on). It all comes together wonderfully. Claim to fame is the fact that Steven Seagal stayed in the Japanese section when in town. **$$$–$$$$**
Tamsui Chinatrust Hotel
91 Zhongzheng E. Rd, Sec. 2,

Danshui
Tel: (02) 8809-1111
Fax: (02) 8809-2346
www.chinatrust-hotel.com.tw
A well-run place in the heart of Danshui (visits to local sites require a taxi ride), with a satisfactory business center and banquet/meeting facilities, average Chinese restaurant, coffee shop, and health center. **$$**
Tien Lai Spring Resort
1-7 Mingliu Rd, Zhonghe Village, Jinshan Township, Taipei County

Tel: (02) 2408-0000
Fax: (02) 2408-0999
www.tienlai.com.tw
A lovely inn-style resort nestled in the mountains north of Taipei, perfect for weekend business or private getaways. Offers a wealth of services, despite having a mere 32 rooms: good restaurant with Western and Chinese food, coffee shop, bar, hot springs/saunas, health center, travel services, and more. **$$$$**

WEST-CENTRAL TAIWAN

Alishan

Alishan House
16 W. Alishan, Xianglin Village, Alishan Township
Tel: (05) 267-9811–4
Fax: (05) 267-9596
www.alishanhouse.com.tw
This is a small, elegant hotel with beautiful decor and lovely gardens, perched high in the mountains. Lots of wood used in the design, unfortunately a rare thing in Taiwan. Caters primarily for hikers and nature-lovers, with limited business or other facilities. **$$**
Alishan Gou Hotel
1 E. Alishan, Alishan Township
Tel: (05) 267-9611
Fax: (05) 267-9614
www.agh.com.tw
Straightforward service with no-frills, clean and spartan rooms and a high-mountain location. The simple restaurant features extremely fresh local produce. There are also pleasant karaoke and meeting facilities. **$$**
Ying Shan Hotel
39 E. Alishan, Zhongzheng Village, Alishan Township
Tel: (05) 267-9803
Fax: (05) 267-9369
www.ying-shan.com.tw
A small place of 45 rooms. Extremely simple, clean, with facilities. Like other local spots, hiking and nature are the attractions, as well as fresh local mountain produce served in the simple restaurant. **$$**

Central Cross-Island Highway

Hoya Resort Wuling
3-16 Wuling Rd, Heping Townshi, Taichung County
Tel: (04) 2590-1399
Fax: (04) 2590-1118
www.hoyaresort.com.tw/wuling
Young, large upscale hotel situated in the high central mountains at Wuling Recreational Farm. Forty-two of the 143 rooms are "family guestrooms," extra large with two large beds and tatami space. Outdoor swimming pool, spa, and good hiking paths nearby. **$$$**
Guguan Hotel
6 Wenquan Lane, Dongguan Rd, Sec. 1, Heping Township Taichung County
Tel: (04) 2595-1355
Fax: (04) 2595-1359
Located in the mountain hot-springs area of Guguan, offers travel services, hot-springs baths, adequate meeting and food/drink facilities. Beyond the hot springs, the attractions are spectacular scenery and great hiking. **$$**
Lishan Guest House
91 Zhongzheng Rd, Lishan Village, Heping Township, Taichung County
Tel: (04) 2598-9501
Fax: (04) 2598-9505
Lovely views of mountains all around and the town perched above a valley. A fair-sized hotel for these parts, with 102 rooms. Hiking and walking are good here; the main attractions are scenery and

fresh mountain produce from many local farms. **$$**
Wuling Farm Guest House
3-1 Wuling Rd, Hoping Township, Taichung County
Tel: (04) 2590-1259
Fax: (04) 2590-1260
www.wuling-farm.com.tw
Offering superb mountain vistas, guests can pick their own produce on the farm or go out on easy/hard hikes. Rooms are dormitory or cabin-style, food/drink facilities basic but good, recreational facilities such as tennis courts good. **$$**

Changhua

Hsiao Yueh Resort Hotel
30 Sanfen Rd, Huatan Township, Changhua County
Tel: (04) 787-2029
Fax: (04) 787-2151
http://tfv.com.tw/tfv/page_e03.htm
Located near Changhua, falls a bit short of being a true resort, but the restaurants and coffee shop are good and there is a good outdoor swimming pool. The hotel is mostly used by people heading off to the mountains to Alishan, Xitou, and elsewhere. Sits outside main gate of Taiwan Folk Village. **$$–$$$**
Hotel Taiwan Changhua
48 Zhongzheng Rd, Sec. 2
Tel: (04) 722-4681
Fax: (04) 724-6474
A small hotel of 50 rooms, clean and simple and offering good, polite service. Has a barber shop.

This is one of the few quality places in Changhua to stay, and is located on a main thoroughfare that is often noisy. Get a room toward the rear. **$$**
Ying Shang Hotel
129 Changan St
Tel: (04) 722-9211
Fax: (04) 727-1858
A small place of 52 clean and simple rooms, this spot is for people looking for a no-surprises place to stay overnight. Has a coffee shop and karaoke facilities and not much more (the latter important for local travelers). **$**

Chiayi

Chiayi Chinatrust Hotel
257 Wenhua Rd
Tel: (05) 229-2233
Fax: (05) 229-1155
www.chinatrust-hotel.com.tw
Like all China Trust hotels, provides good value for money. Large for this area, with 171 rooms, the hotel offers travel services, a business center, gym, meeting and banquet facilities, and a few fair-to-good restaurants. Popular for company trips and those heading off into nearby mountains. **$$$**
Guo Bao Hotel
11F, 617 Zhongshan Rd
Tel: (05) 228-1818
Fax: (05) 229-1850
A fair-sized place with 88 rooms, offers a coffee shop, a couple of decent Chinese restaurants, laundry service, and

transport/shuttle service.
$

Nice Prince Hotel
600 Zhongxiao Rd
Tel: (05) 277-1999
Fax: (05) 276-6388
www.niceprincehotel.com.tw
Stylish younger facility,
modernistic rooms, has a
gift shop, spa and sauna
facilities and a fitness
center. Try The Fusion
restaurant for regional
specialties. **$$$**

Xitou

Chitou Hotel
10 Forest Lane, Neihu Village,
Lugu Township
Tel: (049) 2612-111
Fax: (049) 2612-055
Directly outside the gates
of the forest recreation
area, this place, done with
a pleasant wood motif,
offers rooms in the main
building and comfortable
chalet-style cabins in the
wooded area behind. The
rooms in the newer section
are large, with TVs, and
there is a good restaurant,
KTV (karaoke with music
video) facilities, meeting
facilities, and recreational
facilities. Crowded
weekends/holidays.
$$–$$$

**Chitou Youth Activity
Center**
15 Forest Lane, Neihu Village,
Lugu Township
Tel: (049) 2612-160-3
Fax: (049) 2612-322
http://chitou.cyh.org.tw
Set directly outside the
main entrance of the forest
recreation area, this spot
has a few more facilities
than most hostels,
including karaoke, a good
restaurant serving local
specialties like bamboo
shoots and mountain
mushrooms, a recreation
center including swimming
pool, basic conference
facilities, and more. But the

main attraction is the
extensive local hiking
opportunities. **$$**

Kinmen

Tai Kin Hotel
1 Gaoyang Rd, Jinsha Town
Tel: (082) 353-888
Fax: (082) 353-456
Clean and simple, with
polite and friendly service.
Offers all the standard
budget-hotel services and
facilities: travel services,
shuttle from the airport,
basic meeting facilities,
and karaoke. **$$**

King Ring Hotel
166 Minquan Rd, Jincheng Town
Tel: (082) 323-777
Fax: (082) 325-902
One of the islands' best
tourist hotels, offers above-
average restaurants for the
region (Chinese, seafood),
as well as karaoke
facilities, travel services,
airport shuttle service, and
more. Located in the main
town, with most local
tourist sites within walking
distance. **$$**

Hotel River Kinmen
100 Xihai Rd, Sec. 3, Jincheng
Town
Tel: (082) 322-211
Fax: (082) 323-322
www.riverkinmen.com
The best and largest (122
rooms) hotel in Kinmen.
The restaurants (Fujian-
style, seafood) are quite
good and reasonably
priced. Offers good travel
services, karaoke facilities,
meeting facilities, shuttle
service, and more. Good
views from many rooms,
but be choosy. **$$**

Mazu

Shennong Hotel
84-2, Qingshui Village,
Nangan Island
Tel: (0836) 26333
Fax: (0836) 26330
www.shennong.com.tw
Newer 63-room hotel in the
center of the island at one
of its highest points, with
far-reaching views from
rooms on the upper floors.
Service is not quite up to
international standards, but
staff try hard and the place
is very clean. Chinese and
Western restaurants are

ABOVE: the exterior and interior of Lalu Sun Moon Lake Hotel.

decent and about as good
as others available in
Mazu. **$$**

Penghu (Pescadores)

Bao Hwa Hotel
2 Zhongzheng Rd, Magong
Tel: (06) 927-4881/8
Fax: (06) 927-4889
www.bao-hwa.com.tw
This mid-sized hotel has
acceptable service and
amenities; the bar and
business center are
notable. It has a good
central location in this
small, slow-paced island
town. Staff will help with
setting up day trips and
other tourist needs. **$$**

Penghu Royal Hotel
33, Lane 64, Xinsheng Rd, Magong
Tel: (06) 926-1182
Fax: (06) 926-1128
A small place, with 45
rooms, quiet and pleasant
and within easy walking
distance of just about
everything. Has pretty good
restaurants and a
comfortable coffee shop,
travel services, and
karaoke facilities to cater
for the local traveler's
night-time entertainment.
$$

**Penghu Youth Activity
Center**
11 Jieshou Rd, Magong
Tel: (06) 927-1124
Fax: (06) 927-4565
http://penghu.cyh.org.tw

Simple, clean, and well run.
Convenient, located down
by the waters of the bay.
Has an in-center Chinese
restaurant (per table fee).
$$

Sheng Guo Hotel
2-12 Shuiyuan Rd, Magong
Tel: (06) 927-3891
Fax: (06) 927-3836
Large for the islands, with
129 rooms, this
establishment offers travel
services, karaoke facilities,
large and clean rooms, and
enthusiastic service.
Food/drink facilities are
merely adequate,
concentrating on seafood
and fresh produce. **$–$$**

Sun Moon Lake

**Fenisia Hotel Sun Moon
Lake**
23 Zhongzheng Rd
Tel: (049) 285-5500
Fax: (049) 285-6600
www.fenisiahotel.com
This large resort hotel,
recently completely
overhauled, on Taiwan's
loveliest mountain lake,
has a lakeside restaurant,
boating facilities, and a
private observatory. It
offers a shuttle service for
guests to and from major
urban centers. **$$$$**

The Lalu Sun Moon Lake
142 Zhongxing Rd
Tel: (049) 285-6888
Fax: (049) 285-5688
www.thelalu.com.tw

This place oozes luxury (be sure you are in the new section, not the renovated older hotel adjoining). The dark-wood rooms are as if from a Bond movie, with lakeside terraces, hidden TVs and fireplaces, and mirrored sections. The edge of the outside pool "bends" perfectly with the lake's waters. $$$$

Sun Moon Lake Youth Activity Center
101 Zhongzheng Rd
Tel: (049) 2850-070
Fax: (049) 2850-037
http://sun.cyh.org.tw

For those on limited budgets, the China Youth Corps (CYC) centers that dot the islands are safe bets. Each provides clean and simple rooms (dorm and sometimes private room; this facility also has a lodge-type villa), shower facilities, and simple restaurants with straightforward local fare. Most, like this one, also have camping facilities and nature recreation areas. $$

El Dorado Hotel
5 Mingsheng St

Tel: (049) 2855-855
Fax: (049) 2856-656
www.sun-moon-lake.com.tw

This spot offers straightforward service and facilities, with simple food/drink and meeting facilities; appropriate for those who want a good place to sleep but plan to do all other activities elsewhere. It is clean and relatively quiet, with a good location off the lake. $$$

Taichung

Evergreen Laurel Hotel Taichung
6 Taichunggang Rd, Sec. 2
Tel: (04) 2313-9988
Fax: (04) 2313-8642
www.evergreen-hotels.com

With a central location near the downtown business area, this hotel is noted for having the best restaurants locally. Facilities include a large outdoor pool and squash courts. A sleek, expansive fitness center was added recently, which includes a sauna, men's and women's water-therapy rooms, steam room, and

gym, all with the best equipment. Relaxed atmosphere. $$$$

Grand Formosa Taichung
1049 Jianxing Rd
Tel: (04) 2328-8000
Fax: (04) 2322-9000
www.grandformosa-taichung.com.tw

This is a new upscale entry into the local hotel fray, fast improving the good yet over-hyped service. There are panoramic views, luxurious accommodation, full-service health spa, and a prime location near downtown sights. $$$$

Howard Prince Hotel Taichung
129 Anhe Rd
Tel: (04) 2463-2323
Fax: (04) 2463-3333
www.howard-hotels.com

Offers a business center, special "executive" floors, private dining rooms, and conference facilities for business guests, along with rooms designed for disabled persons, a fitness center with sauna, good Taiwanese seafood and Shanghainese restaurants, and a pleasant lobby bar. $$$

The Landis Taichung Hotel
9 Taichunggang Rd, Sec. 2
Tel: (04) 2326-8008
Fax: (04) 2326-8060
www.landis.com.tw

Located in the heart of the city, with personalized service, complimentary city shuttle, fine restaurants and bars, a health club, and a high-tech business center, this is the best upscale pick in the city. $$$$

Marshall Hotel
58 Guangfu Rd
Tel: (04) 2226-7589
Fax (04) 2226-2709

This is, by necessity, a well-soundproofed hotel in the city center near the dance clubs, theatre and other nightlife. $$

Plaza International Hotel
431 Daya Rd
Tel: (04) 2295-6789
Fax: (04) 2295-0099
www.taichung-plaza.com

Features a nice range of bars, restaurants, and coffee shops (Taiwanese and Cantonese recommended). Also noted for its rooftop pool, sauna and health center. $$$

SOUTHWEST TAIWAN

Kaohsiung

Ambassador Hotel Kaohsiung
202 Minsheng 2nd Rd
Tel: (07) 211-5211
Fax: (07) 281-1115
www.ambhotel.com.tw

This is a large hotel on the Love River in the central business district. It has good outdoor pool (May–Oct), health-club, and business-center facilities, and is located quite close to the harbor area, main night markets, and most popular entertainment hotspots. $$$

Grand Hi-Lai Hotel
266 Chenggong 1st Rd
Tel: (07) 216-1766
Fax: (07) 216-1966
www.grand-hilai.com.tw

A large hotel, considered by many to be the city's best, with numerous restaurants (stick to those serving regional cuisines), an

executive club, and a pleasant shopping complex. $$$$

The Grand Hotel Cheng Ching Lake
2 Yuanshan Rd, Chengqing Lake
Tel: (07) 370-5911
Fax: (07) 370-4889
www.grand-hotel.org

This outsized hotel is a copy of its classical Chinese-style sister in Taipei. It is located 25 minutes outside Kaohsiung's business district, in a large and popular lake-centered resort area. The hotel has extensive recreational facilities (Olympic-size swimming pool), and offers guests access to some of the region's best golf and tennis facilities. $$$

Han-Hsien International Hotel
33 Siwei 3rd Rd
Tel: (07) 332-2000
Fax: (07) 336-1600

www.hhih.com.tw

Located near the stately Kaohsiung City Hall. Has a solid reputation for attentive service and attention to detail; ample business and leisure facilities. $$

Howard Plaza Hotel Kaohsiung
311 Qixian 1st Rd
Tel: (07) 236-2323
Fax: (07) 235-8383
www.howard-hotels.com

Located near the harbor and business district, the hotel features good in-room and business-center facilities, though it does not have either the quality or social atmosphere found in the restaurants and public places of its sister hotels in Taiwan. $$$

Hotel King's Town
362 Jiuru 2nd Rd
Tel: (07) 311-9906
Fax: (07) 311-9591
www.kingstown-hotel.com.tw

A smaller premium hotel, with 160 rooms, this establishment caters mainly to businesspeople (more from Japan than the West). Nicely decorated in an "imperial" style. $$

Kaohsiung Toong Mao Resort and Hotel
394 Qixian 2nd Rd
Tel: (07) 282-2151
Fax: (07) 281-4540
www.toongmao.com.tw

144 luxury and executive suites in this recently refurbished facility, under new management. Aimed at the business traveler, has conference facilities, business center, free tea room, even a children's play area for tagalongs. $$

The Splendor Kaohsiung
37–85F, 1 Ziqiang 3rd Rd
Tel: (07) 566-8000
Fax: (07) 566-8080
www.thesplendor-khh.com.tw

Formerly called the Grand Formosa Kaohsiung, the

Splendor is located in the upper reaches of Taiwan's second tallest building, overlooking the bustling harbor. Both the rooms and the several good restaurants here offer great views, especially in the evenings. Located near the main business district. **$$$$**

Kending

Caesar Park Hotel Kenting
6 Kending Rd, Hengchun Township
Tel: (08) 886-1888
Fax: (08) 886-1818
www.caesarpark.com.tw
A resort hotel fronting Kending's best beach, this is the former queen of the beach, completely refurbished and reopened in 2006. The hotel has very good sports and recreational facilities (including scuba diving and snorkeling), and offers shuttle service to/from Kaohsiung. **$$$$**

Howard Beach Resort Kenting
2 Kending Rd, Hengchun Township
Tel: (08) 886-2323
Fax: (08) 886-2359
www.howard-hotels.com
This is the new resort queen of Kending, with easy access to the local beaches and other tourist facilities. It also has its own extensive entertainment and recreational facilities, and an adjoining science-fiction and water theme park for the kiddies and young at

heart. Comfortable rooms. **$$$$**

Kenting House
101 Gongyuan Rd,
Hengchun Township
Tel: (08) 886-1371/5
Fax: (08) 886-1377
www.caesarpark.com.tw
Offers 69 bungalow-style rooms, many in classical Chinese style. There are only simple food and beverage services, for this place caters to a younger crowd on a limited budget. It is close to the local beaches and the area's best nightlife. **$$**

Kentington Resort
205 Zhongshan Rd,
Manzhou Village
Manzhou Township
Tel: (08) 880-2880
Fax: (08) 880-2609
A lovely resort isolated from the more hectic area of tourists and party animals near the town of Kending. This place is very quiet, with easy access to hotspots in the area, and offers a wide range of outdoor recreational and business facilities, a good bar/nightclub, a health center, KTV (karaoke with music video), and more. **$$$**

Tainan

Asia Hotel
100 Zhongshan Rd
Tel: (06) 222-6171
Fax: (06) 221-9373
www.asiahoteltaiwan.com
A hotel with 145 rooms smack in the center of the

city. Faces a busy street, so avoid rooms in the front. Service is very polite and helpful (excels at travel services), rooms clean though a bit cramped. The place is getting old, but most tourist sites are within easy walking distance. **$$**

Dynasty Hotel Tainan
46 Chenggong Rd
Tel: (06) 225-8121
Fax: (06) 221-6711
www.hotel-dynasty.com.tw
One of the elite of Tainan's limited supply of good hotels, this establishment, on the main thoroughfare heading away from the pretty colonial train station, has good restaurants, a bar, karaoke, travel services, and meeting facilities. Façade is a bit faded, but interior décor is very nice. **$$**

Evergreen Plaza Hotel Tainan
1, Lane 366, Zhonghua E. Rd, Sec. 3
Tel: (06) 289-9988
Fax: (06) 289-6699
www.evergreen-hotels.com
One of the city's triumvirate of International Tourist Class spots, with Hotel Tainan and the Tayih Landis. Has good restaurants, no smoking floor, ladies floor, (one) room for the physically challenged, business center, gym, outdoor scenic swimming pool, sauna, and professional spa-aromatherapy facilities. **$$$**

Premier Hotel
128 Gongyuan Rd
Tel: (06) 225-2141
Fax: (06) 228-6018
www.premier.com.tw
This is a 2006 renovated hotel in a central location within walking distance of most local tourist sites. It offers polite service and is pleasantly calm and quiet, with clean accommodation and limited amenities (gym, laundry room). **$$**

Hotel Tainan
1 Chenggong Rd
Tel: (06) 228-9101
Fax: (06) 226-8502
www.hotel-tainan.com.tw
Tastefully decorated with a pool, business center, and limousine service, this was long this slow-paced (for Taiwan) city's prime upscale hotel, before the Tayih Landis. The service is at times inconsistent, especially among younger staff, with oddly questionable behavior toward fellow locals. **$$$**

Tayih Landis Tainan
660 Ximen Rd, Sec. 1
Tel: (06) 213-5555
Fax: (06) 213-5599
www.tayihlandis.com.tw
Located in the bustling West Gate commercial area, this new enterprise is the only truly international hotel in the city. Managed by the group that runs Taipei's prestigious Landis hotel, the business, convention, leisure, and entertainment facilities are all five-star quality. Modern décor. **$$$**

EAST COAST

Green Island (Ludao)

Green Island Hotel
56 Wenzhen, Gongguan Village
Tel: (089) 672-244
Fax: (089) 672-314
A pleasant little place of 40 rooms, offering both dormitory and private rooms. Has a nice restaurant with inexpensive fare presented with little flourish, karaoke facilities, travel services, and

camping facilities. **$**

Kai Hsing Hotel
102-12 Nanliao Village
Tel: (089) 672-033
Fax: (089) 672-050
www.kaihsing-hotel.com.tw
The largest and best hotel on the island, with 101 rooms of differing styles. Has good travel services (will arrange bike rentals), motorbike rentals, karaoke facilities, and a good restaurant with simple fare and an

interesting local specialty or two. **$$**

Songrong Hotel
42 Nanliao Village
Tel: (089) 672-515
Fax: (089) 672-208
Close to the airport, this spot offers simple and spacious accommodation. Many rooms look out to sea. Staff will help with bike and scooter rentals, taxi rentals, and other travel matters. Amenities are simple but well-maintained. **$–$$**

Hualien

Astar Hotel
6-1 Minquan Rd
Tel: (038) 326-111
Fax: (038) 324-604

TRANSPORTATION
ACCOMMODATIONS
EATING OUT
ACTIVITIES
A – Z
LANGUAGE

www.astar-hotel.com

This mid-sized hotel is near the waterfront, which becomes very quiet at night. Some rooms can seem small because of peculiar design, so check first. There are adequate recreational and food/drink facilities, though nothing fancy, and limited business facilities. **$$–$$$**

Azure Hotel Hualien
590 Zhongzheng Rd
Tel: (03) 833-6686
Fax: (03) 832-3569
www.azurehotel.com.tw

A smaller place (100 rooms) on one of the main drags (beware rooms at lower levels facing the street). Locals consider the Western restaurant one of the better ones in the area. Offers tours, airport and train station transport, and a car rental service (this is a region of driving, not walking, tours). **$$**

Chinatrust Hualien Hotel
2 Yongxing Rd
Tel: (038) 221-171
Fax: (038) 221-185
www.chinatrust-hotel.com.tw

This is perhaps the city's best hotel, pleasantly low-rise, with a good outdoor pool, fitness center, and in-house travel service. The Chinese restaurants are perhaps the best in the region. **$$–$$$**

Parkview Hotel
1-1 Linyuan Rd
Tel: (038) 222-111
Fax: (038) 226-999
www.parkview-hotel.com

This is a large hotel with pleasing, broad views from most rooms (too rare in crowded Taiwan). It is near a golf club and Taroko Gorge, the two main attractions for guests, and has a pool, karaoke facilities, tennis courts, games arcade, and health club. **$$$**

Hualien County

Hualien Farglory Hotel
18, Shanling, Yanliao Village,
Shoufeng Township
Tel: (03) 812-3999
Fax: (03) 812-3988
www.bellevista.com.tw

Nestling atop a Coastal Mountain ridge facing the ocean, with Hualien Ocean Park directly below, this luxurious young 391-room Victorian-style facility is just 25 minutes from Hualien. Guests enjoy reduced prices to theme park. Shuttle service from Hualien train station and airport is available. **$$$$**

Hualien Promised Land Resort
1, Lixiang Rd, Shoufeng Township
Tel: (03) 865-6789
Fax: (03) 865-6555
www.plcresort.com.tw

On the plain between the Coastal Mountains and the Central Mountain Range, in East Rift Valley National Scenic Area, this young resort is just 30 minutes from Hualien. Individual luxury townhouse-style accommodation, 260 rooms in all, with central eating facility. **$$$$**

Shin Kong Chao Feng Recreation Farm
20 Yongfu St, Linwang Ward,
Fenglin Township
Tel: (03) 877-2666
Fax: (03) 877-1433
www.skcf.com.tw

Quiet rural village with charming Dutch-style cottages, 122 rooms in total, at north end of East Rift Valley National Scenic Area. Large rooms are designed for family stays; central dining facilities, hot-spring spa, aviary, and nature walks. Cottages on outer ring face outwards, allowing for unobstructed views of mountain and surroundings. **$$$/$$$$**

Orchid Island (Lanyu)

Lanyu Villa Hotel
9 Renai St, Hongtou Village
Tel: (089) 732-111
Fax: (089) 732-189
www.lanyu.com.tw (Chinese only)

This is a mid-sized hotel with no-frills clean rooms and polite service. Apart from the fair-sized rooms, facilities are basic. Provides easy access to all the local sights. The staff are good at helping with little things like bike rentals and such. **$$**

Orchid Island Villa Hotel
7 Hongtou, Hongtou Village

Tel: (089) 731-611
Fax: (089) 325-701

Same as above, basic and with nary an unpleasant surprise. The hotel offers convenient access to all of the island's attractions and, like the Lanyu Hotel, offers refreshing ocean views in quiet, slow-paced village surroundings. **$$**

Taitung/Zhiben

Formosan Naruwan Hotel and Resort Taitung
66 Lianhang Rd, Taitung
Tel: (089) 239-666
Fax: (089) 239-777
http://naruwan.myhotel.com.tw

Large facility on the edge of town toward the sea, the Naruwan incorporates attractive aboriginal motifs throughout; the roomy wood-decor rooms are particularly pleasant as a result. Entertaining native performances are given in the lobby daily. **$$$$**

Jyh Been Hotel
35 Longquan Rd, Wenquan Village
Zhiben
Tel: (089) 512-220
Fax: (089) 513-067
www.tangno.network.com.tw

Of small size in comparison to some other top-level hotels in the area, this is the oldest of the local oldies. It is still a good place to stay, with a karaoke and other local-style entertainment facilities. Prime attraction is the great outdoor mineral pools (to be avoided when there are holiday crowds). **$$$**

Hotel Royal Chihpen
23, Lane 113, Longquan Rd,
Wenquan Village, Zhiben
Tel: (089) 510-666
Fax: (089) 510-678
www.hotel-royal-chihpen.com.tw

This is the top hotel in the area, offering comfortable and luxurious open-air and in-room spa facilities. It has the district's best food (various Chinese cuisines, teppanyaki, and Western buffet) and drink facilities, and is by a forest reserve and hiking trails. **$$$$**

Lion King Hotel
572 Zhonghua Rd, Sec. 1, Taitung
Tel: (089) 328-878
Fax: (089) 322-378

This is a smaller hotel with basic amenities and services, located near the heart of this small city, near the sea and making walks to all local tourist sites easy and convenient, **$$**

Taroko Gorge

Catholic Hostel
24 Tianxiang Rd, Xiulin Village
Tel: (038) 691-155
Fax: (038) 691-736

A long-time favorite with foreign budget travelers, this spacious, clean, and friendly spot, at the top end of the gorge like most of the area's accommodation, offers dorm and simple double rooms. Located on a hill overlooking, unfortunately, a parking lot; nevertheless, the scenery is still great. Facilities very basic. **$**

Grand Formosa Taroko
18 Tianxiang Rd, Xiulin Village
Tel: (038) 691-155
Fax: (038) 691-160
www.grandformosa-taroko.com.tw

The only international hotel in the gorge, located at the top end. Naturally, offers great views and pristine surroundings. Offers an airport shuttle service from Hualien airport, tour and travel arrangements, and a host of top-flight recreational facilities. **$$$$**

Tianxiang Youth Activity Center
30 Tianxiang Rd, Xiulin Village
Tel: (038) 691-111/3
Fax: (038) 691-171
http://tienhsiang.cyh.org.tw

Like all of Taiwan's youth activity centers, they provide great value for little money. In the striking gorge setting, offers simple and clean dorm and private rooms, a simple cafeteria, spartan yet clean showers, simple karaoke facilities. **$$**

PRICE CATEGORIES

Price range indicated are for two people, including breakfast:
$$$$ more than NT$6,000
$$$ NT$3,500–6,000
$$ NT$1,500–3,500
$ NT$2/300–1,500

E ATING OUT

RECOMMENDED RESTAURANTS AND CAFÉS

WHAT TO EAT

Eating is one of the single greatest pleasures Taiwan holds in store for the traveler. Almost any eatery in Taiwan serves good food, but approach the so-called Western restaurants with caution – outside of the major hotels and fast-food chains, these may serve food that bears little resemblance to the dishes you are familiar with.

Selecting a Restaurant

If you are a novice to Chinese food, the best places to try local cuisine are the hotel restaurants in Taipei, Kaohsiung and the other major urban centers. These serve probably the best (and most expensive) Chinese food available in Taiwan.

An alternative for lunch, and sometimes for dinner, is to visit one of the many eateries on the basement floors of the main department stores. Everything is freshly cooked, and the prices are quite low. If you see one eatery with no customers waiting, chances are that the food is not very good. It is better to go to another where you have to wait in line. The rule-of-thumb therefore is to patronize eateries which are the most popular.

The third suggestion is to go to an ordinary restaurant. Remember that large Chinese restaurants most often cater to groups rather than individuals. Four people at a table should be the minimum, and don't expect the food to be cheap.

Don't be afraid to experiment because of the language barrier; there are so many items on a Chinese menu that most foreigners become daunted and hesitate to order unusual dishes, thereby missing out on local specialties and delicacies. The first few times you dine locally, if possible bring along a local friend, who will show you how you've been led miserably astray when eating Chinese cuisine back home; after this, each meal becomes a pleasant adventure.

Types of Cuisine

The majority of Taiwanese can trace their origins to Fujian province, across the strait in China, yet there are people from every corner of the mainland. All have distinctive culinary traditions, making Taiwan perhaps the best spot in the world to explore the many different types of Chinese cuisine.

Northern Style (Beijing, Inner Mongolia). Recommended dishes: Beijing duck, lamb and leek, hot and sour soup, celery in mustard sauce, cold shredded chicken with sauce, sweet and sour yellow fish, steamed vegetable dumplings.
Southern Style (Cantonese). Recommended dishes: roast duck, poached chicken with onions and oil, greens with oyster sauce, steamed whole fish, dim sum, roast pigeon, cabbage with cream.
Western/Central Style (Hunan, Sichuan). Recommended dishes: (Sichuan) steamed pomfret, chicken "Duke of Bao," "pockmarked grandma's beancurd," fragrant egg sauce, duck smoked in camphor and

BELOW: the flaming wok of Cantonese cooking.

tea, twice-cooked pork; (Hunan) frog legs in chili sauce, honeyed ham, beggar's chicken, minced pigeon in bamboo cup, steamed whole fish.

Eastern/Coastal Style (Shanghai). Recommended dishes: West Lake vinegar fish, river eel sauteed with leek, braised pork haunch, sauteed sweet pea shoots, "drunken chicken," "lion-head meatballs," braised beef loin.

Taiwanese Food. Recommended dishes: steamed crab, poached squid, fresh poached shrimp, shrimp rolls, grilled eel, sashimi, grilled clams, turtle soup.

Chinese Vegetarian Cuisine. Recommended dishes: try the various types of "beef," "pork," and "chicken," made entirely from various forms of soybean curd and different types of mushrooms, as well as fresh and crispy vegetables.

Street snacks

Some of the best known and most loved local foods, however, are the *xiaochi*, or "small eats." Throughout Taipei, many of the city's devoted foodies will be found in neighborhood nightmarkets eating hot snacks from temporary tables. The food is invariably freshly cooked because the turnover is high.

Chopsticks

Nothing appears on the Chinese banquet table that cannot be single-handedly manipulated with a pair of chopsticks, save soup of course.

A Few Dining Hints

Locals boil their drinking water. If you are not sure of the quality of the water, do not drink it when dining at simple (cheap) restaurants. Though fine at its source, trace elements of metals sneak into the water in underground pipes.

Ask for bottled water, though steaming hot coffee or tea is likely better, having been boiled.

A fair amount of monosodium glutamate (MSG) is used locally, especially in soups. Have someone write a note in Chinese asking the kitchen not to use any MSG in preparing your food, and show it to the waiter. Most places are happy to oblige.

Today, as the popularity of Chinese cuisine spreads throughout the world, it is considered de rigueur to use chopsticks when eating Chinese food. And in Taiwan you'll find abundant opportunities to practice.

The Chinese only use forks and knives in the kitchen – and when eating Western food. For their own cuisine, they prefer to have everything cut, sliced, diced, or otherwise prepared in the kitchen, so that the food is in bite-sized pieces when served. Those who wield their chopsticks too slowly often miss the choicest morsels whenever a new dish appears on the table. However, for reasons of hygiene, some

restaurants now serve so-called set menus with portions of everything on individual plates.

Chopsticks can also be used to select choice morsels from the best dishes for the guest-of-honor or friend at the table. The polite way to do this is to turn the sticks around so that you use the clean blunt ends to serve food to others.

Wielding Chopsticks

When using chopsticks, some foreigners stick them in their rice, standing straight up, when not being used. Never do this, for the sight resembles incense sticks burning in a censer during funeral rites, and will bring bad fortune. When wielding your chopsticks, avoid pointing the tips at anyone, which is as bad as pointing a dagger at their hearts (ie wishing them bad luck). Placing your chopsticks across your bowl indicates you want more; leaving food in your bowl (beyond a few grains of rice) indicates you were dissatisfied with your host's food.

Reusable Chopsticks

Many eating establishments in Taiwan provide disposable chopsticks made of wood. The government is asking people to bring their own reusable chopsticks, to prevent the great waste of wood and paper wrapping. Metal chopsticks are best, for the surfaces of those made of wood and plastic are flawed and may hide unhygienic matter despite washing.

R E S T A U R A N T   L I S T I N G S

TAIPEI

Beijing cuisine

Celestial
3F, 1 Nanjing W. Rd
Tel: (02) 2563-2380
Clean and functional décor; real Peking duck is slowly disappearing from Taipei, but this place (with several other outlets) is still going strong; Beijing-style vegetables are also excellent; Chinese beers and liquors, and a very limited selection of average wines. **$$–$$$**

King Join Restaurant
18 Siwei Rd
Tel: (02) 2701-3225
Recognized as the best of

the bunch (four other outlets in Taiwan); lovely, sumptuous Qing-dynasty décor; especially famous for Chinese delicacies; no smoking, no alcoholic beverages, but you can bring your own wine (no corkage fee); cold dishes only after 8pm. Vegetarian fare only. **$$$**

Cantonese

Jing Yuan
2 Lane 199, Xinyi Rd, Sec. 4
Tel: (02) 2705-8066
Elegant classic Chinese décor; small selection of French wines; English-

speaking staff offer knowledgeable advice on ordering; set lunch menus, with good food in small servings, is available for around NT$700. **$$$$**

Kwei Hwa
13F, 600 Linsen N. Rd
Tel: (02) 2596-5110
In the Imperial Hotel, with refurbished classy design; has very good weekday dim sum lunch menu that runs to less than NT$500 per person; wines available, but you can bring your own – corkage fee of NT$500 per table. **$$$**

Chaozhou

Zui Hong Lou
9 Tianshui St
Tel: (02) 2559-7089
Close to Dihua St, here you'll find regional specialties such as lobster Chaozhou style, and shark's-fin soup. English menu. **$$**

Chinese Muslim

Shao Shao Ke
15, Lane 41, Renai Rd, Sec. 2
Tel: (02) 2351-7148
One of Taipei's more unusual culinary retreats, serving dishes from

China's Shaanxi province, where the owner studied traditional medicine. Contemporary recipes offered, plus delicious old creations now extinct. The theme, food and décor is Muslim-inspired, with unleavened bread, lamb, and fragrant spices at core. Popular with Westerners, despite total lack of English. **$$–$$$**

Hunanese

Ji Yuan
324 Dunhua S. Rd, Sec. 1
Tel: (02) 2708-3110
Good combination of dishes – not just spicy, but sweet, sour, and salty as well; a good number of fish dishes (fish is usually served whole), of which the carp and pomfret are particularly outstanding.
$$$

Peng Yuan
2F, 380 Linsen N. Rd
Tel: (02) 2551-9157
Simple in décor, all effort

is placed on the food here; busy, large, noisy; of special interest is the *mizhi huotui* (ham cooked with honey); a favorite with locals is *mala tianjitui* (frog's legs in hot sauce).
$$$

Shanghainese

Fang's
7 Tianmu E. Rd
Tel: (02) 2872-8402
Established in 1970, Fang's has a solid reputation; fast, efficient service, simple décor; both Shanghai and Jiangzhe cuisine; around 200 dishes on the menu, with an extensive range of steamed dumplings; the *zuiji* ("drunken chicken") is a treat; beer and sorghum spirits only. **$$**

Shanghai Court
2F, 2 Songshou Rd
Tel: (02) 2720-1234, ext. 3198)
In the regal Grand Hyatt Hotel, offers top-flight service, a grand outside

BELOW: steamers of dumplings and buns.

view, and haute cuisine done in the old Shanghai style, with colonial touches; rotating menu ranges from the simple, like steamed dumplings, to the exotic, like bird's-nest soup.
$$$–$$$$

Sichuanese

Chinese Dining Room, Grand Hotel
1F, 1 Zhongshan N. Rd, Sec. 4
Tel: (02) 2886-8888, ext. 1211
An elegant restaurant in the Grand Hotel, this place is home to some of the island's best chefs; especially good are the *mapo doufu* ("pockmarked grandma's beancurd"); brave souls can try the steamed fatty pig intestines. **$$$$**

Ning Chi
398-1 Xinyi Rd, Sec. 4
Tel: (02) 2703-4961
Part of a popular chain; known for its *mala huoguo* ("numbingly spicy" hot pot), a popular winter dish; the caldrons have a dividing wall, allowing a not-so-hot broth as well; beer chasers de rigueur with *mala huoguo*; the larger your group, the cheaper per person for hot pot. **$$$**

Szechuan Court
12F, 63 Zhongshan N. Rd, Sec. 2
Tel: (02) 2100-2100, ext. 2383
In the old Ambassador Hotel, loyal regulars have been coming here for decades; especially good are the *gongbao jiding* (stir-fried diced chicken with dried chili peppers; also, try the *guaiwei ji* ("strange-tasting" chicken). **$$$$**

Taiwanese

Kudu
205 Jilin Rd
Tel: (02) 2536-8642
http://kudu.khnet.tw
Family-run place that grew from kiosk outside. Modish Japanese décor, polished wood everywhere, but traditional Taiwanese recipes. Décor reasonably stylish, excellent food, friendly and efficient service. Very inexpensive

considering the quality and quantity of food. Seafood good, as well as marinated sausage with scallions and meats braised in soy sauce. **$**

Orchid
2/3F, 255 Nanjing E. Rd, Sec. 3
Tel: (02) 2712-3456
In the Brother Hotel, formerly one of the better hotels; popular with locals, the décor is a little tattered, but food is very good; many seafood selections; hot pot is available; very limited wine selection, but normal "Chinese" drinks available.
$$–$$$

Tainan Tan Tsu Mien
31 Huaxi St
Tel: (02) 2308-1123
Named after a famous Tainan noodle specialty, it has probably the most expensive noodles in Taiwan; also known for its seafood; somewhat incongruous Wedgwood china, chandeliers, and Corinthian columns.
$$$–$$$$

Vegetarian

Dharma
140 Jinhua St
Tel: (02) 2351-6651
A simple place, resembling a shop more than a restaurant, run by pleasant elderly ladies; great range of dishes, including delicious vegetarian "meat" such as mutton and chicken; cash only. **$–$$**

Health Natural Vegetarian
2F, 108 Xinsheng N. Rd, Sec. 2
Tel: (02) 2560-1950
One of the few upscale vegetarian restaurants in Taiwan (seven outlets island-wide); the buffet offers a tremendous range, and service is polite and professional; no alcoholic beverages.
$–$$

PRICE CATEGORIES
Prices below are for two people, including drinks:
$$$$ more than NT$3,000
$$$ NT$2,000–3,000
$$ NT$1,000–2,000
$ NT$1,000 or less

La Marquise
11, Alley 2, Lane 345, Renai Rd,
Sec. 4
Tel: (02) 2773-8529
This simple, cozy spot is
the only French-style
vegetarian outlet on the
island; offers savory French
fare; no alcohol – serves
wide range of coffees,
herbal teas and non-
alcoholic beers. Regulars
are especially fond of the
crispy pastry of the
vegetable pies. **$$**

American

Dan Ryan's Chicago Grill
8 Dunhua N. Rd
Tel: (02) 2778-8800
www.danryans.com
Extremely popular with the
after-work crowd; cozy place,
done in 1930s Chicago jazz-
era style, with a moosehead
on one wall and a poster of
Michael Jordan on another;
standard American fare,
consistent quality; great
high-stool bar in front.
$$–$$$

Ruth's Chris Steak House
2F, 135 Minsheng E. Rd, Sec. 3
Tel: (02) 2545-8888
www.ruthschris.com
Outlet of successful US
chain; old British style with
dark wood paneling and
leather upholstery; features
prime cuts of US beef à la
carte; wide range of French
and Californian wines, from
NT$1,000 to NT$4,000.
$$$–$$$$

Continental

Uli's Euro Deli
17 Keqiang St
Tel: (02) 2831-2741
German master butcher Uli
Lengenberg is part of the
Tianmu District cultural
palette. His busy shop-
cum-restaurant serves up
many European meat-based
specialties, a house
favorite being
Currywuerstchen sausage.
There are also many
European cheese imports,
plus German beer. **$$**

The Windsor
2, Alley 16, Lane 38, Tianyu St,
Tianmu
Tel: (02) 2875-4038
In the hills of Tianmu,
resembles a European

ABOVE: fine dining at the Grand Hotel.

chalet; great beer garden,
popular in steamy
summers; reservations
often needed. **$$$$**

French

Antoine Room
2F, 12 Zhongxiao E. Rd, Sec. 1
Tel: (02) 2397-8080
In the Sheraton Taipei,
long in the elite of
Taiwan's French dining
experiences. Executive
Chef Noel Bernard (3
Michelin stars) flourishes
traditional recipes from all
French regions, and
particularly likes his
Napolean fish with
creamed spinach and
tomato in champagne
sauce, and his home-made
paté with spicy-fruit
chutney bread. **$$$–$$$$**

Paris 1930
2F, 41 Minquan E. Rd, Sec. 2
Tel: (02) 2597-1234
Located in The Landis
Taipei, considered Taiwan's
best French restaurant by
many; has elegant décor
with sophisticated service;
offers the island's most
extensive cellar of imported
French wines. **$$$$**

Italian

Capone's
312 Zhongxiao E. Rd, Sec. 4
Tel: (02) 2773-3782
www.capones.com.tw
Upscale American-style
Italian restaurant, a favorite

with expatriates; ample
portions, good service in
intimate, low-lit surround-
ings; live music from 9am–
12.30pm Wed–Sat; right
outside Sun Yat-sen
Memorial Hall MRT station.
$$$–$$$$

Toscana
1F, 111 Minsheng E. Rd, Sec. 3
Tel: (02) 2718-1188, ext. 3001
Located in the upscale
Sherwood Hotel,
considered by many to be
Taiwan's best Italian
restaurant; sumptuous
Mediterranean décor; both
Italian and regional
favorites. **$$$$**

Japanese

Izu
B1, 69, Lane 133, Linsen N. Rd,
Sec. 1
Tel: (02) 2567-1881
One good indication is that
the customers here are
mostly Japanese; smack in
the heart of Taipei's
burgeoning Little Tokyo;
food is extremely fresh;
beer or *sake* usually taken
with the sushi and rolls; a
Chinese- or Japanese-
speaking friend is a must.
$$

Shintori
B1, 80 Jianguo N. Rd, Sec. 1
Tel: (02) 2501-7000
Staff are extremely
efficient and, unlike many
upscale dining spots in
Taiwan, discreet as well;
classical Zen Buddhist-

décor, subtle and small-
scale yet beautiful; ultra-
expensive, with an exotic
special that changes
monthly, delicious
specialties, and a huge
range of wines and *sake*.
$$$$

Korean

Der Lih Korean BBQ
1F, 13, Lane 160, Dunhua S. Rd,
Sec. 1
Tel: (02) 2771-2728
Known both for its
barbecue and its fiery
Korean hot pot; offers a list
of over 100 items for hot
pot; constantly
experimenting, regulars
come back to try new hot-
pot items. **$$$**

Han He Ting
447-40 Guangfu S. Rd
Tel: (02) 2758-0027
Though in fact just a side
dish, the delicious *kimchi*
(pickled vegetables) are
hard to stop eating; food is
great, compensating for the
"unenthusiastic service."
Another must-try is the
bulgogi (marinated beef
charcoal-grilled at your
table). **$$$**

NORTH TAIWAN

Danshui

Red Castle
6, Lane 2, Sanmin St
Tel: (02) 8631-1168
Situated in a three-story Victorian-style heritage building, looking down a slope over the Danshui River. The menu is changed every three months, depending on what's in season – try the Taiwan seafood specialties. Open until 1am weekdays, 2am weekends. $$

Shrimp Feed Fish BBQ
145 Zhongzheng St
Tel: (02) 2621-2639
Sits among a crowd of seafood eateries on the riverfront that brings in the crowds for Danshui's famously lovely sunsets. A friendly mom-and-son team run things; their best offerings are fresh barbecue crab, clams, and other shellfish from Danshui's fishermen. Ready yourself for the second-floor pass-the-mike-around karaoke. $$

South Train
1, Lane 51, Boai St
Tel: (02) 2629-2688
Train aficionado Wang Zhi-bi has created a diner that is part restaurant, part museum, stuffed with train models and paraphernalia. One half is a mock-up railroad dining car. Wang, a trained chef, makes everything from scratch, and recommends his casseroles (beef, seafood, vegetarian), baked thyme chicken in spicy sauce, and ginger-garlic beef teriyaki. Daily 11.30am–10pm. $$

Wen Hong Hot Pot
3 Boai St
Tel: (02) 2625-3352
The Taiwanese love their steaming hotpot, especially during the winter months. All good hotpot locations have their secret house sauce that foods plucked from the pot are dipped into. The heavy strongly flavored sauce here is tangy and savory, the hotpot ingredients myriad and very fresh. $$

BELOW: City of Sadness Restaurant, Jiufen.

Ilan

Coconut Palm Forest
1F, 6 Deyang Rd, Jiaoxi Township
Tel: (03) 988-2011
In the new Art Spa hot-springs hotel, this bright and airy facility primarily offers Chinese, Japanese, and Western selections, with a smattering from other cuisines. The Taiwan-style crispy pig's foot and the Japanese seafood pot and stone-baked shrimp are recommended. Alfresco tables available. $$$

Jiufen

City of Sadness Restaurant
294-2 Qingbian Rd
Tel: (02) 2406-2289
Just on the corner of Shuqi and Qingbian roads. On Jiufen's most famous stone-step alleyways, this wood-frame, three-story teahouse was a location for the local shoots of the City of Sadness film. The interior evokes the Japanese-occupation era. The big bay windows offer grand views, but best is the rooftop teahouse/dining area, the bulk of the town looming above, sea crashing ashore far below. Perhaps Jiufen's best visual tableau. $$

Grandma's Fish Stew
9 Jishan Rd
Tel: (02) 2497-6678
Each tourist destination in Taiwan has its renowned local famous products, called *mingchan*, and fish stew is among Jiufen's most popular, along with fried taro and sweet-potato balls. Open daily 10am–10pm. $

Jiufen Old Noodle House
45 Jishan Rd
Tel: (02) 2497-6316
Another Jiufen specialty is spicy beef-noodle soup. Here the secret house ingredients add a unique twist to the beef-noodle broth in which the thick beef slices and noodles are marinated. Open 10am–9.30pm. $

Keelung

Evergarden Chinese Restaurant
5F, 62-1 Zhongzheng Rd
Tel: (02) 2427-9988
In Keelung's best hotel, the Evergreen Laurel, specializes in Cantonese dishes, especially "Hong Kong" dim sum. The harbor views at night are superb. $$$

Muzha

Big Teapot Teahouse
37-1, Lane 38, Zhinan Rd, Sec. 3
Tel: (02) 2939-5615
The Big Teapot rests atop pillars over tiered tea-plantation slopes. The red-brick, timber-interior, two-story facility offers great night views of the city. Try the three cup range-chicken *(sanbei yeji)*; Taiwan-invented *sanbei* dishes have meat chunks simmered in vinegar, soy sauce, and sesame oil. Open until 2am. $$

Yaoyue Teahouse
6, Lane 40, Zhinan Rd, Sec.3
Tel: (02) 2939-2025
In the Muzha tea-plantation area, serves Taiwan-style "tea cuisine" – snacks and heavier dishes that complement tea drinking. Yaoyue (Inviting the Moon), sporting wooden pavilions and outdoor picnic tables, is also renowned for another area specialty, range-chicken. Open until 2am. $$

Yangmingshan

Arum Lily Restaurant
2F, 237 Gezhi Rd
Tel: (02) 2861-6661
The Arum Lily is closely identified with Yangmingshan in spring. Chinese commonly add parts of flowers to their dishes, with results Western palates can accept, so explore the arum-lily soup and salad here. The menu is international fusion. There are great views from this bay-windowed white-and-cream art-deco venue. $$$

Chang Qing Restaurant
63 Bamboo Lake Rd
Tel: (02) 2861-2453
A wonderful converted old stone ploughman's residence. NT$800 minimum per person on the tree-shaded outdoor patio. Chewy range-chicken, a local specialty, and fresh greens from owners' farm, washed down with big mugs of draft. **$$–$$$**
Chin Tein Restaurant
237 Gezhi Rd

Tel: (02) 2861-6661
On the rooftop of the ritzy Landis Resort Yangmingshan, the views of mountains and Danshui River far below are a big draw. Packed for breakfast weekends, quieter on weekdays, be sure to take in the traditional Chinese purple-yam porridge. At night the stars and a full BBQ menu come out (for groups), with traditional Chinese sauces. **$$$**

Shan Lan Café
1F, 237 Gezhi Rd
Tel: (02) 2861-6661
Taiwan's Landis hotels are known for top-quality kitchens. The outdoor patio overlooking a vista of green – a rare gem in busy Taipei – is a treat. Chinese, American, and Continental breakfasts, plus standard Taiwan café selections other hours, of which the classic north China beef-noodle soup and other

noodle dishes are recommended. **$$**
Shanmu Lin
55-12 Bamboo Lake Rd
Tel: (02) 2861-7159
Shanmu Lin means "fir forest," and it is rare in Taipei to dine outdoors amongst the birds and trees. In the Bamboo Lake cash-crop farm district, the range chicken is very good. Try the soups, which feature arum-lily and orchid flowers. **$$**

WEST-CENTRAL TAIWAN

Central Cross-Island Highway

Wuling Farm
3-1 Wuling Rd
Heping Township, Taichung County
Tel: (04) 2590-1259
In the main guest house of this recreational farm there are spectacular views of mountains all round. Chefs concentrate on seasonal local produce: try gourmet dishes building on cabbage, apples, and even tea, for example, organic vegetables like water celery and water spinach, plus pickled cabbage. Per table fee NT$2200 (7 dishes, one soup). Also has good Chinese/Western buffet breakfast (NT$150 person). **$**

BELOW: neon noodle sign.

Changhua

Grand Chinese Restaurant
1F, 30 Sanfen Rd, Huatan Township, Changhua County
Tel: (04) 787-2029
In the Hsiao Yueh Resort Hotel, which serves Taiwan Folk Village, amidst elegant antique-style Taiwanese furniture, enjoy dishes from all Chinese cuisines. However, the main draw here is the many traditional Taiwanese classics, representing all Taiwan areas. **$$**

Chiayi

The Fusion Restaurant
7F, 600 Zhongxiao Rd
Tel: (05) 277-1999
The Nice Prince Hotel

serves regional delicacies: traditional Chiayi snacks, Budai (local fishing village) seafood, Alishan mountain treats, and fusion creations. Open kitchen, decorative theme Alishan wood with flowing waters. **$$–$$$**

Mazu Islands

Grandma's Eatery
143 Niujiao (Rhino Horn) Village
Tel: (0836) 26125
One of the few nightlife spots on the islands (there is also a small bar in the fishing village), in a lovely restored stone residence in the north Fujian style. Unusual north Fujian food – savor the barnacles – there are also Chinese beers, supposedly illegal but all over Mazu, and island-specialty spirits. **$$–$$$**

Penghu

Chrysanthemum Island Cafe
11 Jieshou Rd, Magong City
Tel: (06) 927-1124
White-stucco, breezy cafe with outdoor ceramic-tiled patio that draws crowds for the grand views over wide Penghu Bay. Offers a variety of pastries, coffees, other beverages, and ice shakes – many unique Taiwan variants of Western familiars, and featuring fresh, exotic local produce. **$**
Hongyang Lobster and Local Specialties
20 Minfu Rd, Magong City

Tel: (06) 926-7792
Beyond the lobster, caught in area seas, be sure to try the Penghu specialty black-sugar cake, made from local sugarcane, laver, and peanut candy, and squash cake. This spot also offers a popular takeaway service, perfect for seaside picnics. **$$**
Huanxilou Seafood Restaurant
15-3 Zhiping Road, Magong City
Tel: (06) 927-7775
This popular seafood establishment is one of Penghu's more venerable. The cobia is especially good, but be sure to try the various approaches used for the calamari, caught by Penghu fishermen. **$$**
North Sea Fish Village Seafood Restaurant
2 Zhongzheng Rd, Magong City
Tel: (06) 927-4881
In the Baohua Hotel, with elegant decor not found in most other barebones-décor Penghu dining spots. A banquet-style approach, meaning per table costs, this large place is considered among Penghu's elite seafood locations. Try the inshore-raised cobia, autumn-harvested, a Penghu specialty. **$$**
Ridong
15 Haipu Rd, Magong City
Tel: (06) 927-7300
Bright and comfy, always filled with loyal, long-term, local patrons. The freshest in seafood,

always catch of the day, cooked up in the spicy Sichuan style. For many dishes, pick your own at the aquarium tanks in the front. **$$**

Sun Moon Lake

Andre's
23 Zhongzheng Rd
Tel: (049) 285-5500
In the posh Fenisia Hotel, with superb views of lake and mountain, the menu here jumps around the Western map. The Italian dishes are notably good, but try the Westernized versions of local specialty produce, especially the lake fish (President fish most famous). Attractive open kitchen. **$$$**

Lake View
142 Zhongxing Rd
Tel: (049) 285-6888
A cozy, sophisticated location, seating just 42, in the ultra-sleek Lalu Hotel. Fabulous lake and mountain views. Dripping in Western finery – candelabras, silver cutlery, fine linens – the house specialties concentrate on dishes beloved by late President Chiang Kai-shek, who had a favorite villa on this site. **$$$**

Taichung

Evergarden Chinese Restaurant
6 Taichunggang Rd, Sec. 2
Tel: (04) 2313-9988, ext. 2882
Perhaps the best of the F&B bunch at the Evergreen Laurel Hotel, known for its fine dining. Elegant classical Chinese décor. Top-flight Hong Kong chefs are brought in for the highlighted Cantonese fare. The best regional teas are also stocked. **$$$**

La Mode
4F, 9 Taichunggang Rd, Sec. 2
Tel: (04) 2326-8008
Elegant food and decor in the ritzy Landis Taichung Hotel, with both buffet offerings and entrées, the latter menu renewed each month. The appetizers, presented buffet-style, are in wide range and are tantalizing. **$$$**

Tian Hsiang Lo
2F, 9 Taichunggang Rd, Sec. 2
Tel: (04) 2326-8008
In the Landis Taichung Hotel, serene and subdued, with quiet black, brown, and soft white tones, the main draw here is Hangzhou selections. Dinner set menus start at NT$800. Perhaps the most popular dish is sweet and sour yellow croaker. **$$$**

SOUTHWEST TAIWAN

Kaohsiung

75 Lounge and Grill
75F, 1 Ziqiang 3rd Rd
Tel: (07) 566-8000
In the Splendor Kaohsiung Hotel, the highest place in Kaohsiung to eat, with spectacular views of the city far below. The chef recommends the grilled sea bass with spring chicken and the grilled chop, fillet steak, or rib-eye with half-lobster. Fee for elevator ride. **$$$**

Former British Consulate
20 Lianhai Rd, Gushan District
Tel: (07) 525-0007
www.khhuk.org.tw
Terrific views of harbor below on the left, vast ocean on the right, from inside and outside patio at this important heritage site, Taiwan's first Western-style building. Try the Blue Fin tuna dumplings, followed with the Queen's Choice – a deluxe 3-layer dessert tower ("night tea"). No service charge, open to midnight. **$$**

The Pig and Whistle
199 Siwei 4th Rd
Tel: (07) 330-1006
www.pigandwhistle.com.tw
A Kaohsiung icon, this is where you'll find the city's expats. Very extensive menu, New Zealand lamb cutlets and fish and chips (cod) especially good. Daily lunch and dinner specials, great value. Pub downstairs, music/dance main floor. **$$**

Kending

Cactus Café
126 Dawan Road, Kending Town
Tel: (08) 886-2747
Home-style cookin' from the always attentive Ping, who also serves up great beachside views. Try the breakfast burritos and buttermilk pancakes. Whatever time of day, get there early to get a seat. Open to 2 am. **$$**

Warung Didi
186 Dawan Rd, Kenting Town
Tel: (08) 886-2747
Along with Cactus Café forms perhaps the most popular eatery duo in Kending. The food and view combo are hard to top. Filled with beach-bum regulars. Recommended are the Thai seafood curry, Thai boneless chicken with basil sauce, and Thai yom-yom soup. **$–$$**

Meinong

Meinong Yizhan Hakka Leicha Shop
142 Chenggong Rd
Tel: (07) 681-8475
Leicha is ground tea with peanut, spices, and much else mixed in, a Hakka perennial, very thick and nutritious. Customers get to make their own, guided by staff dressed in traditional Hakka blue-dyed garb, another old-time Meinong craft. **$**

BELOW: Taiwan's cuisine emphasizes fresh seafood.

PRICE CATEGORIES

Prices below are for two people, including drinks:
$$$$ more than NT$3,000
$$$ NT$2,000–3,000
$$ NT$1,000–2,000
$ NT$1,000 or less

TRANSPORTATION

ACCOMMODATIONS

EATING OUT

ACTIVITIES

A – Z

LANGUAGE

ABOVE: Taiwan has some of the best teas in the world.

Evergarden Chinese Restaurant
2F, 1, Lane 366, Zhonghua E. Rd, Sec. 3
Tel: (06) 602-3863
In the high-end Evergreen Hotel, part of a chain known for fine dining. The Evergarden proffers Hong Kong, Sichuan, and Taiwan delights, its Hong Kong dim sum the biggest draw, with over 100 unique house-invention variations. Unusual appetizers include pickled tomatoes flavored with plums, and pickled pumpkin. **$$$**

Uehara
39 Yiping Road
Tel: (06) 299-6226
One of Tainan's better Japanese restaurants. Try to sit in the lovely courtyard. Embraced by wafting jazz music, the set meals (shark fin with pumpkin, salted scallops, or Korean-style beef roll) run NT$800–1,200. Drink wine, whisky or *sake*. **$$$**

Yuan Xiang Yuan Restaurant
178 Zhongxing Rd
Tel: (07) 681-0678
All the best in traditional Hakka fare: stewed pig foot, wax-gourd stew, white-cabbage stew, and something not always seen in Hakka eateries outside Hakka towns, hearty and delicious roast duckling with taro stuffing. Associated with Yuan Xiang Yuan Cultural Village. **$$**

Zhen Haowei Restaurant
78 Zhongshan Rd, Sec. 1
Tel: (07) 681-2165
Meinong is a Hakka town, so where else would you go? This spot, run by the same family for over 40 years, has a homey feel. There are secret home recipes for most everything, but be sure to order old Hakka favorites such as white-cabbage stew and wax-gourd stew. **$$**

EAST COAST

Lotus Pavilion
2 Yongxing Rd
Tel: (03) 822-1171
Located in the Chinatrust Hotel. The restaurant does big business with tour buses on weekends and holidays, so beware. Top-flight Cantonese selections, with the Shansu salmon roll and Fugui prawn ball highly recommended. The window seating above the outdoor pool, lined with palm trees, makes a pleasant place to sit. **$$$**

The Village Chinese Restaurant
1F, 1-1 Linyuan Rd
Tel: (038) 222-111
In the spacious Parkview Hotel, this first-floor facility looks out over romantic tropical scenery. The kitchen concentrates on Cantonese cuisine, with the lunchtime dim sum especially popular.

Selections from other regional Chinese cuisines. **$$$**

Joki
3 Shimen, Fengbin Township, Hualien County
Tel: (038) 781-616
www.joki.com.tw
On the coastal highway, this bizarre coffeeshop and art gallery (think native Austronesian sculpture mixed with Picasso) is a favorite stopping point for expats heading south of Hualien City. Superb views down over the rocky coast. Simple, traditional Taiwanese snacks, with some Western-style sandwiches, thick toast with peanut butter. **$**

Esod Vegetarian Restaurant
320 Zhongxing Rd, Sec.
Tel: (89) 232-106
True vegan fare is what you get here at this 40-seat eatery in the main downtown area. The food is king, meaning little décor adornment. There are many selections, all with the freshest ingredients, the core being rice, noodle, and pasta dishes. The ramen is notably good, as are the teas and shaved-ice treats. **$$**

Tian Hsian Chinese
B1, 18 Tianxiang Rd, Xiulin Village
Tel: (038) 691-155
Located in the international-class Grand Formosa Taroko Hotel, with a décor built around Chinese classical furniture, the Tian Hsian offers good dining options and features regional indigenous produce. Try the Chinese medicinal/tonic dishes and the aboriginal specialties.

The locally sourced trout and sunfish are also savory. **$$$**

Naruwan
1F, 23, Lane 113, Longquan Rd
Tel: (089) 510-666
In the greenery-soaked Hotel Royal Chihpen, the Naruwan offers diners a buffet of Chinese, Japanese, and Western selections as well as a Chinese-cuisine menu that has a smattering of good local aboriginal dishes. Room open and airy, floor-to-ceiling windows, décor loosely aboriginal, much wood. **$$$**

PRICE CATEGORIES

Prices below are for two people, including drinks:
$$$$ more than NT$3,000
$$$ NT$2,000–3,000
$$ NT$1,000–2,000
$ NT$1,000 or less

A CTIVITIES

FESTIVALS, THE ARTS, NIGHTLIFE, SHOPPING AND SPECTATOR SPORTS

THE ARTS

General

The three English-language papers each carry weekend culture and entertainment supplements, which come out on Friday or Saturday. The bimonthly *Travel in Taiwan* has sections on the upcoming month's cultural activities, arts and entertainment events. For the most part, tickets must be purchased from the venue staging an event; this can often be frustrating because of language problems, so it is always best to have a local friend handle the purchase, either by phone or by accompanying you in advance to the ticket office.

Art Galleries

Galleries exhibit works of art by both old masters and promising young local artists. They display an impressive range of styles, from traditional Chinese landscape painting and calligraphy to contemporary Western abstracts and still lifes, and the artists employ both Eastern and Western materials and methods. For detailed information on exhibitions, check the weekend arts and entertainment supplements in the local English-language newspapers.

The spacious Taipei Fine Arts Museum is at 181 Zhongshan N. Road, Sec. 3, tel: (02) 2595-7656, www.tfam.gov.tw. This modernistic facility frequently sponsors exhibitions of arts and crafts by renowned international and local talents. There are other fine-art museums in Kaohsiung and Taichung.

The Taipei Museum of Contemporary Art at 39 Changan W. Rd, tel: (02) 2552-3720, www.moca taipei.org.tw, is another of the city's culture venues in a heritage-site facility, once the city hall. It juxtaposes works by foreign and local artists, following three themes: art, design, and architecture practices.

Taipei's private galleries represent a wide range of styles, from traditional landscapes to modern abstract. Some of the more interesting art galleries in Taipei are listed below:

Apollo Art Gallery
2F, 218-6 Zhongxiao E. Rd, Sec. 4
Tel: (02) 2781-9332
Asia Art Center
177 Jianguo S. Rd, Sec. 2
Tel: (02) 2754-1366
www.asiaartcenter.org
Caves Art Center
B1, 138 Zhongxiao E. Rd, Sec. 1
Tel: (02) 2396-1864
www.gallery.com.tw

Chi-Wen Gallery
3F, 19, Lane 252, Dunhua S. Rd, Sec. 1
Tel: (02) 8771-3371
www.chiwengallery.com
Crown Art Center
50, Lane 120, Dunhua N. Rd
Tel: (02) 2716-8888
Eslite Gallery
B2, 245 Dunhua S. Rd, Sec. 1
Tel: (02) 2775-5977, ext. 582
IT Park
2/3F, 41 Yitong St
Tel: (02) 2507-7243
Kander's Museum
1F, 25 Zhongxiao W. Rd, Sec. 1
Tel: (02) 2361-4644
Lung Men Art Gallery
2F, 2, Alley 150, Xinyi Rd, Sec. 5
Taipei Artist Village
7 Beiping E. Rd
Tel: (02) 3393-7377
www.artistvillage.org
Taiwan Crafts Center
9F, 20 Nanhai Rd

BELOW: exhibit at the Museum of Contemporary Art.

Tel: (02) 2356-3880, ext. 302
(closed Monday)

Classical Music and Dance

Taiwan has produced numerous world-class musicians. Western music is regularly performed at various venues in Taipei by the Taiwan Provincial Symphony Orchestra and the Taipei Municipal Symphony Orchestra. The favorite venue for most Taipei-based expats is the National Concert Hall, on the grounds of the National Taiwan Democracy Memorial; many top musicians from around the world come to the island for special performances. Consult your hotel, or the English-language papers, for details on performances and venues. Traditional Chinese music has its roots in temple ritual, court traditions, and village music. Try catching temple music at the elaborate rituals held annually, on September 28, to celebrate the birthday of Confucius.

There are few traditional dances in Taiwan, mostly performed by minority groups. Snippets of dances can be seen at the various tourism centers around the island. On the other hand, modern dance has gained popularity in Taiwan over the last decade or so.

The Cloud Gate Dance Theater (www.cloudgate.org.tw), led by Lin Hwai-min, has spearheaded the movement. It combines both Chinese and Western techniques and ideas, choreographed to the music of contemporary Chinese musicians. The internationally acclaimed group holds regular performances in Taipei.

The Taipei Dance Circle (www.taipei-dance-circle.com.tw), a breakaway from the Cloud Gate Theater, also perform their own unique style of modern dance regularly.

Chinese Opera

Taiwan is one of the best places in the world to attend Chinese-style opera. From the melodies sung by magnificently costumed performers and the orchestral accompaniment, to the astounding acrobatics and martial-arts displays of the performers, a night at the Beijing or Taiwanese opera is both an entertaining and educational experience.

The Taipei Eye stages special performances of opera, puppetry, and other traditional folk arts especially tailored for tourists, introducing numerous forms in an exciting 90-minute program each Friday and Saturday night. Intros are given and showtime subtitles. Located in the heritage-site Taiwan Cement Hall, 113 Zhongshan N. Rd, Sec. 2, tel: (02) 2568-2677, www.taipeieye.com.

For a taste of Beijing or Taiwanese opera, try the television set – live performances are broadcast almost every day. In the back alleys of Taipei and outside the capital city, keep your eyes open for traveling opera companies that set up and stage performances, lasting several days, in temple courtyards and other public places. These performances are generally sponsored by the government in an attempt to keep traditional culture alive, or by a rich local, who will gain merit in the eyes of the gods (to whom the show is actually presented, not the local mortals) by sponsoring a benevolent act.

Crafts

The Taiwanese take great pride in the things they can make with their hands: from lanterns and toys, handbags and baskets, bamboo and rattan crafts, rugs and carpets, to knitwear and embroidery.

In Taipei, an excellent selection of local handicrafts (including those of the aborigine tribes) are on display for sale at the Taiwan Handicraft Promotion Center, at 1 Xuzhou Street, tel: (02) 2393-3655, fax: (02) 2393-7330, e-mail: thpc@handicraft.org.tw, www.handicraft.org.tw. This is a good place to do souvenir and gift shopping, with reasonable prices. Prices are set, rising progressively as one moves from the first to the fourth level. Overseas shipping for purchased items can be handled by the center. Other similar display centers, linked to various government units and thus with good reputations, dot the island. (For more details on other types of shopping *see page 107*.)

Cinema

Residents of Taiwan are enthusiastic moviegoers, mostly watching Hong Kong and Western films. Taiwan is one of Hollywood's most lucrative markets, and all major Hollywood studios have permanent representatives here.

Most of the foreign films that come to Taiwan are from the United States, and they are always shown in English, with Chinese subtitles. This means that traveling movie fans need not fear a shortage of Western film entertainment when in Taiwan.

The daily English-language newspapers carry information on English-language films currently playing in Taipei. There are usually

BELOW: a fluid performance from the Taipei Dance Circle..

three to five performances per day, with the last show beginning around midnight. By far the most popular movie-viewing venue for foreigners in Taipei is Warner Village Cinema Center, in the city's posh east district. New, clean and comfortable, the theater complex also houses Taiwan's first Planet Hollywood outlet, making for the ideal night out.

NIGHTLIFE

Nightlife options in Taipei, Kaohsiung, Taichung and Tainan, are varied and plentiful. A night on the town usually begins with a meal; beer, wine, and spirits are ordered along with dinner, and the liquid refreshment rarely stops flowing (*see page 103* on beer-houses). "When drinking among intimate friends, even a thousand rounds are not enough," proclaims an ancient Chinese proverb, and many of the people of Taiwan take that advice to heart. Inebriation is a form of convivial communication here, an opportunity to drop the formal mask of business and reveal the "inner person." Since the Chinese are food fanatics who appreciate good cuisine of all kinds, Taipei also has a range of Western restaurants, many operated by accomplished European chefs.

Karaoke/KTV

A familiar part of the Taipei night scene is the karaoke/KTV club. Venues are decorated in a variety of themes, from Versailles palaces to high-tech chrome-and-neon space stations. After selecting the appropriate-size private room, customers can order drinks and snacks while leafing through a catalog of traditional, pop, Western and Asian songs. Desired selections are keyed in via a small terminal in the room. Songs can be selected any time and are queued in line. Wall outlets allow for plenty of microphones. A note of caution: in the late 1990s there were a series of disastrous fires at KTVs around the island; safety standards are now enforced much more strictly, but it is still best to get local acquaintances to confirm the safety of a place.

Taipei Pubs and Bars

Taipei abounds with pubs and bars. One of the easiest places to go bar-hopping is the so-called Sugar Daddy

ABOVE: ready for a night out in Taipei.

Row area around Shuangcheng Street, off Linsen N. Road near the Imperial Hotel. There are lots of establishments within easy walking distance of one another. Also called "the Zone" or "the Combat Zone" by expats, this area used to be a favorite place for R&R for US servicemen in the 1960s and 1970s. Now much toned down, the Zone is still a popular haunt for those who just can't sit down in one spot for very long, and think more action is always waiting in the next watering hole.

45 Pub
2F, 45 Heping E. Rd, Sec. 1
Tel: (02) 2321-2140
An "in" place with the young foreign-language student and teacher crowd, with record industry paraphernalia and 1960s music. Has very affordable, good menu, with special deals for big groups.

Bacchus Wine Bar
176 Xingan St
Tel: (02) 2716-9179
Has over 30 imported wines on the menu. Happy hour is 4–8pm, and prices on bottles are reduced NT$200 from 11pm until closing (3am). Closed Sunday.

Brown Sugar
101 Songren Rd
Tel: (02) 8780-1110
www.brownsugar.com.tw
Live music nightly, primarily local artists, regular overseas imports. Groups primarily jazz and blues, some soft rock. Events, artists, menu online.

The Brass Monkey
166 Fuxing N. Rd
Tel: (02) 2547-5050
www.brassmonkeytaipei.com
Sports bar with big screen – concentrating on the

Commonwealth" crowd, meaning lots of rugby, soccer/football, and hockey – that also offers Wednesday pub quizzes and Thursday ladies' night. Aficionados say the food at this pub is among the city's best.

Carnegie's
100 Anhe Rd, Sec. 2
Tel: (02) 2325-4433
www.carnegies.net
Perhaps the city's most popular bar at the moment. Over 300 shooter selections, dance poles on the bar, must be over 21 (bring ID) – you get the picture. Expect long lines on Fridays, Saturdays, and on Wednesday Ladies Nights.

Driftwood
4, Alley 9, Lane 316, Roosevelt Rd, Sec. 3
Tel: (02) 2365-7413

Drinking Games

A popular method of downing liquor or beer other than toasting is a kind of "rock, paper, scissors" finger game, in which the loser must drain his glass dry. Also popular are various forms of a "fingers-guessing game." The basic form: two contestants each shoot out a number of fingers, at the same time. As this is done, one guesses how many fingers in total will be exposed. If wrong, the other gets a chance to guess next round. If right, the other must down his full glass.

Locals can be seen engaging in these spirited contests in restaurants and pubs throughout Taiwan. One who walks away sober is either considered a cheat or a man with the "capacity of an ocean."

Gay Hangouts

The Beach
B1, 3, Lane 152, Xinyi Rd, Sec. 3
Tel: (02) 2702-7113
Stylish décor, physically very
attractive bar. Resident DJ
weekends, small dance area. Cover
on Friday and Saturday (one free
drink); free entry until about 10pm,
but crowds arrive later. Parties with
erotic male dancers, generally, once
a month or more.

Fresh
7 Jinshan S. Rd, Sec. 2
Tel: (02) 2358-7701
www.fresh-taipei.com
Big complex, four floors. Veggie
restaurant on the first floor, main
bar and two lounges on the second,
dancing on the third, and a rooftop
garden terrace. Gets very crowded,
a good thing, runs until almost
sunup. Fri–Sat night cover. Some
staff speak English.

Gingin's
8, Alley 8, Lane 210, Roosevelt Rd,
Sec. 3
Tel: (02) 2364-2006
A laid-back coffeeshop/teahouse
combo, frequented by folk visiting
the gay-lifestyle bookstore across
the street.

Go Fish
B1, 6 Anhe Rd, Sec. 1
Tel: (02) 2755-1076
A spot for women exclusively,
featuring a dance floor and
karaoke.

I.T. Park
2/3F, 1 Yitong St
Tel: (02) 2507-7243
A chic, comfy art gallery-cum-bar,
there is a cozy terrace here –
perfect for tea or coffee and a chat.

Jailhouse
2F, 3-1, Alley 8, Lane 316,
Roosevelt Rd
Tel: (02) 2364-1623
Lesbian bar; there is a cover
charge, which goes up Fridays and
Saturdays. Opens 9pm.

A relaxed, easygoing and compact
aboriginal bar that offers an eclectic
mix of live native (weekends), Canto-
pop and Western music. Wood and
native Taiwanese (ie, aboriginal)
items dominate.

The Green Bar
84-1 Tianmu E. Rd, Tianmu District
Tel: (02) 2873-3263
A hybrid roadhouse/café bar where
beers are a low NT$90 each from
3pm to 8pm. An expat favorite, with

darts and sports on TV (standing
room only on major sport events).

Jurassic Park
196 Bade Rd, Sec. 2
Tel: (02) 2741-0550
Beerhouses are large, open places
(think of Valhalla), with long tables,
kegs of beer pulled up alongside, and
a steady flow of greasy Chinese
foods. Each has a theme: this iconic
spot, long called the Indian Beer
House, crawls with three floors of

Red Indian heads, dinosaur bones,
gargoyles that serve as urinals, and
petrified tables and stools.

Lane 86
7, Lane 86, Xinsheng S. Rd, Sec. 3
Tel: (02) 2367-1532
A hole-in-the-wall neighborhood
watering hole popular with the expat
student and language-teacher
community. Quiet and comfy, this is a
good spot to come to chat.

Luxy
5F, 201 Zhongxiao E. Rd
Tel: (02) 2772 1000
www.luxy-taipei.com
One of the sleekest and ritziest of
the city's growing coterie of glitzy
dance clubs. In fact it is two clubs in
one, each with a very different
atmosphere and top DJs, plus
lounges and VIP rooms.

Malibu West
9, Lane 25, Shuangcheng St
Tel: (02) 2592-8228
One of the more popular Combat
Zone watering holes, sporting a
sports-and-local-pretties theme, this
large establishment does above-
average local and Western pub food.
This, and the all-day buy-two-get-one-
free deal on Taiwan Beer, brings
them streaming in.

Ploughman Inn
8, Lane 232, Dunhua S. Rd, Sec. 1
Tel: (02) 2773-3268
An old expat favorite, a pub with bar
downstairs featuring live music
nightly; NT$300 on Sunday to
Thursday, NT$400 on Friday and
Saturday, including buffet, excluding
drinks; wide selection of wines and

BELOW: drink with the dinosaurs at Jurassic Park beerhouse.

other drinks from pub's stock. Happy hour 6–8.30pm, 40 percent off alcoholic drinks.

Q-Bar

16, Alley 19, Lane 216
Zhongxiao E. Rd, Sec. 4
Tel: (02) 2771-7778
www.qbartaipei.com

On a quiet side street, fixed up with chic Art Deco trappings, this is one of those places where each member of the after-work crowd seems to recognize someone as they stroll through the door. Has a very good cocktail menu.

Roxy 99

B1, 218 Jinshan S. Rd, Sec 2
Tel: (02) 2351-5970

One of the more popular bars in the growing bar and pub district surrounding Shida Road, home to language-study institutes and thus young locals and expats. The music covers jazz and blues to rock and other forms, but the local DJs always seem to know the classics. Free entry and four drinks free for those arriving before 11pm on Wednesday Rock Nite.

Saints & Sinners

114–116 Anhe Rd, Sec. 2
Tel: (02) 2739-9001

A favorite, part of a one-two punch with Carnegie's in the emerging Anhe Road party area. The long wraparound bar is a favorite, its backdrop a salivating array of imported beers, wines, and spirits. Often filled with boisterous expat sports teams celebrating wins, or losses.

The Tavern

415 Xinyi Rd, Sec. 4
Tel: (02) 8780-0892
www.tavern.com.tw

Bills itself a "theatre of sports," perhaps Taipei's best sports bar, with 48 flat-screen TV monitors and a super-large screen for the day's biggest event. Great pub fare. Close to Taipei World Trade Center. Check website for games/specials.

Live Music/Clubs

Taipei's, and Taiwan's, live music scene is vibrant and growing of late. Outside of Taipei, expat bands in Western-style bars are the main attractions for foreigners. In Taipei the variety is more robust; certain clubs/bars such as Zee Live House put leading local and regional singers on stage; other places such as the Farmhouse and The Pig, old-time favorites, feature local bands with talented Westerners, Filipinos and local Chinese; upscale spots like Ziga Zaga, TU, and Brown Sugar bring in quality acts from overseas –

generally jazz or rhythm and blues acts. Almost all venues with live entertainment have a cover or minimum charge.

Blue Note

4F, 171 Roosevelt Rd, Sec. 3
Tel: (02) 2362-2333

A favorite night-time destination for lovers of jazz. A different band moves in each night – either pros (both locals and expats) or the eclectic house band. The latter accepts "volunteer" vocalists. During the slower daytime hours patrons can choose from a selection of thousands of CDs. Live music starts at 9.40pm; cover.

Brown Sugar

101 Songren Rd
Tel: (02) 8780-1110
www.brownsugar.com.tw

A lively spot featuring live bands every night. These are mostly local, with irregular foreign bands from North America, mainly playing jazz, blues, and soft rock at times.

EZ5

211 Anhe Road, Sec. 2
Tel: (02) 2738-3995

Taiwan's Canto-pop singing stars pay part of their bills plying their trade in local clubs. This is one of the best, bringing in some of the island's top recording talent. The early-evening crowd will also come for dinner; the kitchen has a wide menu of Chinese favorites. Entry tickets redeemed for two drinks or snacks.

The Farmhouse

5, Lane 32, Shuangcheng St
Tel: (02) 2595-1764

The focal point of the Zone district, decorated in a country-inn style, The Farmhouse seems to have been here forever. A different band takes to the stage each night, most doing rock and pop cover tunes. Closed Monday.

The Party Room

12F, 138 Bade Rd, Sec. 4
Tel: (02) 3762-1289
www.partyroom.com.tw

A large dance venue in the Living Mall complex, one of Taipei's most popular. Large in scale, plush amenities, good music and, key, top-flight bookings for live music and DJs. Good food too.

The Pig

78 Tianmu E. Rd, Tianmu District
Tel: (02) 2874-0631

A spacious British-style pub that tends toward a club atmosphere with a sit-down crowd after the bands hit the stage each night from 9.30pm onwards. Styles range through the week, but light rock dominates weekends. Happy hour daily noon–8pm.

Plush

12F, 138 Bade Rd, Sec. 4

Bottle Clubs

A popular form of Taiwan nightlife is the so-called bottle club. Customers buy liquor by the bottle; it is later stored in special racks for future use. These clubs are generally upmarket, with expensive furnishings, tasteful decor, low lights and "atmosphere." Some provide live entertainment. Wealthy local patrons popularly keep bottles of good French cognac. The island's businessmen often choose bottle clubs for entertaining friends and associates on corporate expense accounts.

Tel: (02) 3762-1600
www.plush.com.tw

Large, rambunctious dance club, plush trappings. Ladies' night Wednesdays, B-52 and Tequila happy hours (buy one, one free), Friday is Miniskirt Party night, wear one, get in free. Cover charge.

Spin

B1, 91 Heping E. Rd, Sec. 1
Tel: (02) 2356-9366

In the basement of an older business building, this popular, small disco brings in an intriguing mix of regulars that range from very offbeat arts types to students and language teachers to young professional yuppies. The popular Ladies' Night is on Thursday.

TU

B1, 249 Fuxing S. Rd, Sec. 1
Tel: (02) 2704-7288

A smoky and tightly packed basement hotspot for the singles' crowd, DJs play hip-hop, R&B, and reggae. Thursday, Ladies' Night, brings in droves of well-dressed members of both sexes, with all-you-can-drink admission, men NT$500, ladies NT$100.

Zee Live House

10, Lane 190, Dunhua S. Rd,Sec. 1
Tel: (02) 2711-8766
www.zeelive.com.tw

Opened in 1968, this club has been around forever. Three local Canto-pop stars hit the stage each night, playing to the 30-ish yuppie crowd until the wee hours. There is a good range of Chinese and continental dishes.

Ziga Zaga

2 Songshou Rd
Tel: (02) 2720-1234, ext. 3198

Located in the palatial Grand Hyatt Taipei, this is Taipei's favorite dance club for the 30-something professional crowd; live jazz, funk, and some pop. Opens 9.30pm Mon–Wed, 9pm other days.

Winehouses

One of the quintessential forms of post-dinner activity for groups of Taiwan's men is the *jiujia*, or winehouse. People begin to arrive at about 9pm. Most serve food and expect guests to order several dishes, but the main meal is usually taken elsewhere. Winehouse specialties usually include a variety of "potency foods" like snake-bile soup, turtle-bile stew, sauteed eel, or black-fleshed chicken. All are alleged to be aphrodisiacs.

At least four persons should participate in a winehouse party and at least one should be a local man who is familiar with the routine. Without enough guests, the party cannot reach that vital stage of excitement the Chinese call *jenao*, literally "hot and noisy." A Chinese-speaking guest helps translate the nuances of the conversation and activity. Beyond the cultural experience, this type of establishment may not be to the taste of foreigners; they are very expensive, and in many cases you must pay for the drinks, and the time, of the "hostesses" who entertain guests with conversation.

Note: winehouses are different from beerhouses *(page 103)*.

FESTIVALS

In addition to ancient festivals such as the Lunar New Year and the Mid-Autumn Festival, national holidays such as Double Tenth National Day and the Mid-Autumn Moon Festival, and commemorative days, there are scores of other local Taiwanese festivals known as *baibai*, which are colorful celebrations held in honor of local deities. There are over 100 popular gods in Taiwan, and not only are their birthdays commemorated, each of their "death days" and "deification days" are also occasions for celebration.

The celebration of *baibai* days begins with the faithful offering the best food and wine to the respective deities, and ends with the devotees themselves gorging on the offerings – but not before they are sure that the deities have had their fill. This is usually the time taken for a joss stick (incense stick) to burn out. Few Taiwanese remain entirely sober on these occasions, and everyone spends a lot of money to *qingke*, or "invite friends out."

National holidays and commemorative days, of more recent

origin, follow the Western solar calendar, but most festival dates still follow the lunar calendar. Thus, they vary from year to year and can fall any time within a two-month period. Check exact dates at the time of planning for your trip.

January/February

Foundation Day of the Republic of China: Celebrated every January 1, this day commemorates the founding of the republic on January 1, 1912. On that day, Dr Sun Yat-sen was inaugurated as the first president of the newly founded Republic of China. Also on that day, China officially switched from the lunar to the Gregorian calendar. This occasion is celebrated annually in Taipei with parades, dragon and lion dances, traditional music, patriotic speeches, and, of course, lots of firecrackers.

Chinese Lunar New Year: Most important time of year in the Chinese calendar, beginning the first day of the first lunar month. A time for families to be together. Some private companies will give holidays longer than the official holiday period.

Traditionally called the Spring Festival, the Lunar New Year remains the biggest celebration of the year in Taiwan, as it has for millennia in all Chinese communities. The festival is observed in various stages for a full month, from the 16th day of the 12th lunar month, although offices and shops generally close for only a week around New Year's Day.

BELOW: Baosheng Festival warrior.

Many ancient customs are associated with the Lunar New Year. For example, all outstanding debts must be paid off before New Year's Eve; failure to do so is a grave affront and an omen of bad luck for the coming year. Many wealthy Chinese businessmen in Taiwan keep running accounts in their favorite restaurants and clubs, paying their bills only once a year, just before Lunar New Year's Eve. Another custom is exchanging gifts, especially little red envelopes (*hongbao*) stuffed with "lucky money," the amount depending on the closeness of the relationship between the giver and recipient. Everyone dresses up in new clothes at New Year, from hats down to shoes; this symbolizes renewal and a fresh start in life for the coming year. People visit family and friends and spend a lot of money on entertainment. Indeed, local banks are sometimes plagued with cash shortages at this time of the year. The dominant color is red, which is universally regarded as auspicious among the Chinese; red flowers, red clothing, red streamers, red cakes and candies and the ubiquitous red envelopes appear everywhere.

At the stroke of midnight on New Year's Eve, the entire island suddenly reverberates to the staccato explosions of millions of firecrackers and skyrockets, as every temple and household in Taiwan lights the fuses which will frighten evil spirits from their thresholds, ensuring an auspicious start to the Chinese Lunar New Year. The Chinese invented gunpowder for this very purpose over 1,000 years ago.

The stock phrase to offer all your friends and acquaintances whenever and wherever you encounter them during the period is "*gongxi facai*," which means "I wish you happiness and prosperity" (literally, "Congratulations! Get rich!"). The rhyming retort to this greeting is "*hongbao nalai*," or "hand over a red envelope."

February/March

Lantern Festival: This festival, which falls on the first full moon of the Lunar New Year, marks the end of the Spring Festival. Celebrants appear at night in the streets, parks, and temples of Taiwan carrying colorful lanterns with auspicious phrases inscribed on them in elegant calligraphy. This tradition is supposed to insure against evil and illness in the coming year. The festival food associated with this event is a sweet dumpling of glutinous rice stuffed with bean- or date-paste and called *yuanxiao*. Major temples are excellent places to observe the Lantern Festival. Prizes are awarded for the most beautiful and original lantern designs.

The largest celebrations on this day are the Taipei Lantern Festival, which is held in the grounds of the National Taiwan Democracy Memorial, Kaohsiung Lantern Festival, held along the Love River and the official national event, rotated among cities. Over 100,000 people cram into each venue to watch the respective giant theme floats, see the thousands of lanterns, enjoy the traditional snacks, and take part in the many demonstrations and activities.

Yanshui Rocket Hives Festival: Definitely one of the world's most bizarre celebrations. Yanshui is a fishing town north of Tainan city; the madness takes place on Lantern Festival eve, when tens of thousands of danger-seekers converge on the narrow streets. Large mobile platforms laced with honeycombs stuffed with thousands of rockets – the infamous "rocket hives" – are fired off one after another. Rockets shoot off almost horizontally. All Dante-esque hell breaks loose.

Two centuries back, plague descended on the town. The God of War, Guangong, was called in. Townsfolk guided him about in his life-and-death battle with the plague demons by the light of fireworks. Today the big blast continues from about 7pm into the early hours; smart revelers wear motorcycle helmets and thick old clothing for protection. This is a rite of passage for Old Taiwan Hands.

Pingxi Sky Lantern Festival: Pingxi, a small town southeast of Taipei, sits in a narrow valley on the upper Keelung River. Over 10,000 revelers crowd in and around town on the 15th lunar night of the new year, the Lantern Festival, and the night before, to watch "sky lanterns" journey upwards into the night. Upwards of 3,000 rising, flickering, slow-shooting stars may fill the darkness at any moment. The effect is one of surreal and sensual beauty.

The largest sky lantern to date was 18 meters tall. Each, even the smallest, contains at least one prayer/wish, written on the outside, the mini unmanned hot-air balloons delivering them to the gods. Buy your own small and simple wish-deliverer on-site for as little as NT$250. The origin of sky lanterns is ancient and military in nature, used for

ABOVE: the icon of Mazu at Baoan Temple.

communications; it is said the isolated Han Chinese settlers in this valley used them to signal each either when bandits and aborigine warriors were about.

Birthday of Guanyin: Guanyin, Goddess of Mercy, is one of the most popular Buddhist deities in Taiwan, Korea, and Japan. Known for her compassion and love for people, she is one of Taiwan's patron protective deities. Her birthday is celebrated with colorful *baibai* ceremonies in major temples throughout Taiwan.

April/May

Tomb Sweeping Day: Traditionally calculated as the 105th day after the Winter Solstice and called the Qingming (Clear and Bright) Festival, Tomb-Sweeping Day in Taiwan is now celebrated annually on April 5, which coincides with the date of President Chiang Kai-shek's death, in 1975. Though April 5 remains the date of the traditional Chinese festival it is no longer a national holiday in Taiwan.

During this festival, entire families travel to their ancestral burial grounds to sweep accumulated dirt and debris from the tombs, place fresh flowers around the graves, and perhaps plant some new trees,

flowers and bushes in the area.

Birthday of Mazu: One of the biggest *baibai* of the year in Taiwan, this festival is dedicated to Mazu, Goddess of the Sea, patron saint of Taiwan, and guardian deity of the island's fishermen. It is celebrated with great fanfare in the over 870 temples where Mazu is enshrined. The biggest festival takes place in Central Taiwan, at the elaborate Mazu temple in Beigang, near Chiayi. But you can also get an eye- and earful at the famous Longshan (Dragon Mountain) Temple in the oldest section of Taipei. Sacrificial offerings of roast pig and boiled chickens, billows of smoke from incense and burning paper money, undulating lion and dragon dances, colorful parades and lavish feasting comprise some of the festivities.

Cleansing of the Buddha Festival: This day commemorates the birth of Sakyamuni (the historical Buddha) some 2,500 years ago. The festival is marked in temples throughout the island with cleansing-of-Buddha ceremonies, during which all statues of Buddha are ritually washed while monks recite appropriate sutras. Many of the icons are then paraded through the streets to the sound of gongs and drums.

Additional Festivals Background

A superb and wonderfully informative booklet, *Festivals in Taiwan*, is available from the tourism bureau, providing detailed, accurate and consistent information (often frustratingly difficult to get) on Taiwan's major festivals.

ABOVE: two dragon teams seize the flags at the finishing line of the Dragon Boat Festival.

May/June

Dragon Boat Festival: One of China's most ancient festivals, this event commemorates the death of Qu Yuan. An accomplished poet and upright minister, he plunged to his death in a river about 2,500 years ago to protest at the corruption and misrule of his king, who had banished him from the court. According to the legend, on hearing of his tragic death, the local people rowed their boats out on the river and dropped stuffed rice dumplings tightly wrapped in bamboo leaves into the water, to both supplicate and nourish his spirit and to distract the fishes from eating him. These dumplings, called *zongzi*, remain this festival's major food item.

The Dragon Boat Festival is celebrated with colorful dragon-boat races, which in recent times have become a major sporting event in Taiwan. Teams from all around Taiwan and around the world compete for top honors in various divisions. The Taipei event is the biggest. The bows of the boats are carved into elaborate dragon heads, and the crews row vigorously to the resounding beat of large drums placed at the stern of each boat.

June/July

Birthday of Chenghuang: This *baibai* festival is celebrated with great pomp and ceremony at Taipei's Xiahai Chenghuang (Xiahai City God) Temple at 61 Dihua Street, Sec. 1. The worship of city gods is a practice that has been recorded in China as far

back as the early Xia dynasty (2200–1524 BC), and remains one of Taiwan's liveliest celebrations. City gods are said to have the power to protect a city's inhabitants from both natural disasters and enemy intruders, and they also advise the Lord of Heaven and the King of Hell regarding appropriate rewards and punishments for the city's residents after death. No wonder the Chinese pay them such lavish homage!

Among the colorful festivities of this *baibai* are parades with icons of the City God held high upon pedestals, offerings of whole pigs

Festival Foods

Traditional foods are associated with specific festivals, and visitors should try them where possible. During Chinese New Year people eat *fagao* and *jiaozi*; radishes and pineapples are both eaten and used as decorations. The characters for *fagao*, which are little cupcakes, are homonyms for "go up," as in to rise to a better social position. *Jiaozi*, meat- and vegetable-filled dumplings, are shaped like ingots, and denote prosperity. The characters for "radish" and "pineapple" are homonyms for, respectively, "good fortune" and "prosperity." *Yuanxiao* are enjoyed during the Lantern Festival; the round balls represent the "unity" of the family in the New Year season. *Yuebing*, or moon cakes, eaten during the Mid-Autumn Festival, are also symbols of family unity.

stretched on bamboo racks, processions of celebrants wearing stilts and colorful costumes, lion and dragon dances and lavish feasts.

July/August

Chinese Valentine's Day: Chinese Valentine's Day is derived from the legend of the herd boy and the spinning girl. The herd boy (a star formation in the constellation Aquila, west of the Milky Way) and the spinning girl (the star Vega in the constellation Lyra, east of the Milky Way) appear closest together in the sky on this night, and all the magpies on earth are said to ascend to the sky to form a bridge across the Milky Way so that the lovers may cross over for their brief once-a-year tryst. This is a festival for young unmarried girls and for young lovers, who observe the romantic occasion by exchanging gifts, strolling in moonlit parks, and praying in temples for future matrimonial bliss.

August/September

Ghost Month: The Chinese believe that on the first day of the seventh lunar month the ghosts of deceased relatives return to their earthly homes for a visit. In order to placate the spirits and discourage their mischief, trays of succulent foods are set out before each home as an offering to them, and Buddhist priests are invited to every neighborhood and alley to bless these offerings and supplicate the spirits with prayer. Incense is burned and bundles of paper "clothing" and spirit money are set alight for use by the spirits in the other world. These offerings are also meant to prevent the ghosts of criminals and spirits whose living descendants neglect to honor them from entering one's home and causing trouble. It is not an auspicious time for marriage or commencing important new ventures. Rites are held daily in all Buddhist temples during Ghost Month, which formally ends on the last day of the seventh month, when the spirits return to the underworld and the gates slam shut for another year.

Birthday of Confucius: Celebrated as Teachers' Day on September 28, this day commemorates the birth of the sage Confucius in 551 BC. Known as China's greatest teacher, Confucius continues to exert profound influence on culture and society in Taiwan. Elaborate traditional ceremonies are held every year on this day, the most extensive at 6am at Taipei's Confucius Temple (at 2 Nanmen St), complete with ancient musical instruments, formal court attire, ritual dances and other Confucian rites as old as the sage himself.

Tickets to attend this ceremony must be reserved in advance. Reservations can be made through local tourism authorities. Three hundred tickets are handed out on a first-come, first-served basis at the temple gate on the day itself, but note that many people come the night before to line up.

September/October

Mid-Autumn Festival/Moon Festival: The Chinese believe that the harvest moon is the fullest, brightest moon of the year, and they celebrate its annual appearance by proceeding en masse to parks, hillsides, riverbanks and seashores to gaze at "The Lady in the Moon," nibble on tasty snacks, and drink wine.

The festival is celebrated by exchanging gifts of *yuebing*, or mooncakes, which are large, round pastries stuffed with sweet-bean paste, mashed dates, chopped nuts, minced dried fruits, and other fillings. Exchanging *yuebing* also has patriotic overtones, because during the successful overthrow of the Mongol Yuan dynasty by the Chinese Ming, secret plans for the insurrection are said to have been concealed in moon cakes and distributed to patriots.

Double Tenth National Day: "Double Tenth," or "*shuangshi*," refers to the tenth day of the tenth month in the Western calendar, and commemorates the overthrow of the Manchu Qing dynasty, China's last, by revolutionaries on October 10, 1911. It is celebrated with parades of honor guards from all branches of the armed forces, commando-landing demonstrations, patriotic speeches by top government leaders, and displays of folk dancing, sword-fighting, martial arts, and other cultural activities. In recent years, the military aspects have been toned down somewhat. Most of the action takes place in the huge plaza in front of the Presidential Building in Taipei.

Hotels and restaurants in Taipei are full throughout the week prior to Double Tenth day, as tens of thousands of overseas Chinese from all over the world pour into town for the festivities. Tourists who intend to visit Taiwan at this time should make early reservations for hotels and flight space.

SPORT

General

In recent times, organized sports and strenuous outdoor activities have been enjoying increasing popularity in Taiwan. Local health experts have been informing people that traditional Chinese approaches to health and longevity are not enough; rigorous physical exercise is also required. The island frequently hosts international sports events, and regularly sends teams to compete abroad. (To avoid confrontation with China, Taiwan is officially named "Chinese Taipei" in many international competitions.) The sports most easily accessible to the tourist in Taiwan are golf, tennis and swimming.

Golf

Golf is the oldest organized sport in Taiwan, and all of Taiwan's golf clubs are open to foreign visitors for guest memberships. The clubs are open year-round. Many are private, but others are open to all, although they offer preferential rates and tee-off times to members on weekends and holidays.

Arrangements for guest privileges in Taiwan's golf clubs may be made through hotel travel desks and local travel agencies, who will also arrange for regular club members to accompany or sponsor temporary guests in those clubs whose rules require it. Clubs, shoes, caddies, and food and beverage facilities are available at all of the clubs.

Further inquiries regarding golf in Taiwan may be directed to the **ROC Golf Association**, 12F-1, 125 Nanjing E. Road, Sec. 2, Taipei, tel: (02) 2516-5611, fax: (02) 2516-3208; www.twgolf.org.

Tennis

Tennis has been the fastest-growing sport in Taiwan in recent years, and hundreds of new courts have been constructed around the island to meet the demand for tennis facilities. Ask your hotel for the nearest available tennis courts, or just make a booking at a hotel with its own tennis courts.

More information is available at the **Chinese Taipei Tennis Association**, Room 705, 7F, 20 Zhulun Street, Taipei, tel: (02) 2772-0298, fax: (02) 2771-1696; email: ctta@tennis.org.tw

BELOW: a morning tai chi session in the park.

TRANSPORTATION

ACCOMMODATIONS

EATING OUT

ACTIVITIES

A – Z

LANGUAGE

Diving Revisited

The Taiwan Visitors Association publishes the best available English-language source of information on diving in Taiwan, a free booklet entitled *Diving in Taiwan: Guide to Scuba Diving in Taiwan*. It is chock-full of detailed information on dive sites, diving associations, gear rental shops, and more. Solid English information can also be found online at www.taiwanscuba.com.

Martial Arts

The Chinese have always kept themselves in shape by practicing various ancient forms of martial arts and related breathing and meditation exercises.

Every morning at dawn, thousands of people pour into parks, temple courtyards and other public places around the island to practice *taiji quan*, martial arts, yoga, sword dances, or simple aerobics. Visitors may also get a good workout each morning by simply joining whatever group interests them and mimicking their gentle movements. The most popular places in Taipei for early-morning exercise sessions are 2-28 Peace Park (formerly Taipei New Park, near the Taipei Main Railway Station), the landscaped grounds of the National Taiwan Democracy Memorial, the compound of the Sun Yat-sen Memorial and Daan Forest Park.

Even if you don't participate, you should try to catch this scene at least once while in Taipei. If you are interested in serious study, information is available from the **National Tai Chi Chuan Association of Taiwan**, 6F, 20 Zhulun St, Taipei, tel: (02) 2778-3887, fax: (02) 2770-3890, www.cttaichi.org.

Swimming

In addition to public beaches, there are numerous swimming pools at various upscale hotels, clubs, and resorts around the island. If your hotel does not have swimming facilities, ask the concierge for assistance.

The Taiwanese have of late been taking to swimming in greater numbers, and public-use facilities are increasing. The following two locations are recommended; go on weekdays:
My Island Spa
31-33, Lane 505, Zhongshan N. Rd, Sec. 5
Tel: (02) 8861-4633
Adults NT$400, NT$500 holidays,

children NT$200, for an all-day pass to a large heated pool plus whirlpool, sauna, fitness equipment, and more. Daily 24 hours.
Tropic Diving Center
34 Zhishan Rd, Sec. 2
Tel: (02) 2880-1231
Near the National Palace Museum, NT$300 brings full-day entry. Indoor and outdoor pools; also serves as a scuba training center. Daily 6.30am–9.30pm.

Scuba Diving and Snorkeling

The coral reefs off Kenting National Park, at the southern tip of Taiwan, offer spectacular diving. The rocky, shallow shoreline here also permits excellent snorkeling. In the north, divers can explore underwater coral kingdoms off the coast of Yeliu, which is famous for the strange formations of coral protruding from its seaside promontory. The islands of Lanyu, Ludao and Penghu are other good diving locales, with the possibility of sighting larger marine life off the latter.

Several local diving clubs organize regular excursions to popular diving areas. For further information, contact the following organization:
Chinese Taipei Diving Development Association
509 Zhongyang Rd, Nangang District
Tel: (02) 2786-3092
www.cdda.org.tw

Outdoor Adventure

Taiwan is a mountainous island that offers great opportunities for hiking

and trekking. The following operations are recommended:
Forestry Bureau
Tel: (02) 2765-3366, ext. 107
http://trail.forest.gov.tw
The Forestry Bureau has established a National Trail System that includes easy hikes close to the big cities, routes with historical significance, coastal mountain trails, and routes to the highest mountain peaks. For more information on the routes, as well as general information on island hiking, contact the Forestry Bureau.
FreshTreks
4F, 50 Zhongxiao W. Rd
Tel: (02) 2388-6565
e-mail: FreshTreks@FreshTreks.com
www.freshtreks.com
Taiwan's rugged, mountainous wilderness is little explored by foreigners because of difficulties with language, transport, and navigating the confusing pass system. Thankfully, things are now changing. Visitors are turning to a young firm called FreshTreks, based in Taipei and founded by a Frenchman, to handle everything from pickup to drop-off and everything in between, including equipment provision and the obtaining of passes. FreshTreks organises everything from mountain hiking and biking to river tracing and sea kayaking. Both package tours and tailor-made ones are available, and conducted in English, unlike its competitors.

Sightseeing Tours

The most popular city and island tours offered by travel agencies in Taipei are briefly introduced below.

Whale and Dolphin Watching

Environmental consciousness has been on the rise in Taiwan in recent years, and eco-tours are becoming popular. However, a lack of supervision and systematic regulation means that in some areas more harm is being caused than good. Local academics are openly fearful (government bodies privately so) that dolphins and whales are harassed and quite possibly harmed. Some believe the whales are changing their migratory patterns to avoid the boats which come too close, linger too long, and, worse still, chase dolphins and whales. Readers are asked not to join such tours for the moment, to avoid harming nature's ecological balance.

Tourist boat tours are called Blue Highway tours. Beyond whale and dolphin watching tours, pure

scenery-enjoyment tours are available at the following places:
● Danshui *(see page 163)*;
● river cruises from the wharfs at Guandu, Dadaocheng, and Dajia Riverside Park in Taipei;
● northeast tours from Bisha Harbor on the coast just south of the city of Keelung;
● tours to Guishan (Turtle) Island on the east coast, launched from the small harbor directly across from the mainland; and
● harbor/sea cruises from Kaohsiung Harbor.

Your best single source of general info on Blue Highway tours is the Tourism Bureau, but local English-speaking travel agencies will also be able to help arrange tours. Save from Kaohsiung, most tours do not run in winter.

"Taiwan Tour Bus" Service

The Tourism Bureau launched this service on the first day of 2004. This program aims to have local tour operators provide high-quality, standardized services. Among the recognized tours involved are those listed above. Each bus will be staffed by tourism professionals

proficient in English; English-language brochures with details of the tour destinations will be provided. The program currently has 28 distinctive tour products.

For more information visit the Tourism Bureau website at www.taiwan.net.tw.

Agencies tend to have the same basic tours and prices. Extra charges are levied if you want a single room on overnight stays.

Taipei City

This half-day tour covers the National Palace Museum, Martyrs' Shrine, Longshan Temple, and other city sights, and offers glimpses of contemporary urban life along the way. (NT$900)

Taipei by Night

An enduring favorite, this nocturnal tour commences with a Mongolian barbecue dinner, then proceeds to the famous Longshan Temple and the Huashi Street/Snake Alley (Huaxi Jie) tourist night market. (NT$1,300)

Wulai Aborigine Village

This is a half-day excursion to the colorful ethnic-minority village at Wulai, about an hour's drive south of Taipei. There you can watch native song and dance performances, hike through lush mountain terrain, and enjoy spectacular scenery. (NT$1,300)

North Coast

A half-day tour of Taiwan's scenic northern coastline, this excursion takes you to the port city of Jilong and the fantastic rock formations at Yeliu, then proceeds down the north coast to Danshui and back to Taipei. (NT$1,000)

Sun Moon Lake

This two-day tour takes you to Taiwan's favorite honeymoon resort, a lake located 760 meters (2,500 ft) above sea level in Taiwan's only landlocked county. This year-round resort is famous for its landscape, hiking, temples, and pagodas. The tour departs Taipei by air-conditioned bus and arrives in Taichung for lunch. The bus then proceeds to Sun Moon Lake, about an hour's drive from Taichung, passing through lush scenery of rice paddies, sugar cane, tea, banana, and pineapple plantations. After checking into a hotel, there is a leisurely two-hour boat cruise on Sun Moon Lake. Visits to Puli, famous for its rice-wine production, and to Lugang are also included. (NT$6,000)

Taroko Gorge and East Coast

The Taroko Gorge is considered to be one of the wonders of Asia, and it remains the single most popular tourist attraction outside of Taipei. About 20 km (12 miles) of craggy canyon are enclosed by towering cliffs of marble that soar up to 915 meters (3,000 ft) high. Taroko Gorge is bisected by the Central Cross-Island Highway, with marble bridges and 38 tunnels cut into solid rock.

This two-day tour goes by air to Hualien from Taipei on the first

morning, then heads up the gorge for a bus tour through breathtakingly beautiful landscape.

Lunch is served in the alpine environment of the Tianxiang Lodge, then the bus returns to Hualien in time for performances by the Ami minority, and a tour of Taiwan's biggest marble factory and showroom.

The next day is spent visiting the East Coast National Scenic Area, with an evening return to Taipei. (NT$8,700; there is also a one-day tour of the gorge for NT$4,900)

Round-the-Island Tour

This five-day tour takes in almost all of the island's major sights. The first day is spent touring the Formosan Aboriginal Culture Village, the second touring the Sun Moon Lake area and Puli. The third day is spent at Kenting National Park, the fourth in and around Kaohsiung. On the final day there is a drive up Taroko Gorge, then a return to Hualien for Ami performances and a tour of the marble factory. The tour flies back to Taipei in the early evening. (NT$16,200)

Kaohsiung, Kenting National Park and Taroko

This three-day excursion is a reduced version of the five-day outing described above, with visits to a selection of the same sites. (NT$12,600)

SHOPPING

Where to Shop

As explained on page 107, the Taiwanese have taken a deep liking to upscale shopping venues. Large-scale department stores, department store-based shopping centers, and now massive malls are the very definition of what is perceived as sophisticated, cosmopolitan living.

Many make a shopping trip a full-day outing, and centers seek to attract visitors by almost always having a department store, scores of fashion boutiques, and upscale outlets selling everything a consumer could possibly desire – DVDs, CDs, gift items, books, jewelry, watches, electronic goods, cameras, and of course, clothing and accessories.

A wide selection of restaurants and eateries, as well as a food court, are de rigueur, and most shopping centers will have a cinema complex and a number of nightlife venues such as pubs, bars, and perhaps dance establishments. Almost all are open daily from about 10am–11am

BELOW: shopping at the Tapei 101 Mall.

TRANSPORTATION ACCOMMODATIONS EATING OUT ACTIVITIES A – Z LANGUAGE to 9.30pm–10pm. Cinemas and nightlife venues located within shopping malls are open till late.

Malls

Breeze Center
39 Fuxing S. Rd, Sec. 1
Tel: (02) 6600-8888
www.breezecenter.com.tw
A huge shopping center with both upscale and mid-range fashion and accessories outlets. Also features a supermarket, department store, and cinema complex. Conveniently located right off Muzha MRT line.

Core Pacific City Living Mall
138 Bade Rd, Sec. 4
Tel: (02) 3762-1888
http://web01.livingmall.com.tw
This massive complex is a tourist attraction in itself for locals, with a giant globe as its entrance. Scores of boutiques, numerous restaurants, a cinema complex, and a clutch of large, upscale lounge bars and dance clubs attract the crowds to this mall.

Miramar Entertainment Park
20 Jingye 3rd Rd (in Neihu)
Tel: (02) 2175-3456
www.miramar.com.tw
Super-mall positioned as an entertainment-orientated facility targeting young families and youth, offering theme-park options complementing mid-range, top-end consumer products.

Taipei 101 Mall
45 Shifu Rd, Xinyi District
Tel: (02) 8101-7777
www.taipei-101.com.tw
In a large five-level structure fronting the new Taipei 101 tower, this location is proving a major draw with its large bookstore – Taiwan's best for English titles – and its many boutiques, restaurants, and other retail outlets. There is a shuttle bus service from/to Taipei City Hall MRT station (exit 2), daily 11am–9pm.

Taipei Metro (The Mall)
203 Dunhua S. Rd, Sec. 2
Tel: (02) 2378-6666, ext. 6580
www.themall.com.tw
Connected to the Far Eastern Plaza Hotel, this mall is a multi-level circular complex with skylight. Upscale boutiques predominate here.

Department Stores

Pacific SOGO Department Store
45 Zhongxiao E. Rd, Sec. 4
Tel: (02) 2776 5555
Taiwan's most popular and profitable department store, part of a Japanese chain and featuring upmarket brand-name fashions and accessories. It is located outside Zhongxiao-Fuxing MRT station, and connected to a bright new underground mall beneath Zhongxiao East Road, Sec. 4. Many

Antiques

Taipei is one of the better places in the region to search for Chinese antiques, designated as anything over 100 years old. The best outlets, and those most experienced in dealing with foreigners, are located in Tianmu, the expat enclave in northern Taipei; check the English language papers for ads. Most items are of wood and are sourced in mainland China, Taiwan having already been scoured almost dry. Tianmu area outlets are reputable, staff speak English, and they can arrange shipping. Items run the gamut, as do prices. Here is a selection of outlets with long track records.

Bai Win Antiques
1F, No. 2, Lane 405,
Zhongshan N. Rd, Sec. 6
Tel: (02) 2874-5525
http://baiwinantiques.com

Cherry Hill Antiques
6, Lane 77,
Zhongshan N. Rd, Sec. 2

Tel: (02) 2541-7575
http://cherryhill.antiques.com.tw
Chinese Handicraft Mart
1 Xuzhou Rd
Tel: (02) 2393-7330, 2393-3655
www.handicraft.org.tw
Run by the government as a promotional enterprise. Items available at the mart range from small gifts, souvenirs, and curios to pricey artifacts and antiques. Overseas delivery available.

Pierre's Gallery
14, Lane 291, Jianguo S. Rd,
Sec. 1
Tel: (02) 2702-8555
The gallery owner, Pierre, speaks English, and specializes in paintings, statues, and carvings. There are auctions on the 8th of each month.

Taiwan Arts and Crafts Center
577 Beian Rd
Tel: (02) 2553-5018
Good supply of rosewood, teakwood, and lacquer-finish furniture.

big sales throughout the year.
Shin Kong Mitsukoshi Department Store
66 Zhongxiao W. Rd, Sec. 1
Tel: (02) 2388-5552
The first Mitsukoshi chain outlet in the city, with two others in the Taipei World Trade Center area. Location in skyscraping Shin Kong Life Tower across from Taipei Main Station means ultimate transport convenience for shoppers.

Duty Free Shop

Ever Rich Duty Free Shop
B1, 72 Minquan E. Rd, Sec. 3
Tel: (02) 2502-8899

Customer Service Hotline:
0800-098-668
www.everrich.com.tw
Ever Rich Duty Free Shop operates an outlet close to Zhongshan Junior High School MRT station in Taipei. This is Taiwan's only such government-recognized operation outside the transit areas in the major international-travel departure points, meaning you can either buy taxed goods to take away immediately or pay for duty-free merchandise and then pick it up at the airport before departure. Discounts on most available items at Taiwan's duty-free shops are usually 10–20 percent.

BELOW: Bai Win Antiques has an array of exquisite collectable items.

A – Z

A HANDY SUMMARY OF PRACTICAL INFORMATION, ARRANGED ALPHABETICALLY

A ddresses

Taipei's address system may at first appear a bit complicated, but once you get the knack of it you'll find it is quite logical and negates the need to memorize countless names in this densely populated metropolis.

All addresses have building number, alley or lane number, street name, and section. Here is an example: No. 15, Lane 25, Zhongxiao East Road, Section 3. The city is broken down into a grid, north-south Zhongshan Road and east-west Zhongxiao Road serving as axes. All city-stretching arteries are broken down into sections; for Zhongxiao East Road, Section 1 is that closest to Zhongshan Road, Section 2 further away, and so on. The pattern is repeated, headed west, for Zhongxiao West Road.

On each section building numbers start counting at "1." Thus, there can be a No. 1 Zhongxiao E. Rd, Sec. 1, a No. 1 Zhongxiao E. Rd, Sec. 2, and so on. Referring to our sample

address again, if you see "lane" in an address it means you go to Sec. 3 of Zhongxiao East Road and find building

BELOW: temples are free to visit.

No. 25; right beside that building will be a lane – Lane 25. Go down that lane and find building No. 15.

If you see something like "No. 15, Alley 6, Lane 25," go to Lane 25 and find building No. 6. Alley 6 will be beside that building. Then go down the alley to building No. 15. The key is that "alleys" are bigger, leading off major arteries, and lanes lead off alleys. Once you get the hang of it you can quickly guess what area any address is in – much different from facing such addresses as No. 12896 Interminable Boulevard in other places.

This same system is used throughout the island. But since Taipei is the only place divided into a grid, you won't see the "north/south/east/west" designations used elsewhere.

Admission Charges

Temples and shrines are free, and welcome visitors. Public museums are often free or have a nominal entrance fee, though larger facilities like the National Palace Museum will have fees over NT$100.

Privately-run museums will usually have entrance fees of a few hundred NT$. National parks and scenic areas are either free or have a nominal entry fee, usually per vehicle, but may have entry fees for special designated areas; these will be under NT$

B arbershops

Two of the favorite creature comforts of Taiwanese men are relaxing in the pampered luxury of barbershops and bathhouses. Unlike bathhouses though, barbershops provide more than just grooming services. So-called "luxurious tourist barbershops" dot Taipei city and other urban areas.

Many are now more circumspect than in their heyday when they were easily identified by electrified barber poles spinning by their neon-lit entrances. You are greeted by young women clad in long gowns, who guide you to a chair, refresh you with a hot hand towel, and offer you tea and cigarettes.

Some men have their hair cut and styled, while others may just have a shampoo, manicure and massage. The latter is a curiously refreshing finger-pressure massage that covers the scalp, neck, and spine. Those with the time and inclination may then stretch out in a reclining position with a towel wrapped over their eyes and indulge in the great Chinese tradition of *xiuxi* (short rest).

Taipei once had a reputation for its

notorious "barbershops." Only a complete Taiwan newbie would wander into one of these establishments for a haircut – they were well known to be fronts for prostitution. But times have changed and very few of these "barbershops" have survived the major clean-up operations imposed by successive mayors. A sprinkling of such places still exist on Yanping Road near Ximending.

Women can get the same stimulating treatment (without the accompanying sexual connotations) at any Taiwan beauty salon, where shampoos, perms, hairstyling, manicures, and massages are performed in the same luxurious comfort. Almost all international tourist hotels in Taipei have both barbershops and beauty salons, but these offer Western-style service, with a less traditional flavor.

Budgeting for Your Trip

The Tourism Bureau has the best information on budget travel, contained in the free booklet *Taiwan Homestay Accommodation for International Youth Travelers*. The booklet details 51 of the best homestay facilities (there are now over 1,400 locations) and nearby attractions, in English and Japanese. The guidebook is available at overseas bureau offices, international and domestic airports in Taiwan, as well as visitor-information centers around the island. The facilities listed are not exclusive to young travelers.

Business Hours

Official government business hours in Taiwan are 8.30am–12.30pm and 1.30–5.30pm, Monday–Friday. Banks are open 9am–3.30pm Monday–Friday. Business hours are 9am–5.30pm Monday–Friday.

Stores and large shops are open from 10 or 11am until 9 or 10pm Monday–Saturday; most now keep the same hours on Sunday, or close a little earlier. Many smaller shops and stalls keep longer hours and remain open all week. Museums are usually closed on Mondays; many are also closed the day after national holidays. While offices and banks close on public holidays, many retail outlets remain open at least part of the day.

Business Travelers

Work and play are convenient for those traveling on business to major urban centers. All international tourist hotels have business facilities, and most now have business centers.

Taxis are ubiquitous and almost always clean, and fares are low compared to other countries. Get your hotel to write out your destination in Chinese to show to drivers, who almost never speak English. In Taipei some drivers have received English training; look for the plum-blossom logos on their cars, neon-lit at night, or call (02) 2799-7997. In cities, drivers are obliged to give receipts, though most store them away; ask for a *shouju* (receipt).

Traffic is a headache in Taiwan's cities, so give yourself plenty of extra time when going to meetings. If late, a grace period of about 20–25 minutes is given by locals, who fight the traffic every day, before mild irritation sets in. Be sure to apologize anyway.

C hildren

Though Taiwanese take their children to places that would be thought of as "adult" in the West, such as cafés, upscale restaurants, and so on, there are precious few facilities set up for special needs – especially for those with babies. All international tourist hotels will go out of their way to help, though to date only the Westin Taipei has specifically set up facilities and programs for children. Rarely will you find diaper- (nappy-) changing tables or rooms, high chairs, and so on.

Taiwan is not a place friendly to

BELOW: a popular ride at the Children's Recreation Center, Taipei.

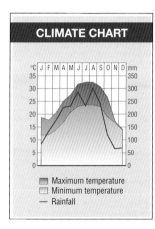

CLIMATE CHART

°C J F M A M J J A S O N D mm

Maximum temperature
Minimum temperature
— Rainfall

pedestrians, though Taipei is working hard to widen main-artery sidewalks and get scooters off them, so few parents use strollers (pushchairs); local mothers prefer papooses, with baby in front rather than back. To find out about child-friendly places to visit, there is no better source than the Community Services Center (see Orientation box, page 331).

The island has come a long way in the past ten years with child-friendly recreation facilities, including quality theme parks and supervised beaches with proper facilities. The Tourism Bureau website (www.taiwan.net.tw) has a special section on theme parks, and detail on tourist-friendly beaches.

Climate

Taiwan has a humid subtropical climate, with long hot summers and moderate winters. In the north and east of the island and in the mountains, the months from December to March are often damp and chilly, with strong winds and frequent rain. The Taipei area is notorious for this, and snow occasionally falls on the summits of the Central Mountain Range (Zhongshan Shanmo). Further south and west, winters are noticeably sunnier and warmer.

Temperatures begin to rise in March, and by early May everywhere is hot and humid. The heat lasts until October. Most of Taiwan's rain falls from May to September, mostly in intense but short-lived showers and thunderstorms. Mean annual rainfall ranges from 2,500 to 5,000 mm (100 to 200 inches).

Taiwan's location also subjects it to annual typhoons, which pass through between July and October. Most of these cause little more than strong winds and heavy rains over the island, but there are occasional powerful winds and severe storms.

The most pleasant time of the year to visit is mid-September through November, especially in Taipei and the mountains. The southwest is usually very pleasant from October until March.

Crime and Safety

Taiwan, though not without crime, is a safe place to visit, with little in the way of violent crime.

Drivers in Taipei, however, are quite aggressive, and often nudge their vehicles through pedestrians at crosswalks, so be alert when crossing the street.

Almost all private residences have bars over windows to prevent burglary. Generally, private homes have only a front entrance, with two doors – an outer one with a metal frame, and an inner one; both are kept locked.

Customs Regulations

All inbound passengers must fill in a customs declaration form upon arrival. The following items are strictly prohibited from entry into Taiwan: gambling apparatus or foreign lottery tickets; pornographic materials; publications promoting communism or originating in communist countries; firearms; toy guns; all drugs or narcotics of a non-prescription and non-medical nature.

All personal belongings such as clothing, jewelry, cosmetics, food and similar items may be brought into Taiwan free of duty. Items such as computers, stereo equipment, TV sets and video recorders, though also duty-free, must be declared on arrival. Each passenger over 20 is also permitted to bring in duty-free alcoholic beverages (1,000cc or less without limitation on number of bottles) and tobacco products (200 cigarettes, 25 cigars or 450 grams/1 lb of pipe tobacco. Gold exceeding a total value of US$20,000 is not permitted.

Passengers must declare the amount of foreign currencies they carry upon arrival. If not declared, the portion of foreign currencies in excess of US$10,000 (or its equivalent in other foreign currency) shall, upon arrival, be subject to confiscation. The unused balance may then be declared on the Outbound Passenger Declaration Form upon departure.

Otherwise, outbound passengers are limited to taking US$10,000 or the equivalent in other currencies out of Taiwan. Up to NT$60,000 in cash may be carried. Visitors who want to bring in more than NT$60,000 in cash must apply for a permit from the Central Bank of China before entering Taiwan.

For more detail, visit the **Directorate General of Customs** website at: http://eweb.customs.gov.tw.

Outbound Declaration

An outbound passenger declaration form must be completed when carrying any of the following items:
● foreign currency, local currency, gold and silver ornaments in excess of allowed amounts (see below).
● any unused foreign currency declared upon arrival.
● commercial samples and personal effects such as cameras, calculators, recorders, etc, which you wish to bring back to Taiwan duty-free in the future.
● computer media, discs, tapes, etc.

Passengers who have not declared gold, silver, and foreign currencies on arrival and are then discovered to be carrying these items in excess of the legally designated quantities will have the excess amount confiscated by customs, and may be subject to punishment by law. The designated legal limits are as follows:
● foreign currency – US$10,000, or equivalent, in cash (excluding unused portion of currency declared upon arrival).
● ROC currency – NT$60,000 in bank notes.
● gold/silver ornaments or coins – US$10,000.
● articles that may not be taken out of the country include unauthorized reprints or copies of books, records, videotapes, and so on; genuine Chinese antiques (over 100 years old), ancient coins and paintings.

Airport Tax

All outbound passengers (save diplomatic personnel and dependents, etc) must pay an airport exit tax of NT$300. You must present the receipt when checking in.

Disabled Travelers

Unfortunately, Taiwan is not a friendly place for travelers with disabilities. The international airports do have facilities for the physically challenged. Top-class hotels and a few museums have special access ramps installed at lobby entrances, and a dedicated cubicle in public-area washrooms, but beyond this there is not much that is helpful. More hotels are now offering rooms and other facilities for the disabled,

TRANSPORTATION · ACCOMMODATIONS · EATING OUT · ACTIVITIES · A – Z · LANGUAGE

but it is best to confirm this beforehand.

Each MRT station provides elevator access from street level, there is also a reserved spot for wheelchairs in the first and last car of each train.

E mbassies and Consulates

The Republic of China (Taiwan) has formal diplomatic relations with 24 sovereign political entities. Countries outside this group set up trade and commerce offices, quasi-embassies that handle all the responsibilities that a full embassy does.

Australia: Australian Commerce and Industry Office
27-28F, President International Tower, 9-11 Songgao Rd, Taipei
Tel: (02) 8725-4100
www.australia.org.tw

Canada: Canadian Trade Office
13F, 365 Fuxing N. Rd, Taipei
Tel: (02) 2544-3000
www.canada.org.tw

UK: British Trade & Cultural Office
26F, President International Tower, 9-11 Songgao Rd, Taipei
Tel: (02) 8758-2088
www.btco.org.tw

US: American Institute in Taiwan
7, Lane 134, Xinyi Rd, Sec. 3, Taipei
Tel: (02) 2162 2000
www.ait.org.tw

Emergencies

When traveling in Taiwan, have your passport with you. In case something untoward happens and you cannot identify yourself, have a note in Chinese attached to the passport; this will identify your hotel or a Chinese-speaking person to contact in case of emergency.
Fire: 119
Ambulance: 119
Police: 110
Women and Children Protection Hotline (113 0) 24-hour emergency, legal information, and psychological services for victims of domestic violence and/or sexual abuse.

Entry Requirements
Visas and Passports

Citizens of Australia, Canada, Costa Rica, Japan, Korea, Malaysia, New Zealand, Singapore, the United Kingdom, the United States and most EU countries – with passports valid for at least six months and confirmed onward or return tickets – are allowed visa-free entry to Taiwan for a period of 30 days. The period is not extendable.

Citizens of Slovakia, Poland, and Hungary are eligible for 30-day landing visas. Documents needed from travelers are the same as for those above. The processing fee is NT$1,200, save for countries with reciprocal agreements. No extensions are permitted.

Other nationalities and those who wish to stay in Taiwan for longer than 30 days must apply for visitor visas before arriving in Taiwan. Foreigners applying for visitor visas must hold valid passports, incoming and outgoing travel tickets (or a letter from your travel agent), three photos, documents stating the purpose of the visit (except for sightseeing or transit), and a completed application form.

Such visitor visas are good for 60 days and may be extended twice for 60 days, for a total of 180 days. Foreigners entering Taiwan on a visitor visa may not work without official authorization.

Visitors from countries without Taiwanese embassies or consulates may approach the designated

Electricity

Taiwan uses electric current of 110 volts at 60 cycles; appliances from Europe, Australia, and Southeast Asia will need an adaptor or transformer. Many buildings have sockets with 220 volts especially for the use of air conditioners.

Taiwanese representatives in their respective countries for letters of recommendation. These letters may then be exchanged for visitor visas at any Taiwanese embassy or consular office en route to Taiwan, or on arrival at Taiwan Taoyuan International Airport or Kaohsiung International Airport, the only points of entry to Taiwan at which such letters may be exchanged for a visa.

More detailed information regarding ROC visitor visas can be obtained from the **Bureau of Consular Affairs**, Ministry of Foreign Affairs, 3-5F, 2–2 Jinan Road, Sec. 1, Taipei, Taiwan, tel: (02) 2343-2888; e-mail: post@boca.gov.tw, www.boca.gov.tw. Visa application forms can now be downloaded.

Visa Extensions

Apply for extensions at least three days before your regular visa expires. To extend a regular tourist visa in Taipei, visit the **National Immigration Agency (NIA)**, 15 Guangzhou St, Taipei, tel: (02) 2388-9393 or 24-hour service hotline at 0800-024-111.

Etiquette
Greetings

The Taiwanese, like the Koreans and Japanese, used to bow and clasp their hands together when being introduced to someone new, but today the Western handshake has displaced the ancient custom. Nevertheless, locals still shy away from boisterous greetings in public, such as hugs, kisses, and resounding slaps on the back. A firm handshake, friendly smile, and slight nod of the head are appropriate gestures of greeting.

Names

In Chinese, a person's family surname precedes both given name and formal title. For example, in the name Li Wuping, Li is the surname and Wuping is the given name. In the expression "Li *Jingli*," Li is the surname and *jingli* (manager) is the title. Chinese language names generally consist of three names – one surname and two given names – but many people use only two. The majority of Chinese family names come from the *Lao Bai Xing* (Old Hundred Names), first formulated over 3,000 years ago in feudal China. Among the most common are Li, Wang, Chen, Huang, Zhang, Yang, Liang, and Sun. Locals prefer to be addressed by their family name and title, as above, rather than by their full name.

Business Cards

During formal introductions, locals today usually exchange business cards, which has become the tradition throughout Asia. In fact, many people don't even listen to oral introductions, but wait instead to read the person's card. It is a good idea to have some personal cards printed before traveling anywhere in East Asia, even if not traveling on business. Always hand and take a card with both hands, and be sure to take a close look at the card given, to show you take the other person and his/her position and authority seriously. Place the card on the table in front of you during meetings. Do not toss it in your briefcase or wallet when getting ready to leave; slide it into a place that shows you value the person and the relationship that has been established. These things will be noticed, and if handled improperly will create negative feelings.

Entertaining

The Chinese term *qingke* literally means "inviting guests" and refers to the grand Chinese tradition of entertaining friends and associates with lavish generosity, usually at banquets. In Taiwan, locals are often perplexed when they see Westerners call for their bill at restaurants, then pull out pocket calculators and proceed to figure out precisely how much each person at the table must contribute. The Chinese tradition, on the contrary, is to compete for the privilege of paying the bill for the whole table – though it is understood that in the end the person who has done the inviting will almost always be "allowed" to pay.

To the Taiwanese, inviting guests out for dinner and drinks is a delightful way to repay favors or to cultivate new business relationships, and they do so often, for this is a gift that the giver always shares with the recipients. And the very moment you've paid a hefty dinner bill, everyone at the table is immediately obliged to invite you out as their guest sometime in the near future. This way, although the bill is high when it's your turn to *qingke*, you only end up paying for one out of, say, 12 banquets. In the final analysis, it all balances out, and everyone takes turns earning the "big face" that comes with being a generous host. If in Taiwan for a limited time, do try if possible to entertain anyone who has entertained you before heading home. Not doing so is bad form.

Toasts

When toasted at dinner parties, it is good manners to raise your wine glass with both hands: one holding it and the other touching the base. The host will take his seat opposite (not beside) the guest-of-honor, and it is fitting to have the host's back to the door and the guest-of-honor facing it. It is said this is because, long ago, the host gave you a wall to sit in front of to show you would not be attacked from behind; both hands raised when toasting kept any hands from going for weapons under the table.

Tea

Tea served at the end of a meal is your host's polite insinuation that the party is over and that it is time for you to leave. So don't overstay your welcome, even though your host may insist. Do not let the host leave before you, and thank him heartily for his hospitality when departing.

Polite Courtesy

Chinese-style courtesy may be confusing to Westerners. For example, even though it is late and the host would love to call it a day, he will gently persuade his guest to stay longer. In this case, it is up to the guest to detect from the host's tone what is the best thing to do. This requires skill and cultural sensitivity. An experienced traveler once ventured, "The rule of thumb is to do the exact opposite that your Chinese friend suggests." Try this if you must, but with discretion.

Titles

Some of the most common titles used in Chinese during introductions are as follows.
Xiansheng/Mister (as in Li *Xiansheng*)
Taitai/Mrs (Li *Taitai*)

BELOW: it is essential for the hosts to entertain guests generously.

Giving Gifts

Some don'ts: No knives or scissors; sharp objects are not auspicious, and suggest you wish to cut off the friendship. No clocks or watches; also inauspicious, these suggest "deliverance" of the receiver to their final end. No handkerchiefs; connotations of the crying done at funerals. No towels; traditionally given as gifts to those attending funerals. Always present gifts formally, with two hands, palms up.

Xiaojie/Miss (Li *Xiaojie*)
Furen/Madame (Li *Furen*)
Laoban/Boss (Li *Laoban*)
Jingli/Manager (Li *Jingli*)

ay and Lesbian Travelers

Though the Taiwanese have a strange fascination with cross-dressers and transvestites in a performance context – men have traditionally played female roles in Beijing opera – gay men and women generally hide their same-gender preferences from relatives and colleagues. There are clubs and bars in Taipei that cater to gay men and women (for more details *see page 316*), but these are less common in the smaller towns and cities. Much greater tolerance is being shown in the city of Taipei now, and the city even publishes its own free guide for the gay community. There is also an annual Gay Pride Festival held in the city. Good information can be found online at www.utopia-asia.com and www.gay-taiwan.net.

ealth and Medical Care

Tap water is not recommended for drinking, and avoid ice in drinks. Most people boil water, and many hotels provide boiled drinking water. Bottled water is available at convenience stores and supermarkets, but make sure the seal is intact.

In Kaohsiung people do not drink boiled tap water, because of trace levels of arsenic.

Effective cholera inoculation certificates are required for passengers coming from certain countries or who have stayed more than five days in infected areas. Visitors staying over three months are required to have an HIV test. Otherwise, health certificates are not normally required. It is recommended to have inoculations against tetanus, Hepatitis A and, in some cases,

The Number of Death

In the West we often see elevators without a 13th floor. In Taiwan, in hospitals and many public buildings, you will be whisked directly from the third to the fifth floor. This is because the words for "death" and "four" are pronounced the same. No need for tempting ill fortune by sending people to the "floor of death" in a building.

Hepatitis B well in advance if traveling to remote areas. If you are visiting rural areas in summer, the Japanese encephalitis vaccine is recommended. Malaria is not a problem in Taiwan. Contact the **National Quarantine Service**, Department of Health, 6 Linsen N. Road, Taipei, tel: (02) 2395-9825, fax: (02) 2395-9830. In case of emergency, dial 119 (note that the operators speak limited English). In the UK, detailed health advice for visits anywhere in the world is available from MASTA (Medical Advice for Travelers Abroad), tel: 09068 224-100 (premium rate). It has a website at www.masta.org.

Medical Treatment

The quality of medical facilities and services is excellent in the major cities, and medical treatment and dental work generally cost far less than in any Western country or Japan.

It is advisable to inform your country's representative office where you are staying when in Taiwan. In the event of a medical emergency, they should be able to help. Avoid using the services of small clinics and the smaller hospitals, whose doctors and nurses are often overworked and speak limited English. Following is a list of major hospitals:

Taipei
Chang Gung Memorial Hospital
199 Dunhua N. Rd
Tel: (02) 2713-5211
Mackay Memorial Hospital
92 Zhongshan N. Rd, Sec. 2
Tel: (02) 2543-3535
National Taiwan University Hospital
7 Zhongshan S. Rd
Tel: (02) 2312-3456
Taiwan Adventist Hospital
424 Bade Rd, Sec. 2
Tel: (02) 2771-8151

Taichung
Taichung Veterans General Hospital
160 Zhonggang Rd, Sec. 3
Tel: (04) 2359-2525

ABOVE: preparing a herbal prescription.

Hualien
Tzu ohi Buddhist General Hospital
707 Zhongyang Rd, Sec. 3
Tel: (03) 856-1825

Tainan
Father Fox Memorial Hospital
901 Zhonghua Rd, Yongkang City,
Tainan County
Tel: (06) 252-1176
National Cheng Kung University Hospital
138 Shengli Rd
Tel: (06) 235-3535
Taiwan Provincial Tainan Hospital
125 Zhongshan Rd
Tel: (06) 220-0055

Kaohsiung
Chang Gung Memorial Hospital
123 Dabei Rd
Tel: (07) 731-7123

Traditional Medicines

Beyond popular and well-known medicines such as tiger balm, foreigners can take the opportunity to learn about other traditional medicines while in Taiwan. Many of these are extremely effective. However, be sure you do not purchase items made in mainland China, which are common despite prohibitions on direct trade; such items are not subject to the same high testing and quality control production standards as in Taiwan.

I nternet

All international tourist hotels provide internet access in private rooms, and many regular tourist hotels now do as well. All the international tourist hotels provide internet access for guests in business centers, charging in the area of NT$200 per hour. Libraries often have free internet access. There are a great many internet cafés in the major cities, both stand-alone and chain outlets, but be advised that most cater to teen aficionados of video games. These places aren't quiet. Fees are calculated by the minute, and because of heavy competition are most often NT$1 per minute or less. This same competition means locations open and close with impressive speed. Be aware that staff will have some trouble communicating with you in English, save techno-jargon. Look for true cafés and coffeeshops that have wireless internet access as a bonus for customers. In Taipei some pubs and bars are now also offering wireless access.

Taipei is also engaged in an expanding program whereby payphone internet terminals are set up in MRT stations, you'll need a phone card. A much-used terminal bank is next to Kingstone Bookstore on Zhongxiao W. Rd, across from Taipei train station. There are also free-use terminals on the second level of the National Central Library, across Zhongshan S. Rd from National Taiwan Democracy Memorial Hall.

The city is also engaged in a large-scale program to bring, eventually, wireless access to the entire metropolis. At the moment the Xinyi District around Taipei 101 is wireless, as is the Ximending shopping area, and all MRT stations in the city itself. For detail access the city administration's website (www.taipei.gov.tw).

Orientation

For anyone planning to be in Taiwan for more than just a few days, a visit to the Community Services Center in Taipei can be invaluable. A non-profit foundation run by expatriates, the center can help answer most questions on Taiwan.

Community Services Center
25, Lane 290, Zhongshan N. Rd, Sec. 6
Tianmu, Taipei
Tel: (02) 2836-8134
Fax: (02) 2835-2530
e-mail: csc@community.com.tw
www.community.com.tw

Lost Property

Local folk will most likely turn in any found property at the local police precinct, especially if they discover any non-Chinese documents. Staff at the precinct may not be able to speak English, so contact the Foreign Affairs Police, who do, and who can help you trace the valuables.

In the Taipei MRT system, fill out a lost-property form at the information counter (in all stations), or at the Lost and Found Service Center, tel: (02) 2389-4710, at Taipei Main Station, B3 level, next to Information Counter No. 1.

For lost passports, contact the National Immigration Agency (NIA), 15 Guangzhou St, Taipei, tel: (02) 2388-9393 or 24-hour service hotline at 0800-024-111.

Maps

Good maps are found in all major bookstores – but in Chinese. You'll find little if anything in English. Your best bet are the free maps available at the tourist-service counters at the country's major entry points, in the major cities, and at entry points to major tourist areas such as national scenic areas and national parks. Staff at all these places, save perhaps some scenic areas and national parks, should be able to converse with you in English.

Media

Print

Three English-language newspapers, all of less than international quality but useful for local news, are published daily in Taiwan. They are the *China Post* (www.chinapost.com.tw), *Taiwan News* (www.etaiwannews.com) and *Taipei Times* (www.taipeitimes.com). All

are morning papers. In addition to international and regional news, these newspapers carry financial news, entertainment sections, features, sports reports, and guides to English-language programs on TV and radio. Most hotel newsstands carry all three.

The Xinwenju (Government Information Office) publishes an illustrated monthly magazine in English, *Taiwan Review* (http://taiwan review.nat.gov.tw), which features articles on local politics and culture, travel in Taiwan, and other aspects of local life; unfortunately its journalistic integrity has slipped, the result of constant political pressures from the powers that be. The *Review* now more obediently follows the agenda set on-high, notably for articles affecting Taiwan's overseas image. *Taiwan Panorama* (www.taiwan-panorama.com), a glossy bilingual monthly, covers Taiwan society and culture. The Tourism Bureau sponsors an illustrated bimonthly, *Travel in Taiwan* (www.tit.com.tw), that explores local travel and cultural subjects; it is available free from Tourism Bureau offices and at major hotels.

The American Chamber of Commerce puts out a quality monthly entitled *Topics* (www.amcham.com.tw) that provides good overview articles on the workings of Taiwan's economy, as well as pieces on specific firms.

The Taipei City Government publishes *Discover Taipei Bimonthly* (http://english.taipei.gov.tw) exploring travel and culture topics related to the capital-city region. In Taichung, *Compass Magazine* (www.taiwanfun.com) is a comprehensive glossy providing timely info on where to go and what to do in greater Taichung.

Foreign periodicals available in Taiwan include *Time*, *Newsweek*, *Life*, *the Economist* and many other major publications; these are sold at large bookstores and hotel newsstands.

Television and Radio

Cable is now ubiquitous in Taiwan. Private homes enjoy up to 80 channels. Quality hotels will carry international mainstays such as HBO, CNN, Star TV, ESPN, and more. Program schedules for the international networks are carried in the English dailies. ICRT (International Community Radio Taipei) is the only English-language radio station available. It can be received in the north and south at FM 100.7/AM 576, in Hsinchu and the Taichung area at 100.1. Local radio stations broadcast a wide variety of Chinese, Taiwanese, and Western music.

Almost all radio and TV stations broadcast 24 hours a day.

Money

The Taiwanese currency is the New Taiwan Dollar, written as NT$. There are 100 cents to one dollar. At the time of writing the exchange rate was NT$32 to US$1.

Major foreign currencies can be easily exchanged for NT$ at major local and foreign banks, international tourist hotels and the two international airports. In smaller towns or in the countryside, however, it is practically impossible to change foreign currency into NT$. In smaller towns usually only the Bank of Taiwan changes foreign currency; the procedure is complicated and time-consuming.

Important: Be sure to obtain receipts of all such transactions; you'll find they save you a lot of hassle with the bank when you try to reconvert unused New Taiwan dollars on departure. Usually you can change US$ for your surplus NT$. The banks at Taiwan Taoyuan International Airport outside Taipei are best. There is also a bank at Kaohsiung International Airport.

Travelers' checks are widely accepted at most hotels, foreign-tourist-oriented restuarants and souvenir shops, major department stores, and local branches of the issuing banks. Major credit cards such as American Express, Visa, MasterCard, and Diners Club are now accepted at almost all urban establishments.

VAT Refunds for Foreign Travelers

Foreign tourists who spend more than NT$3,000 (approximately US$90) in the same **TRS** (tax-refund shopping) outlet in a single day and take the goods out of the country within 30 days will be eligible for tax refunds worth 5 percent of the value of the goods, providing they complete the necessary forms in the shop and get the forms endorsed at the airport or harbor before departure.

More than 30 department stores around the island, including eight in Taipei, now sport the TRS logo. For more details, and a list of TRS outlets, visit www.ntat.gov.tw. (National Tax Administration "VAT-refund" section on home page).

Photography

Taipei is in a sub-tropical country and is plunked down in a mountain-surrounded basin that keeps

Public Holidays

Traditional holidays correspond to dates in the lunar calendar and thus change from year to year. Taiwan comes to a virtual standstill during the minimum four-day holiday at Chinese New Year; depending on the days of the week on which these fall, the government may grant a full work week off.

- **Foundation Day of the Republic of China**: January 1
- **Chinese Lunar New Year**: January/February
- **Peace Memorial Day**: February 28
- **Tomb Sweeping Day**: April 5
- **Dragon Boat Festival**: May/June
- **Mid-Autumn Festival/Moon Festival**: September/October
- **National Day (Double Tenth)**: October 10

humidity in along with vehicle exhaust and air-conditioner heat. Thus, keep camera and film cool and dry as best you can. A haze settles over the city many days, some days man-made and some days natural from warmer air traveling over the nearby cool ocean and vice-versa, so get those big-sweep shots early.

Film is easy to find, at any convenience store, drugstore, or photo shop. Most photo shops handle processing in an hour or two; remember that prints on Fujifilm tend to have a greenish tint in comparison to other stock. For professional-quality results, and where some English is spoken:

Tianmu Photo Lab
15 Zhongshan N. Rd, Sec. 7
(at Tianmu Circle)
Tel: (02) 2873-0368
Jazz Photo Lab
431 Bade Rd, Sec. 2
Tel: (02) 2721 8681
This is a favored place among professionals. Exotic film stock available.

Postal Services

Taiwan has one of the fastest and most efficient postal services in the world. Post offices are open from 8am–6pm Monday–Friday; select major offices open 8am–4pm on Saturday. Letters mailed to the US from Taiwan usually arrive at their destinations within five to seven days of posting. Local mail is delivered within 24 to 48 hours.

Taipei's **Central Post Office** is

located at the North Gate intersection, close to the Taipei Main Railway Station. This is the best place to collect and post mail in Taipei; some clerks speak passable English at the international counters. This office also provides inexpensive cartons and packing services for parcel posting.

Stamps may be purchased at the mail counter of any hotel in Taiwan, and letters may be dropped in any hotel or public mailbox. Local mail goes into the green boxes, and international airmail goes into the red boxes.

For more information, call 0800-700-365 or visit the Chunghwa Post website at www.post.gov.tw.

R eligious Services

The country's main mosque is **Taipei Grand Mosque** (tel: (02) 2321-9445) on Xinsheng S. Rd across from Daan Forest Park. It is not open to non-Muslims.

Approximately 6 percent of the population is Christian, the aboriginal peoples almost fully Christian. Protestants, mostly Presbyterian, take up about 80 percent, Roman Catholics the remainder. Some 150,000 guest workers from the Philippines are overwhelmingly Christian.

The following Taipei churches provide services in English:

Anglican/Episcopalian
Church of the Good Shepherd
509 Zhongzheng Rd. (Shilin District)

BELOW: prayers at Longshan Temple.

Tel: (02) 2873-8104
http://arc.episcopalchurch.org/taiwan/goodshepherd
Sunday services at 9.30am, normally combined English/Chinese service 10.30am on fourth Sunday each month.

Roman Catholic
Mother of God Church
171 Zhongshan N. Rd, Sec. 7
(Tianmu District)
Tel: (02) 2871-5168
Sunday services at 10am, 12.15pm, and 7pm.

For more details on English services, the best source is the weekend editions of the English daily papers.

S tudent Travelers

The government of Taiwan has introduced many programs specifically targeted at attracting student travelers in recent years. Both study and work travel are possible, special rail passes and accommodations are available, and a Tour Buddy program has been set up so students can tour with knowledgeable local youths. Visit the Tourism Bureau website (www.taiwan.net.tw) or a special website targeted at the youth traveler (www.youthtravel.tw).

T elecommunications
Long-distance calls

Long-distance calls within Taiwan can be made from private or public pay phones. Just punch in the correct area code and number. The number of digits in the telephone number varies from eight in Taipei, to five in Mazu.

Local calls

Local city calls may be dialed from any public pay telephone. Public phones in Taiwan are divided primarily into two types, coin and card. Coin-operated phones accept coins in denominations of NT$1, NT$5, and NT$10. For local calls, NT$1 buys one minute of phone time. Phone cards are divided into magnetic-strip stored-value cards and IC stored-value cards, and can be used all over Taiwan. Magnetic-strip cards sell for NT$100 each, and IC cards are available in NT$200 and NT$300 versions. The cards are sold in railway stations, bus stations, scenic spots, and convenience stores. You need to dial the area code first if calling from one county/city to another; if calling within the same county/city, there is no need to dial the area code.

Telephone Codes

Country code: 886
Area codes:
Taipei area, incl. Keelung	02
Kaohsiung	07
Changhua County	04
Chiayi	05
Hsinchu	03
Hualien County	038
Ilan County	039
Miaoli County	037
Nantou County	049
Penghu County	06
Pingtung County	08
Taichung	04
Tainan	06
Taitung County	089
Yunlin County	05

International calls

IDD calls can be made by dialing the international dialing code 002 + country code + city code + local number. International reverse-charge (call collect) and credit calls can be made through dedicated phones at airports and major hotels.

Calls to the USA can be made through AT&T Direct, and to over 100 other countries through AT&T World Connect, by dialing 0080-102880. The access code for Sprint is 0080-140877 while MCI Worldcom Connect is 0080-134567.

For reverse charges or credit calls, dial 008 + the communication number for the country being called, as follows:
Australia: 008-061-0061
Canada: 008-012-0012
Germany: 008-049-0049
Hong Kong: 008-085-2111
Italy: 008-039-0039
Japan (via KDD): 008-810051
Philippines: 008-630063
Singapore: 008-065-6565
UK: 008-044-0044
US (AT&T): 008-010-2880

On private phones, the overseas operator may be reached by dialing 100. For directory assistance in English dial 106 or (02) 2311-6796. For international information, call this free number: 0800-080-100. International direct dialing is available from many public phones, marked in English as IDD-capable, especially in hotels. Visa, MasterCard and JCB cards can be used, as well as IC cards that can be purchased at 7-Elevens.

Facsimile

In Taipei, fax services are available 24 hours for Taiwan or overseas at the Chunghwa Telecom offices at 162 Dunhua S. Road, Sec. 2, and at 5 Xinyi Road, Sec. 5 (Taipei World Trade Center). Service is also available at international hotels, convenience stores, and post offices throughout the city.

Tipping

Generally speaking, tipping is not expected in Taiwan, although token gratuities are always appreciated. Hotels and restaurants automatically add a 10 percent service charge to bills, but this money rarely gets distributed in full among the staff, so a small cash tip of 5 to 10 percent is always welcome in restaurants. An NT$50 tip per piece of luggage tip is usual for hotel and airport porters, and for assistants providing special services in hair salons.

Tipping is not necessary for taxi drivers, unless they load luggage for you. Taxis still cost far less in Taiwan than most places of similar economic development, but the cost of gas (petrol) and maintenance here is quite high, so drivers appreciate even the smallest tips. Oversupply, fierce competition, and low fares mean that most taxi drivers nowadays spend 12 or more hours on the road, many of them for seven days a week, often transferring their vehicle to another driver when they go off-shift.

The only places in Taiwan where heavy tips are routinely expected are in wine houses and bottle clubs, where big tipping wins you "big face."

Toilets

Taipei provides relatively clean public washrooms in the larger parks, but not the smaller ones.

Around Taiwan, public-use washrooms are provided at most major tourist sites. However, the facilities are generally overwhelmed by the sheer numbers of visitors on weekends and holidays, and cleanliness falls by the wayside. Few such places provide toilet paper, so always have your own handy. Unlike some other Asian destinations, there are no charges for the use of public washrooms in Taiwan. If nature calls and you are away from a tourist site, your best bets are temples, fast-food outlets, shopping malls, and the larger hotels (the last will have paper). The mass rapid-transit systems in Taipei and Kaohsiung have clean washrooms and toilet paper, but this may not be true during the heavy-use rush hours. Around the island, more and more 7-Elevens in scenic areas are providing clean washroom facilities, though usually no paper. Note that parks, temples, and major tourist sites will most likely solely have squat toilets.

Time Zone

Taipei and all Taiwan is +8 hours from Greenwich Mean Time (GMT). It is +13 from Eastern Standard Time (EST) in the eastern US and Canada, +12 during EST daylight savings time. The time difference with Sydney is -3 hours in summer, -2 in winter.

Tourist Information Offices

Service and information centers are located at both international airports. The receptionists speak English, and can help with transport, accommodation and other travel requirements.

There are two organizations in Taiwan that oversee and promote the tourism industry. The Tourism Bureau is the official government organ responsible for tourism in Taiwan. The Taiwan Visitors Association is a private organization that promotes Taiwan tourism abroad and provides travel assistance to visitors in Taiwan. Since neither of these organizations is blessed with a generous budget, the facilities they offer to travelers are limited. Nevertheless, they do their best to assist with inquiries. Major cities are also now setting up tourist-assistance services, in English. Visit their respective websites.

Taipei

Tourism Bureau, Ministry of Transportation and Communications
9F, 290 Zhongxiao E. Rd, Sec. 4
P.O. Box 1490
Tel: (02) 2349-1635
Fax: (02) 2771-7036
e-mail: tbroc@tbroc.gov.tw
www.taiwan.net.tw
Travel Information Service Center (TISC)
240 Dunhua N. Rd. Just south of Songshan Airport
Tel: 0800-011765
Email: tisc@tbroc.gov.tw

Taichung

Taichung Travel Section
4F, 216 Minquan Rd
Tel: (04) 2254-0809/0800-422-022
Fax: (04) 2223-3549
e-mail: tisctch@ms39.hinet.net

Tainan

Tainan Travel Section
10F, 243 Minquan Rd, Sec. 1
Tel: (06) 226-5681/0800-611-011
Fax: (06) 226-4905
e-mail: traintna@ms48.hinet.net

Kaohsiung
Kaohsiung Travel Section
5F-1, 235 Zhongzheng 4th Rd
Tel: (07) 281-1513/0800-711-765
Fax: (07) 281-4660
e-mail: trainkhh@ms48.hinet.net

Visitor Information Center, Tourism Bureau
CKS International Airport
Terminal I
Tel: (03) 398-2194
Terminal II
Tel: (03) 398-3341
Kaohsiung International Airport
Tel: (07) 805-7888/0800-252-550
The Tourism Bureau provides a toll-free number (0800-011-765) for visitors in Taiwan with travel inquiries. Service is 24 hours, in Chinese, English, and Japanese.

Tour Operators
Taipei
Travel agencies operate daily tours using air-conditioned buses and English-speaking guides. Tickets for these tours may be obtained through your hotel, or by contacting these agencies directly:
Bobby Travel Service
11F, 88 Changan E. Rd, Sec. 2
Tel: (02) 2505-5677
Fax: (02) 2505-5777
e-mail: chou@bobby.com.tw
www.bobby.com.tw
Edison Travel Service
4F, 190 Songjiang Rd
Tel: (02) 2563-5313
Fax: (02) 2563-4803
e-mail: edisonts@ms6.hinet.net
www.edison.com.tw
Golden Foundation Tours
5F, 142 Zhongxiao E. Rd, Sec. 4
Tel: (02) 2773-3266, ext. 138
Fax: (02) 2772-3449
e-mail: gftour@gftours.com.tw
www.gftours.com.tw
Gray Line Tours
4F, 46 Zhongshan N. Rd, Sec. 2
Tel: (02) 2541-6466
Fax: (02) 2522-1960
Huei Fong Travel Service
8F, 36 Nanjing E. Rd, Sec. 2
Tel: (02) 2551-5805
Fax: (02) 2563-5791
e-mail: service@havefuntravel.tw
www.hftravel.com.tw
South East Travel Service Co.
60 Zhongshan N. Rd, Sec. 2
Tel: (02) 2571-3001
Fax: (02) 2523-6981
e-mail: web-service@settour.com.tw
www.settour.com.tw

U seful Numbers
Tourist Information Hotline:
(02) 2717-3737 (8am–8pm)

0800-011-765 (24 hr, toll-free)
International Community Service Hotline (National Police Administration): 0800-024-111
Foreign Affairs Police:
Taipei: (02) 2381-7494
Taichung: (04) 2327-3875
Kaohsiung: (07) 221-5796
Keelung: (06) 222-9704
Jilong: (02) 2425-2787
Hsinchu: (03) 555-7953
Consular Affairs, Ministry of Foreign Affairs:
Taipei: (02) 2343-2888
Taichung: (04) 2222-2799
Kaohsiung: (07) 211-0605
Bureau of Entry and Exit, Ministry of the Interior, Taipei: (02) 2389-9983
English Speaking taxi (Taipei): (02) 2799-7997

W ebsites
www.taiwan.net.tw
The government tourism bureau site is good on general information, and is offering more and more practical info.
http://iff.npa.gov.tw
A wide range of practical info specifically for foreigners living/traveling in Taiwan, from the National Police Agency.
www.hotelstaiwan.com
Discounts on accommodation.
www.roomz.com
Provides links to groups offering deals on accommodation and other travel-related expenses.
www.gio.gov.tw
Government Information Office site; very informative on all aspects of Chinese/Taiwanese culture from architecture to philosophy, and useful links.
www.romanization.com
A wealth of information on Taiwan's numerous Romanization systems, Taipei street names, and more practical material, plus links to numerous digital versions of important out-of-print book titles on Taiwan's politics, culture, and history.
www.taipei.org
Good source of news on Taiwan.
www.taiwanfun.com
Helpful reviews on restaurants, bars, and other fun spots, plus an eclectic mix of local and foreign CD and movie reviews, and much more.
www.taiwannights.com
Good info on clubbing, restaurants, bars, and other sources of night-time fun on the island.

What To Wear
During the hot season, appropriate clothing should include light and loose cotton clothing and

comfortable walking shoes. Many Chinese businessmen prefer to wear leisure suits with open collars to beat the heat, although if you come for business, it is better to be overdressed. Hotels, restaurants and offices are air-conditioned.

During the winter months, be sure to bring some comfortable woolens to help protect you from the chilly, moisture-laden winter air. Sweaters, woolen jackets and dresses, warm trousers and socks will all come in handy during Taiwanese winters, especially in Taipei. People in Taiwan tend to dress a bit more formally on winter evenings than in summer.

During both seasons, it is advisable to bring along some sort of rain-gear; thunderstorms can occur at any time. Most local people use umbrellas, which can be purchased at convenience stores, drugstores, supermarkets, and department stores.

Women Travelers
Taiwan is a safe travel destination for women, though as with anywhere else it is not advisable to walk alone or take taxis alone at night. For any specific medical needs, doctors at major hospitals will be able to communicate in English, though most other staff will not. Among others, the Community Services Center (see Orientation on page 331) specifically recommends the Priority Care Center, tel: (02) 2771-8151/2776-2664, ext. 2670/2672, (www.tahsda.org.tw) at the Taiwan Adventist Hospital in Taipei.

Weights and Measures
Metric system in most instances. However, in both public markets and small local shops throughout Taiwan, vendors still often weigh and measure using traditional Chinese units. If on your own without an interpreter, the following conversion table will help figure out the unit price of items. Length: The Chinese "foot" is called a chi: 1 chi = 11.9 inches or 0.99 feet (0.32 meters). 1 zhang = 10 chi Weight: The Chinese "pound" is called a catty or jin: 1 jin = 1.32 pounds/21.2 ounces (0.6 kg). The Chinese "ounce" is called a liang: 1 liang = 1.32 ounces (37.5 grams). Area: The Chinese measure area in units of ping and jia: 1 ping = 36 sq. feet (3.3 sq. meters) 1 jia = 2.40 acres

L ANGUAGE

UNDERSTANDING THE LANGUAGE

Written Script

Chinese writing is based on ideograms, or "idea-pictures," which graphically depict ideas and objects with written characters derived directly from actual diagrams of the subject. The oldest recorded Chinese characters appeared on oracle bones excavated last century in China and dating from the ancient Shang dynasty (1523–1028 BC). At that time, questions of vital interest to the emperor were inscribed upon the dried shells of giant tortoises and ox scapulae, which were then subjected to heat. The heat caused the shells to crack, and diviners then interpreted Heaven's answers to the emperor's questions by "reading" the cracks. The answers were then inscribed on the shells, which were then stored in the imperial archives. Based on the number and complexity of the characters inscribed on these oracle bones, Chinese historians concluded that Chinese written language was first invented during the reign of the Yellow Emperor, around 2700 BC.

The written characters reached their current stage of development about 2,000 years ago during the Han dynasty, and they have changed very little since then, which makes Chinese the oldest ongoing writing system in the world. The importance of China's written language cannot be overstated: it held together a vast and complex empire composed of many different ethnic groups, and due to its non-phonetic nature, it formed a written common denominator among China's various dialects. Once the symbols were learned, they gave the reader access to an enormous wealth of historical and literary writings accumulated in China over a long period of continuous cultural development – now thought to be more than five millennia. Written Chinese has evolved continuously from generation to generation, transmitting with it the accumulated treasures of Chinese culture right down to the present era. The simple act of writing one's own surname in Chinese immediately recalls and identifies one with a host of historical and literary heroes, spanning five millennia, who shared the same name.

There are about 50,000 Chinese characters listed in Chinese dictionaries, but the vast majority are either obsolete or used in highly specialized branches of learning. About 3,000 characters are required for basic literacy, such as reading newspapers and business documents, and about 5,000 are required for advanced literary studies. About 2,000 Chinese characters are still used in the written languages of Korea and Japan. Few scholars, however, are capable of using over 6,000 characters without resorting to dictionaries.

Spoken Language

There are only several hundred monosyllabic vocal sounds in the Chinese spoken language, which means that many written characters share the same pronunciation. To somewhat clarify matters, the Chinese developed a tonal system which uses four distinctive tones in Mandarin Chinese to pronounce each syllable. Even so, many characters share both common syllables and tones, and the only way to be really sure which words are meant when spoken is to consider the entire context of a statement, or demand a written explanation.

Grammatically, spoken Chinese is simple and direct. There are no conjugations, declensions, gender distinctions, tense changes, or other complicated grammatical rules to memorize. The spoken language consists of simple sounds strung together in the "subject/verb/object" construction common to most Western languages. Tones, while foreign to Western tongues, come naturally with usage and are not difficult to master. Even within mainland China, the various provinces give different tonal inflections to the various sounds. Proper word order and correct context are by far the most important elements to know about spoken Chinese grammar.

In Taiwan, the Mandarin dialect (known as *guoyu*, or the "national language") was declared the official lingua franca by the government in the late 1940s. Mandarin is based upon the pronunciations that prevailed in the old imperial capital of Beijing. In addition to Mandarin, the local "Taiwanese" dialect is derived from China's Fujian province, ancestral home of the vast majority of Taiwan's populace of Han Chinese descent. Taiwanese is commonly spoken among locals, especially in the rural regions, and many local television stations broadcast programs in the dialect. The older generation still speaks some Japanese – a remnant of Japan's colonial occupation – and younger people tend to understand at least basic English. Though English is a required subject for all students in Taiwan throughout high school, it is spoken fluently by very few.

Body Language

The Taiwanese do not engage in much casual contact, except between good friends. What is seen as friendly touching by Westerners is seen as advances by members of the opposite sex. So be careful. Many a Western expat, especially in office situations, has been surprised to find he is perceived as a *selang* – a "color wolf," or playboy – by local colleagues.

When pointing to themselves, locals point to their nose with their index finger. To beckon a person over, extend your arm, palm down, and make a gentle scooping motion toward yourself; a common way Westerners beckon, making a hooking motion with the index finger, palm up, means someone/something is dead. Touching the index finger to the cheek, scratching it up and down, indicates a person has *diulian*, or "lost face." Pressing the index and middle finger together, then tapping them gently against the temple a few times rapidly, means a person is crazy or unstable; the term "*shodo*" is often uttered, from the Japanese pronunciation of "short," as in an electrical short in the brain.

Transliteration

A number of transliteration systems are used in Taiwan, causing endless confusion and consternation for visitors and expat residents. The country now "officially" uses a self-invented system called Tongyong Pinyin, but it is voluntary and thus roundly ignored, even by some central government departments. The system, seen as a politicized Democratic Progressive Party (DPP) invention, is said to be 85 percent similar to Hanyu Pinyin, which the DPP sees as a mainland Communist system, the 15 percent divergence said to incorporate sounds unique to Taiwan's Hoklo (Taiwanese), Hakka, and aboriginal dialects.

Pointedly, the KMT-run Taipei City Government uses Hanyu Pinyin, so visitors will see all street signs in Hanyu in the city but in Tongyong when stepping out into surrounding Taipei County. To make matters more confusing, many ignore both systems, with Wade-Giles and a number of other systems still much used; misspellings are also common because of lack of familiarity with

any system by non-English speakers. This guidebook uses the Hanyu Pinyin transliteration system, except where non-Hanyu spellings are more familiar (Taipei, Chiang Kai-shek, etc).

Useful Phrases

Greetings

Hello, how are you? *Ni hao ma?*
Fine; very good *Hen hao*
Not so good *Bu hao*
Goodbye *Zai jian*
See you tomorrow *Mingtian jian*
Good morning *Zao an*
Good evening *Wan an*
You; you (plural) *Ni; nimen*
I; we *Wo; women*
He, she, it; they *Ta; tamen*
Who? *Shei?*
Mr Li *Li Xiansheng*
Miss Li *Li Xiaojie*
Mrs Li *Li Taitai*
Thank you *Xie-xie*
You're welcome *Bu keyi*

Time and Place

Where? *Nali?*
What time? *Jidian zhong?*
What day? *Libai ji?*
Today *Jintian*
Tomorrow *Mingtian*
Yesterday *Zuotian*
One o'clock *Yi dian zhong*
Two o'clock *Liang dian zhong*
Very far *Hen yuan*
Very close *Hen jin*

Food and Drink

Restaurant *Canting*
Bar *Jiuba*
Let's eat; to eat *Chifan*
Let's drink; to drink *Hejiu*
Ice; ice-cubes *Bing; bingkuai*
Water; cold water *Shui; bing shui*
Soup *Tang*
Fruit *Shuiguo*
Tea *Cha*
Coffee *Kafei*
Hot *Re*
Cold *Leng*
Sugar *Tang*
A little bit *Yidian, Yidiandian*
A little more *Duo yidian*
A little less *Shao yidian*
Bottoms up! *Ganbei!*
Settle the bill *Suanzhang*
Let me pay *Wo (lai) qingke*

Numbers

One *Yi*
Two *Er (liang)*
Three *San*
Four *Si*
Five *Wu*
Six *Liu*
Seven *Qi*

Eight *Ba*
Nine *Jiu*
Ten *Shi*
Eleven *Shiyi*
Twelve, etc. *Shier, etc.*
Twenty *Ershi*
Thirty *Sanshi*
Forty, etc. *Sishi*
Fifty-five *Wushi wu*
Seventy-six *Qishi liu*
One hundred *Yibai*
One hundred and twenty-five *Yibai ershi wu*
Two hundred, etc. *Liangbai*
One thousand *Yiqian*
Ten thousand *Yiwan*
Fifty thousand *Wuwan*

Transportation

Hotel *Fandian*
Room *Fangjian*
Airport *Feijichang*
International airport *Guoji jichang*
Bus/coach *Bashi*
Bus (public) *Gonggong qiche*
Taxi *Jichengche*
Telephone *Dianhua*
International call *Guoji dianhua*
Telegram *Dianbao*
Airplane *Feiji*
Train *Huoche*
Reservation *Dingwei*
Key *Yaoshi*
Clothing *Yifu*
Luggage *Xingli*

Shopping

How much? *Duoshao?*
Too expensive *Tai gui*
Make it a bit cheaper *Suan pianyi dian*
Money *Qian*
Credit card *Xinyong ka*
Old *Lao*
New *Xin*
Big *Da*
Small *Xiao*
Antique *Gudong*
Red *Hong*
Green *Lu*
Yellow *Huang*
Black *Hei*
White *Bai*
Blue *Lan*
Gold *Jin, huangjin*
Jade *Yu*
Wood *Mu*
Proprietor, shopowner *Laoban*
Wrap it up *Bao qilai*

Basic Sentence Patterns

I want... *Wo yao...*
I don't want... *Wo buyao...*
Where is...? *...zai nali?*
Do you have...? *Ni you meiyou...?*
We don't have... *Women meiyou...*
I like... *Wo xihuan...*
I don't like... *Wo bu xihuan...*
I like you *Wo xihuan ni*
I wish to go... *Wo yao qu...*

FURTHER READING

History

From Far Formosa: The Island, Its People and Missions by George Leslie Mackay, D.D., SMC Publishing, Taipei (1996). Reprint of 1896 edition; a look at Formosa by a respected figure whose name is still familiar in Taiwan, with a hospital and other organizations named after him.

Islands in the Stream: A Quick Case Study of Taiwan's Complex History by April Lin and Kerome Keating, SMC Publishing, Taipei (2005). An easy-read primer, focused on political history, that will bring you up to the present in just a few hours.

Japanese Rule in Formosa by Yosaburo Takekoshi, SMC Publishing, Taipei (1996). Reprint from 1907 edition; a demanding and detailed anthropological look at Taiwan's people from the imperial Japanese perspective.

Sketches from Formosa by Rev. W. Campbell, SMC Publishing, Taipei (1996). Reprint of 1915 edition; an intriguing look at late-19th and early-20th century Taiwan through a contemporary's eyes.

Statecraft and Political Economy on the Taiwan Frontier, 1600–1800 by John Robert Shepherd, SMC Publishing (1995). A dense, scholarly book (in fact, the author's dissertation), this is the best single English source for the period in question.

Taiwan: Nation-State or Province by John F. Copper, SMC Publishing (2003). Update of 1996 edition; perhaps the best primer on the island, with eminently readable sections on geography, economy, history, and more.

Business Reading

Directory of Taiwan, The Taiwan News, Taipei (2008). An indispensable annual that bills itself, correctly, as "the most authoritative bilingual directory of government, business and cultural organizations in Taiwan."

Taipei Living, Community Services Center, Taipei (2007). Updated biannually by the center, which helps expats settle in, this handy reference

book expands sixfold on the type of information found in this guide's Travel Tips.

The Taiwan-China Connection: Democracy and Development across the Taiwan Straits by Leng Tse-kang, Westview Press, Boulder (1996). Concise yet penetrating analysis of the changing nature of Taiwan and the business community regarding the formation of economic policy toward China.

Culture and Food

Animals and the Chinese, Sinorama Magazine, Taipei (2000). Slightly dated regarding official animal-protection policies, but the essays offer good insight into how the Chinese co-exist with the animal world.

Birdwatcher's Guide to the Taipei Region by Rick Charette, Taipei City Govt. (2004). Colorful illustrated guide to birdwatching trails in and around the city, with maps.

Culture Shock! Taiwan: A Guide to Customs and Etiquette by Chris and Ling-li Bates, Times Books International, Singapore (1995). A concise and lighthearted primer for confused foreigners on the ins and outs, dos and don'ts of getting along with the locals.

Formosan Odyssey: Taiwan, Past and Present by John Ross, Taiwan Adventure Publications, Taichung (2002). A lighthearted, highly entertaining, and insightful account of a New Zealander's north-south trek down the island.

Private Prayers and Public Parades by Mark Caltonhill, Taipei City Government (2002). Answers all your questions on Taiwan's religious life – which gods you're looking at, origins of festivals, explanations of practices such as tomb-sweeping, throwing of oracle blocks, and more.

Reflections on Taipei by Rick Charette, Taipei City Government (2003). A look at Taipei's people, their culture, and the city's development in modern times via discussions with long-term expatriate residents.

Taiwan: A Political History by Denny Roy, Cornel University Press (2003). Detailed, reliable, easy-reading travel down Taiwan's road to democracy.

The Ugly Chinaman by Bo Yang, translated by Don J. Cohn and Jing Qing, Allen and Unwin, Sydney (1992). For centuries the Chinese have been navel-gazing, wondering how their culture has become so petrified; this modern classic, by a famous dissident, caused great controversy in the 1980s.

Window on Taiwan by Mark de Fraeye, Petraco-Pandora, Brussels, (1999). An expensive and beautifully illustrated work by photographer de Fraeye, with accompanying essays by a range of experts.

Other Insight Guides

Insight Guides cover nearly 200 destinations, providing information on culture and all the top sights. **Insight FlexiMaps** are laminated, easy-to-fold, weather- and tear-proof informative maps which include top 10 tourist attractions.

Hong Kong is one of the titles in the Insight's **Smart Guide** series. Arranged in handy A–Z sections, the comprehensive listings allow the visitor to make their own decisions about where to go and what to see.

Other Insight Guides which highlight destinations in this region include *China*, *South China*, *Beijing*, *Hong Kong*, *Japan* and *Korea*.

Send Us Your Thoughts

We do our best to ensure the information in our books is as accurate and up-to-date as possible. However, some mistakes and omissions are inevitable and we are ultimately reliant on our readers to put us in the picture.

We welcome your feedback, especially your experience of using the book on the road and will acknowledge all contributions. We'll offer an Insight Guide to the best letters received.

Please write to us at:
Insight Guides
PO Box 7910
London SE1 1WE
Or email us at:
insight@apaguide.co.uk

ART & PHOTO CREDITS

Alamy 85, 253
Apa Publications 33, 56
Tibor Bognar/Trip 2B, 133, 186
Frank Broekhuizen 5B, 10/11, 14
Central News Agency, Inc. 18, 34, 35
Rick Charette 93
Chyou Su-ling 154/155, 193
Corbis 128
Mark Downey 118
R Etter/Trip 12/13, 138, 142M, 210, 237, 241
Alain Evrard back flap bottom, 80
Veronica Garbutt 184
Glyn Genin 130, 130M, 131M, 147, 169, 230, 279
Government Information Office 32
Heidrun Guether 79
Brent Hannon 44, 211M, 221, 223M, 266, 270, 272M, 273, 276
D & J Heaton back cover centre top, 288
Bernd Helms front flap top, 114/115
Jack Hollingsworth 204M, 209, 209M, 242M, 276M
Imaginechina 195, 265
Istock 40
Jupiter Images 181
Catherine Karnow 201
Bob Krist 163
Taras Kovaliv/Apa 269
T Lester/Trip 133M, 165
Manfred Morgenstern 16/17, 20, 27, 28, 29, 30L/R, 31, 70, 77, 152
Kal Müller 64
National Palace Museum 25, 63, 68, 69, 71, 76, 78
Onasia 189
Erhard Pansegrau 148
Photobank back cover left, back cover right, 122, 129, 146, 153, 198, 200, 203, 208, 244M, 265M, 278, 285

Photolibrary 99, 206, 219, 239, 242, 252
Catherine Platt/Panos Pictures 141
Dan Rocovits 1, 3B, 58, 59L/R, 61, 72, 74, 75, 86, 87, 267, 268
H Rogers/Trip 47, 111, 148M, 159, 167M, 170, 175M, 194M, 199, 200M, 202, 216, 217, 218M, 252M, 281, 282, 284
David Ryan 37
D Saunders/Trip 131
Frank Salmoiraghi 19, 45, 48/49, 89, 100, 149, 218, 220, 236, 248
Chris Stowers 39L, 41, 50, 52, 65, 94, 106, 126, 143, 150, 150M, 151, 167, 174, 182/183, 188M, 222, 223, 226/227, 232, 233M, 245, 249, 280M, 283, 286M
Chris Stowers/APA 6, 7, 8, 9, 39R, 54, 62, 73, 81, 82, 88, 90, 95, 101, 103, 107, 108, 109L/R, 110, 127, 132, 135, 136, 137, 139, 140, 142, 143, 150, 151, 158, 160, 162, 163, 164, 166, 168, 171, 172, 172M, 173, 176, 177, 178, 293, 294, 295, 297, 299, 305, 307, 308, 309, 310, 311, 312, 313, 314, 315, 316, 318, 319, 320, 321, 323, 324, 325, 326, 329, 330, 332
Chris Stowers/Panos Pictures 2/3, 5, 38, 53, 97, 128M, 129, 136M, 224, 225, 234, 250, 254, 271
Tainan Historical Museum 23, 24, 26
Taiwan Provincial Museum 21
Chris Taylor 46, 92, 161, 161M, 162M, 178M, 190, 190M, 191, 202M, 234M
Mark Theiler 83
J Trapman/Trip 140M
A Tovy/Trip 274
Ariadne Van Zandbergen 255M
R Vargas/Trip 51

Vision Photo Agency 134, 179, 197, 256
Bill Wassman back flap top, front flap bottom, back cover centre bottom, spine, 4L/R, 22, 36, 42/43, 55, 57, 60, 62L, 84, 86, 91, 112/113, 116/117, 175, 180, 187, 192, 194, 196, 204, 205, 207, 211, 213, 214, 215, 231, 233, 235, 238, 243, 244, 251, 255, 257, 258/259, 260, 262, 263, 275, 277, 280, 286, 287
Kosima Weber-Lim 98
Martin Westlake 268M
Andrew Wheeler 102, 212, 266M

PICTURE SPREADS

Pages 66/67: All by Chris Taylor, except top row, right: Yack Fielos/Corbis.
Pages 104/105: All by Chris Stowers, except top row left: Nik Wheeler/Corbis.
Pages 144/145: Clockwise from top: Dan Rocovits, Glyn Genin, Glyn Genin, R Etter/Trip, Glyn Genin, Chris Stowers, Photobank, Michael S Tamashita/Corbis, Michael S Tamashita/Corbis, Chris Stowers
Pages 246/247: All by Chris Stowers

Map Production:
Colourmap Scanning Ltd.

© 2008 Apa Publications GmbH & Co.

Verlag KG (Singapore branch)

INDEX

A
B
C
D
E
F
G
H
J
a
b
c
d
e
f
g
h
j
k
l